Collins

Atlas of 20th Century History

Collins

Atlas of 20th Century History

RICHARD OVERY

Collins

An Imprint of HarperCollins*Publishers*

ISBN-10: 0-00-720170-2
ISBN-13: 978-0-00-720170-9

ISBN-10: 0-06-089072-X (in the United States)
ISBN-13: 978-0-06-089072-8
FIRST U.S. EDITION Published in 2006

Atlas prepared for Collins by Martin Brown

Editorial Direction: Fiona Hobbins, Philip Parker
Proofreading: Margaret Gilbey
Index: Janet Smy

Text © Richard Overy
Professor of History
University of Exeter, 2004

Cover photograph
© Stephen Jaffe/Getty Images

10 09 08 07 06
9 8 7 6 5 4 3 2 1

Printed and bound in Hong Kong by Printing Express

It is a truism that the past century has witnessed the most profound changes of any century in human history. Yet the dimensions of that change are still worth recalling. In 1900 most people were wretchedly poor, by modern standards, and led lives of monotonous and physically demanding work, with almost no access to the services and goods enjoyed by small wealthy elites. The advances that have transformed the century—scientific and medical discoveries, new forms of production and exchange—were largely confined to the prosperous areas of Europe and North America.

Although this division between rich and poor, developed and developing, has scarcely diminished since 1900, the fruits of modernity, bitter though they have sometimes been, have spread worldwide. The catchphrase of the modern age is globalization. The world can be reached through new routes of access: air travel; satellite television; the computer superhighway. The tentacles of thousands of multinational organizations have spread worldwide. Half of all people live in cities; most work in industry and services, generating levels of income undreamed of in 1900. The collapse of empire and the spread of mass culture have now produced very different elites, whose horizons are global rather than parochial. In 1900 kings and emperors still mattered. Now they are merely ornaments.

This transformation was neither preordained nor inevitable. By 1945, after two massively destructive wars in the developed world and an almost terminal crisis of capitalism in 1929, the century seemed to be going from bad to worse. The horrors of trench warfare, followed 25 years later by the revelations of German genocide and Stalinist terror, eroded the confidence in progress inherited from the 19th century. The English novelist, George Orwell, despaired of the future of the century as the war with Hitler drew to a close. He saw persistent "Führer-worship" replacing democracy, rigidly planned economies destroying economic freedom, and an almost permanent state of war between "great superpowers unable to conquer one another." The result was the novel *1984*, published just before the middle of the century, a savage indictment of the drift to state power and a regimented society.

Orwell was wrong, though not entirely. The abuse of state power has persisted. The Cold War produced unimaginable dangers of global destruction. But when 1984 actually came, a large part of the world enjoyed levels of political freedom, economic prosperity, and personal security that barely seemed possible in 1945. The problems that remain are more often than not the result of weak states, not the threat of Big Brother. The revival of the century's fortunes after 1950 resulted from three things: the power of the United States, which was now exerted globally; an exceptional economic boom; and the end of imperialism, an institution almost as old as human history. Empire collapsed everywhere between 1900 and the emancipation of Europe's colonies in the 1960s and with it the idea that one state could physically and permanently control others, though this has not prevented violent and one-sided intervention by bigger powers in the affairs of smaller states. Now this picture is changing again: Religious conflict, environmental crisis and the "war on terror" declared by the west have created new uncertainties and opened up new areas of political conflict. The collapse of communism in Europe, widely welcomed in 1990, has not produced a more secure capitalist world. Anti-globalism and the growing military power of communism in Asia will provide new challenges. Nothing, in the modern age, can ever be taken for granted.

Richard Overy

CONTENTS

The world in 1900 was poised on the threshold of one of the most remarkable periods of change in human history. An old order was giving way to a new. Under the impact of industrialization and the rise of mass politics, the established monarchical order, whose dynasties stretched back for centuries, began to crumble. The coming of mass urbanization and new technologies in the 19th century in Europe and the United States transformed societies traditionally based on landed power and peasant farming. In 1900 most of the world was still ruled by old empires—Manchu China, Ottoman Turkey, Romanov Russia, Habsburg Austria. In 1900 most of the world's population still earned its living from primitive farming. But change was irresistible and worldwide. The dominant theme of the 19th century was emancipation from royal autocracy, from imperial oppression, from poverty and ignorance, above all from political exclusion. The demands for national independence, democracy, and a better way of life, with their roots in North America and western Europe, worked like a strong acid on the old structures of power and wealth. As they dissolved, the world entered an era of exceptional turbulence and violence.

Stretcherbearers at
the Battle of Ypres, 1915

PART I   **THE END OF THE OLD WORLD ORDER**

the **world** in 1900: **empires**

- **1880–1914** 25 million migrants leave Europe
- **1895** Japanese acquire Formosa and Korea (1910)
- **1899–1902** Boer War
- **1900** Boxer Rebellion in China
- **1900** Sigmund Freud publishes *The Interpretation of Dreams*
- **1900** Max Planck discovers quantum theory
- **1902** electron isolated by British physicist Joseph Thompson
- **1915** Albert Einstein's theory of relativity

At the beginning of the 20th century, the political map of the world was overwhelmingly imperial. There were old empires in China and the Ottoman Middle East. There were European colonial empires which stretched back to the 16th century—Spanish, Portuguese, Dutch. There were newer colonial empires which reached their fullest extent in the half century before 1900—British, French, German, Italian.

Even the Americas, most of whose states were republics, had once been part of Europe's empires, and still shared the language and culture exported there. In Europe there were empires built by the Austrian Habsburg dynasty and the Russian Romanovs. They had no overseas possessions, but ruled a conglomeration of subject peoples stretching from Italy in the west to the shores of eastern Asia.

1 Much of the world in 1900 was divided into empires (map below). They were ruled, except for the French empire, by old dynastic houses. In the Far East the Chinese empire was in decline, that of the Japanese, invigorated by a modernizing revolution in 1868, was still expanding. The European empires covered half the globe, much of the area taken over during the previous century. Spain and Portugal were the exceptions. Their vast empires in Latin America, built in the 16th century, had won independence during the 19th century. During the 20th century, the other empires disappeared, to be replaced by the modern nation state.

In 1900 the colonial empires were at their zenith. Starting in the 1870s a new wave of imperialism had brought most of Africa and the Pacific islands under European rule. The last native independent state in Africa—Abyssinia (Ethiopia)—withstood Italian efforts at conquest, inflicting a humiliating defeat on Italian forces at Adowa in 1896. In southern Africa, the British fought the Dutch settlers in Transvaal and the Orange Free State in the Boer War (1899–1902) and brought both under direct British rule. The British empire was the world's largest, covering one quarter of the globe. At its heart lay India, where Queen Victoria was declared empress in 1876. A few thousand officials ruled an area of 350 million people.

Europeans looked out upon the wider world confident that what they offered was civilization and technical progress. They saw the world in their own image. European languages replaced native tongues as the medium of administration and commerce. European religion was exported along with the fruits of European technical and scientific development. In 1900 most of the world outside China was nominally Christian or was ruled by Christian officials. A flood of

www.empiremuseum.co.uk/main.htm
British Empire & Commonwealth history museum
www.channel4.com/history/microsites/H/history/guide20/part04d.html
Guide to world empires in 1900

migrants left Europe—25 million between 1880 and 1914. European trade dominated the world's markets. European armies and navies, armed with the most modern weapons, gave the new European empires the power to impose European interests. Japanese leaders were so impressed with European expansion they adopted western technology and military reforms, and set out to build a colonial empire of their own in east Asia. Formosa (Taiwan) was acquired in 1895, Korea in 1910. Japanese officials were made to read Sir John Seeley's *Expansion of England* as an example to follow.

Appearances in 1900 proved deceptive. As a form of political organization, empire was in its very final stages. In fact, the buoyant colonial empires of Europe contributed to the decline of Ottoman Turkey and Manchu China, which Europeans wished to dominate for themselves. Europe was in the process of generating the social and political forces that were to transform empire in the 20th century. The unification of Italy in 1860 and Germany in 1871 showed the importance of nationalism as a political force. By 1900 agitation for national autonomy was widespread in Europe—in Ireland, Bohemia, Poland, Ukraine, Finland—while nationalist opponents of the old dynasties in China and Turkey undermined the established order.

Nationalism was one component of the development of mass politics. Social and economic modernization in

1 colonial empires in 1900

British	Spanish
French	Dutch
Portuguese	Russian
Italian	American
German	Danish

Belgian
Japanese
Ottoman
other countries

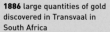

1886 large quantities of gold discovered in Transvaal in South Africa

by 1900 world trade expanded more than threefold in preceding 40 years

1900 Eastman Kodak company sells first Brownie Box Camera for $1

1901 mass production of cars begins in the United States

1903 first powered flight

by 1905 United States world's leading manufacturing nation

Europe in the 19th century produced new social classes no longer prepared to accept traditional dynastic or aristocratic rule. European liberals succeeded in establishing constitutional parliamentary rule and civil rights in Britain, Italy, and France (though not in their empires). Their demands for modern freedoms—democracy, the rule of law, respect for the individual, the right to self-determination—filtered beyond Europe to encourage political protest in the very areas that Europe now ruled. Europe was also the home of modern socialism. Taking inspiration from the German philosopher Karl Marx, socialists argued for a revolutionary transformation of existing society, and the rule of the laboring masses. By 1900 there were movements for civil rights or revolution worldwide.

No single factor was as important in explaining the decline of the old world order as industrialization. Industrial growth overturned the traditional balance of power as established states failed to modernize economically or modernized only slowly, while other states—Germany, the United States, Japan—grew industrially powerful in the last third of the 19th century. The political success of Europeans overseas rested on the great wealth and technical progress brought by industrial expansion. Their appetite for empire owed much to the search for new sources of food and raw materials. In 1900 Britain was at war with the small Boer republic of Transvaal in southern Africa where, in 1886, large quantities of gold had been discovered.

Yet even in Europe the pace of industrial growth was uneven. In 1900 Europe produced more than 17 million tons of steel, but two-thirds of it was produced in just two countries—Britain and Germany. Britain, the oldest industrial power, produced more coal and manufactured more textiles than the whole of the rest of Europe together. But with industrial growth concentrated in particular regions, the rest of Europe's economy remained agrarian, and most Europeans, like most of the world's population, worked on the land. Outside Europe, industrialization was limited everywhere except in the United States, where abundant raw materials and an inventive and skilled workforce turned the country in the 40 years after the Civil War (1861–65) into the world's leading manufacturing nation.

Economic modernization outside Europe depended almost entirely on European investment and European or American technology. Such development as there was could be found in the processing of foodstuffs—pressed canned beef from Latin America, cocoa from West Africa—or in the extractive industries. By 1900, the Transvaal gold mines had more than 100,000 workers. Tin from Malaya or copper from Canada provided much of the world's supply of these commodities. Yet outside the small enclaves of exploited resources the rest of the world remained wedded to traditional methods of production and farming.

The process of modernization relied on the growth of commerce. By 1900 a sophisticated system of trade and currency payments was in operation. It was based on London as lender of last resort and the major center for shipping, insurance, and commodity brokerage. In 1900 Britain controlled one half of the world's merchant tonnage, while her overseas investments were greater than those of the rest of the world together. Fueled by British credit and rising incomes in America and Europe,

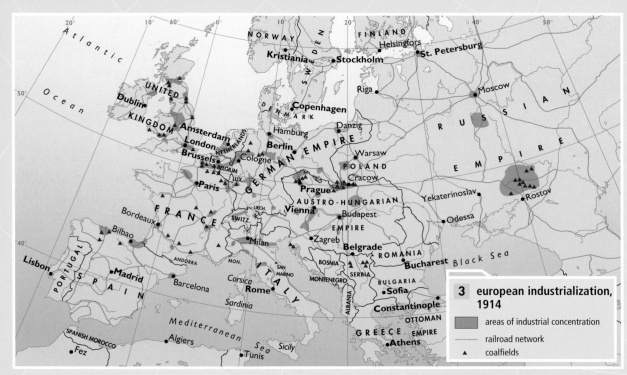

3 european industrialization, 1914

areas of industrial concentration

railroad network

▲ coalfields

www.mindfully.org/WTO/Trade-Progress-1850-1940.htm
Trade facts and figures, 1850–1940
www.census.pro.gov.uk/
National Archive site for 1901 Census of England and Wales

world trade expanded more than threefold between 1860 and 1900. The fruits of this commerce were very unevenly spread. The highest incomes were earned in the United States and Britain, but even here the standard of living of most of the population was low and wealth was concentrated in the hands of only a few. In the less developed regions of Europe and in areas only feebly affected by economic change life was lived at, or occasionally below, the barest level of subsistence.

The transformation of material life depended on the progress of science and technology. The 19th-century industrial revolution was based on iron, coal, and railroads. By 1900 the components of a new wave of technical change were available, drawing on chemicals, electricity, and the internal combustion engine. The first cars were developed in the 1880s; the first powered flight came in 1903; the electron was isolated by the British physicist Joseph Thompson in 1902; the German scientist Max Planck laid

the basis for the quantum theory in 1900; Albert Einstein's theory of relativity came in 1915. The modern age of computers, jets, satellite communication, and nuclear power was born in the flowering of scientific and technical development at the turn of the century. In 1900 the building blocks of a remarkable century of political, intellectual, and technical change were cemented in place.

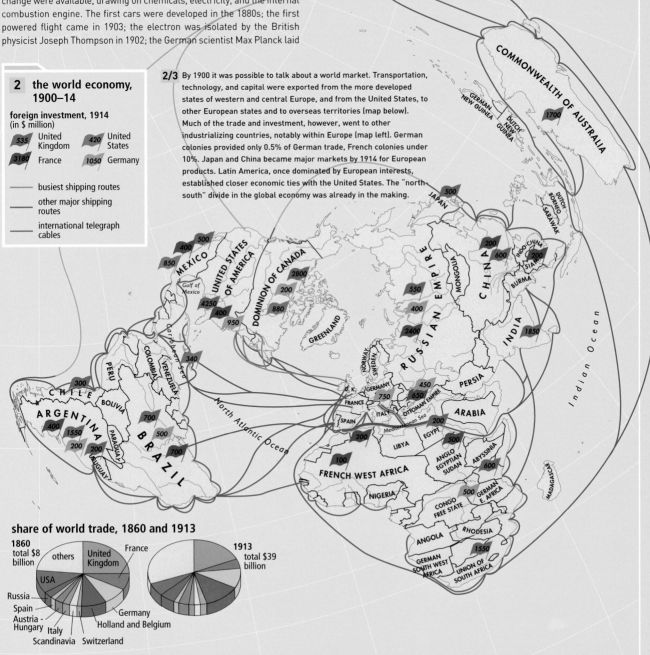

2 the world economy, 1900–14

foreign investment, 1914
(in $ million)

535 United Kingdom	420 United States
3180 France	1050 Germany

— busiest shipping routes

— other major shipping routes

— international telegraph cables

2/3 By 1900 it was possible to talk about a world market. Transportation, technology, and capital were exported from the more developed states of western and central Europe, and from the United States, to other European states and to overseas territories (map below). Much of the trade and investment, however, went to other industrializing countries, notably within Europe (map left). German colonies provided only 0.5% of German trade, French colonies under 10%. Japan and China became major markets by 1914 for European products. Latin America, once dominated by European interests, established closer economic ties with the United States. The "north-south" divide in the global economy was already in the making.

share of world trade, 1860 and 1913

1860 total $8 billion — others, United Kingdom, France, USA, Russia, Spain, Austria-Hungary, Italy, Scandinavia, Switzerland, Holland and Belgium, Germany

1913 total $39 billion

china: from empire to republic

No country exemplified better the tensions between the old world and the forces of change than the Chinese empire of the Manchus. For centuries China was the dominant political and economic power in Asia.

The Manchu dynasty ruled over a vast area from Mongolia to Indo-China; Chinese scientific and intellectual achievements rivaled those of Europe; China's ruling classes regarded the outside world as barbarian and until the middle of the 19th century succeeded in closing China off from the inexorable tide of European expansion.

That tide breached Chinese defenses in 1842. Britain defeated China in an argument over the British opium trade, and was granted a lease to Hong Kong. Five so-called "Treaty Ports" were opened to foreign merchants. Thus began a slow process of encroachment by the European colonial powers, anxious to tap what they saw as the vast potential trade with the Chinese empire. Russia seized the area of north eastern China between 1858 and 1861; defeat by France in 1885 in Indo-China finally excluded

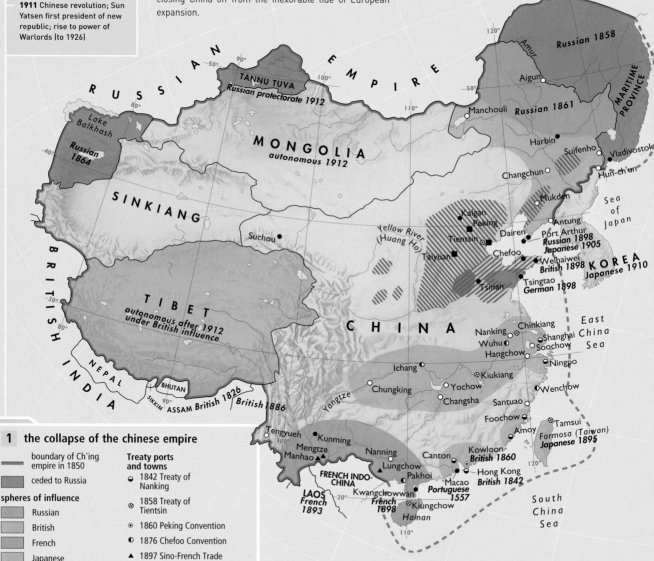

1 the collapse of the chinese empire

- ▬ boundary of Ch'ing empire in 1850
- ▬ ceded to Russia

spheres of influence
- Russian
- British
- French
- Japanese
- German
- Italian

Boxer rebellion, 1899–1900
- original core, 1899
- additional areas affected in 1899

Treaty ports and towns
- ◖ 1842 Treaty of Nanking
- ⊗ 1858 Treaty of Tientsin
- ◉ 1860 Peking Convention
- ◐ 1876 Chefoo Convention
- ▲ 1897 Sino-French Trade Convention
- ○ additional ports opened by 1911
- ● other towns and cities

- ▨ additional areas affected in 1900
- ■ chief towns held by the Boxers in June–July, 1900

1 The collapse of the Chinese empire (map above). During the 19th century China was forced to open up much of her territory to the influence of European powers, the United States, and Japan. Foreigners enjoyed extraterritorial rights and economic concession. Territory was lost in the north and northeast to Russia and Japan and in the southeast to Britain and France. Former vassal states such as Nepal, Burma, Laos, the Ryukyu Islands, and Korea came under foreign influence or control. When the empire collapsed in 1911, China also lost control of Tibet and Mongolia.

www.lcsc.edu/modernchina/u3s1p8.htm
Introduction to the Boxer rebellion
www.wsu.edu:8080/~dee/MODCHINA/REV.HTM
History of the 1911 revolution

Chinese political influence from South East Asia. China also suffered from the ambitions of her Asian neighbour, Japan. Following a revolution in 1868, Japan embarked on western-style modernization. Her armed forces were reformed and re-armed, and Japanese leaders sought to imitate the west by seizing colonies. They joined the scramble for China, exerting pressure in Formosa (Taiwan), the Ryukyu Islands and in Korea and Manchuria. Finally, in 1894-5, Japan defeated China in a full-scale war and seized the island of Formosa.

The onset of European pressure provoked serious crisis in Chinese society and exposed the Manchu's military and economic weakness. The Chinese political and administrative system remained unreformed, with power in the hands of the traditional bureaucracy. Except for the European-dominated Treaty Ports, there was little modern industrial or commercial development. A burgeoning population brought growing pressure on the food supply. The Manchu defence of tradition provoked long periods of domestic unrest, just as the European version of modernity provoked waves of popular Chinese xenophobia, directed both at westerners and at the feeble regime that had been forced to admit them. Chinese leaders were aware of the need for change, but were fearful of the effects of adopting western methods, despite the evident success of Japanese emulation of the west, which was highlighted by the defeat of Chinese armies in 1895.

Gradually the Manchu regime lost effective control of the major provinces. In 1898 the emperor, Kuang-hsü, at last tried to introduce a range of radical reforms to prevent the disintegration of the empire. He was overthrown by the dowager empress, T'zu-hsi, who rejected reform.

In 1899, as the European powers closed in for what they saw as the death of the old empire, a wave of anti-western rebellion swept northern China. The "Boxer Rebellion" was directed at foreign missionaries and legations, and at Chinese who traded or collaborated with westerners. A European and American expeditionary force suppressed the revolt with a good deal of violence, while Russia took the opportunity to occupy most of Manchuria.

The Boxer Rebellion, though unsuccessful, spelled the end for the old system, as the 1905 revolution did in Russia. In 1901 the reformists won power and a program of state modernization and economic development was launched. Military, educational, and legal reforms that ended the power of the old bureaucracy were matched by a program of railroad building and the establishment of modern banks and trading houses. Progress went furthest in the areas more strongly under European influence. It was here that reformist politicians gathered, and young educated Chinese were brought into contact with western ideas and techniques.

These more radical elements were unwilling to accept the survival of the Manchu dynasty, even in its reformed guise. By 1911 the moral authority of the old regime was dead. A small army revolt in Wuchang sparked a rejection of Manchu rule across China's many provinces. The T'ung-meng-hui party (Revolutionary Alliance) set up a provisional government at Nanking. The Alliance leader, Dr. Sun Yat-Sen, was proclaimed president of the new Republic of China on January 1, 1912. In ten years the world's largest and oldest empire collapsed, the weightiest victim of the European drive to modernize the world in its own image.

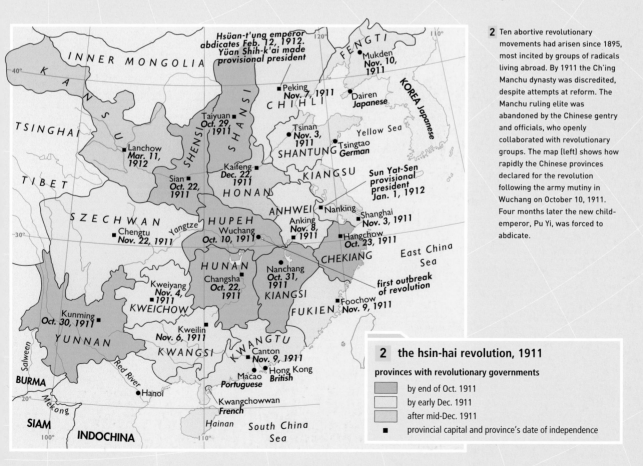

2 Ten abortive revolutionary movements had arisen since 1895, most incited by groups of radicals living abroad. By 1911 the Ch'ing Manchu dynasty was discredited, despite attempts at reform. The Manchu ruling elite was abandoned by the Chinese gentry and officials, who openly collaborated with revolutionary groups. The map (left) shows how rapidly the Chinese provinces declared for the revolution following the army mutiny in Wuchang on October 10, 1911. Four months later the new child-emperor, Pu Yi, was forced to abdicate.

2 the hsin-hai revolution, 1911

provinces with revolutionary governments

- by end of Oct. 1911
- by early Dec. 1911
- after mid-Dec. 1911
- ■ provincial capital and province's date of independence

the decline of the **ottoman empire**

What China was to the Far East, the Ottoman Turkish empire was to the Middle East and North Africa. The Turkish advance ended in the 18th century with domination of the Balkans, the Middle East to the frontiers of Persia and North Africa as far as Morocco. Throughout the 19th century, however, the Ottoman empire slowly broke apart.

In the 1830s, Egypt, which was only a nominal part of the empire, almost succeeded in overthrowing Ottoman rule throughout the Middle East in eight years of warfare. Greece won its independence in 1830; Algeria was conquered by the French from 1830; Romania, Serbia, Bulgaria, and Montenegro won effective autonomy in 1878.

During the latter half of the century the European imperial powers, Britain, France, and Italy, began to encroach on Ottoman interests throughout the Mediterranean and Middle East, partly to protect the interests of Christian subjects of the Ottomans, partly to extend or preserve economic interests, particularly after the opening of the Suez Canal in 1869. In 1882 the British formally occupied Egypt, in 1898 establishing Anglo-Egyptian control of the Sudan. In Palestine and Syria the French and British acted as protectors of the native Christian communities.

The presence of the Christian West in areas of former Ottoman control produced a mixed response. In the middle years of the 19th century, liberal reformers tried to imitate the West in order to strengthen the Ottoman empire, but they were resisted by reactionaries wedded to traditional

1 the decline of the ottoman empire by 1920

Ottoman empire by 1800   Turkey in 1920

Ottoman empire by 1914

Areas of rule or control after the First World War

British   Spanish

French   Russian

Italian   frontiers after the First World War

www.allempires.com/empires/ottoman/ottoman1.htm
The rise and fall of the Ottoman empire
www.wsu.edu:8080/~dee/OTTOMAN/EUROPE.HTM
History of the Ottomans from the 19th century

Islamic values and culture, and by nationalists who, while rejecting western values, nonetheless sought secular, centralized states. In the 1870s, the reform initiative, the *Tanzimat*, succeeded in establishing a modern constitution for the empire, but when Sultan Abdul Hamid II came to the throne in 1876 he suspended the new parliament and began a 30-year reign of repressive personal rule. He encouraged those reforms which increased central power, but his rule was incompetent and corrupt. The empire's finances were a constant source of friction between the sultan and foreign creditors, and between the sultan and his long-suffering soldiers and officials, whose salaries were always in arrears.

Abdul Hamid alienated most groups in the empire during his long reign: nationalists disliked his dependence on western money and the incursions of western imperialism; traditional Islamic leaders urged a return to fundamental Islamic life. The liberals and reformers, meanwhile, many in exile in Paris or Vienna,

kept up a constant cry for constitutional rule and more effective modernization. The exile movement, usually referred to as the Young Turks, established contact with disgruntled army officers and intellectuals in the empire. In 1908 widespread mutiny broke out in the Ottoman army in Macedonia and Thrace. Though the sultan hurriedly restored the constitution, his authority collapsed.

With revolution in Turkey the Christian parts of the empire began to break away. Crete joined with Greece, Austria-Hungary seized Bosnia and Herzegovina, and Bulgaria declared full independence. In 1909 hardline Islamic elements staged a coup under the dervish leader Vahdeti. It was suppressed by the Young Turk reformers led by Enver Pasha and the Paris-based Committee of Union and Progress. Abdul Hamid was forced to abdicate, and starting in 1913 a three-man military junta effectively ruled what remained of the empire down to 1918. The Young Turks proved anything but liberal in power. They embarked on a program to impose the Turkish language and Turkish interests on the Arab and European parts of the empire, imprisoning and executing opponents, including the sultan's chief eunuch, Nadir Aga, who was hanged in public in Istanbul. His execution marked a symbolic break with past Ottoman practice. The Young Turks sought a centralized, Turkified, modern state. They introduced the western 24-hour clock, western modes of dress, education for women, and military reforms. Yet for the Ottoman empire, the change came too late. In 1911 Italy conquered Libya, the last Ottoman outpost in North Africa. A year later the tenuous Ottoman grip on their European possessions was torn loose by an alliance of Balkan kingdoms.

1 The Ottoman empire, which at its zenith in the 17th century reached as far as Budapest in eastern Europe, and included the Crimea and southern Ukraine, had shrunk by the end of the 19th century to its heartland around the eastern Mediterranean (map above). Its last footholds in Africa were eliminated one by one. Algeria was conquered by the French in 1857; Tunisia, on which Italian hopes for a North African empire were based, was taken over by France in 1881 as a protectorate. In September 1911 Italy attacked Tripoli in Libya, and the following year seized the whole area as an Italian colony.

the **balkan** wars

- **by 1900** the Radical Party in Serbia and the Agrarian Union in Bulgaria both mobilize vote
- **1908** Bulgaria becomes independent; Austria annexes Bosnia and Herzegovina
- **1909** Romanian mass peasant revolt leads to 10,000 deaths
- **1909** military revolt in Greece, brings liberal reformer Eleftherios Venizelos to power
- **1912** Balkan states negotiate treaties of mutual assistance
- **1912 (8 October)** Montenegro opens the war against Ottoman forces; Serbia, Greece, and Bulgaria join in
- **1913** Treaty of Bucharest; Macedonia divided between Serbia and Greece; independent Albania established

2 In June Bulgaria attacked Serbia and Greece , whose armies were soon joined by those of Montenegro, Romania, and Turkey (map below). During the second major battle at Tsarevo Selo, Bulgaria sued for an armistice.

2 the second balkan war, 1913

— boundaries of areas lost by Bulgaria

territories gained according to the 1913 Treaties of London and Bucharest

▨ Romania	▨ Greece
▨ Serbia	▨ Ottoman empire

At the beginning of the 19th century, the Balkan peninsula was ruled entirely from Constantinople, the center of a genuinely multiracial empire. These European provinces were sparsely populated, poor, and provincial. They bordered the Christian empires of Catholic Austria and Orthodox Russia, both of which saw themselves as the natural ally of Balkan Christians.

Over the course of the century Austria and Russia strove to increase their influence in the peninsula as that of the Ottomans declined, but the chief beneficiaries of Ottoman weakness were the Balkan nationalities themselves. One by one the peoples of the Balkan area achieved their independence from Ottoman rule. Greece became independent in 1830. At the Congress of Berlin in 1878, following a war between Russia and the Ottoman empire over the Bulgarian struggle for independence, the political map of the region was redrawn. The independence of Serbia and Romania was assured; Bulgaria became a self-governing province within the Ottoman empire, independent in all but name; and the Habsburg empire took control over Bosnia, Herzegovina, and the Sanjak of Novibazar. Turkish rule in the Balkans was restricted to Albania, Macedonia, and Thrace and substantial parts of this legacy were ceded to Greece in 1881 and Bulgaria in 1885.

For the Balkan states, however, independence brought substantial problems. Not only were they economically backward and dominated by a numerous and impoverished peasantry, but high population growth in the second half of the 19th century led to smaller and smaller holdings of land. The average in Serbia was five acres, barely sufficient to feed a family. The only escape was emigration, most of it to the United States, or into the cities, where limited attempts were made to ape the industrial modernization of the rest of Europe. Chronic capital shortages and technical backwardness made economic progress difficult. In Romania, the most advanced Balkan economy, industry contributed only 1.5% of national wealth in 1914.

1 In October 1912 the Balkan League (Serbia, Montenegro, Bulgaria, and Greece) launched what became the First Balkan War against Ottoman Turkey (map right). Reinforcement for the Turks was difficult, because the Greek navy controlled the sea route to Macedonia. Bulgarian forces bore the brunt of the fighting. They besieged Adrianople (Edirne), which they were granted in the peace settlement in May 1913. The Greeks and Serbs attacked Macedonia and Albania, where they surrounded Turkish garrisons. These were poorly prepared for a prolonged siege, and the morale of the Turkish forces was low. The Serbs and Greeks were both ambitious to capture Albania whose ports, including Durazzo offered an opening to the Adriatic Sea. The Great Powers wanted instead an independent Albania. The war ended in May 1913 with the issue unresolved. Serbia and Greece looked to the Macedonian lands captured from Turkey as compensation. They agreed secretly with each other, and with Romania, Montenegro, and the recently defeated Turks, to divide up Macedonia at Bulgaria's expense.

The attempt to create new national states cost the Balkan peoples dearly. Taxation remained high, and governments, keen to build railroads and develop their armed forces, borrowed extensively from foreign lenders. Political power was chiefly in the hands of the royal courts and a small elite of soldiers and bureaucrats, although the states were all nominally constitutional monarchies. By 1900 mass politics began to encroach more. The Radical Party in Serbia and the Agrarian Union in Bulgaria both mobilized the votes of peasants anxious for reform. In Romania a mass peasant revolt in 1909 led to 10,000 deaths. In Greece a military revolt in 1909 brought to power Eleftherios Venizelos, a leading liberal reformer who dominated Greek politics for more than a generation.

For small national states, economically weak but with pretensions to grandeur, the remaining Ottoman territories in Europe were an inviting asset. Encouraged by Russia, which sought to improve its diplomatic standing in the region, the Balkan states negotiated treaties of mutual assistance in the spring of 1912 directed against the Ottoman empire. It was not part of Russia's plan to create stronger Balkan states, and in October Russia and Austria warned the Balkan states to leave Turkey alone.

The warning went unheeded. On October 8, Montenegro opened the war against Ottoman forces. The other Balkan states, Serbia, Greece, and Bulgaria, joined in. Their 700,000 troops were more than a match for the 320,000 Ottoman soldiers, poorly paid and with little stomach for the contest. In May 1913 the First Balkan War ended with only Constantinople and a small strip of territory left in Europe to the Turks (map right). The Balkan states then squabbled over the spoils. In June Bulgaria launched a war against Serbia and Greece to increase its share. She was quickly defeated. At the Treaty of Bucharest in August 1913, Macedonia was divided between Serbia and Greece, and an independent Albania established under an International Control Commission of the Great Powers, with Dutch officials in charge of Albania's tiny security forces. The national principle triumphed over old imperialism. For Russia and Austria, presiding uneasily over creaking multinational empires, this was an alarming precedent.

AUSTRO-HUNGARIAN EMPIRE

Požarevac

R O M A N I A

Vidin
Danube
Iskur
Plevna
Ruschuk
(Ruse)
D O B R U J A

S E R B I A
Nish
independent 1878
Novibazar
Mitrovica
Pirot
Slivnitsa
Sofia
B U L G A R I A
independent 1908
Trnovo
Shumla
Balchik
Varna

MONTENEGRO
Ipek (Pec)
Kostendil
siege of Adrianople;
taken by Bulgarians 1912,
restored to Turkey in
Nov. 1913 by Treaty of
Bucharest

agusa
ovnik)
Podgorica
siege of Scutari
Cetinje
Scutari
Lake
Scutari
Prizren
Debar
Uskub
(Skoplje)
Kumanovo
Oct. 23–24, 1912
Kocani
Philippopolis
(Plovdiv)
Maritsa
Burgas
Black Sea

Durazzo
Tirana
Elbasan
Krushevo
Monastir
Nov. 15–18, 1912
Florina
M a c e d o n i a
Serral
Mesta
Kirdzali
Xanthi
T h r a c e
Adrianople
(Edirne)
Babaeski
Kirk-kilisse
Oct. 22, 1912
Lüle Burgas
Oct. 29–31, 1912
Midia
Constantinople
San Stefano
Nov. 17–19
Tchadalja of
Mamara

A L B A N I A
principality 1913
Valona
Koritsa
Venidje Vardar
Nov. 2–3 1912
Salonica
Nov. 8, 1912:
Salonica capitulates
to the Greeks
Kavalla
Dedeagach
Enos
Thasos
Oct. 30, 1912:
occupied by Greece
Samothrace
Rodosto
Sea
Gemlik
Bursa

Argyrokastron
Santi
Quaranta
Corfu
Janina
Kalabaka
Larissa
Lemnos
Oct. 30, 1912:
occupied by Greece
Imbros
Oct. 30, 1912:
occupied by Greece
Dardanelles
Gallipoli
Balikesir

Epirus
Arta
Preveza
Volos
Thessaly
to Greece 1881
A e g e a n
Skopelos
Skyros
Tenedos
Oct. 30, 1912:
occupied by Greece
Lesbos
Nov. 21, 1912:
occupied by Greece
O T T O M A N

Lefkas
G R E E C E
independent 1830
Euboea
Sea
Chios
Nov. 24, 1912:
occupied by Greece
Gediz
Manisa
Smyrna
E M P I R E

Cephalonia
Gulf of Patras
Corinth
Piraeus
Athens
Andros
Tinos
Samos
Aydin
Menderes

Zakinthos
Peloponnese
Tripolis
Nauplia
Saronic
Gulf
Syros
Naxos
Cyclades
Nikaria
Nov. 17, 1912:
occupied by Greece
Mugla

Milos
Santorini
Simi
Rhodes
occupied by
Italy 1912
Rhodes
Scarpanto
Dodecanese

1 the balkans, 1912–13

western frontier of the Ottoman empire,
1912

position of armies, Oct. 18–20, 1912

⊠	Bulgarian	⊠	Serbian
⊠	Greek	⊠	Montenegrin
⊠	Ottoman	★	battle

**areas of opposition to Ottomans at the
armistice, Dec. 1912**

⧄	Bulgarian	⧄	Serbian
⧄	Greek	⧄	Montenegrin

**territory gained according to the
1913 Treaty of London by:**

▨	Bulgaria	▨	Serbia
▨	Greece	▨	Montenegro

C R E T E
independent 1898
to Greece 1913
Candia

M e d i t e r r a n e a n
S e a

19

european alliances

The crisis in the Balkans proved to be more than a local conflict over the Ottoman succession. The other European powers took a keen interest in the outcome. For more than a century the so-called Eastern Question—the balance of international power in the Near East—had been a central issue in the diplomacy of the major states.

The Balkans themselves were of little value beyond the insecure investments placed there, but they were long regarded as the frontier between the interests of three great empires whose preservation was thought to be in the wider interest of European security. When Ottoman power was eclipsed, the balance was rudely overturned, with neither Austria nor Russia willing to see the other fill the vacuum created by the end of Turkish rule.

The traditional solution was for the European powers to act in concert on issues that threatened to divide them. The Balkan crisis in the 1870s was resolved by the Congress of Berlin in 1878, orchestrated by the German chancellor, Otto von Bismarck, its prime motive being to maintain stability. Agreement was similarly reached on the Partition of Africa in 1884 and over the influence of the European powers in China. When the Balkan issue flared up again in

1912, the powers convened in London to do what they had done for decades: adjudicate disputes by common agreement.

Two factors undermined the concert tradition revived in London. Starting in the 1870s there had developed in Europe a system of alliances between two or more of the major states that cut across efforts at multilateral cooperation. By 1913 these had solidified into two blocks. On the one hand were the Central Powers, Germany, Austria, and Italy; on the other were the so-called "Entente" powers, built around the long-running military pact between France and Russia, to which Britain had finally adhered in order to settle colonial issues, first with France in 1904 and then Russia in 1907. Though the alliances were defensive in intent, they encouraged a competitive military buildup that left Europe less rather than more secure.

The second factor was the growing domestic weakness of the two empires, Russia and Austria-Hungary, whose interests were most affected by events in the Balkans. The attempts by the monarchy in both empires to maintain the old order, while encouraging economic and social modernization, produced serious tensions. Liberals and

1 Between 1879, when Germany and Austria-Hungary allied together, and 1907, when Britain signed an Entente agreement with Russia, Europe slowly divided into two alliance blocs. Britain remained aloof until signing an alliance with Japan in 1902, and a further agreement with France in 1904. Until then Germany had hoped to bring Britain into some kind of alliance against Russia and France. When the Balkan crises (1912-13, see page 18) flared up, the two alliance blocs were drawn inexorably into the conflict (map right), until all the major states of Europe, save Italy, were at war.

2 Morocco provided a key flashpoint in relations between the major European states. By agreements with Italy, Britain, and Spain (1902-4), France hoped to extend its influence in Morocco. German objections in 1906 led to the conference at Algeciras (map below). Five years later a second crisis developed when the German gunboat *Panther* was sent to Agadir in a show of strength to prevent France from establishing further control in Morocco. Conflict was averted in November 1911 when France granted Germany territory in the Congo in return for German recognition of French interests.

1 the outbreak of world war one, 1914

- mobilizations, with date
- ultimata issued, with date
- declarations of war, with date
- Entente Powers at outbreak of war
- joined Entente Powers during the war, with date
- Central Powers at outbreak of war
- joined Central Powers during the war, with date
- frontiers, 1914

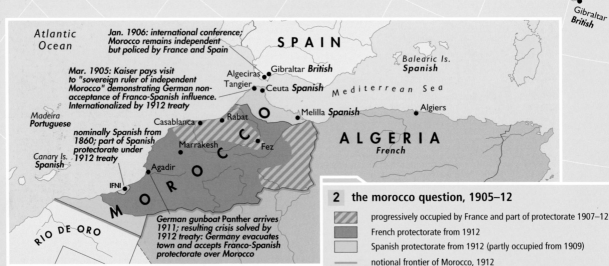

Atlantic Ocean

Jan. 1906: international conference; Morocco remains independent but policed by France and Spain

Mar. 1905: Kaiser pays visit to "sovereign ruler of independent Morocco" demonstrating German non-acceptance of Franco-Spanish influence. Internationalized by 1912 treaty

SPAIN

Algeciras • Gibraltar *British*
Tangier • Ceuta *Spanish*

Balearic Is. Spanish

Mediterrean Sea

Madeira Portuguese

Casablanca • • Rabat

nominally Spanish from 1860; part of Spanish protectorate under 1912 treaty

Marrakesh • • Fez

Melilla *Spanish*

Algiers •

A L G E R I A
French

Canary Is. Spanish

• Agadir

M O R O C C O

IFNI

RIO DE ORO

German gunboat Panther arrives 1911; resulting crisis solved by 1912 treaty: Germany evacuates town and accepts Franco-Spanish protectorate over Morocco

2 the morocco question, 1905–12

- progressively occupied by France and part of protectorate 1907–12
- French protectorate from 1912
- Spanish protectorate from 1912 (partly occupied from 1909)
- notional frontier of Morocco, 1912
- frontiers, 1912

www.firstworldwar.com/source/pre1914.htm
Archive documents from the years preceding the outbreak of WW1
www.worldhistory.com/wiki/n/nationalism.htm
Concepts of nationalism in the early 20th century

socialists wanted to scrap the old political system; nationalists demanded autonomy for the national minorities. Both empires sought to stem domestic decline through an active foreign policy. The Near East was a natural area of influence for both. Their mutual defense of the old status quo in the Balkans gave way to a growing rivalry. The area became a testing ground for the survival of the dynastic empires as great powers.

For Austria the threat was immediate. The success of Serbia against Turkey encouraged a general southern Slav movement among the Slavic peoples of the Habsburg empire. Austria, like Turkey, faced the nationalist fragmentation of its empire. On June 28, when a Bosnian nationalist, primed by Serbian military intelligence, assassinated Franz Ferdinand, heir to the Austrian throne, in Sarajevo, the Austrian authorities determined to launch a third Balkan war to punish the Serbs. They

expected a small war and remained blind to the wider European crisis provoked by their gesture. Inevitably, the Serbian crisis interlocked with the wider system of alliances. Russia gave Serbia qualified support, enough for her to reject an ultimatum from Vienna that would have turned Serbia into a satellite state. Germany encouraged Austria to act quickly, but to avoid a wider war. France encouraged Russia to stand firm and mobilize. In the confusion, states believed the worst of each other. Germany mobilized and moved preemptively against the powers that, in her view, "encircled" her. Russia and France mobilized to avoid the German danger. Britain sided with her allies only after German troops invaded Belgium in early August on their way to fight the French. Within a week the great powers found themselves at war over a Balkan issue that a year before they had been able to resolve around the conference table.

21

the **great war**: the western front

1914 to 1918

- **1914 (July)** outbreak of WWI
- **1914 (September 5-10)** Battle of the Marne
- **1916** Battle of the Somme
- **1917** first use of massed tanks (Battle of Cambrai)
- **1917** Americans enter the war; Russians withdraw
- **1918** Armistice

In the years before 1914 imperialism, economic rivalry and the rise of popular nationalism at home encouraged a widespread fatalism about the inevitability of conflict. Yet in July 1914 few Europeans expected the Balkan crisis to result in a general European war.

The network of alliances and the arms race all pointed to a different conflict. In the event, it was the crisis of traditional dynasticism rather than the forces of change that produced war, the old order rather than the new.

The general assumption was that war would be over by Christmas. Military leaders prepared for a single decisive battle with the weapons available. There was little planning for a longer war. The German general staff exemplified this outlook. As early as 1904 the chief-of-staff, Alfred von Schlieffen, drew up a plan for a short two-front campaign. German forces were to be concentrated against France in a quick knockout blow before wheeling eastward to defeat the more slowly mobilizing Russian army.

It was a risky strategy, forced by necessity. When war really came in 1914 Schlieffen's successor, Helmuth von Moltke, hesitated to take the risk. He kept some forces in reserve in case the French attacked southern Germany; other forces had to be pulled back hastily to the east when Russia mobilized faster than anticipated. As a result, the German blow against France lacked sufficient strength to be decisive. French forces, reinforced by the speedily assembled British Expeditionary Force, counter-attacked the German forces 40 miles from Paris. The Battle of the Marne (September 5-10) forced a German withdrawal to the Aisne River and effectively ended the Schlieffen Plan. Both armies dug in, with artillery amd machine guns, behind a rampart of barbed wire.

Both sides sought to break the deadlock. In the east, German forces were more successful. Together with Austro-Hungarian armies, Germany pushed Russia back hundreds of miles across Russian Poland. The western Allies planned to circumvent the trenches by moving from southern Europe. Italy was induced to join the Entente Powers and a new front opened against Austria. When Turkey joined the German side late in 1914, attacks were launched by British Empire forces in the Middle East. Neither new front broke the stalemate.

In 1916 the British under Field Marshal Douglas Haig prepared a more carefully planned frontal assault on German lines in the west. The Battle of the Somme began on July 1st against strongly defended German positions. Haig planned to smother the German trenches with a five-day artillery barrage and then mass divisions for a "Big Push" to break the German front. The reality was grotesquely different. On the first day of the battle the British suffered 60,000 casualties, mowed down as they advanced through barbed wire. For another four months Haig threw forces into an unwinnable conflict. Both sides experienced terrible losses. Little was achieved.

In 1917 morale on both sides was poor. French troops mutinied rather than be pitted uselessly against machine guns. In July the German parliament passed a peace resolution calling for an end to hostilities. The mutineers were promised improved tactics and conditions; the German military leaders, Field Marshal Paul von Hindenburg and General Erich Ludendorff, rejected any thought of peace short of victory. An unrestricted submarine campaign was launched in February 1917 to blockade Britain into defeat. The chief effect of this decision was to bring the United States into the war against Germany.

The last year of the war was fought under rapidly changing circumstances. American entry coincided

1 During the Great War Europe experienced the first continent-wide conflict since the Napoleonic wars a century before. Population growth and industrialization now produced a war of extraordinary scale and destructiveness (maps right and below). In 1916 the Entente Allies had a combined population of almost 300 million, the Central Powers only 142 million. The balance of Europe's mineral production was more even. However, by the end of the war much of the Allied capacity had been captured by German and Austrian forces, in Belgium, northern France and the Ukraine. The Allies were saved in 1917 by the addition to their strength of the resources of the United States.

2 the western front, 1914–18

→ Entente offensives

→ German offensives

━ farthest German advance, Sep. 5, 1914

━ trench line from Nov. 1914

━ Armistice line, Nov. 11, 1918

★ battle

★ battle costing more than 250,000 lives

naval blockade of Germany effective end 1916

1916: Battle of Jutland

1914: Tannenberg counteroffensive

1917: Riga offensive

1914: Russian offensive in East Prussia

1916: Brusilov offensive

1918: Central Powers advance through Ukraine

Kiev 1918

1914

1915: Gorlice campaign

1917

1916: Asiago offensive

1918

1915 Isonzo

1915: conquest of Serbia

1916: Central Powers conquest of Romania

Kolubara 1914

1916 Tirana

1918: Allied advance into Serbia

1915: British land at Salonica to support Serbia

1915: Gallipoli offensive

see inset below left

with Russian withdrawal following the second revolution there in October 1917. Germany swung more forces to the west, and Ludendorff prepared for a final assault to break the deadlock. The March offensive of 1918 used specially trained "storm battalions" to breach the enemy line to allow the infantry mass to follow through. Any initial success was blunted by Allied superiority in material as well as the strategic vision of the Allied supreme commander, Marshal Ferdinand Foch. In June the German effort was over, and the Allies, reinforced by American forces and money, slowly pushed the German army back toward the German frontier. Though technically undefeated in the field, Ludendorff pressed for an armistice in November 1918 to avoid an unambiguous Allied victory.

1 the great war in europe, 1914–18

Entente Powers

Central Powers

major Entente Power offensives

major Central Power offensives

farthest advance by Entente Powers: (east 1914, west 1918)

farthest advance by Central Powers: (west 1914, east 1918)

★ battle

★ battle costing more than 250,000 lives

⚓ naval base

- **1914** attacks launched by British forces on Middle East
- **1914 (late)** Turkey joins Central Powers
- **1914-15** French, British, and South Africans conquer German colonies except German East Africa; German concessions in China and colonies in Pacific are taken over by Japan, Australia, and New Zealand
- **1915** Gallipoli campaign; troops withdrawn January 1916
- **1915 (April)** Treaty of London
- **1916** Romania occupied by German forces after declaring for entente powers
- **1917** Greece enters war under Anglo-French pressure
- **1917** General Allenby takes Jerusalem

Victory in the First World War was decided on the Western Front, but the war was fought right across Europe and the Middle East, as well as in Germany's overseas colonies.

German possessions in the Far East and the Pacific were captured in four months. German colonies in Africa fell to French, British, and South African forces, except for German East Africa, where the German commander, General von Lettow-Vorbeck, fought a skillful campaign, in which he remained undefeated when the Armistice came in 1918.

Victory in the Middle East had a number of causes. The Ottoman Turks, still smarting from defeat in Europe in 1913, were pro-Austrian and anti-Serb. The war minister, Enver Pasha, had close contacts with Berlin, and when the Central Powers offered the restoration of Turkish Macedonia in return for Turkish assistance, he persuaded his government to declare war on the Entente Powers in November 1914. The closure by Turkey of the straits to the Black Sea cut Russia off from her trade lifeline with the West, undermining the Russian war effort. The Turkish forces were sent east into the Russian Caucasus, where they were annihilated in the snowbound mountains. In April 1915 the Turkish army prevented the British seizure of Gallipoli and the Dardanelles. More British disasters followed. A small Anglo-Indian force advanced into Mesopotamia (modern Iraq), but was besieged and forced to surrender to the Turks at Kut el Amara in April 1916. A Turkish attack on the Suez Canal was repulsed by British empire forces, but the effort to dislodge the Turks from Sinai was ineffectual until General Allenby broke through in the fall of 1917 and pushed on to take Jerusalem. In the last year of war a widespread Arab revolt helped the British cause. When Turkey sued for an armistice in October 1918 most of her remaining empire had already been occupied.

In the Balkan peninsula loyalties were divided between the two sides. Bulgaria, anxious, like Turkey, to reverse the outcome of the Balkan Wars, sided with Austria and Germany. In October 1915 Bulgaria entered the war against Serbia, whose small population had kept the Habsburg empire at bay for a year. Serbia was quickly defeated. Romania and Greece both hesitated, waiting to see which side would prevail. Romania overestimated Russian strength and when she declared for the Entente Powers in 1916 was occupied by German forces. In Greece a fierce domestic political struggle developed over intervention. British and French troops landed at Salonica in October 1915 to aid Serbia, but remained bottled up there until September 1918. Under British and French pressure Greece finally joined the war effort in June 1917. When the western powers liberated the Balkans against feeble resistance in September-November 1918, there were nine Greek and six Serbian divisions fighting alongside the British and French.

1 The Ottoman empire entered the war at the side of Germany and Austria in October 1914, hoping to resurrect her fading fortunes in the Middle East (map right). Her actions tied down western forces in Egypt, the Persian Gulf and at Salonica in the Balkans. Turkey's major battles were fought against the Russians on the Trans-Caucasian front. The army was weakened by the confrontation with Russia, and in 1916 a widespread Arab revolt in Arabia forced Turkey to abandon much of the southern empire before an armistice was signed aboard the British warship *Agamemnon* on October 30, 1918, moored off the coast of Lemnos.

2 When, after a great deal of domestic argument, Italy joined the Entente Powers in May 1915 in the war against Austria-Hungary, she was confined by geography to fight on a narrow stretch of her northeastern frontier (map left). Two years later German forces joined the battle and inflicted a devastating defeat, whose effects were only finally overcome a year later in October 1918 against a weakened enemy at Vittorio Veneto.

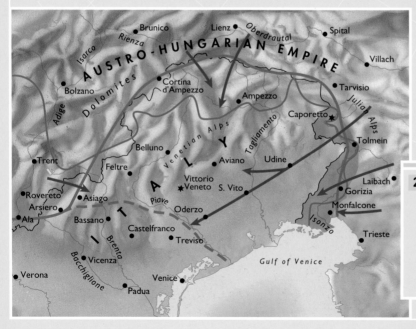

2 the italian campaign, 1915–18

- area of Isonzo campaign 1915–17
- frontline, Oct. 1917
- → German offensive, Oct. 1917–Jan. 1918
- frontline, Jan. 1918
- armistice line, Nov. 1918
- ★ battle

1 the war in the middle east, 1914–18

Entente Powers · Central Powers

Advances
→ British   → Russian
⇢ Arab   → Ottoman
→ French

Offensives
— area of Arab revolt against Ottomans
— Ottoman frontline at time of surrender, Oct. 30, 1918
— railroads

Italian belligerence was also bought by the promise of territory in the Balkans. Italy in 1914 had been formally allied to Austria and Germany, but refused to honor the alliance on the grounds that Vienna had not consulted the Italian government about its plans for a Serbian war. Italian society was deeply divided over intervention in the war: the nationalists hoped to use the conflict to increase Italian power in the Adriatic and Mediterranean; the dominant liberals were split; the left was opposed to the war. In the end the government waited to see which side would offer most. It proved to be the Entente Powers. In the Treaty of London, signed in April 1915, Italy was offered the areas occupied by the Habsburgs in South Tyrol, Trieste, and Istria, a slice of the Dalmatian coast, the Dodecanese Islands, and a share of the German colonies.

The following month Italy duly declared war on Austria-Hungary, though not against Germany. The Italian commander, General Cadorna, mobilized his poorly trained and ill-equipped forces , and, between June

1915 and August 1917, repeatedly attacked the Austrian lines on the Isonzo front in the northeast. By 1917 Italy was also at war with Germany, and when in October 1917 Austria at last persuaded the German Kaiser to supply German forces for Italy a counteroffensive was mounted. The deficiencies of Italian forces were fully exposed when Austro-German forces attacked at Caporetto, smashing all resistance and capturing 250,000 Italians. Cadorna withdrew to the Piave River. Famous for sacking his own generals in droves, he himself was now sacked. His successor, General Diaz, retrained and reequipped the Italian army. Western forces and weapons appeared in larger numbers. Meanwhile, a renewed Austro-German offensive in June 1918 was repulsed. In October Diaz attacked a demoralized and disorganized Habsburg force. In the battle of Vittorio Veneto, Italy gained its first battle honors.

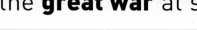
Before the war it was widely assumed that any great power conflict would be both a land war and a naval war. The naval race before 1914 had produced great battle fleets on both sides. Germany and Austria had 56 battleships between them; Britain, France, and Russia had 123, with 74 in the Royal Navy alone.

In practice the naval war took second place to the land battle. There was only one serious clash between the British and German navies, the Battle of Jutland (May 31–June 1, 1916), the last naval engagement with lines of large-gunned battleships.

The German High Seas Fleet was effectively blockaded in its ports by the stronger Allied force confronting it. The sea war became a conflict of blockade and counterblockade, and its chief offensive vessel was the submarine, whose true impact few had foreseen before 1914. The target of both sides was the seaborne commerce of the other. The British began a formal blockade in March 1915, with Orders in Council which permitted the seizure of goods destined for Germany. As the stalemate continued, the blockade was tightened. Britain used her powerful trading and financial position across the world to pressure other states and private firms to limit trade with the enemy. The effects of the blockade on Germany are difficult to estimate precisely, since domestic shortages of food also had domestic causes. The loss of feed-stuffs and fertilizer from abroad crippled German agriculture. By 1917 meat consumption was less than one-third of the prewar level, and grain consumption only half.

Both sides found naval inaction frustrating. In order to give the Navy a clear strategy of its own, the first lord of the admiralty, Winston Churchill, pushed for an attack on the Turkish Straits. The operation began on February 19, 1915 with five French and British battleships blasting Turkish defenses. The subsequent landing was a catastrophe. The mainly Australian and New Zealand troops involved were pinned down for nine months with enormous casualties. In January 1916, they were withdrawn. Churchill resigned, and the Royal Navy developed no further independent strategy.

There were frustrations on the other side, too. In 1916 the commander of the German High Seas Fleet, Admiral Reinhard Scheer, planned to lure the Royal Navy into a major fleet battle in the North Sea, where the British ships would be sunk by a waiting U-boat trap. The plan was a disaster. Alerted by radio intelligence, the British fleet was ready for the engagement. The two met at Jutland off the Danish coast. Outnumbered, Scheer skillfully extracted his ships and retreated back to port. The British lost 14 ships, the Germans 11. The battle confirmed the powerlessness of the German navy, which was forced to sit out the war.

In the last weeks of the war German commanders in Kiel decided on a final do-or-die duel with the enemy. By then the sailors, bored and hungry, had had enough of the war and mutinied. A year later the fleet was scuttled rather than let it fall into British hands.

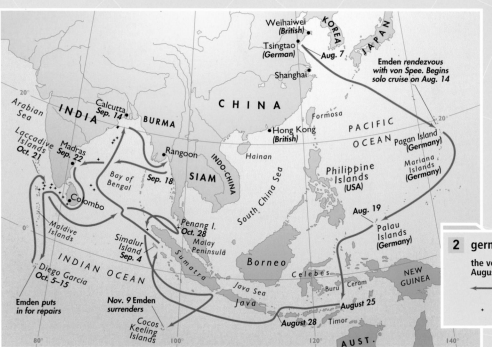

2 In the first year of war Allied shipping was threatened in every ocean by small numbers of German merchant raiders, German warships stranded abroad. The *Emden* and *Königsberg* entered the Indian Ocean in August 1914 from the Pacific, where they had formed part of the German East Asia Squadron under von Spee. The *Emden*'s voyage (map left) led to the loss of 17 merchant vessels before her surrender in November.

2 **german merchant**

the voyage of SMS *Emden*, August 7–November 9, 1914

→ route of SMS *Emden*

+ captures by the SMS *Emden*

www.worldwar1.co.uk/
History of surface warship warfare during WW1
www.bbc.co.uk/history/war/wwone/war_sea_gallery_05.shtml
Battles and themes of British sea power during WW1

1 Overseas trade with the empire and
the Americas was vital to Britain and
France. More than half of British food and
raw materials came from foreign trade. The map
(above) shows the main trade routes bringing supplies of
grain, meat, nitrates, copper, and hides for the western war effort. For the
first year of war individual German warships preyed on merchant vessels. Once
they were eliminated the threat of minefields and submarines remained,
chiefly in the approaches to British and French ports. The admiralty in London
remained strongly opposed to establishing merchant convoys on the grounds
that they would be large and inviting targets and were difficult to organize and
escort. Armed merchantmen fought their way through individually. In 1917
convoys were tried on the Scandinavian route and losses fell from 25% to
0.24%. Convoys were then introduced on all routes. In June/July 1917, 800
ships sailed in Anglo-American convoys and only five were lost.

---

1 the war at sea, 1914–16

* Entente Powers minefield
* Central Powers minefield
— trade route
→ route of von Spee's squadron
  Aug.–Nov. 1914
⊙ area in which German merchant
  raiders made captures,
  Aug. 1914–Feb. 1915
▬ naval battle (see right)

Naval battles

1 Heligoland Bight:
   August 28, 1914

2 Coronel:
   November 1, 1914

3 Falkland Islands:
   December 8, 1914

4 Jutland:
   May 31, 1916

27

the costs of the **great war**

by 1917 40% of British workers are women

1918 outbreak of "Spanish" influenza kills more than 6 million Europeans

When the war ended in November 1918 its costs dwarfed anything imagined four years before. The conflict took the lives of eight and a half million soldiers, and left another 21 million wounded, gassed, or shell-shocked.

The financial cost totaled more than $186 billion worldwide and the economies of every warring state in Europe were brought close to bankruptcy as governments resorted to the printing press to fund the swelling demands of war. Civilians not only bore the financial burden, but suffered high loss rates through famine, disease, or the direct effects of the war. The war also cost the lives of an estimated nine million civilians.

Conflict on this scale was without precedent. States had no experience of mobilizing and equipping forces of this size. As the war progressed the demands of the military machine forced governments to control the production of the whole economy, to ration goods, and to replace male labor with women, young workers, or forced labor. By the end of the war 65 million men had been mobilized, most of them peasants or clerks. Agricultural output declined as a result. In Germany 30 million tons of grain were produced in 1913; in 1917 output was just 15 million.

General Ludendorff, the German quartermaster-general, in 1919 described the conflict as "total war." It was a new kind of war between national communities, not just between soldiers. The scientific, economic, and moral resources of the nation were mobilized as ruthlessly and comprehensively as its military manpower. No state in 1914 had been prepared for such a conflict. The demands of war led to exceptional claims on domestic resources and involved a degree of state direction, even in the democracies, unheard of in peacetime. Widespread propaganda was used to maintain enthusiasm for war. Workers were placed under martial law or subjected to strict labor conscription.

The effects on the home front were often severe. Longer hours of work, declining safety standards, the difficulty of obtaining even rationed goods, the sharp fall in real income, all produced a continuous decline in the standard of life. Conditions were better in Britain, with access to the world market and a strong financial position, and worst in Germany, Austria, and Russia, which were cut off from the world economy by the war. Hunger and overwork took their toll, and when a virulent "Spanish" influenza epidemic hit Europe in 1918, more than six million died.

Worsening conditions provoked widespread unrest. After a period of political truce in the early stages of the war, the parties of the left became increasingly critical of the war, while the unions, their numbers swollen by new recruits to the industrial workforce, pursued improvement in conditions through strikes. In 1915 there had been 2,374 strikes in the warring states, involving 1.1 million workers; in 1917 there were 4,369 with 3.4 million

1 the cost of the war

mobilized forces and losses

5.6 million
Entente Powers

2.8 million
Central Powers

0.6 million
deaths

British and U.S. loans

British (U.S. $)
France $2.17

U.S. (U.S. $)
Italy $1.59

frontiers, 1914

from United States

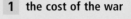

1 The First World War, (maps left and right) took a terrible toll on the men who fought it. Out of more than 42 million mobilized on the side of the Central Powers, 52% were killed, wounded, or taken prisoner. On the other side 67% of all the mobilized men were lost to the war effort. Austria-Hungary lost 90% of her military manpower. The financial burden dwarfed all previous state expenditure. The western Allies were sustained at the end of the war by $10 billion of U.S. aid.

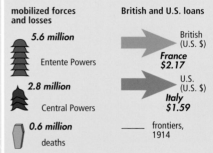

cost per country (U.S. dollars $)

$37.7 bn	Germany
$35.3 bn	Great Britain
$22.6 bn	USA
$24.2 bn	France
$22.6 bn	Russian empire
$20.6 bn	Austria-Hungary
$12.4 bn	Italy
$1.66 bn	Canada
$1.6 bn	Romania
$1.43 bn	Ottoman empire
$1.42 bn	Australia
$1.1 bn	Belgium
$0.8 bn	Bulgaria
$0.6 bn	India
$0.5 bn	other Allies
$0.4 bn	Serbia
$0.37 bn	New Zealand
$0.3 bn	South Africa
$0.27 bn	Greece
$0.13 bn	other British colonies
$0.04 bn	Japan
$186 bn	Total

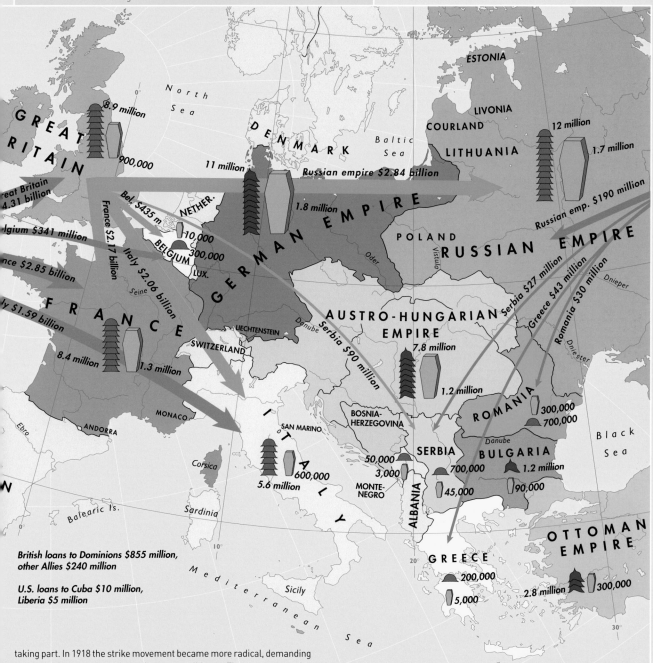

taking part. In 1918 the strike movement became more radical, demanding political change as well as better conditions. There was popular resentment against businessmen who were believed to be making windfall profits out of the war, or against wealthier consumers who could buy on the black market or live life as usual.

By 1918 very few were untouched by war. An army of volunteers, many of them women, helped run the medical services, or staff the new government offices set up to cope with administering the home front, or collect scrap and refuse to recycle for war production. In Germany *ersatz* or substitute materials were unavoidable. Shoes were made of cardboard, paper from potatoes, coffee from nettles. In Austria, Russia, and Italy even *ersatz* could not be produced, and the supply of food and military equipment collapsed under the strain of the war, leading by 1917 to severe shortages both at home and at the front, and to widespread demoralization.

The First World War was a test of endurance—of national cohesion, of moral resilience, of economic capacity. It was also a test of the old European order, and its self-confident, morally assured claim to be the source of peace and progress. Europe's image was irreparably tarnished by the war. Progress was shown to mask barbarism; civilization to be a veneer. The war marked the end of the Europeanization of the world, and opened the way to a new world in which Europe played just one of the parts.

29

russia: from czardom to bolshevism

The bankruptcy of the old order was most clearly evident in the Russia of the Romanovs. In the decades before 1914 Russia presented a curious blend of reform and repression. The czars recognized that the survival of their system of personal rule depended on building a strong state.

Feudalism was ended in the 1860s. The army was modernized and expanded. In the 1890s the finance minister, Sergei Witte, accelerated Russia's industrialization, so that by 1914 Russia was the world's fifth-largest industrial power. These changes helped transform Russian society. A wave of new workers from the land moved into Russia's cities, swamping the traditional urban workforce and straining the supply of housing and food. The gentry declined as a social and political force. Modernization produced a new business class, but it also generated a more numerous class of officials, doctors, teachers, and lawyers, among whose number were many eager to maintain the pace of reform and transform Russia into a modern state. It was here that the czarist regime refused to change. The state remained a royal autocracy, with political power imposed by the army and the bureaucracy.

Nicholas II believed his power was granted by God and that it was his duty to exercise it undiminished.

The contradiction between old-fashioned divine-right rule and the reality of rapid social and economic change encouraged widespread political opposition. When Russia was defeated in a war with Japan over the Far Eastern frontier in 1904-5 the czar's position weakened. Peasant unrest and growing labor protest provoked a revolutionary crisis. In October 1905 the czar consented to a manifesto drawn up by Witte which offered civil liberties and a popularly elected assembly. When popular protest subsided, the concessions were modified. The franchise was limited, the assembly had no real power, and civil rights—freedom of speech and assembly—never activated. Between 1906 and 1914 the czar attempted to rule as he had always done.

By 1914 autocracy was still intact, but it coexisted with growing political movements—conservative, liberal, socialist—whose supporters expected political reform. Protest grew in 1914, and the decision for war with Austria and Germany was taken by the czar in the middle of a general strike in St. Petersburg.

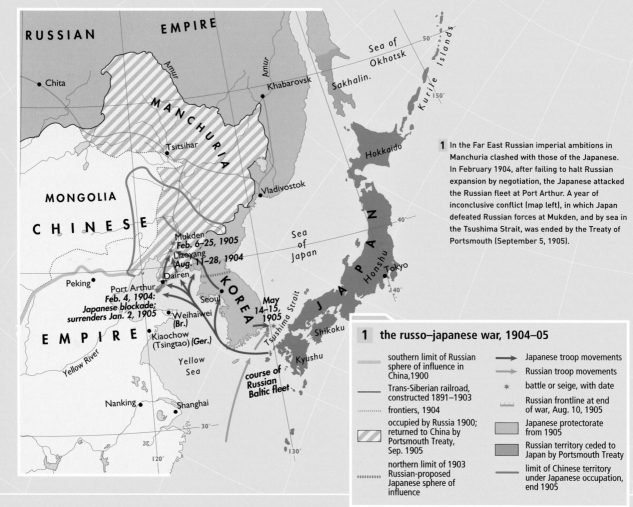

1 In the Far East Russian imperial ambitions in Manchuria clashed with those of the Japanese. In February 1904, after failing to halt Russian expansion by negotiation, the Japanese attacked the Russian fleet at Port Arthur. A year of inconclusive conflict (map left), in which Japan defeated Russian forces at Mukden, and by sea in the Tsushima Strait, was ended by the Treaty of Portsmouth (September 5, 1905).

1 the russo–japanese war, 1904–05

- southern limit of Russian sphere of influence in China, 1900
- Trans-Siberian railroad, constructed 1891–1903
- frontiers, 1904
- occupied by Russia 1900; returned to China by Portsmouth Treaty, Sep. 1905
- northern limit of 1903 Russian-proposed Japanese sphere of influence
- Japanese troop movements
- Russian troop movements
- battle or seige, with date
- Russian frontline at end of war, Aug. 10, 1905
- Japanese protectorate from 1905
- Russian territory ceded to Japan by Portsmouth Treaty
- limit of Chinese territory under Japanese occupation, end 1905

www.dur.ac.uk/~dml0www/Russhist.HTML
Russian history, 1905-30
www.usd.edu/honors/HWB/hwb_l/lenin.htm
Lenin's rise to power in Russia

2 War on the Eastern Front (map left) between 1914 and 1917 was more mobile than in the West. The field of war was much larger, and the number of troops much smaller. Early Russian victories against Austro-Hungarian armies were balanced by major defeat in the advance into Prussia in August 1914. In 1915 the Central Powers pressed Russian forces back. In 1916 Russian armies again inflicted serious reverses on Austrian forces and reached the crest of the Carpathian mountains, only to be pushed back once more by the German army.

2 the eastern front, 1915–17

- controlled by Central Powers, end Apr. 1915
- → Central Powers' advances, 1915
- captured by Central Powers by end Sep. 1915
- → Brusilov offensive (June 4, 1916) and Romanian attack (Aug. 28, 1918)
- Entente Powers frontline, Oct. 18, 1916
- captured by Central Powers by Jan. 1917
- western extent of Russian control at outbreak of Revolution, Feb. 1917
- → czar's failed attempt to reach St. Petersburg, Mar. 1917
- — frontiers, 1914

With the coming of war the political tensions in Russia subsided. Two vast Russian army groups moved through East Prussia toward Berlin and then into Galicia against Austro-Hungarian forces. The Austrians suffered a crushing defeat at Lemberg, but German forces under Hindenburg, hastily deployed against a larger army, inflicted defeats at Tannenberg and the Masurian Lakes, which turned the tide in the East. In 1915 Russian forces were pressed back deep into Russian territory, suffering a million casualties and the loss of a million men captured. In the fall the czar insisted on taking over the high command himself, against almost universal protest. In 1916 Russian offensives, even the early successes of General Brusilov against the Austrians in June, were turned back, and another million men lost.

The effects of defeat on the home front fatally undermined the old order. The incompetence of czarist officials and ministers undermined what voluntary efforts were made by the war industry committees set up by business-

men or by the relief and medical facilities run by the Union of Towns and *Zemstvos* (local councils). The huge losses of men and horses reduced the food supply. In December 1916 the army ration was cut from three pounds of bread a day to one. Officers and men lost confidence in the czar. The court around the czarina, Alexandra, and her mystic adviser, Rasputin, was isolated amid a sea of protest across the political spectrum. In December 1916 Rasputin was murdered by a group of aristocrats. On February 23rd, following a month of city-wide strikes and bread riots in St. Petersburg, a demonstration for International Women's Day turned into a revolutionary protest. Soldiers in the city refused to fire on the demonstrators. The czar's generals and the Duma political parties universally condemned the czar. With no prospect of military support he abdicated on March 2, 1917, and the following day a provisional government was declared, led by Prince Georgii Lvov and composed largely of moderate liberals.

the **russian** revolution

1917 (February-November) membership of Bolshevik party climbs from 22,000 to 200,000

1917 (June) popular revolution declared in Petrograd by angry workers and soldiers

1917 (July) socialist Alexander Kerensky becomes premier of Provisional government

1917 (14 September) Kerensky declares a Republic

1917 (29 October) Petrograd Soviet establishes a Military Revolutionary Committee and seizes control of Petrograd

1917 (November) Bolsheviks take over and first socialist state established

1917 (December) Geman government agrees to Armistice

With the overthrow of the old order in Russia, there was widespread support for the establishment of a liberal, constitutional regime. There was hope that the war could now be prosecuted efficiently and in the people's name. The new regime promised a constituent assembly that would decide the form of the new state.

The bulk of the army remained at the front to prevent a German breakthrough. The Provisional Government faced a chaotic situation. Troops at the front formed popular councils and rejected orders. In cities and villages local committees (soviets) were set up in an attempt to run local affairs in defiance of the government. The Petrograd Soviet set itself up as a rival source of authority; dominated by socialists, it called for immediate social reforms, economic improvement, and an end to the war. But with neither the Soviets nor the Provisional Government able to compel obedience, conditions on the home front deteriorated further.

During 1917 the crisis of food supply grew worse. By October Moscow and Petrograd were down to a few days' supply of what were already meager rations. Real wages fell by more than one-third over the summer, factories were closed down for want of materials, the transportation system was strained to breaking point, and runaway inflation set in. The public mood became more radical. Peasants, who had hoped for a redistribution of land that never came, began to seize the large estates for themselves. Workers, many of whom had not initially been hostile to the regime, were alienated by further deprivation and the decision to renew the war. In April the Provisional Government took in moderate socialists; in July the socialist Alexander Kerensky became premier. As the government moved to the left, it alienated conservative and liberal support without solving popular grievances. When a renewed offensive in Galicia in June 1917 was defeated by German forces with heavy loss of life, a popular revolution was declared in Petrograd by angry workers and soldiers. The "July Days" were ended by repression, but Russia's cities were becoming ungovernable.

The main beneficiary of the radicalization of Russian society was the Bolshevik Party. Support for other socialist parties—the Social Revolutionaries and the moderate Mensheviks—also increased, but it was the spectacular growth of Bolshevism, from around 22,000 party members in February 1917 to more than 200,000 eight months later, that constituted the chief threat. Bolshevik leaders refused to cooperate with the Provisional Government. They argued for an end to the war, the granting of land to poor peasants, and the transfer of power to the local soviets, which Bolshevik sympathizers entered in large numbers. Lenin stressed the importance of propaganda and political activism. By the fall many Russians saw Bolshevism as the only way out of the chaos of war and economic collapse, and the only way to save the revolution.

When in September the army commander-in-chief, General Kornilov, attempted a march on Petrograd to stamp out unrest and stiffen the war effort, Bolsheviks were prominent among the workers who halted his trains and persuaded his soldiers to defect. Russia began to polarize between right and left, and violence increased. On September 14th, Kerensky declared a republic, hoping to appease radical opinion, but the Provisional Government had lost all credibility. Early in October the Bolshevik central committee decided to stage a coup. The Petrograd Soviet established a Military Revolutionary Committee on October 29th, controlled by the Bolshevik, Leon Trotsky. Between November 6th and 8th the Military Committee seized control of Petrograd, while the All-Russian Congress of Soviets, meeting in the city, approved an exclusively Bolshevik Council of People's Commissars as the new government, with Lenin as its chairman.

The new regime announced sweeping changes. Local power was granted to the soviets and popular committees; land was promised to the peasantry (who had already seized most of it); non-Russian nationalities were promised autonomy; the workers were offered control of the factories. Above all, Lenin urged the search for peace. This was almost the only promise he redeemed. In December the German government agreed to an armistice. In March Trotsky traveled to the Polish city of Brest-Litovsk, where he was compelled to recognize the loss of the former czarist territories of Poland, the Baltic States, Ukraine, and Georgia. Two months before, the long-promised Constituent Assembly, called reluctantly by Lenin, returned 75% non-Bolshevik delegates. It was closed down immediately, and a *de facto* Bolshevik dictatorship commenced upon the daunting task of building a new Russia.

1 By the winter of 1916–17 Russia was in crisis (map right). When hostility to the regime reached boiling point in February 1917, there were spontaneous protests in many Russian cities. When the czar abdicated, he was succeeded by a provisional government whose authority was difficult to establish in the country and in the army. Popular local councils (soviets) sprang up in the cities and in the countryside. By October domestic order and military discipline had collapsed to such an extent that the radical socialist Bolshevik movement was able to seize power.

2 The Bolshevik Revolution in November was a carefully planned seizure of power in the capital, Petrograd (map left). On November 6–7 the bridges and the main railroad stations were seized by armed workers and soldiers. On October 25th the cruiser *Aurora* fired blank shells at the Winter Palace, which housed the Provisional Government. On November 8th the palace was occupied and the government disbanded. The Bolsheviks set great store by the use of revolutionary force.

2 the revolution in petrograd, Nov. 1917

❶ first Bolshevik objective

❷ second Bolshevik objective

❸ third Bolshevik objective

○ garrison loyal to Provincial Government

◉ garrison loyal to Bolsheviks

Norwegian Sea

Barents Sea

1 russia in war and revolution, 1917–18

western border of the Russian empire, 1914

front between Russia and Central Powers, Mar. 12, 1917

Lenin's return from Switzerland, Apr. 1917

Russian gains in July 1917 offensive

serious Russian mutinies in Aug. 1917

Central Power gains by Oct. 20, 1917

Kornilov's attack on Petrograd, Sep. 8–14, 1917

principal towns where Bolsheviks took power, Nov. 1917–Feb. 1918

boundary of Russian territory occupied by Central Powers following the Treaty of Brest-Litovsk, Mar. 1918

frontiers, 1916

• Narvik

N O R W A Y

• Trondhjem

S W E D E N

White Sea

Mezen

Archangel
Feb. 17, 1918

F I N L A N D
independence of Finland recognized Dec. 1917

Lake Onega

Onega

Åbo
Helsingfors •

Lake Ladoga

Petrozavodsk
Jan. 17, 1918

• Stockholm

Sukhona

20 Oct. 1917

Baltic Sea

Revel
8 Nov. 1917

Petrograd
Nov. 7, 1917

Vologda
Feb. 8, 1918

Vyatka
Dec. 8, 1917

Yekaterinburg
Nov. 8, 1917

Novgorod
Nov. 27, 1917

Perm
Nov. 14, 1917

Riga
early Sep. 1917

Pskov
Nov. 15, 1917

Yaroslavl
Nov. 9, 1917

Kostroma
Dec. 15, 1917

Izhevsk
Nov. 9, 1917

Dvinsk •

Tver
Nov. 10, 1917

Ivanovo
Nov. 7, 1917

Kazan
Nov. 8, 1917

Danzig •

Königsberg •

Government moved from Petrograd Mar. 1918

Moscow
Nov. 15, 1917

Nizhniy Novgorod
Nov. 10, 1917

Ufa
Nov. 8, 1917

GERMAN EMPIRE

Vilna •

Vitebsk
Nov. 9, 1917

Smolensk
Nov. 12, 1917

Kaluga
Dec. 11, 1917

R U S S I A

Tula *Dec. 20, 1917*

P O L A N D

Warsaw

Minsk
Nov. 7, 1917

Mogilev
Dec. 1, 1917

Penza
Jan. 4, 1918

Samara
Nov. 9, 1917

Lodz •

Brest-Litovsk

Orel
Nov. 14, 1917

Tambov
Nov. 13, 1917

Volga

Orenburg
Jan. 31, 1918

Gomel
Nov. 12, 1917

• Kursk

Don

Voronezh
Nov. 12, 1917

Saratov
Nov. 9, 1917

Cracow •

Zhitomir
Jan. 22, 1918

• Lemberg

Kiev
Feb. 8, 1918

Kassa •

AUSTRO-HUNGARIAN EMPIRE

Vinnitsa •

Kharkov
Dec. 24, 1917

Tsaritsyn
Nov. 27, 1917

Poltava
Jan. 19, 1918

• Debrecen

Dniester

Kishinev
Dec. 10, 1917

Yekaterinoslav
Jan. 11, 1918

Dnieper

Don

Volga

Kolozsvár
early Aug. 1917

Jassy •

Nikolayev
Jan. 27, 1918

Novocherkassk
Feb. 25, 1918

Astrakhan
Feb. 7, 1918

• Temesvár

Brassó •

Odessa
Jan. 31, 1918

Rostov
Nov. 10, 1917

Sea of Azov

Kuma

R O M A N I A

Bucharest •

Caspian Sea

Simferopol
Jan. 26, 1918

SERBIA

Danube Ruse •

BULGARIA

Sofia •

Sebastopol
Dec. 29, 1917

Novorossiysk
Dec. 14, 1917

• Varna

Black Sea

C a u c a s u s

• Burgas

Plovdiv •

Ural

50

40

Salonica •

Adrianople •

G R E E C E

Constantinople

O T T O M A N
E M P I R E

Tiflis •

Baku
Nov. 15, 1917

Angora •

Trebizond •

Erivan •

the **collapse** of the **central powers**

1918 (January) American President, Woodrow Wilson, announces Fourteen Points

1918 (April) Council of the Oppressed Peoples called in Rome

1918 (28 October) independent Czech state declared in Prague

1918 (3 November) Austrian forces sign Padua Armistice

1918 (16 November) Hungary declares its independence

1918 (9 November) German Kaiser flees to Netherlands; German republic declared

1918 (12 November) an Austrian Republic is declared in Vienna

1918 (1 December) Yugoslav state established by Serbs, Croats, and Slovenes

The Treaty of Brest-Litovsk marked the high watermark of the German and Austrian war effort. With the Central Powers now controlling the supplies of much of Eurasia, victory was regarded as a real possibility, not some distant hope.

Plans were drawn up for a German-dominated European order, and for German imperial supremacy in Africa once the war in the west was won.

Triumph over a weakened Russia disguised weaknesses in the Central Powers. The Habsburg empire now faced the very nationalist crisis she had gone to war in 1914 to prevent. In January 1918, President Woodrow Wilson, announced his Fourteen Points for the postwar settlement of Europe. These included an independent Poland and self-determination for other peoples. This was considerably more than the nationalities had been demanding. Whether or not they may have accepted a federal monarchical state, Wilson's promise of genuine independence encouraged the subject races to break away from Habsburg rule.

In April 1918 a Congress of the Oppressed Peoples was called in Rome at which Poles, Czechs, Slovaks, and south Slavs called for the fragmentation of the empire on national lines. Even the Austrian German social democrats called on the emperor to liberate the nationalities. When in October Emperor Karl granted a manifesto giving autonomy to his ethnic minorities, it was already too late.

In Poland a national council was formed with western backing. Polish soldiers stopped fighting for Germany and Austria, and Polish officials resigned their posts. A Czech-Slovak national council in Paris under Edvard Benes was recognized by the West as the *de facto* Czech government, and on October 28th an independent Czech state was declared in Prague. A few weeks earlier a council of Serbs, Croats, and Slovenes set itself up in Zagreb to found a Yugoslav state. Everywhere the authority of the empire crumbled. Local councils sprang up in defiance of the central authority. Soldiers deserted, no longer willing to die for a bankrupt order. In Hungary the prime minister, Count Istvan Tisza, was murdered and amid mounting violence in the capital his successor, Mihály Károlyi, declared an independent Hungary. This was the final blow to the monarchy. On November 3rd the Austrian forces signed the Padua Armistice and stopped fighting. On November 11th the emperor Karl withdrew unconditionally from state affairs. A day later a republic was declared in Vienna. At this final stage of the war the Austrian Germans looked to Germany for salvation. They hoped that the self-determination of peoples promised in the Fourteen Points would apply to them, and they could build a Pan-German state.

1 The collapse of the Central Powers when it came in 1918 was sudden and complete (map right). The three allies, Germany, Austria, and Hungary, recognizing that the war was effectively lost in September 1918, broke away from each other in the hope of securing a separate peace and better treatment. The old ruling classes conceded political reform and peace. In Hungary Mihály Károlyi called for a separate peace on October 16th and broke completely with Austria two weeks later. On October 21st German deputies in the Vienna parliament voted for a "Greater Germany," hoping to persuade the Allies to accept their self-determination. The Allies refused a German-Austrian state and treated each separately.

2 The Habsburg empire was a melting pot of nationalities (map left). Starting in 1867 the two chief "peoples of state" were the Germans and the Magyars, to whom the interests of the other smaller nationalities were subordinate. In the early years of the century a program of Magyarization directed against the subject nationalities drove the different Slav peoples to demand self-determination.

2 austria-hungary

ethnic divisions

Germans		Poles	
Italians		Magyars	
Czechs		Slovaks	
Slovenes		Ruthenes	
Croats and Serbs		Romanians	

www.lib.byu.edu/~rdh/wwi/1918/14points.html
President Woodrow Wilson's Fourteen Point Plan for the ending of WW1
www.onwar.com/aced/nation/hat/hungary/fhungary1918.htm
The Hungarian revolution, 1918–19

1 the collapse of the central powers, 1918

- controlled by Entente Powers, Sep. 30
- limit of Central Powers' control, Sep. 30
- lost by the Central Powers before the Armistices
- evacuated by the Central Powers under the Armistices of Nov. 3–11

- ceded to former nationalities of Austro-Hungarian empire by Dec. 6
- Germany-Austria, declared independent Nov. 12
- Hungary, declared independent Nov. 16
- controlled by Czechoslovakia by Dec. 31
- ✸ social/political unrest
- ◐ troop mutiny
- ◑ naval mutiny
- ◆ Armistice
- ★ declaration of independence
- ▲ overthrow of monarchy

250,000 POWs returning to Germany and 2 million to Austria, bring with them Bolshevik and revolutionary ideas

as determined by the Treaty of Brest-Litovsk, Mar. 1918

independent from Dec. 6, 1917

occupied by Romania, Nov. 11

Romania as agreed by the Treaty of Bucharest

beginning of Entente offensive, Sep. 14

For much of 1918 Germany appeared less crisis-ridden than the Habsburg empire, but there already existed a strong undercurrent of political tension. Hostility to the Kaiser and military rule was widespread and serious strikes broke out in Berlin in the spring. Strikers began to add political demands to the call for higher wages and more food. When news of German reverses in August and September reached the home front, morale declined sharply.

A day later, hoping to satisfy the demands of the Allies and pave the way for an armistice before they reached German soil, Ludendorff recommended to the Kaiser the establishment of a parliamentary government. On October 3rd the autocracy came to an end. While negotiations continued, the home front reached crisis point. When the sailors of the Kiel fleet refused to sail on October 29th there was talk of revolution. On November 9th the Kaiser fled to the Netherlands. The same day a republic was declared and the social democrat leader, Friedrich Ebert, became chancellor.

Within the space of a year the three empires—Romanov, Habsburg, and Hohenzollern—had become republics, with all of them dominated by the popular parties of the left. Of the major prewar empires, the only one to survive and retain its king-emperor was that of the British.

In the aftermath of the First World War the victors hoped to build a better world based on democratic principles and collective efforts for peace. It proved difficult to heal the wounds of war. The world economy grew unevenly in the 1920s and then collapsed in 1929, throwing more than 20 million out of work. The Russian Revolution set the stage for bitter ideological divisions between communist and conservative forces worldwide. The communist threat provoked a new political force, Fascism, committed to destroying Marxism and building modern authoritarian regimes based on mass nationalism. Finally, the legacy of the war's political settlement left a whole number of unsettled scores. When the 1929 slump undermined collective action, there followed a nationalist backlash and escalating international tension. The postwar dreams turned sour. The powers that imposed peace in 1919 found themselves 20 years later facing war once again.

A young Italian Fascist makes the salute

PART II **THE WORLD BETWEEN THE WARS**

the **postwar** settlement in **europe**

On January 2, 1919 the victorious Allies met at the palace of Versailles, on the outskirts of Paris, to draw up a peace settlement. The conference was dominated by the great powers: Britain, France, the United States. Italy and Japan were both full participants, but their political weight was never sufficient to force the hand of the other three powers. The lesser Allies—Greece, Romania, Serbia—were allowed to send representatives to Paris, but had no say in the final settlement except in matters that affected them directly.

U.S. President Woodrow Wilson, represented his country in person at the conference. He came expecting to impose a lasting peace, based on the liberal principles he outlined in the Fourteen Points. Chief of these was the right to national self-determination, a right Wilson thought would encourage popular democratic regimes in Europe. His vision of a new liberal Europe was shared by few of his allies. France came to the conference led by the fiery veteran politician Georges Clemenceau, whose chief concern was to guarantee French security and to make the Germans pay for the physical destruction of much of northeastern France. The British representative, Prime Minister David Lloyd George, shared some of Wilson's hopes for a liberal Europe, but was not willing to put principle before national interest. Britain, too, wanted to repair the economic damage of war.

The resulting settlement was an uneasy compromise between enlightened principle and *raison d'état*. It was agreed that Germany should be disarmed, but no other power was similarly obliged. There was a vague commitment in the League Covenant to the goal of disarmament, but a formal conference to address the issue did not convene until 1932, and broke up two years later with little achieved. Self-determination was applied only loosely, because the confused ethnic pattern of eastern Europe made a neat solution almost impossible. Austrian Germans were denied the right to join with their fellow Germans, while many other Germans were forced to live under Czech rule in the Sudetenland. The American idea to create a peacekeeping League of Nations was enfeebled by the failure to agree on a multinational army to enforce the peace; nor could the architect of the League, Wilson, sell the idea to Congress. The United States remained

2 The disintegration of the Habsburg empire provided the conditions for the creation of a south Slav state. The Serb government, in exile on Corfu, was torn between ideas of a Greater Serbia and a federation with other southern Slav peoples. The Croats and Serbs of the empire formed a Yugoslav National Committee in 1917, which took the lead a year later in establishing a Yugoslav state in collaboration with the exiled Serbs. On December 1, 1918 the Kingdom of the Serbs, Croats, and Slovenes was established in Belgrade, under the Serbian Karadjordjevic dynasty. Fear of Italian ambitions drove the Montenegrins and other minorities into the new Slav state. Over the next two years there developed strong arguments between the federalists—mainly Croats—and the Serbian leadership, which favored a unitary state based around Serb institutions. The constitution of June 1921 was a victory for the Serb idea. Serbs set up a centralized state, dominated by the Serbian political elite and an army officered mainly by Serbs.

2 the formation of yugoslavia, 1919

- Serbia and Montenegro, 1913
- annexed by Serbia and Montenegro from Ottoman empire, 1913
- frontiers, 1914
- annexed from Bulgaria, 1919
- Austro-Hun. territory united with Serbia and Montenegro, 1920, to create the Kingdom of Serbs, Croats, and Slovenes
- remained Austrian by plebiscite, 1920
- Kingdom of Serbs, Croats, and Slovenes in 1929, when renamed Yugoslavia

1 The postwar settlement (map above right) was arrived at in a series of treaties devised by the major powers in sessions in and around Paris between 1919 and 1920. Heavy territorial penalties were imposed on Germany, Austria, Hungary, Bulgaria, and Turkey. Though not party to the settlement, the new Soviet state also lost extensive prewar Russian territory in Poland, the Baltic states, and Romania. The gainers were the eight new national states created in central and eastern Europe. Despite the Allies' desire to satisfy demands for self-determination by the peoples of the old empires, they left large minority groups living under the rule of other nationalities, creating an unstable foundation for the new postwar order.

1 national conflicts and frontier disputes, 1919–36

———	German empire, 1914
———	Austro-Hungarian empire, 1914
———	Russian empire, 1914
———	post-settlement frontiers
———	British mandates
———	French mandates
▲	plebiscites held

	new states
	areas of dispute
	areas temporarily autonomous or independent
	areas under armed occupation
	areas under League of Nations High Commissioners
★	political disturbances

Plebiscites and territorial disputes

1 plebiscite Feb. 1920: divided between Denmark and Germany
2 occupied by France, 1923–25
3 to Belgium 1919
4 to Belgium 1919
5 evacuated 1930, remilitarized 1936
6 League of Nations Mandate by plebiscite to Germany 1935
7 to France 1919
8 divided between Germany and Poland by plebiscite Mar. 1921
9 Allied occupation 1920–23, annexed by Lithuania 1923, autonomous 1924, to Germany 1939
10 to Germany July 1920
11 to Poland Dec. 1918
12 partitioned between Czechoslovakia and Poland 1920
13 to Hungary 1921
14 to Austria 1920
15 annexed by Poland 1920, to Poland by plebiscite 1922
16 to Greece from Bulgaria 1919
17 demilitarized 1924, remilitarized 1936
18 Greek-Bulgarian conflict, 1925

outside the League, leaving the settlement to be dominated by the interests of France, the only major armed power left on the continent.

Nor did it prove possible to impose a settlement in any coherent way. Peace was signed with Germany on June 28, 1919, but the other Central Powers were treated separately. Agreement was reached slowly and only after a great deal of bickering between the Allies and between victors and vanquished. In much of eastern Europe, fighting continued for several years and the settlement in the east was only completed in 1923. A treaty with Austria was signed in St. Germain on November 3, 1918. The loss of the non-German areas of the Habsburg empire was confirmed, together with the loss of about one-third of the German-speaking part of the old kingdom. The Austrian army was limited to 30,000 and reparations imposed on the rump state. In the Trianon Treaty, signed by Hungary on June 4, 1920, two-thirds of the old Hungarian state was lost, principally to Yugoslavia and Romania. Hungary, too, was made liable for reparations, and her armed forces restricted to 35,000.

The gainers were the new republics of eastern Europe. Poland became a sovereign state again after years of partition, and was able to expand her territory at the expense of the weak Soviet state on her eastern borders and a disarmed Germany in the west. Czechoslovakia was carved out of the northern territories of the Habsburg empire. Both contained substantial minorities. Three million Hungarians, eight million Germans, and five million Ukrainians lived under the rule of other races. The other indirect beneficiary of the settlement was Ireland. Granting self-government to Poles and Czechs made it difficult to deny it elsewhere, and in 1921 Lloyd George finally conceded autonomy to all of Ireland save the northern province of Ulster. The national question here, as in much of eastern and central Europe, remained unresolved.

1918 German war debt totals more than 150 billion marks

1919 (May) Germany loses colonies and land; has limits placed on armed forces and must accept war guilt as part of Paris Peace Conference

1919 (28 June) peace signed with Gemany in Treaty of Versailles

1921 German reparations bill set

1923 hyperinflation; mark worth one trillionth its prewar value

1924 currency stabilized; Dawes Plan for German reparations

Of all the states that had sued for peace at the end of the war, Germany was the only one to do so on the basis of Wilson's Fourteen Points, rather than surrender unconditionally. As a result many Germans assumed that Germany would be treated as a participant in the peace settlement, able to negotiate the terms on her own behalf. The achievement of democratic government, confirmed with the election of a Constituent Assembly in January 1919, appeared to fulfill the wishes of the Allied powers. When the German delegation arrived in Versailles, however, they found that the terms were dictated to them, and that far from reflecting any spirit of democratic goodwill the terms were punitive and non-negotiable.

The settlement provoked strong resentment inside Germany at a time when the fragile democratic government was trying to damp down popular revolutionary movements and cope with military threats from newly independent Poland. A heated debate within the new parliament over acceptance or defiance was finally resolved in June in favor of signing because of Germany's feeble military situation and the Allied decision to maintain the blockade, which left millions of Germans close to starvation. Extreme nationalists were never reconciled to the humiliation, and dubbed those who signed the "November criminals" for seeking an armistice in the first place. The main proponent of acceptance, Matthias Erzberger, was murdered in 1921 by a right-wing extremist in the Black Forest.

The Allied powers had two major objectives in imposing the settlement: they wished to weaken Germany so that she would no longer pose a military threat to the other powers; and they hoped to limit Germany's economic revival by stripping her of assets and resources and forcing her to pay reparations. They also wanted Germany to accept responsibility for the war as a moral basis for their own claims against her. In Article 231 of the Treaty, Germany was forced to accept "war guilt." No other provision provoked greater resentment, for the German public believed that the war had been the product of a collective crisis of the Powers.

The rest of the settlement was bad enough from the German viewpoint. One-eighth of the prewar territory was lost, and all German colonies. East Prussia was divided from the rest of Germany by a corridor of territory designed to give Poland access to the sea. German assets abroad were seized and her merchant fleet confiscated. Her armed forces were emasculated. The General Staff was disbanded, training schools closed down, fortifications and munitions works destroyed, while the right to possess or develop any weapons of an offensive character was refused. An Allied Control Commission was established to secure verification of German compliance. Similar bodies were set up for the permanent monitoring of the conditions of the Treaty. Even German missionaries abroad were to be supervised by Allied commissioners of the same Christian denomination.

1 On May 7, 1919 a draft copy of the Treaty of Versailles was handed to the German delegation at the Trianon Palace with 22 days for comment. The German delegation rejected most of the proposals, but the Allies agreed only to a modification of the rate of German demobilization and to a plebiscite in Upper Silesia. The main settlement remained unchanged (map right): Germany lost territory in Poland, Belgium, Denmark, and France, and its western frontier was demilitarized. Its rivers were freed to international traffic and Danzig was made a free city under the League of Nations.

2 One of the most bitterly contested decisions of the peace conference concerned the fate of Upper Silesia—a coal-rich area. The Allies insisted on giving part to Poland, including the bulk of the rich coalfield. This was among the largest single economic losses from the settlement. The Allies also took industrial equipment and agricultural resources, most of Germany's merchant marine, and significant quantities of natural resources (left). The money reparations proved impossible for Germany's economy to cope with and in 1924 and again in 1929 the schedule of payment was adjusted. The 1929 plan caused a nationwide protest in Germany, and first brought Adolf Hitler into the national political limelight.

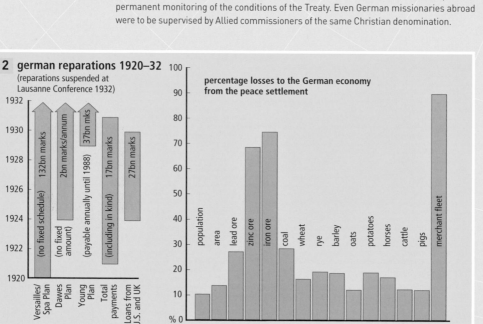

2 german reparations 1920–32
(reparations suspended at Lausanne Conference 1932)

- Versailles/Spa Plan — 132bn marks (no fixed schedule)
- Dawes Plan — 2bn marks/annum (no fixed amount)
- Young Plan — 37bn mks (payable annually until 1988)
- Total payments — 17bn marks (including in kind)
- Loans from U.S. and UK — 27bn marks

percentage losses to the German economy from the peace settlement

- population
- area
- lead ore
- zinc ore
- iron ore
- coal
- wheat
- rye
- barley
- oats
- potatoes
- horses
- cattle
- pigs
- merchant fleet

www.qt.org/worldwar/prelude/prelude1.html
The Treaty of Versailles as a prelude to WW2
www.schoolshistory.org.uk/ASLevel_History/week4_versailles.htm
The Impact of the Treaty of Versailles

LITHUANIA

Memel
Territory
Entente occupation, 1920;
to Lithuania, 1923
141,000

Königsberg

EAST

Danzig
free city, protected
by League of Nations
356,740

WEST
PRUSSIA

PRUSSIA

to Poland
2,700,000

Posen

Vistula

Warsaw

POLAND

Lodz

Breslau

UPPER SILESIA

to Poland
980,926

Cracow

Hultschin to
Czech. 45,000

Northern
Schleswig
to Denmark
164,390

Southern
Schleswig

DENMARK

Copenhagen

Baltic
Sea

North
Sea

Hamburg

Bremen

Stettin

Elbe

NETHERLANDS

Amsterdam

Rotterdam

Hanover

Berlin

Oder

GERMANY

Dresden

Leipzig

Prague

CZECHOSLOVAKIA

Rhine

RUHR

Cologne

Bonn

Brussels

BELGIUM

Eupen-
Malmédy
to Belgium
61,000

LUXEM-
BOURG

Saar

Frankfurt

Alsace-Lorraine

FRANCE

to France
1,874,014

Strassburg

Nuremberg

Stuttgart

Danube

Munich

AUSTRIA

SWITZERLAND

1 the postwar settlement in germany, 1918–35

━━ German empire, 1918

areas lost and retained by Germany

▨ lost, 1919–20

▧ lost by plebiscite, 1920–21

▨ retained by plebiscite, 1920–21

☐ under League of Nations control, plebiscite stipulated for 1935

61,000 population of lost territories

━━ frontiers, 1923

zones occupied by Allied troops

▨ for 5 years

▨ for 10 years

▨ for 15 years

- - - eastern frontier of demilitarized zone

- - - southern frontier of defortified area

━━ line beyond which no repair or fortification was allowed

━━ rivers under international control

At the heart of many of the arguments between the Allies lay the issue of reparations. The Treaty laid down in precise detail what the Allied powers wanted to repair the economic losses of war. The total sum was only finally agreed at a conference in London in 1921, when Germany was asked to pay 132 billion gold marks in annuities down to the year 1988. But well before then large deliveries in kind were made according to the terms of the Treaty, which specified everything from schedules of coal deliveries to the supply of 500 stallions, 2,000 bulls, and 1,000 rams to replenish the stock on French farms caught up in the fighting on the Western Front.

The reparations demands came on top of Germany's own vast war debts, which totaled more than 150 billion marks. The strain of paying for the war and demobilization produced serious inflation, which was exacerbated in 1923 when French and Belgian troops were sent to the Ruhr in January to force the delivery of coal reparations. By November 1923 the mark was worth one-trillionth of its prewar value. The currency collapse wiped out the cost of the war, but it also wiped out the savings of millions of ordinary Germans. In 1924 the currency was stabilized with Allied help, and a new reparation schedule drawn up, geared to Germany's ability to pay. The German public blamed the Treaty for the currency collapse and for Germany's economic weakness. The foreign minister, Gustav Stresemann, argued that fulfillment of the Treaty was the only way to achieve German rehabilitation in the international arena. While Germany settled down to work within the framework of the Versailles system, a legacy of bitterness and a profound sense of injustice lived on in the German mind.

1919 (April 28) League of Nations approved a Versailles conference

1920 League meets for first time in Geneva

1920 U.S. refuses to ratify Paris treaties and withdraws into isolation

1922 Greek army expelled from Turkey; Peace Treaty secured in 1923

1923 League forces Italy to withdraw from occupation of Corfu

1926 Germany admitted to League of Nations; Brazil withdraws from League of Nations

1933 Japan leaves League of Nations

One of the fruits of Stresemann's policy of realism was the admission of Germany to the League of Nations in 1926. The League was approved at the Versailles Conference on April 28, 1919, and it met in formal session for the first time in Geneva in 1920. Its purpose was to preserve the peace through the collective action of its members.

Though the League had no armed force of its own, economic sanctions and the imposition of a kind of quarantine on the offending state were considered sufficient deterrent against aggression. In practice the League spoke with anything but a collective voice. Germany and Communist Russia were both excluded. The United States Senate refused to ratify the Versailles Treaty and never joined the League.

The League Council consisted of four permanent powers—Britain, France, Italy, and Japan—and four others chosen at intervals from the remaining member states. The first four were Belgium, Brazil, Spain, and Greece, but Brazil became the first state to leave the League, in 1926, because of the inferior status enjoyed by the coopted states. The first real success for the League, when it forced Italy to withdraw from its unilateral occupation of Corfu in 1923, was scored against one of the organization's own principal council members.

Subsequent members within Europe

1 Albania, 1920
2 Austria, 1920
3 Bulgaria, 1920
4 Latvia, 1920
5 Estonia, 1921
6 Lithuania, 1921
7 Hungary, 1922–37
8 Germany, 1926–33

www.indiana.edu/~league/
League of Nations archives and historical collections
www.san.beck.org/GPJ21-LeagueofNations.html
Woodrow Wilson and the League of Nations

The League assumed responsibility for important parts of the postwar settlement. German colonies and Ottoman provinces were distributed as territories mandated by the League to Britain, France, and Japan. The city of Danzig in Prussia was placed under a League commissioner as a free city, to allow the Poles to have a port on the Baltic. The most serious test faced by the League came in the effort to impose a settlement on the Balkans and the Near East, the area whose instability had helped provoke the Great War in the first place.

Here was an issue that was difficult to resolve. Italy had joined the war in 1915 after signing a secret convention in London promising her substantial territorial spoils in Dalmatia and Slovenia. At the peace conference Wilson rejected secret agreements, and the London agreement was shelved. The Italian representative stormed out of the conference, but nothing could persuade the other Allies to concede all Italy wanted. In Italy Versailles was christened the "mutilated victory" by angry nationalists. One of their number, the poet Gabriele D'Annunzio, seized the city of Fiume (Rijeka), which had been promised to Yugoslavia. He was driven out by force after a year, though in 1924 the city was finally given to Italy in return for other concessions to the Yugoslavs.

The second problem was Greece. A minor Allied power, Greece's ambitions were fired by the power vacuum which the defeat of Bulgaria and Turkey opened up in the Near East. The Greek premier, Venizelos, looked for compensation in mainland Turkey, where there were large Greek minorities, and in Thrace. Under the Treaty of Neuilly, which Bulgaria signed on November 29, 1919, her gains in the Balkan Wars were largely lost. Serbia retained a large share of Macedonia, while Greece took western Thrace. The Greeks reached a secret agreement with Italy, granting them a free hand in western Turkey in return for Greek support for an Italian mandate over Albania. Here again the League intervened. Albania's independence was guaranteed and the 1913 frontiers restored with minor adjustments in November 1921. Italy's loss in Albania was followed by Greek disaster in Turkey. Venizelos's delusions of grandeur were exposed when Turkish forces crushingly defeated the Greek armies in August 1922. The conflict was settled by the League, which secured a final peace treaty with Turkey at Lausanne on August 23, 1923, and supervised the exchange of national minorities between the two warring states.

By 1923 the postwar settlement was complete. Six new national states had been created, but the principle of national self-determination could not be reconciled with the ambitions of the victors, large and small. Central and Eastern Europe represented an untidy ethnic map, in which sizable and resentful minorities lived in uneasy partnership with the dominant race who ruled over them.

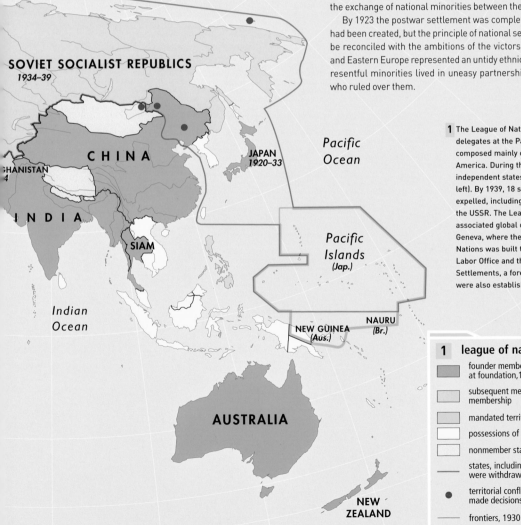

SOVIET SOCIALIST REPUBLICS
1934–39

CHINA

AFGHANISTAN

INDIA

SIAM

JAPAN
1920–33

Pacific
Ocean

Pacific
Islands
(Jap.)

Indian
Ocean

NEW GUINEA
(Aus.)

NAURU
(Br.)

AUSTRALIA

NEW
ZEALAND

1 The League of Nations was founded by the delegates at the Paris Peace Conference. It was composed mainly of states in Europe and Latin America. During the interwar years most other independent states joined, except the U.S. (map left). By 1939, 18 states had left or been expelled, including Germany, Japan, Italy, and the USSR. The League was one of a number of associated global organizations set up in Geneva, where the magnificent Palais des Nations was built to house it. The International Labor Office and the Bank of International Settlements, a forerunner of the World Bank, were also established in Switzerland.

1 league of nations, 1920–39

- founder members and states invited to join at foundation, 1920
- subsequent members, with dates of membership
- mandated territories
- possessions of member states
- nonmember states
- states, including their possessions, which were withdrawn or expelled
- ● territorial conflicts over which the League made decisions
- ——— frontiers, 1930

the **rise** of the **U.S.** as a great power

<table>
</table>

1900 to 1939

- **1898** U.S. annexes Hawaiian Islands
- **1898** U.S. acquires many overseas interests after war with Spain
- **1904** U.S. gains control of Panama; builds canal (completed 1914)
- **by 1914** U.S. world's largest industrial producer
- **1919** first trans-Atlantic flight
- **1920** Prohibition in U.S. (to 1933)
- **1923** General Motors (world's largest manufacturing company) established
- **1936** Pan-American congress; U.S. proclaims good neighbor policy

The central role played in the Versailles Settlement by President Woodrow Wilson highlighted the emergence of the United States as a major player on the world stage. Although European diplomats regarded the New World as a marginal factor in the balance of power, the United States had, since the 1860s, transcended her geographical isolation and come to play a fuller part in the international order.

The basis of the United States' new power was economic. Like Germany, the U.S. was able to use rapid and large-scale industrialization as an entry to the club of great powers. By 1914 the United States was the world's largest industrial producer with vast natural resources, a large population swollen by mass immigration from Europe and a tradition of technical and scientific innovation. Farming remained an important activity, with one-third of the working population still engaged in agriculture in 1910, but heavy investment in transportation and in scientific farming methods turned the United States into a major supplier of world foodstuffs.

U.S. statesmen prided themselves on their nation's republican and democratic foundations, so different from the Europe many had recently left. But in the late nineteenth-century climate of colonization and imperial rivalry even the United States was tempted into an expansion of its territorial claims and political influence, particularly in the Caribbean and the Pacific. The acquisition of Hawaii was a model of colonial expansion—a trade treaty with its native sovereign in 1875, the establishment of a coaling and naval base at Pearl Harbor in 1887, and a final decision to annex the island group in 1898 following the overthrow of the king and the formation of a pro-American republic.

That same year, 1898, the United States fought a war with Spain, one of the oldest and most decrepit of the European empires. The United States' growing naval power made victory a formality. The outcome turned the U.S. into a power with extensive overseas interests. In the Pacific, the Philippines, and the island of Guam were acquired. In the Caribbean, Puerto Rico, and Cuba were brought under U.S. protection, while the other Caribbean imperialists, Britain and France, agreed by the Hay-Pauncefote Treaty of 1901 to give the United States a virtually free hand throughout the region.

Some American imperialists began to dream of turning eastern Asia into an American sphere. Japan was opened up to western influence by U.S. pressure. Manchuria was regarded as an area ripe for economic penetration, and the whole of China was viewed by American businessmen and politicians as a potential sphere of influence. U.S. insistence produced the so-called "open door" policy in China to ensure no one power preempted the others by gaining special economic privileges, but the principle of "open door" trade was soon applied wherever American merchants had strong interests. This was particularly so in Latin America, which was regarded from Washington as the United States' backyard. In 1903 the United States forced Colombia to abandon its claims to Panama; a virtual U.S. protectorate was established and work begun on a U.S. canal across the isthmus. The canal was completed in 1914, linking America's Atlantic and Pacific interests.

2 first world war debt payments to July 1931

- 🪙 $1 billion or less received
- 🪙 $1 billion or less paid out
- *4.05* figures in billions of dollars

total scheduled payments: $52.74 billion

2 The core of U.S. power was money (map below). During the Great War that wealth was used to support the war efforts of the United States' allies. After 1918 U.S. loans were needed for reconstruction. The debtor states fell behind on payments and the issue of war debts poisoned relations between Europe and the United States. The Johnson Act in 1934 banned any further loans to Europe, except to Finland, which honored its obligations.

Iceland

U.S. loans to Europe, 1924–29

CANADA

UNITED STATES OF AMERICA
20.82

NORWAY · SWEDEN · FINLAND

ESTO.
LATVIA
LITHUANI.

DENMARK

UK
10.20 *9.75*
IRELAND NETH.

BELGIUM

GERMANY
25.60
POLAND

AUSTRIA CZECHOSLOVAKIA
HUNGARY

FRANCE SWITZ.
13.65 *10.49*

ITALY
4.05 *3.97*
YUGOSLAVIA

ROM
BULGA

GREECE

PORTUGAL SPAIN

www.smplanet.com/imperialism/teddy.html
History of U.S. interventions in Latin America
www.besthistorysites.net/USHistory.shtml
Early U.S. imperialism

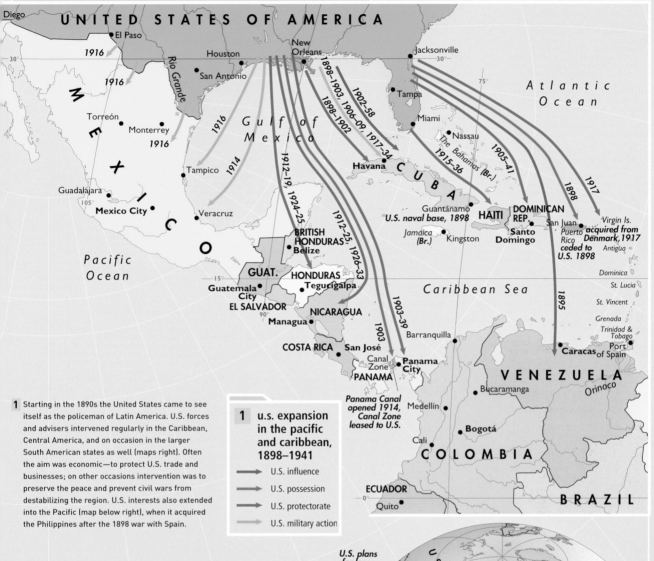

1 Starting in the 1890s the United States came to see itself as the policeman of Latin America. U.S. forces and advisers intervened regularly in the Caribbean, Central America, and on occasion in the larger South American states as well (maps right). Often the aim was economic—to protect U.S. trade and businesses; on other occasions intervention was to preserve the peace and prevent civil wars from destabilizing the region. U.S. interests also extended into the Pacific (map below right), when it acquired the Philippines after the 1898 war with Spain.

1 u.s. expansion in the pacific and caribbean, 1898–1941

→ U.S. influence
→ U.S. possession
→ U.S. protectorate
→ U.S. military action

Increasingly before the Great War, the U.S. came to see itself as an arbiter between the warring monarchies of Europe and Asia. In 1905 the United States hosted the peace conference between Japan and Russia. The U.S was also represented at the Algeciras conference in Morocco in 1906. The eventual decision to enter the war in 1917 was backed by a growing belief that the U.S. was destined to transform the old balance of power. Woodrow Wilson represented a powerful strand of American opinion which wanted to produce a new global order based on open diplomacy, open trade, and liberal values.

Though Wilson failed to carry Congress with him in his effort to remake the world order in 1919, the decade that followed was dominated by American culture and economic power. The Washington Conference of 1921-2 set a new balance of global naval power; the United States intervened regularly over the issue of war debts and reparations; the world economy began to orientate itself away from London and Paris and toward New York. Though formally isolated from international commitments, the aggressive modernity of American life—jazz, cars, the movies—brought the American Dream to millions of non-Americans worldwide.

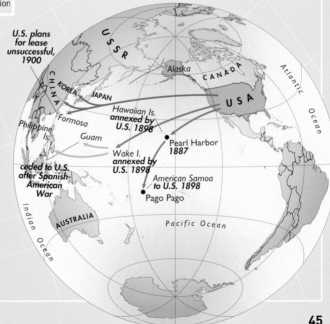

1906 U.S. occupies Cuba (to 1908); and again 1917–1923

1910 Mexican revolution begins; U.S. intervenes (1914); new constitution (1917)

1924 virtual civil war in Brazil; military coup in Chile

1926 U.S. troops occupy Nicaragua (to 1933)

1929 Calles establishes National Revolutionary Party, Mexico

1930 Military revolution in Brazil; Vargas becomes president and launches "New State" (1937)

1932 Chaco War between Bolivia and Paraguay (to 1935)

1934 Cardenas president of Mexico; introduces land redistribution and nationalization of oil (1938)

U.S. influence was widespread in Latin America, but Latin America was never simply the United States' backyard. Emancipation from the Spanish and Portuguese empires early in the 19th century did not end Latin America's close economic and cultural links with Europe. A stream of migrants brought with them new skills and new political ideas, which competed with the liberal republicanism on which the newly independent states had been based.

The traditional social order was sustained by the new export economies. The old land-owning class, based on the large estates (*haciendas*), monopolized the export trade and dominated the Mulatto and Native Indian populations who worked on the land. The landed elite controlled politics by a complicated system of patronage and through rigged elections. Though nominally liberal, the political systems were in reality oligarchies, working for the interests of the rural elites who profited from the exceptional boom in export earnings from the 1870s to the end of the First World War.

The war proved a watershed for Latin American politics and the export economy. In the 1920s and 1930s export growth declined sharply. Overseas protection and chronic oversupply of food and raw materials on world markets ended the decades of prosperity and eroded the economic power base of the old elites. The social balance was also changing. The export economies had produced large new cities with a new educated middle class to service the trade and to run bureaucracies and an urban proletariat whose ties with the land were cut. These groups had no allegiance to the old *hacienda* system and resented the power of the rural elites. Their political hostility to the old system was fueled by European immigrants bringing socialist, anarchist, and nationalist ideas with them. In 1917–20 there occurred a wave of social protest across the continent against low wages and poor conditions. The crisis was brutally suppressed, but the consensus on "order and progress" on which the old system relied collapsed in the years that followed.

1 At the beginning of the 20th century Latin America was mainly ruled by large landowners and rich exporters who relied on money and orders from abroad to keep the traditional elites in power (maps right and below). In the 1920s the decline of the export economies and the rise of a class of educated urban officials and soldiers keen to create vigorous new nation-states less dependent on the developed world produced a period of political instability across the continent. By the mid-1930s the old elites were in retreat and a generation of army-backed authoritarian politicians seized power in a confused series of coups and countercoups.

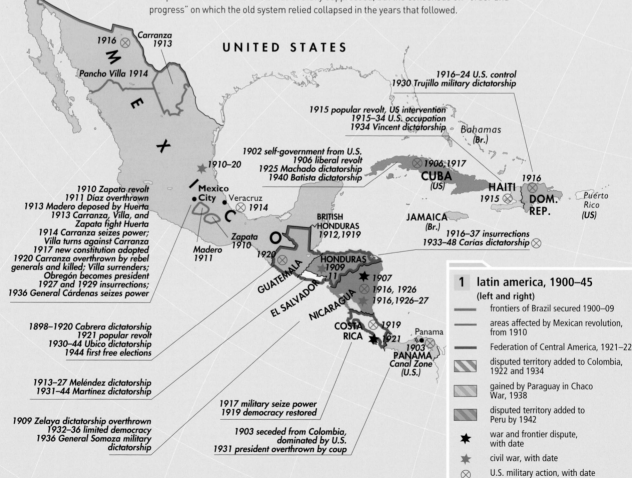

1 latin america, 1900–45
(left and right)

— frontiers of Brazil secured 1900–09

— areas affected by Mexican revolution, from 1910

— Federation of Central America, 1921–22

▨ disputed territory added to Colombia, 1922 and 1934

▨ gained by Paraguay in Chaco War, 1938

▨ disputed territory added to Peru by 1942

★ war and frontier dispute, with date

★ civil war, with date

⊗ U.S. military action, with date

— frontiers, 1945

www.fsmitha.com/h2/ch03mex.htm
The Mexican revolution
www.fsmitha.com/h2/ch17.htm
Latin American politics and economic depression

1904 military rule
1909 limited democracy
1936–40 social disturbances

1925 military coup
1929 democracy restored
1931–35 period of turmoil
1935 military rule
1938 democracy restored again

1914 military revolt
1919–30 Leguia dictatorship
1930 popular military revolt
1931 revolts
1936–39 dictatorship

1899–1908 Castro dictatorship
1908–35 Gómez dictatorship
1935 limited democracy restored

1900–30 limited democracy
1924 military revolt
1930 military revolt
1934–45 dictatorship of Vargas
1935 communist uprising
Nov. 1937 Vargas declares
"New State"

1920 liberal regime overthrown
1926–30 Siles dictatorship
1931 democracy restored
1934–46 military dictatorship

1912–36 limited democracy
1940–48 Morínigo dictatorship
1936–37 military rule

1903–33 democratic rule
1933–34 Terra dictatorship

1890–1912 limited democracy
1912 electoral reform
1930–32 Uriburo dictatorship
1932 democracy restored
1933–34 revolt in north eastern provinces
1933 economic recovery programme launched
1943 military revolt

1891–1925 limited democracy
1924–31 Ibáñez military dictatorship
1931 unrest
1932 democracy restored
1938 aborted Fascist uprising
1938 Popular Front government

There were powerful signs of change before the war. In Uruguay José y Ordónez began a program of democratic and social reform in 1911. In 1912 the urban radicals succeeded in forcing electoral reform, and in 1916 won their first election. The most far-reaching transformation occurred in Mexico, where the reform program of Francisco Madero, begun in 1910, turned into a full-scale revolution against the old order. In the 1920s, with increased urbanization and the export crisis, the grip of the old elites slackened almost everywhere in Latin America. New, predominantly middle-class parties emerged preaching a new nationalism. They had a quasi-fascist outlook, with their emphasis on authoritarian politics, corporatist social policy, and state-led economic modernization. They were based in cities and won support among army officers anxious to create some kind of new order out of the crisis of the declining liberal states. Nationalists all shared a growing resentment against the United States, which had steadily increased its economic presence in Latin America by taking over commodity production (sugar in Cuba, copper in Chile, oil in Mexico, etc.) and repatriating the profits.

The nationalist revolt produced a period of confused and violent politics between landowners, soldiers, and middle-class radicals. In Chile in 1924 the army established a dictatorship for Carlos Ibáñez, but seven years later he was overthrown and one of his successors, Marmaduke Grove, briefly established a socialist republic. In Argentina urban nationalists and the army took control in 1930, but an effective corporatist dictatorship was only finally established by General Juan Péron in 1943. In Brazil, too, the military and the urban radicals ended the old order in 1930, and Getúlio Vargas set up a single-party dictatorship to establish a "New State." The new regimes attempted to create a consensus by making concessions to labor and by encouraging *indigenismo*, a movement to revive Native culture and values and to reject U.S. and European influence. But the rift between rich and poor, rural and urban proved difficult to bridge and more and more Latin American regimes relied on crude authoritarianism to survive.

The challenge to European influence was not confined in the interwar years solely to the independent states of Latin America. Though the European empires reached their fullest extent during the period, with the acquisition of Turkey's Arab provinces at the end of the war and with Italy's later conquest of Abyssinia, nationalist forces in the empires began to challenge the whole basis of imperial power.

The main beneficiaries of the postwar settlement were Britain and France. The League gave Britain trusteeship for Palestine, Iraq, and Transjordan, as well as former German colonies in Samoa, New Guinea, Togoland, and Tanganyika. France gained Syria, Lebanon, and German Cameroon. These areas were integrated into the global economic interests of the two metropolitan powers. Oil discoveries in the Persian Gulf area gave a new strategic significance to the Middle East.

The expansion of territory disguised a great number of weaknesses in the whole imperial structure. There was growing criticism of colonialism from the United States and the Soviet Union. The empires were expensive to maintain, despite the very real economic rewards they brought with them. Above all the European empires faced growing opposition from within their territories, led by educated elites who sought a role in local administration or even national autonomy. There were serious, sometimes violent, challenges to colonial rule.

Nowhere was opposition to British rule more apparent than in India, where the nationalist Indian Congress party gathered widespread popular support. In 1935 the British conceded the India Act, which gave self-government to

1 During the interwar years European overseas empires remained an important economic asset against a background of economic stagnation and recession (map right). But the material advantages were offset by growing political and social conflict. Some of this was the result of impoverishment and trade decline, but much of the protest came from nationalists hostile to colonial rule. In the Middle East, India, and the British Dominions concessions were made. By 1939 the long-term prospects for the survival of colonial empires were bleak.

Map labels:

European population in 1935: 50,000 and 100,000 Greeks with Turkish nationality (less than 1%). Indigenous banks and beginnings of coal mining and iron and steel industry.

French investment in public utilities. Iraq Petroleum Company pipeline from Iraq to Tripoli.

Jewish population of mainly European origin in 1939: 429,605 (28%). By 1948, Jewish population own 14% of cultivable land. Iraq Petroleum Company pipeline from Iraq to Haifa.

European population in 1936: 213,000 (8%) own one-tenth of cultivated land.

European population in 1931: 881,600 (15.7%) own one-third of cultivated land.

The Rif 1921–26

Some French investment; major agricultural development of Jezira (northeast) after 1938.

European (or European-protected) population in 1937: 225,000 (1.5%). Considerable French, British, and Belgian investment mostly in mortage banks and land companies. Indigenous industry beginning with Banque Misr group in 1920s.

European population in 1936: c.202,000 (3.4%)

Petroleum begins to be produced by Arabian-American Oil Company. 0.7 million tons produced in 194[...]

Resistance by Sayyid Muham[...] "the Mad Mullah" 1891–1920.

conquered by Italy 1936

ANGLO-EGYPTIAN SUDAN
Condominium shared between Britain and Egypt. Cotton produced by partnership between government, tenants and British-owned Sudan Plantations Syndicate.

Ashanti rebellion 1900

Anyang revolt, 1904

Nandi resistance 1895–1905

Maji-Maji revolt 1905–07

anti-Portuguese risings 1913

1898-1904

Herero and Hottentot revolts 1904–06

Zulu revolt, 1906

Autonomous Dominion within British empire starting in 1926

★1906,1919

Cyrenaica 1914-32

Place names: Istanbul, Ankara, TURKEY, CYPRUS, LEBANON, SYRIA, IRAQ, Baghdad, Tehera[n], PERS[IA], KUWAIT, BAHRAIN, TRUC[IAL] OMAN, Mecca, SAUDI ARABIA, YEMEN, Sana, Aden, ADEN PROTECTORATE, OMA[N], ERITREA, FRENCH SOMALILAND, BRITISH SOMALILAND, Addis Ababa, ABYSSINIA (ETHIOPIA), ITALIAN SOMALILAND, Khartoum, Red Sea, Alexandria, Cairo, Aswan, EGYPT, LIBYA, Tripoli, Tunis, TUNISIA, Algiers, ALGERIA, PORTUGAL, SPAIN, FRANCE, ITALY, Tangier, Rabat, Casablanca, MOROCCO, SPANISH MOROCCO, RIO DE ORO, FRENCH WEST AFRICA, THE GAMBIA, PORT. GUINEA, SIERRA LEONE, LIBERIA, GOLD COAST, TOGOLAND, NIGERIA, Lagos, FERNANDO PO, SAO TOME & PRINCIPE, SPANISH GUINEA, BRITISH CAMEROONS, FRENCH CAMEROONS, FRENCH EQUATORIAL AFRICA, BELGIAN CONGO, CABINDA, ANGOLA, RUANDA URUNDI, UGANDA, BRITISH EAST AFRICA, KENYA, Mombasa, TANGANYIKA, ZANZIBAR, Dar-es-Salaam, NORTHERN RHODESIA, NYASALAND, SOUTHERN RHODESIA, MOZAMBIQUE, MADAGASCAR, SOUTH WEST AFRICA, BECHUANALAND, SWAZILAND, BASUTOLAND, UNION OF SOUTH AFRICA, Durban, Cape Town, PALESTINE, TRANSJORDAN

Indian Ocean

www.international.ucla.edu/article.asp?parentid=7158
An exploration of decolonization in the 20th century
www.bbc.co.uk/history/war/iraq/britain_iraq_03.shtml
The British in Iraq after WW1

the 11 provinces and set up an All-India Federation of provinces and the remaining principalities. The Act satisfied neither old elites nor new nationalists, and by 1939 British rule rested on fragile foundations. Congress refused to assist the war effort between 1939 and 1945 and began a "quit India" campaign under the radical nationalist, Jawaharlal Nehru.

Nationalist opposition was less developed elsewhere, but was still significant. In the Dutch East Indies and French Indo-China nationalism was sustained by communist opposition. In the Dutch East Indies a communist revolt was mounted in 1926, and communist resistance reached a climax in Vietnam in the early 1930s, led by, among others, the young revolutionary Ho Chi Minh, who had picked up his radical politics in Paris. In North Africa the European powers faced attacks not only from popular native uprisings —the Rif revolt in Morocco led by Abd el-Krim, the Sanussi resistance to Italian conquest in Cyrenaica—but also from more organized political movements, such as the Etoile Nord-Africaine in Algeria or the Destour in Tunisia, which drew on the example of European radicalism.

In the former Ottoman territories of the Middle East European rule was difficult to establish in the face of Arab nationalism, mobilized to throw off Turkish rule. Britain conceded independence to Egypt in 1922 and to Iraq in 1932, though both had to accept a continued British military presence. A Syrian revolt against French rule (1925-7) was suppressed and a harsh authority imposed. In Palestine the British faced a prolonged crisis, made worse by the promise to grant the Jews a homeland. When Jewish emigration from Europe expanded following Hitler's achievement of power in 1933, a virtual guerrilla war between Arabs, Jews, and the British tied down more British troops than were stationed in mainland Britain. In sub-Saharan Africa resistance to Europeanization, which had produced decades of violent conflict, developed into more formal political protest movements: the Young Kikuyu Association set up in Kenya in 1921; the African Nation Congress founded in 1923 in South Africa; the National Congress of British West Africa established in 1920.

All these movements, and those in the Caribbean and South Asia, were fueled by the economic distress following the slump of 1929. Falling prices, high unemployment, and restricted rights to the land produced serious unrest among the sugar islands of the West Indies, in the Gold Coast (Ghana), and the Rhodesian copper belt. The gulf between the metropolitan powers, mainly democracies, and their undemocratic colonies became harder to justify or sustain.

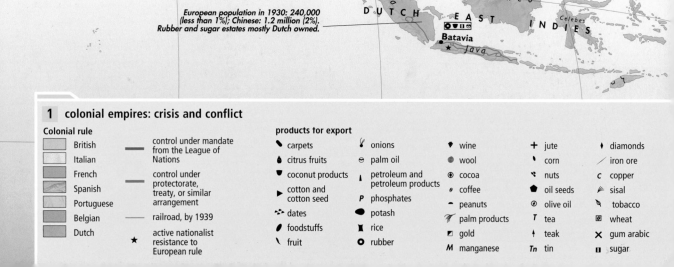

...produced by Iraq Petroleum Company ...ish, Dutch, French, and American). ...5 million tons produced in 1940.

Oil (Anglo-Iranian Oil Company— British control) forms two-thirds of all exports. 8.62 million tons produced in 1940.

...l (Bahrain Petroleum ...mpany—American). ...million tons produced ...1940.

...l discovered but not yet ...ploited (Kuwait Oil ...mpany—British and American).

...ropean interests in tea plantations ...and jute factories. Beginnings of ...digenous Indian-owned textile, iron, ...and steel industries.

Petroleum produced by Burmah Oil Company (British).

Production of tin and rubber largely controlled by Europeans and Chinese. Processing and marketing of rice by Chinese.

European investment in tea and rubber.

Large Chinese, smaller Indian population (majority Malay). Tin-mining under British and Chinese ownership; also rubber but with South Indian labor. Trade of Singapore mostly controlled by Chinese.

European population in 1930: 240,000 (less than 1%); Chinese: 1.2 million (2%). Rubber and sugar estates mostly Dutch owned.

European population in 1936: 40,000 (less than 0.5%); Chinese: 325,000 (1%). Rubber mainly produced by French companies, rice cultivation mainly French or Indo-Chinese, mostly processed and marketed by Chinese. 6% of cultivated land owned by French with some French-owned industries in north.

Amritsar 1919

Bengal 1923-32

1930-4

1 colonial empires: crisis and conflict

Colonial rule

	British
	Italian
	French
	Spanish
	Portuguese
	Belgian
	Dutch

control under mandate from the League of Nations

control under protectorate, treaty, or similar arrangement

railroad, by 1939

★ active nationalist resistance to European rule

products for export

carpets	onions	wine	jute	diamonds
citrus fruits	palm oil	wool	corn	iron ore
coconut products	petroleum and petroleum products	cocoa	nuts	copper
cotton and cotton seed	P phosphates	coffee	oil seeds	sisal
dates	potash	peanuts	olive oil	tobacco
foodstuffs	rice	palm products	T tea	wheat
fruit	rubber	gold	teak	gum arabic
		M manganese	Tn tin	sugar

Many anti-imperialist politicians followed the beacon of the Soviet Union. The triumph of communism in the Russian empire demonstrated the power of popular politics directed to a clear revolutionary ambition. The new communist state was regarded as a rallying point for all those struggling against exploitation and imperial rule. To Sidney Webb, the veteran British socialist, the Soviet Union was the "New Civilization," an island of progress amid a sea of reaction.

The reality was very different. The infant revolutionary movement became isolated internationally and was almost stifled in Russia itself. Russian communists were a minority in the new state and had to fight to establish their political survival. The first priority was to end the war. At Brest-Litovsk in March 1918 the new Russian leaders had to concede extensive territorial losses, including the Baltic states and Ukraine. By July 1918 full-scale civil war had broken out. Anti-Bolshevik forces were supported by contingents of foreign troops, some of them, like the Czech Legion, prisoners of war fighting to get back to Europe, others sent from abroad to get Russia back into the war and to overthrow communism. British, French, American, and Japanese forces, together with the so-called "White" Russian armies, succeeded in controlling large areas of the old Russian empire, leaving the Bolsheviks with the Russian heartland around Moscow and Petrograd. By 1919 the survival of the new state was in the balance.

1 Following the Bolshevik revolution in November 1918, the former czarist empire broke down into civil war (map right). The battle lines remained exceptionally confused. The communist Red Armies fought against the "White" armies, which were made up of a mixture of monarchists, anticommunists, and nationalists, who wanted the independence of the non-Russian peoples. Foreign armies also intervened from north, east, and south, while former Czech POWs fought the communists along the Trans-Siberian railroad in their effort to return to Europe. A fragile peace came in 1921 with the final defeat of anticommunist forces.

2 the foundation of the ussr

- Russian Soviet Federative Socialist Republic, Oct.1922
- Far Eastern Republic, incorporated into RSFSR Nov. 19,1922
- other constituents of the USSR, Dec. 30, 1922
- independent People's Republics incorporated into the USSR by 1925
- under Japanese occupation to May 1925
- other communist states
- frontier of the USSR,1923

The Bolsheviks won the civil war in 1921 only by imposing a brutal dictatorship on the areas they controlled, and by militarizing both the Party and society. Five million were called into the Red Army set up at the start of 1918. More than 50,000 former czarist officers, under the command of Leon Trotsky, commissar for defense, fought for the Reds. Under a system of "War Communism" all Russian businesses, except the very smallest, were nationalized and the "money economy" widely suspended. Grain was requisitioned, workers regimented. Bolshevik Russia became an armed camp, and the new Party members who joined after 1918 did so in most cases via the army. The civil war also forced Lenin's government to run the state from above. All potential sources of opposition, from separatist movements in the non-Russian areas to workers' groups demanding greater democracy, were ruthlessly crushed. The soviets, instead of becoming the instruments of democratic participation, were sidelined. The regime set up a new secret police force, the Cheka, in November 1917, which murdered and imprisoned anyone accused of counterrevolutionary activity. When the civil war finally ended in 1921, the political system had crystallized into a virtual one-party state, ruled from above by the Council of People's Commissars in tandem with the Central Committee of the Communist Party.

When the dust of the civil war settled the renamed Soviet Union was in chaos. Much of the area ceded at Brest-Litovsk had been recaptured. But the economy was close to collapse, with raging inflation, falling grain

2 A 1922 treaty established the USSR, linking Russia, Belorussia, the Ukraine and Transcaucasia (map above). Other former tsarist territories were absorbed later.

production, and a shrinking urban and industrial population. By 1920 only 1.5 million factory workers remained of the 3.6 million in 1917. The peasantry had retreated into subsistence agriculture, seizing the estates and converting 99 percent of the land area into old-fashioned communes. Among the peasantry fewer than one percent of households had a Communist Party member.

For the urban radicals who led the revolution, the prospects for turning a peasant society into a modern workers' state were bleak. Revolution failed everywhere else outside Russia. In 1921 Lenin reluctantly proposed economic reforms designed to restore private trade and production and to create an orthodox central banking system. The reforms became known as the New Economic Policy (NEP). Lenin saw them as a necessary retreat in order to rebuild Russian industry and stabilize the social order after six years of war. When Lenin died in 1924, the Party was left with the unhappy compromise of a radical socialist political system trying to rule a deeply conservative, peasant-dominated society.

1 russia in war and revolution

- ━━━ boundary of Russian empire, 1914
- ▲ towns occupied by Entente forces, Aug. 1918–19
- ╌╌╌ area controlled by Bolsheviks, Aug. 1918
- ┈┈┈ eastern boundary of area controlled by Bolsheviks, Apr. 1919
- ▨ controlled by Bolsheviks, Oct.1919
- ━━━ boundary of areas controlled by anti-Bolshevik forces, Apr. 1920
- ─── deepest advance of Red Army into Poland, Aug. 1920
- ╌╌╌ final anti-Bolshevik advance, Oct. 1920
- ━━━ boundary of Soviet territory, Mar. 1921
- ⟵ movement of White Russian armies
- ⟵ movement of non-Russian anti-Bolshevik forces
- ⟵ anarchist military activities
- ⊙ centers of Confederation of Anarchist Organizations
- ○ Makhno's headquarters, 1918-20
- ─── frontiers, 1923

Entente fleet
Barents Sea

Murmansk

British French Canadians Italians Serbs

White Sea

Canadians Americans

Archangel

British French

SWEDEN

FINLAND
independence of
Finland recognized
Dec. 1917

Finns

Petrozavodsk

Lake Onega

Lake Ladoga

Helsinki

Revel (Tallinn)

British/French naval assistance

Narva

Yudenich
ESTONIA

Petrograd
(Leningrad)

Novgorod

Vologda

Vyatka

Perm

Izhevsk

Yekaterinburg
(Sverdlovsk)

Riga **Letts**

LATVIA

Baltic Germans

Pskov

Kornilov's attack
on Petrograd
Sep. 1917

Kostroma

Yaroslavl

Ivanovo

Nizhniy Novgorod
(Gorkiy)

Kazan

Kolchak 1918-19

Ufa

**Nicholas II
and family shot
by Bolsheviks
July 1918**

LITHUANIA

Tver (Kalinin)

Moscow

R U S S I A

GERMANY
(E. PRUSSIA)

B O L S H E V I K

Vitebsk

Smolensk

Kaluga

Trans-Siberian Railway

Samara
(Kuybyshev)

Czechs

Warsaw

Minsk

Mogilev

Tula

Orel

Tambov

Penza

Orenburg
(Chkalov)

POLAND

Brest-Litovsk

Poles

Gomel

Voronezh

Saratov

Ural Cossack Army
1918-20

CZECHOSLOVAKIA

Kiev

Zhitomir

**Denikin
1919**

Kharkov

Poltava

Peregonovka

Lozovaya

**Don Cossacks
1917-19**

Tsaritsyn
(Stalingrad)

HUN.

Dibrivki

Yekaterinoslav
(Dnepropetrovsk)

Nikopol

Gulyay-Pole

Mariupol

Novocherkassk

Rostov-on-Don

Astrakhan

Romanians

BESSARABIA

Kishinev

Berdiansk

Cossacks

ROMANIA

Odessa

Wrangel 1920

Sevastopol

Simferopol

Novorossiysk

Caspian Sea

BULGARIA

French

Black

British

Sea

Georgians 1919-20

Mensheviks

Entente fleet

Batum

Tiflis (Tbilisi)

Baku

Istanbul

Krasnovodsk

T U R K E Y

Kars

Tabriz

**British
1918-19**

PERSIA

www.departments.bucknell.edu/russian/chrono3.html
A chronology of Russian history from 1917
www.johndclare.net/Russ6.htm
The Bolshevik state, 1917–21

ussr: modernization and terror

1920 Comintern set up in Moscow

1922 Joseph Stalin appointed Party General Secretary

1928 first Five-Year Plan for industrial development and collectivization of agriculture (1929) launched

1929 Trotsky expelled from USSR

1935 Franco-Soviet Pact

1936 Great Terror launched in Russia

by 1937 93 percent of peasant households collectivized

1937–38 Soviet show trials of senior communists

In the period after Lenin's death, the Communist Party in the Soviet Union searched for ways to modernize the new state while retaining the momentum of revolutionary progress. There was some hope that a new socialist international organization, Comintern, set up in Moscow in 1920, would encourage revolution outside Russia, but that prospect seemed a distant one by 1924.

The Party divided into those who believed that NEP would gradually produce a successful urban economy that would evolve through Party guidance into a socialist system, and those who urged rapid modernization from above before communism was swamped by peasant capitalism.

This "Great Debate" was resolved by the drift of internal Party politics. The moderates around Bukharin, who probably represented the majority in the Party and in the country, became the enemies of the Party General Secretary, Joseph Stalin. He was appointed in 1922 after years of distinguished revolutionary service. He used his powers of patronage to build up a power base in local Party branches, from where he then strengthened his political position in the national leadership following Lenin's death. He thought there was little prospect of revolution abroad and argued for a strategy of "socialism in one country."

1 In the late 1920s the Soviet regime embarked on a colossal experiment in social engineering and forced industrial growth. The object was to turn the Soviet Union from a mainly peasant society into a mainly urban-industrial one within ten years (map below). In 1926, 81 percent of Russians worked on the land. In 1939 the figure was only 52 percent. The city population expanded by 30 million from 1926 to 1939. For those who

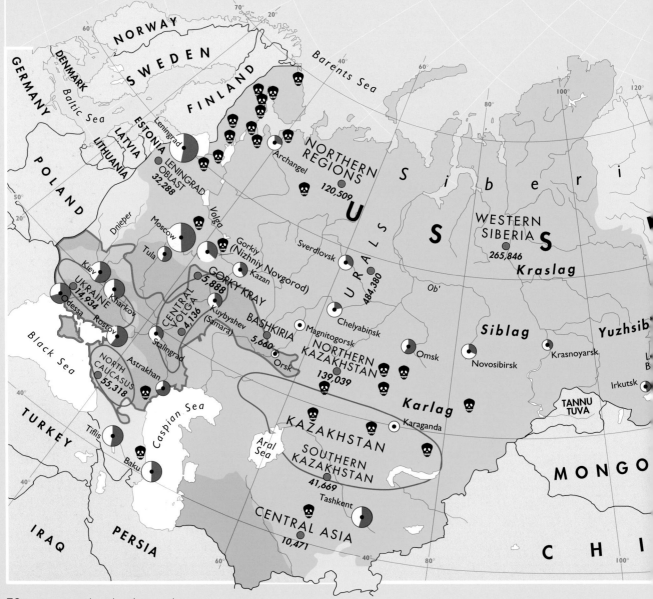

www.loc.gov/exhibits/archives/reps.html
Repression and terror in Stalin's early USSR
www.fordham.edu/halsall/mod/1936purges.html
Stalin's purges in the mid-1930's

opposed the "second revolution" a system of camps was set up across the northern and central USSR, operated by the interior commissariat (NKVD) through the Gulag camp organization. In 1930 there were 179,000 in the camps; by the time of Stalin's death in 1953 there were 2.4 million, 23 percent of them political prisoners.

This strategy, in Stalin's view, was to push through a second revolution from above, stamping out any vestiges of political pluralism or cultural diversity in the name of a rigorous communism, while at the same time transforming Soviet society and the economy to match the communist model. This policy meant rapid industrial and urban growth, and the bringing to an end of free-market peasant agriculture.

The trigger for the second revolutionary wave came in the winter of 1927–28 when falling grain supplies to the cities coincided with a series of war scares prompted by a breach in Anglo-Soviet diplomatic relations. Stalin threw his weight behind those who argued for rapid industrialization, the enforced modernization of agriculture and a buildup of military power to defend the revolutionary achievement. The Bukharin moderates were defeated and Stalin's vision of a communist reform imposed. In 1929 the first Five-Year Plan for industrial development was launched. In the summer of the same year, following an unsuccessful campaign to persuade the peasantry to adopt large-scale "collective" farming, a revolutionary wave was unleashed against the countryside. The chief victims of collectivization were the so-called "kulaks," the richer and more successful farmers, but all peasants suffered the widespread destruction of their traditional way of life. Village communal farming was replaced by large farms based around the Motor Tractor Station (MTS), where the peasants were mere wage-laborers. A decree in 1935 gave them the right to cultivate a small gardens, and many were forced to live off its proceeds. Millions of other peasants went off to the cities to form the basis of a new wage-labor force, where they had to learn habits of timekeeping and factory discipline entirely foreign to them. The result was further conflict with the authorities and accusations of sabotage, which were harshly dealt with. More than a million peasants worked in forced labor settlements. By 1937 some 93 percent of peasant households had been collectivized, and their centuries-old way of life dismantled. The church was almost destroyed as an institution; in its place came an endless diet of socialist propaganda.

The revolution from above had many consequences. The Soviet Union did become a major industrial power by the late 1930s. But above all the modernization drive allowed Stalin to complete his progress toward personal dictatorship. To push through the reforms it became necessary to rely on increased state power. The police forces of the interior ministry, the NKVD, were used indiscriminately against anyone, even those in the Party, deemed an enemy of Stalinist modernization. The regime adopted a propaganda of frantic revolutionary endeavor and isolated those who stood outside it as saboteurs and capitalist spies. The "cult of personality" built Stalin up as the supreme hero of the revolution. Those who opposed him, such as Bukharin, were forced to confess to outlandish crimes in a series of staged show trials in 1937 and 1938. Stalin arranged the death of almost all the old cadre of Bolsheviks. The tally of those who died under Stalin was probably in excess of eight million. By 1940 the Soviet Union was unarguably more modern, but the New Civilization was sustained by a vicious despotism.

70°

Dalstroi

140°

160°

60°

EASTERN
SIBERIA
91,720

Sea of
Okhotsk

ALDAN
4,724

FAR EAST
Burlag 40,440
Komsomolsk
(founded 1932)
Amur
50°

Amur

Khabarovsk

140°

Vladivostok

40°

Sea of
Japan

120°

A   N

1 collectivization and population movements, 1923–39

principal areas of collectivization

2–10% of all farms collectivized by 1928

25–50% of all farms collectivized by 1933

50–70% of all farms collectivized by 1933

70–85% of all farms collectivized by 1933

principal famine areas, 1932

Kraslag labor camp administration zone

corrective labor camps, 1932

location of "special settlers," 1932

city populations by census of Jan. 1939

(in thousands)

more than   500–   250–   100–   50–
1 million   1,000   500   250   100

population
by census
of Dec. 1926

growth of
population
Dec. 1926
to Jan. 1939

frontiers, 1930

the **world economy**

- **from 1914** U.S. replaces Britain as primary lender
- **1929** Wall Street crash precipitates world Depression
- **1930** Hawley-Smoot Act: U.S. puts increases on tariffs
- **1931** President Hoover announces one-year suspension of war dept payments
- **1931** collapse of Central European Bank begins major recession
- **1933** President Roosevelt introduces New Deal
- **1934** approx. 17 million Americans living on relief

The growth of the Soviet economy in the 1930s contrasted sharply with the rest of the capitalist world. The depression that gripped the world economy in 1929 produced the biggest business slump of modern times. Economic crisis undermined confidence in the survival of capitalism as an economic system, just as the Russian Revolution had hit confidence in the survival of the liberal political order.

The seeds of the economic crisis can be found buried in the more prosperous decade which followed the end of the war. For many the 1920s were years of boom, though not for all. After the initial disruption caused by massive demobilization in 1919, the world economy began to expand again on the lines of the prewar years. The core of that expansion was the American industrial economy. The war turned the United States into the world's banker and the world's largest trader. Industrialization also made strides in those areas cut off from European imports during the war. The flow of U.S. funds helped drag the more backward parts of the world economy towards the modern age.

The boom years were sustained by a whole range of new products—cars, radio, movies, chemicals—and by the development of large industrial corporations, like Ford or Dupont, which used the most up-to-date techniques in management and production. Improvements in efficiency boosted profits and lowered prices, releasing more money for investment and encouraging a boom in consumer durables, such as cars.

The American-led boom disguised many surviving weaknesses. The prewar trading economy, based on the gold standard and free convertibility, proved impossible to resurrect. Free trade gave way to widespread protectionism as states sought to shield the living standards of their own populations. The United States replaced Britain as the primary lender. More than $6 billion were invested overseas between 1925 and 1929. Unlike Britain, however, the U.S. economy had a weak international finance sector. Many of the

1 The Depression in the United States created poverty on a massive scale. In 1934 some 17 million Americans lived on relief, many in the poorer southern states (map below right). Even by the late 1930s there were still more than eight million unemployed. The Depression produced mass migration from the impoverished small-farm states of the Midwest and South to new industrial regions in the far West, Florida, and to established northern industrial cities. Others obtained temporary work from the Works Project Administration, which provided 500,000 temporary jobs from public funds.

2 german unemployment, 1933–37

0–2.5	15.1–25
2.6–5.0	25.1–35
5.1–15	35.1–50
	50.1–over 75

(unemployment per 1,000)

October 1933

October 1937

2 In four years German unemployment was almost eliminated (maps above). The main cause lay with state efforts to revive employment through work-creation projects, the building of the new highways, and investment in house-building, canals, and other major construction projects. Marriage loans, introduced in 1933, were designed to remove women from the job market. The compulsory state labor service, for men and women, took more than 250,000 18-year-olds off the unemployment totals. By 1939 unemployment was down to just 33,000—most of whom were largely unemployable.

loans were speculative or short-term, subject to sudden recall. Moreover the U.S. economy was self-sufficient in many commodities, unlike the British, and so imported less, blunting the trade growth of other states. If the American boom was good for Americans, the impact abroad was more mixed.

The fragility of the new boom was glaringly exposed when in October 1929 a sustained speculative investment bubble finally burst. American creditors began to call in

overseas loans, causing panic among debtors who had reloaned the money for long-term projects, as had been the case in Germany. As the arteries of world finance began to silt up, the U.S. economy reacted by putting up prohibitive tariffs in the 1930 Hawley-Smoot Act, thereby cutting off imports from economies desperate to pay back dollar debts. Competitive protection followed, cutting world trade by almost two-thirds of its value between 1929 and 1932. Prices and profits collapsed, and in the United States, Germany, and half a dozen other developed states, industrial output sank by more than one-third in three years.

The most conspicuous element of the slump was unemployment and the miserable poverty that marched with it. In the developed world alone by 1932 there were more than 24 million out of work. At its peak, it affected one in four of the American workforce; in Germany the figure by 1932 was two in every five. At its worst almost nine million Germans were thrown out of work in a

farm workers begin organizing, 1933

San Francisco general strike, May–July 1934

1 the depression in the united states

population decrease or increase:

decrease	10–15
0–5%	15–20
5–10%	20% and over

workforce of 20 million. The figures for the registered unemployed told only part of the story. Many of the long-term unemployed disappeared from the registers as their entitlement to unemployment relief lapsed. Even in those states with welfare systems the scale of unemployment soon exhausted the relief budgets. As state revenues fell it proved impossible to give adequate welfare. In cities across Europe and the United States there sprang up hundreds of unofficial charitable projects giving out a hot meal or bread and fuel for starving families.

The Depression was a social catastrophe for which governments were ill prepared. Not until the very end of the slump, when the damage had been done, did governments recognize that recovery was only possible with more state intervention. In the United States, under the presidency of Franklin Roosevelt, a package of welfare and economic reforms was introduced, known collectively as the New Deal. The National Recovery Act of 1933, a program of public works was established to restore output and employment. By the end of the decade more than $10 billion had been spent and 122,000 public buildings, 664,000 miles of road, 77,000 bridges, and 285 airports constructed.

In Europe recovery was patchy. It went furthest in Germany following Hitler's appointment in 1933 as chancellor. A package of state-backed programs soaked up many of the unemployed, including a new system of multilane highways, the *Autobahnen*. Investment was pumped into building houses, agriculture, and rearmament. By 1936 the pre-Depression position was restored; by 1939 the German economy was one-third larger than in 1929. In Britain, home of free trade, the state began to institute a higher level of economic management, backed by a new tariff structure established at the Commonwealth Conference in Ottawa in August 1932. Home demand expanded rapidly as the British consumer benefitted from cheap food imports. For those still employed, the 1930s brought a remarkable consumer boom.

The gradual recovery of national economies did little to stimulate the world market. The 1930s saw a wave of competitive protectionism designed to stimulate domestic production and to avoid reliance on an uncertain export economy. In Germany a Four-Year Plan launched in 1936 aimed to reduce Germany's dependence on overseas supply by producing synthetic oil, rubber, and textiles and by mining low-grade German ores. In 1938 a large program of import substitution was set up in Japan, centered around synthetic oil. Much of world trade was reduced to a simple barter system. International efforts to combat the recession were confined to a World Economic Conference in London in 1933 whose failure highlighted the changed outlook of post-Depression governments.

There existed a widespread belief that the days of liberal economics and global trade were over, to be replaced by state-regulated economic development and small self-contained trading blocs. Even in the United States, where the idea of an open world economy still had powerful advocates, state intervention and tariff protection were the key features of the Depression decade.

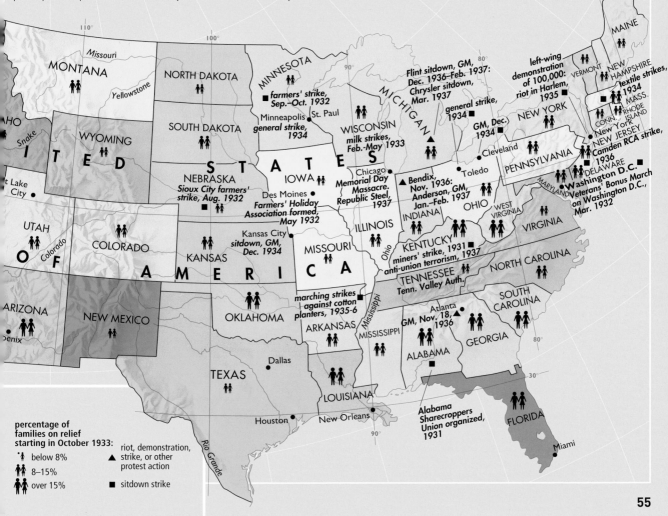

percentage of families on relief starting in October 1933:

below 8%

8–15%

over 15%

riot, demonstration, strike, or other protest action

sitdown strike

states of the "new order": japan

1931 Japanese occupy Manchuria

1932 "Manchukuo" Republic set up in China by Japan

1933 Japan leaves League of Nations

1934 Japan declares "Aman Doctrine" (Japanese sphere of influence in East Asia)

1936 Japanese military take over government

1936 Japanese sign anti-Comintern pact with Germany

1937 beginning of full-scale war between Japan and China

1938 Japanese install puppet government of Chinese Republic of Nanjing

2 the manchurian campaign, 1931–32

— railroads under Japanese control

→ Japanese advances, 1931

■ Japanese garrisons, 1931

▲ Japanese control by Sep. 1931

— railroads under Soviet control, 1931

● Japanese control by Aug. 1932

▮ areas of Manchurian resistance

▮ target area of Japanese subversion and inducement, 1932–37

▮ area from which Chinese regular forces effectively expelled, 1935

— area of Japanese attempt to establish puppet North China State, 1935

The political consequences of the slump were profound. The breakdown of international collaboration and the collapse of world trade undermined willingness to sustain the postwar settlement. The search for a new economic order, based on economic nationalism, was soon followed by efforts to construct a new international political order to replace that established by Britain, France, and the United States in the early 1920s.

The driving force behind this New Order was a triumvirate of states, Germany, Italy, and Japan, where militaristic nationalism was in power, trading on resentment toward other races and harboring ambitions to launch a new wave of imperial conquests. Japan exemplified this profound dissatisfaction with the existing order. In the 19th century, following a revolution in 1868 against the old feudal system, Japanese leaders made a sustained effort to imitate the West in order to build a strong and prosperous state. Modern industry was adopted; the armed forces were reformed along European lines; European styles of dress and European culture were imitated. In 1902 Japan consolidated her new international role when she signed a treaty of friendship with Britain. Two years later she defeated imperial Russia at sea and on land and became the major power in East Asia. Japan saw herself as an imperial power, like Britain or France. By 1910 Japan had acquired control of Korea and Taiwan, and a string of islands and mainland bases, which were treated like colonial possessions. When war came to Europe in 1914, Japan joined the Allies and sat at the Versailles Conference as one of the five major powers. At the Washington Conference, which opened in November 1921, she signed a Four-Power Treaty with Britain, France, and the U.S. confirming the existing territorial settlement in the Pacific region, and in 1922 was party to a Nine-Power Pact guaranteeing the sovereignty and independence of the Chinese Republic.

The policy of integration with the West had brought Japan great gains, but it also provoked widespread criticism at home among a new generation of young nationalists, who wanted to reassert traditional Japanese culture and values, and who rejected what they saw as Japan's humiliating dependence on the West. When the slump of 1929 shattered the Japanese silk industry and closed the door to overseas trade, the nationalists, prominent in Japan's armed forces, agitated for a new direction in Japan. The military leadership

2 On September 18, 1931 Japanese soldiers of the Manchurian Kwantung army blew up a short stretch of line on the South Manchurian railroad near Mukden, run by Japan. The "incident" was taken as the opportunity to extend Japanese control (map below) over an area rich in mineral resources, particularly coal and shale oil. Chinese resistance was vigorous but sporadic. By March 1, 1932 the area was under Japanese control.

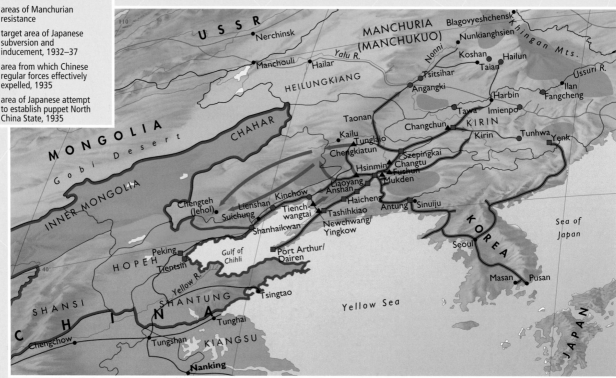

www.microworks.net/pacific/road_to_war/
The road to war in Asia
www.fas.harvard.edu/~asiactr/sino-japanese/
A study of the Sino-Japanese war

1 During the 1930s Japan embarked on a program of imperial expansion into China (map right). Encouraged by the army and by patriotic associations in Japan, the Japanese government approved the army's initiative in seizing the Chinese province of Manchuria in 1931. A year later Japanese forces threatened the port of Shanghai, with its large European population. After a restless peace, full-scale war came in 1937, which brought Japanese forces down the eastern seaboard, threatening European colonies in the Far East.

1 japanese expansion starting in 1914

- Japanese territory, 1914
- spheres of Japanese influence in 1918
- expansion to 1933
- expansion to Dec. 1941
- spheres of Japanese influence in 1941
- ✳ Japanese conflict with USSR
- → Japanese attacks
- ■ Chinese capitals
- ▪ Allied bases

began to dominate the cabinet and override parliament; military radicals assassinated hundreds of politicians and businessmen with Western links; radical nationalists mobilized popular support for Japanese imperialism in Asia.

The obvious area for Japanese expansion was mainland China. In September 1931, in defiance of the Washington agreements, the Japanese army in Manchuria seized the whole province for the Japanese empire. Though Japan had long enjoyed an extensive economic presence in Manchuria, its seizure was the first serious challenge to the League of Nations and the postwar settlement. Japan was censured by the League, and left it in 1933. In 1934 the nationalist politician, Prince Konoye Fujimaro, declared the Amau Doctrine, which amounted to a rejection of Western influence in China and the establishment of a new Asian order, centered on Japan.

The Western states, anxious about their own economic interests, did nothing to obstruct Japan. Following Manchuria, which was turned into a puppet kingdom under the Manchu Pu Yi Hsüan-t'ung—who had been the last Ch'ing emperor of China—Japan continued to put pressure on China for further concessions, while embarking on an extensive program of rearmament. Elaborate schemes were drawn up to create a new regional economy, the "Greater East Asia Coprosperity Sphere," with Japan at the core and a circle of other Asian and Pacific states tied to her economically and politically. In July 1937, following a clash between Chinese and Japanese forces in Peking, full-scale war was launched against China. Japan seized much of northern and eastern China, including the capital, Nanking, captured with huge loss of life in December 1937. In 1938 Japan announced that a New Order was in the making, which would restore Asia to the Asians.

- **1915** Italy joins Allies
- **1922** Mussolini takes power in Italy
- **1928** Abyssinia signs friendship treaty with Italy
- **1929** Mussolini signs Lateran Accord with Papacy
- **1934** Italians suppress Senussi resistance in Libya
- **1935** Italy invades Abyssinia
- **1936** Italian troops enter Addis Ababa
- **1936** Mussolini delares Rome-Berlin Axis

Italy, like Japan, was a new power. Unified between 1859 and 1870, the Italian state, weak economically and militarily, remained marginal to the European power balance. In the two decades before 1914, Italy acquired a colonial empire in Africa and, like Japan, began to dream about becoming a major regional power.

When in 1911 Italy defeated Ottoman forces in Libya, her ambitions turned toward the Middle East and the Mediterranean basin as a natural area of Italian dominance. The Great War exposed the feebleness of this ambition. Italy made few gains from the conflict, despite the promises made by Britain and France when Italy intervened on their side in 1915. Like the Japanese, Italian leaders found themselves compelled to work within an international framework manipulated by Britain and France.

Italy's weak international standing was one of the factors that fueled the rise after the war of a radical nationalist movement, which found its chief expression in a small party of veterans led by an ex-socialist agitator, Benito Mussolini. His Fascist Party, founded in 1921 (named after the bundle of rods and axes, fasces, carried by those who executed the law in ancient Rome), attracted support from those Italians— veterans, students, intellectuals—frustrated with the existing parliamentary system and from businessmen hostile to Labor. The fascists developed a reputation for brutal anti-Marxist activism and for tub-thumping patriotism. Though with only 35 seats in the national assembly, Mussolini was invited by the king, on the advice of leading conservatives, to become prime minister in October 1922. His success was sealed by a mass demonstration of uniformed Fascist militia whose black-shirted members converged on Rome on October 30th, the day of Mussolini's appointment.

For all the nationalist rhetoric, Mussolini's Italy remained within the League system in the 1920s. Mussolini was concerned with the establishment of domestic power. In 1926 Italy became a one-party state, with Mussolini as its undisputed leader, or *Duce*. By mobilizing business support, the economy was stabilized and labor unrest died down. In 1929 the Lateran Accords signed with the Papacy ended the conflict between church and state that dated back to 1870. In foreign policy Mussolini sought to have Italy taken seriously as a great power. Italian foreign policy was respectable. Italy worked within the League and supported the Locarno Pact of 1925, which reaffirmed the territorial settlement in western Europe from which Italy had profited little. In April 1935 at Stresa, Mussolini hosted a meeting of British, French, and Italian representatives, which was the last occasion on which the three European victor powers publicly endorsed their commitment to the survival of the Versailles Settlement.

By 1935, however, Italian foreign policy had taken a new turn. In the aftermath of the slump, Mussolini saw an opportunity from the domestic preoccupation of the other powers and the collapse of international collaboration. His nationalist supporters were keen for Italy to overturn her reliance on the West, and to develop an independent and imperial policy in the areas of historic Italian interest—North Africa, the Middle East, and the Balkans. Mussolini was also anxious to keep the Fascist revolution boiling; he saw himself as a new Caesar, called to build a second Roman empire.

For nationalists the natural area for empire-building was independent Abyssinia, where Italy had been humiliatingly defeated in 1896 and where there were extensive Italian economic interests. On October 3, 1935 Italian forces invaded Abyssinia, and by May had brought it under Italian rule. The League again faced a challenge from one of its most prominent members. Sanctions were imposed, which had little effect, but so alienated Italian opinion that Italy left the League in 1937. Mussolini now burned his boats. In July 1936 he committed Italian forces to help nationalist rebels in Spain overturn the republican regime in defiance of Britain and France. In 1937 Italy aligned herself publicly with Hitler's Germany when she signed the Anti-Comintern Pact (directed against international communism) to which Japan had already subscribed the previous year. From an attitude of cooperative internationalism, Italy had become by 1938 a power committed to challenging the status quo.

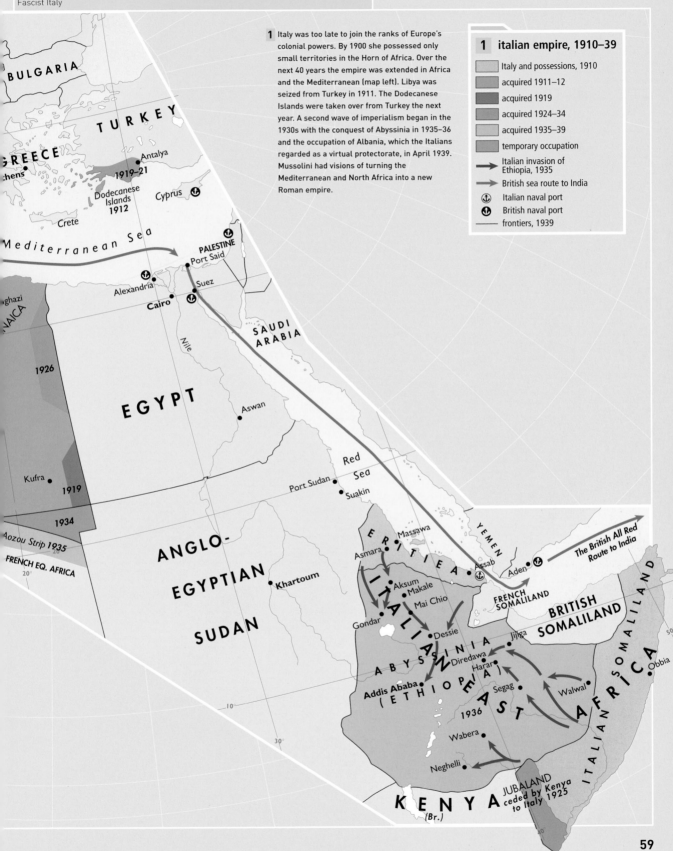

1 Italy was too late to join the ranks of Europe's colonial powers. By 1900 she possessed only small territories in the Horn of Africa. Over the next 40 years the empire was extended in Africa and the Mediterranean (map left). Libya was seized from Turkey in 1911. The Dodecanese Islands were taken over from Turkey the next year. A second wave of imperialism began in the 1930s with the conquest of Abyssinia in 1935–36 and the occupation of Albania, which the Italians regarded as a virtual protectorate, in April 1939. Mussolini had visions of turning the Mediterranean and North Africa into a new Roman empire.

1 italian empire, 1910–39

- Italy and possessions, 1910
- acquired 1911–12
- acquired 1919
- acquired 1924–34
- acquired 1935–39
- temporary occupation
- → Italian invasion of Ethiopia, 1935
- → British sea route to India
- ⚓ Italian naval port
- ⚓ British naval port
- — frontiers, 1939

BULGARIA

TURKEY

GREECE

Athens

Antalya

1919–21

Dodecanese
Islands
1912

Cyprus

Crete

Mediterranean Sea

PALESTINE
Port Said

Benghazi

CYRENAICA

Alexandria

Cairo

Suez

SAUDI
ARABIA

1926

Nile

EGYPT

Aswan

Kufra

1919

Red
Sea

Port Sudan

Suakin

1934

Aozou Strip 1935

FRENCH EQ. AFRICA

ANGLO-
EGYPTIAN

SUDAN

Khartoum

ERITREA

Massawa

Asmara

Aksum

Makale

Mai Chio

Gondar

Dessie

YEMEN

Assab

Aden

FRENCH
SOMALILAND

*The British All Red
Route to India*

BRITISH
SOMALILAND

ITALIAN

ABYSSINIA
(ETHIOPIA)

Addis Ababa

1936

Jijga

Diredawa

Harar

Segag

Walwal

EAST

AFRICA

ITALIAN SOMALILAND

Obbia

Wabera

Neghelli

KENYA

JUBALAND
ceded by Kenya
to Italy 1925

(Br.)

states of the "new order": **germany**

Italy's decision to move closer to Hitler's Germany in 1937 tied her to the most dangerous and powerful of the states seeking political revision in the 1930s. Hitler and his Nazi party colleagues made no secret before 1933 of their hostility to the Versailles Settlement. When Hitler was appointed chancellor on January 30, 1933 as part of a conservative scheme to stabilize the German political system following the political turmoil of the years of depression, Germany was ruled by a man convinced that she would rise again as a great power, and that he was the chosen instrument of destiny to achieve it.

For Hitler there were two sides to the idea of a New Order—a political and social revolution in Germany itself; and a revolution in the international order established at the end of the Great War. Within 18 months Germany was turned into a one-party state, dominated at every level by the Nazi Party and its numerous affiliated organizations and, following the death in 1934 of the president, Field Marshal von Hindenburg, a one-man dictatorship. Hitler merged the offices of chancellor and president, and declared himself to be simply the leader—*der Führer*. Trade unions were abolished, political prisons and a political police force, the Gestapo, set up. The latter was run by Heinrich Himmler who, by 1936, was in control of all the country's police and security services. In 1935 the first active steps were taken to remodel Germany racially with the notorious Nuremberg Laws denying Jews full civil rights. This was part of a more general program of "racial hygiene," which included racist teaching in schools and the compulsory sterilization of the hereditarily ill and mental patients.

On the international front Nazi goals were less clear. There was general agreement in German society on the justice of overturning Versailles. Hitler wanted to create a pan-German state in central Europe and to remilitarize Germany. For many in the Nazi movement this was the limit of German ambition. But from the early 1920s Hitler had harbored the desire for a war of revenge which would turn Germany into a world power. He had no fixed plan or blueprint, but his long-term goal was to build up German power to the point where Germany could carve out a large territorial empire in Eurasia and become an imperial superpower. Hitler regarded war as an integral feature of relations between states, to be welcomed rather than avoided. Nevertheless the early years of the Nazi regime saw a cautious approach to foreign policy, from fear of provoking other states while Germany was still relatively powerless. Rearmament began slowly, and was not publicly declared until March 16, 1935, when Hitler announced a new 36 division army, five times larger than the 100,000 force allowed in the Versailles Treaty. In March 1935 the Saarland returned to German sovereignty when 90.8 per cent of its citizens voted for union. In March 1936 German forces reoccupied the demilitarized zone of the Rhineland, which Allied forces had vacated in 1930. The Allies did nothing to maintain the postwar settlement on these issues, partly because of hostility to the risk of war among their home populations, partly because they privately recognized the futility of maintaining a punitive peace on questions that did not constitute a serious threat to western interests.

In 1936 Hitler stepped up the pace. New military programs were authorized for the modernization and expansion of the armed forces, which were intended to make Germany the foremost military power in Europe by the early 1940s. In November 1937 Hitler announced a new course in German foreign policy: union with Austria and possible war with Czechoslovakia to return three million Sudeten Germans to German rule.

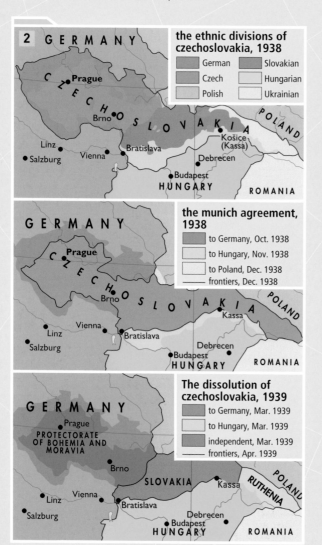

2 Germany's military spending increased rapidly after 1935, buttressing Hitler's foreign policy ambitions. In spring 1938 he turned his attention to Czechoslovakia (maps left), where the large German population in the west gave him a pretext for intervention. In September 1938, Britain and France acquiesced to his occupation of the Sudetenland. Six months later, Hitler seized the rest of the Czech lands, leaving a rump Slovakia as a Nazi client state, while Hungary and Poland each took a share of the spoils of what had been central Europe's most democratic and stable country.

1 german expansion, 1935–39

Germany, 1935

Saarland, incorporated by plebiscite, 1935

Rhineland (demilitarized zone) reoccupied by Germany, 1936

frontiers, 1937

Slovakia (client state of Nazi Germany), nominally independent from Mar. 1939

German annexations:

Mar. 1938

Oct. 1938

Mar. 1939

In March 1938 German forces entered Austria and an *Anschluss*, or annexation, was imposed. In May 1938 Hitler ordered plans for war with the Czechs in the fall. This did alarm the West. Although Britain and France pressured the Czechs to concede German occupation of the Sudetenland in October 1938, both states prevented outright conquest. At the Munich Conference in September 1938—the first occasion on which Versailles was revised through discussions on German soil—Hitler backed away from full-scale war. By the end of 1938 he had achieved much of his domestic and international ambition. Germany was poised to begin a more radical revision of the international order.

1 In the 1930s Germany, under Hitler's leadership, began to reverse the conditions imposed under the Versailles Settlement (map above). The Saarland returned to German control in 1935; the demilitarized Rhineland was occupied by German forces in March 1936 and, by 1939, a wall of fortifications (the Siegfried Line) had been built on the western border. In 1938 Austria was united with Germany, the dream of Austrian nationalists in 1919, achieved by the ex patriate Austrian, Hitler. Three million Germans who had been Austrian subjects in 1918 lived under Czech rule. In 1938 Hitler planned to seize these German areas by force, but they were achieved by negotiation with Britain and France. The Sudeten Germans, who had organized themselves in the Sudeten German Party, with more than 1.3 million members in 1938, welcomed the unification with Germany with overwhelming enthusiasm.

the **spanish civil war**

1918–20 the Trieno Bolshevista

1923 military coup in Spain

1931 Spanish Second Republic formed

1932 September Law aimed to transform Spanish agriculture

1936 Spanish civil war begins

1939 Nationalist victory ends Spanish civil war

The struggle between an old and new political order in Europe came to be exemplified in the 1930s by the civil war that tore Spain apart between 1936 and 1939. It was a conflict widely regarded as a struggle between the forces of light— socialism and liberalism—and the forces of darkness—fascism and reactionary nationalism. In reality the issues at stake in Spain were far more complex.

In many respects Spanish politics and society in the early part of the century resembled Latin America. Spain, too, was dominated by a traditional rural elite, with a large mass of impoverished and landless rural workers. The Catholic Church was a major force, and the military had a tradition of intervention in Spanish politics. Spanish modernization was slower than in other parts of western Europe. Agriculture was the main source of livelihood even in the 1930s, while Spain relied on exporting food and raw materials. But, as in Latin America, the cities expanded starting in the late 19th century, particularly Barcelona, center of Spain's limited industrial development. In the cities flourished a liberal middle class, keen to shift political power to the urban populations, anticlerical in outlook, radical in their desire for social reform and effective democracy. There also developed a new urban proletariat, entirely hostile to the old order and attracted to the more radical wing of European socialism, anarchism, and syndicalism.

The old political system was based on a parliament—the *Cortes*—which was dominated by the traditional elites, who rigged elections and stifled popular political participation. It was a system in decay. In 1918–20 there was widespread and violent political unrest—the *Trieno Bolshevista*—fueled by the rural and urban poor. In 1923 the army overthrew the feeble constitutional monarchy of Alfonso XIII, and General Primo de Rivera became military dictator, committed to a program of social and economic modernization. Unable to cope with the effects of the slump, de Rivera was overthrown in turn, and in April 1931 the urban radicals, in alliance with Labor, established a republic under the radical intellectual, Miguel Azaña.

The republic embarked on a thorough program of reform directed against the Church, which was disestablished; the army, which was much reduced in size; and the landlords. The rural issue was the most bitterly contested. The September Law of 1932 aimed to transform Spanish agriculture by giving rural workers minimum wages, regular all-year employment, and the chance to own land seized from absentee landlords. Within two years conservative opinion in Spain was mobilized in mass nationalist movements: the CEDA (Spanish Confederation of Autonomous Rights), the Nationalist Party, and the fascist Falange. This bloc achieved power in the elections of November 1933 and set out to reverse the reforms and enforce landlord power with savage violence. The republican forces divided between the moderate liberals and socialists, who sought reform

2 The political map of Spain (below left) roughly followed the pattern of landholding. In the more prosperous farming communities of the north was found the heartland of Spanish support for Catholicism and the conservative order. In the tenant farming areas of the south were found the supporters of anarcho-syndicalism, hostile to the landowners and the state. In the central area of large estates the laborers were predominantly socialist. In Catalonia there existed an independent movement for Catalan autonomy, dominated by the left-wing *Esquerra*. A statute of autonomy was granted to the Catalans in September 1932, but then rescinded when the right came to power. There was a separate Basque nationalist movement in the north hostile to the Republic.

3 Spain between the wars was faced with a serious crisis on the land (below right). Overpopulation, soil erosion, and the slump in food prices added to the traditional tensions between landlords and the rural poor. The areas of greatest poverty in the south and southeast were also the areas of greatest aridity. In the north of the country agriculture was more prosperous, and small peasant-owned farms were common. In the south small tenant farmers and share-croppers prevailed. In the central regions large landlord estates had survived, worked by an army of impoverished laborers. In 1932 the Republic pushed through an agrarian law to improve wages and working conditions against fierce resistance. With global recession in the background, the law achieved little.

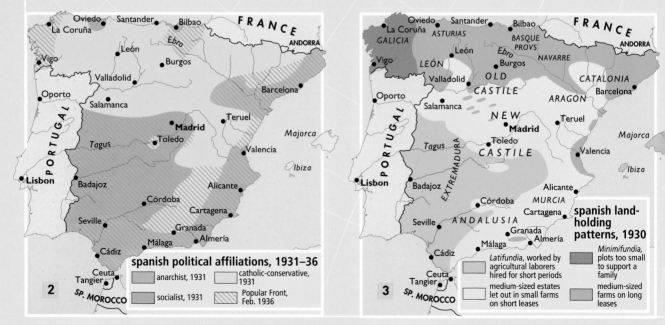

spanish political affiliations, 1931–36

- anarchist, 1931
- socialist, 1931
- catholic-conservative, 1931
- Popular Front, Feb. 1936

spanish land-holding patterns, 1930

- *Latifundia*, worked by agricultural laborers hired for short periods
- medium-sized estates let out in small farms on short leases
- *Minimifundia*, plots too small to support a family
- medium-sized farms on long leases

www.spartacus.schoolnet.co.uk/Spanish-Civil-War.htm
Comprehensive guide to the Spanish civil war
www.english.uiuc.edu/maps/scw/scw.htm
Artistic impressions and artefacts of the Spanish civil war

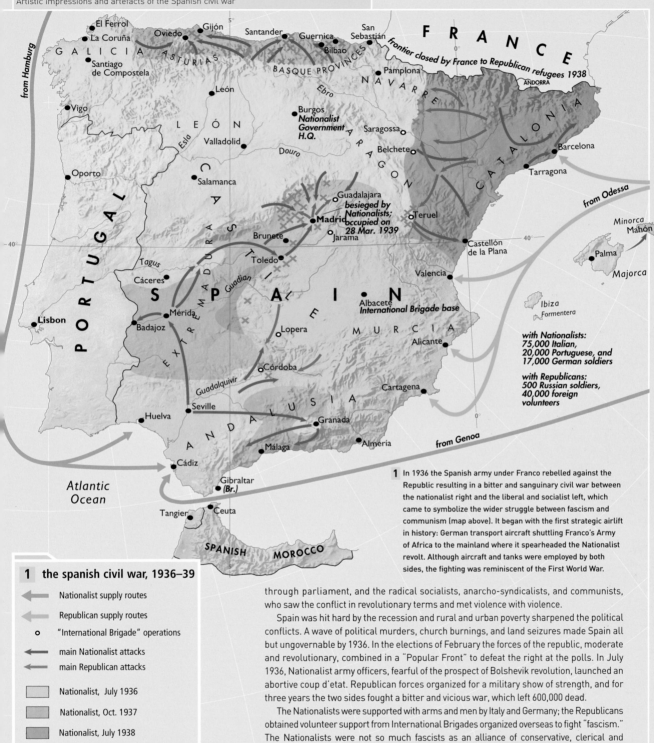

1 In 1936 the Spanish army under Franco rebelled against the Republic resulting in a bitter and sanguinary civil war between the nationalist right and the liberal and socialist left, which came to symbolize the wider struggle between fascism and communism (map above). It began with the first strategic airlift in history: German transport aircraft shuttling Franco's Army of Africa to the mainland where it spearheaded the Nationalist revolt. Although aircraft and tanks were employed by both sides, the fighting was reminiscent of the First World War.

1 the spanish civil war, 1936–39

← Nationalist supply routes

← Republican supply routes

o "International Brigade" operations

← main Nationalist attacks

← main Republican attacks

☐ Nationalist, July 1936

☐ Nationalist, Oct. 1937

☐ Nationalist, July 1938

☐ Nationalist, Feb. 1939

☐ Republican, Mar. 1939

✕ areas of most intense fighting

with Nationalists:
75,000 Italian,
20,000 Portuguese, and
17,000 German soldiers

with Republicans:
500 Russian soldiers,
40,000 foreign
volunteers

through parliament, and the radical socialists, anarcho-syndicalists, and communists, who saw the conflict in revolutionary terms and met violence with violence.

Spain was hit hard by the recession and rural and urban poverty sharpened the political conflicts. A wave of political murders, church burnings, and land seizures made Spain all but ungovernable by 1936. In the elections of February the forces of the republic, moderate and revolutionary, combined in a "Popular Front" to defeat the right at the polls. In July 1936, Nationalist army officers, fearful of the prospect of Bolshevik revolution, launched an abortive coup d'etat. Republican forces organized for a military show of strength, and for three years the two sides fought a bitter and vicious war, which left 600,000 dead.

The Nationalists were supported with arms and men by Italy and Germany; the Republicans obtained volunteer support from International Brigades organized overseas to fight "fascism." The Nationalists were not so much fascists as an alliance of conservative, clerical and nationalist forces with some fascist support. Their leader, General Franco, came from the tradition of *caudillismo*, or military dictatorship. He succeeded in welding Nationalist forces into a modern armed force. After early defeats the Nationalists captured Barcelona on January 6, 1939 and Madrid on March 28th, ending the war. Franco became head of an authoritarian regime committed to a strategy of modernization within a conservative framework.

1919 "May 4th" movement launched by Chinese student protesters

1921 Chinese communist party formed

1921–22 Washington Conference attempts to regulate situation in East Asia

1924 Kuomintang government established in Canton

1926 Chiang Kai-shek begins reunification of China (Northern Expedition)

1927 Chiang Kai-shek suppresses communists in Shanghai

1930 Chaing Kai-shek launches operations against Chinese communists

1934 Long March of Chinese communists begins

Civil war between nationalists and communists was not confined to Europe. In the 1930s China was plunged into a war between rival political factions until the common threat of Japanese aggression in 1937 brought an uneasy truce. The roots of the Chinese civil war went back to the revolution of 1911 (see page 14). The overthrow of the Manchu emperors led to a period of turmoil throughout China as Chinese political forces struggled to find a post-imperial state which could command widespread allegiance.

The first Chinese president, Yüan Shih-k'ai, elected in 1912, though nominally in favor of a constitutional democracy, by 1915 turned his office into a virtual dictatorship, based on the military force of the northern Chinese generals. When he tried to make himself emperor in 1916 his allies deserted him. His death a few months later ushered in a period of warlord rule which lasted until 1927. China fragmented into a number of military dictatorships whose forces fought among themselves for regional advantage. In the absence of a settled central government the other powers maintained the privileged position they had enjoyed under the emperors, dominating Chinese trade, customs, railroads, even the post office, while enjoying extraterritorial rights on Chinese soil.

The rise of warlordism and the continued presence of foreigners prompted a nationalist revolt in the 1920s. The call for national unity and sovereignty was loudest in China's universities, where students demanded social reform. The May 4th Movement, named after a demonstration by Peking students in May 1919, sparked a wave of strikes and boycotts which were crudely suppressed. The "New Culture Movement" that followed produced a period of intense intellectual debate on the path of modernization China should follow.

1 From 1928 to 1937 much of China was brought under the control of Chiang Kai-shek after a period of warlordism had brought China into political chaos. Chiang, who became a methodist after his marriage to one of the powerful Christian families of Shanghai—the Song—set up his capital in Nanking, where he launched the "New Life Movement," a quasi-fascist renewal of Chinese culture and values against westernism and Marxism.

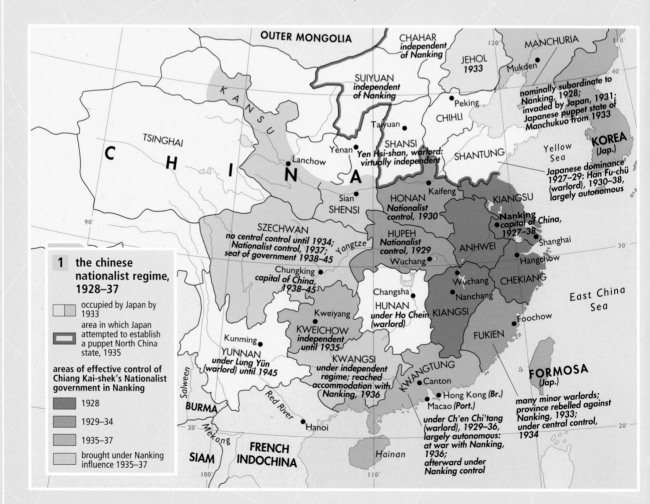

1 **the chinese nationalist regime, 1928–37**

☐ occupied by Japan by 1933

☐ area in which Japan attempted to establish a puppet North China state, 1935

areas of effective control of Chiang Kai-shek's Nationalist government in Nanking

■ 1928

■ 1929–34

■ 1935–37

☐ brought under Nanking influence 1935–37

www.wsu.edu:8001/~dee/MODCHINA/COMM.HTM
Modern China: the communist party
www.spartacus.schoolnet.co.uk/2WWchaing.htm
Chiang Kai-Shek and the Kuomintang

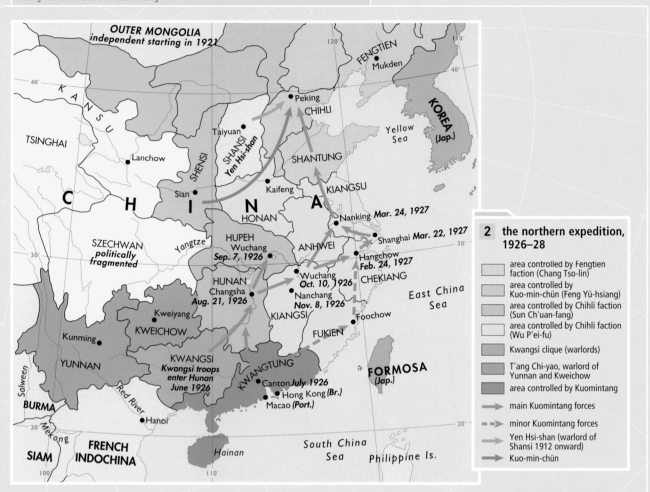

2 the northern expedition, 1926–28

area controlled by Fengtien faction (Chang Tso-lin)

area controlled by Kuo-min-chün (Feng Yü-hsiang)

area controlled by Chihli faction (Sun Ch'uan-fang)

area controlled by Chihli faction (Wu P'ei-fu)

Kwangsi clique (warlords)

T'ang Chi-yao, warlord of Yunnan and Kweichow

area controlled by Kuomintang

main Kuomintang forces

minor Kuomintang forces

Yen Hsi-shan (warlord of Shansi 1912 onward)

Kuo-min-chün

Two major political groups emerged from the debate. The first was based on Sun Yat-sen's National People's Party (Kuomintang), first founded in 1912 and revived by Sun in 1924; the second was the Chinese Communist Party, set up in July 1921. The two cooperated on a shared anti-imperialism, the communists winning support among the working classes of the main ports and the Kuomintang recruiting from among the educated urban classes and native Chinese businessmen of the south. Following Sun's death in 1924, a Kuomintang government was set up in Canton as a rival to the government in Peking dominated by the northern warlords. Sun had learned from the warlord era and the Kuomintang had its own trained army by the mid-1920s, run by a young officer, Chiang Kai-shek, who by 1925 was the leading figure in the movement.

In July 1926 Chiang began a year-long war against the north—the so-called Northern Expedition—which led a year later to the consolidation of much of China under one regime, based in Chiang's new capital in Nanking. Up to this point Kuomintang and communists cooperated, but Chiang's fear of a broader social revolution turned him against communism. In 1927 his forces destroyed the communists in the major cities. However, one young communist leader, Mao Tse-tung, kept resistance alive in the province of Kiangsi and when Chiang attacked his group in 1934, the fragments of the Chinese movement trekked 6,000 miles to the northern province of Shensi. In the 1930s Chiang became undisputed leader of the new national China; sovereignty was largely restored, though China remained reliant on western help. The social issue of China's millions of poor peasants and workers remained unresolved.

2 In 1926 the Kuomintang and the communists allied to launch a military campaign against the northen warlords to unify the country (map above). Despite their numerical inferiority, Chiang's forces defeated the divided warlord armies and brought much of central China under nationalist rule.

democracy and dictatorship

1919 to 1939

1922 Mussolini takes power in Italy

1923 Military coup in Spain

1926 Military seize power in Poland

1926 Antanas Smetona seizes power in Lithuania

1932 Antonio de Salazar becomes dictator of Portugal

1933 Germany becomes single-party dictatorship

1934 Konstantin Päts imposes one-party rule in Estonia

1935 Greece becomes a military dictatorship

The history of China between the two wars exemplified the problem of adapting to modern politics in the vacuum left by the collapse of an old imperial order. The assumption held by most radical modernizers was that some form of parliamentary democracy was the natural successor to old-fashioned authoritarianism. In reality most democratic experiments soon collapsed. China was democratic for a brief moment in 1912 when a president was popularly elected; Russia's short taste of democracy in the elections of 1917 was crushed in the civil war; Turkey held free elections in 1920, but from 1924 Kemal Atatürk's Republican People's Party operated a one-party system.

Democracy survived little longer in postwar Europe. In 1920 most European states were parliamentary democracies in imitation of the victorious democratic powers. But one by one the new democratic regimes gave way to dictatorships. The first transformation was in Italy, where the Fascist Party leader, Benito Mussolini, became prime minister in a right-wing coalition, then in 1926 head of a one-party state. Spain followed suit in 1923 when the military seized power. A brief democratic interlude between 1931 and 1936

2 The most disruptive change came in Germany. The electoral triumph of Nazism (maps below left), which secured 44% of the vote in March 1933, encouraged radical right-wing movements in the rest of Europe. Hitler and his closest associates used the means of democracy in order to subvert it.

3 The secret of the Nazi Party success was to organize a parallel state based on the party regions or Gaue and to create institutions—youth groups, labor service, the Labor Front—which forced ordinary Germans to collaborate or face party hostility or worse. By 1945 1.3 million Germans had been imprisoned at one time or another for political crimes (map bottom left).

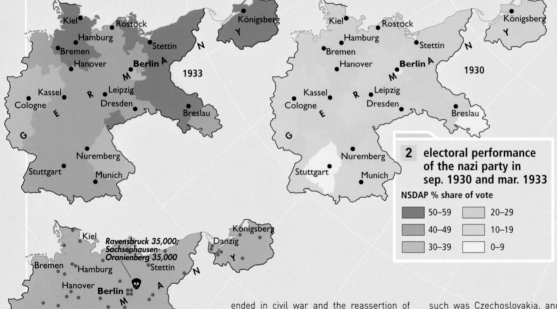

2 electoral performance of the nazi party in sep. 1930 and mar. 1933

NSDAP % share of vote

50–59	20–29
40–49	10–19
30–39	0–9

1932: Salazar dictatorship declared
1934: general strike

3 germany: concentration camps, 1937–38

concentration camp with potential capacities, including ancillary camps

site of divisions 1–80 of General SS

ended in civil war and the reassertion of military dictatorship under Franco (see pages 62–63). In Poland the military seized power in 1926 under Marshal Pilsudski, and was run by the so-called "Colonels' Group." Democracy collapsed in the Baltic States between 1926, when Antanas Smetona seized power in Lithuania, and 1934 when Konstantin Päts imposed one-party rule in Estonia. In Portugal a weak parliamentary state was overturned in 1926, and in 1932 Antonio de Salazar, leader of the National Union Party, became dictator. Hungary was ruled by Admiral Horthy's National Union Party starting in 1919, and Austria was turned into an authoritarian state in 1933 under Engelbert Dollfuss until it was absorbed by Hitler's Germany five years later. Greece became a military dictatorship in 1935, Bulgaria in 1936. Romania became a royal dictatorship under King Carol in 1938, and a military dictatorship three years later. The only one of the new postwar democracies to survive as

such was Czechoslovakia, and even this fell victim to German expansion in 1939. By the time Germany became a single-party dictatorship in the summer of 1933, democracy was already deep in crisis. By 1939 it survived as a political form only in Britain, France, the United States, the Low Countries, Scandinavia, and a handful of British Dominions.

The failure of democracy had many causes. There developed in the 1920s a powerful movement against liberal politics, which were seen as serving the interests of the wealthy western elites rather than meeting the needs of the masses. Democracy gave the masses the chance to express their hostility to the old elites, but neither the new mass right nor left was particularly democratic in outlook except where parliamentary government was well entrenched, as in Britain and France. The new authoritarian parties made a striking contrast with liberal organizations. They were militaristic, violent, active: the endless rallies, marches, and rituals gave them an appeal which staid parliamentary politics lacked in a period of

www.freedomhouse.org/reports/century.html
Survey of democracy in the 20th century
www.giles.34sp.com/
Irreverent guide to 20th century dictators

1 At the beginning of the 1920s most European states were democracies. By 1939 most were dictatorships, some fascist, some nationalist, some royalist. The new states created at Versailles were faced with numerous difficulties in establishing a modern parliamentary system. The slump exacerbated domestic political tensions. Europe's population began to move toward radical extremes—communist, nationalist, or fascist. Democracy survived in Britain and France, the Low Countries and Scandinavia, but in these too there developed native fascist and communist movements which threatened democratic stability.

crisis and transition. They also provided a source of status and power to those who lacked wealth and social position. They were genuinely populist movements, led by men such as Stalin and Mussolini, the sons of craftworkers or, like Hitler, the son of a clerk. Dictators, left or right, imposed consensus and persecuted opponents in order to build their version of the modern state.

1 **social and political change in europe, 1929–39**

political regimes

- fascist or communist
- repressive or not fully democratic
- democratic
- percentage of industrial workers unemployed (23.2)

major movements of protest and dissatisfaction, 1929–39

- ◆ strike wave
- ■ riot or demonstration
- ● right-wing activity
- — frontiers, 1937

overture to the second world war

1936 German reoccupation of Rhineland

1936 Britain and France begin to rearm

1937 U.S. neutrality laws passed through Congress

1937 Neville Chamberlain becomes British Prime Minister; follows policy of appeasement

1938 Germany occupies Austria

1939 (March 31) Chamberlain gives unconditional guarantee to Poland

1939 (September 1) German forces attack Poland

1939 (September 3) Britain and France declare war

The rise of authoritarian dictatorships in states with a vested interest in revising the international order established in the early 1920s posed a severe challenge to the democratic powers. The sharp polarization between liberal democracy, communism, and fascism produced a period of intense crisis in the 1930s, a form of European civil war. By 1939 the optimism of the peacemakers of 1919 gave way to a growing fatalism about the inevitability of another great war.

1 The Prussian city of Danzig at the mouth of the Vistula River became the cause of war in 1939 (map right). In 1919 under the terms of the Versailles Settlement, Danzig was made a free city under the League of Nations. The object was to allow Poland access to the Baltic here for trade. A corridor of Prussian territory between Danzig and the rest of Germany was given to the Poles for the same reason. The Corridor contained substantial German minorities. However, instead of using Danzig, the Poles developed the port of Gdynia as their outlet to the sea, while the Danzig enclave, populated largely by Germans, came to be dominated in 1933 by a Nazi government. In 1939 Hitler's Germany asked for the return of the city. Poland refused to revise the League settlement. Hitler prepared for war with Poland and, to prevent outside intervention, sent Foreign Minister Ribbentrop to sign a pact with Stalin in August 1939.

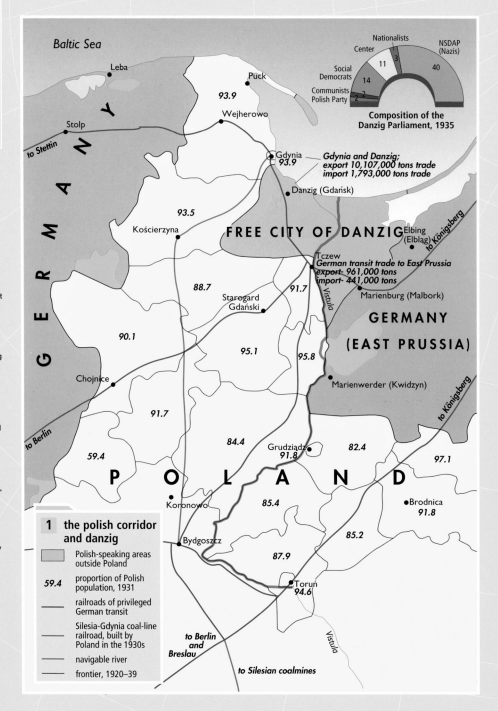

Composition of the Danzig Parliament, 1935

Gdynia and Danzig; export 10,107,000 tons trade import 1,793,000 tons trade

German transit trade to East Prussia export: 961,000 tons import: 441,000 tons

1 the polish corridor and danzig

- Polish-speaking areas outside Poland
- **59.4** proportion of Polish population, 1931
- railroads of privileged German transit
- Silesia-Gdynia coal-line railroad, built by Poland in the 1930s
- navigable river
- frontier, 1920–39

www.fsmitha.com/h2/ch21b.html
Europe:1937 to the outbreak of WW2
www.fsmitha.com/h2/ch22.htm
American and European approach to German aggression

The international order which the democratic states set up after the Great War contained fundamental flaws. Two major powers, the U.S. and the USSR, effectively stood outside it, though both possessed great potential weight in the balance of power. The United States refused to join the League of Nations or ratify the Versailles Treaty, and in 1937 isolationist opinion at home forced neutrality legislation through Congress. The Soviet Union was never fully integrated within the postwar order, even during a brief period as a League power between 1934 and 1939. Germany also stood outside the system, whose treaty structure most Germans wished to overturn. In the 1920s when Germany was disarmed these ambitions did not matter, but when Germany became a real military force again in the 1930s under Hitler, she was a permanent threat to the status quo.

In effect the postwar order was dominated by Britain and France. Neither power was in a position to afford the military and economic effort required to defend the status quo, particularly in the 1930s when their priority was to rebuild their economies after the recession and to avoid domestic social conflict. The system always depended on the collective goodwill of other states, and when that evaporated in the 1930s Britain and France found themselves overstretched defending global empires with shrunken resources. The weakness of their position encouraged them not to run risks in foreign policy and to try to meet the revisionist states halfway. The policy of "appeasement," as it became known, was a recognition of realities by statesmen who knew that their electorates were hostile to war and their forces too weak to restrain aggression by force.

Nonetheless, in 1936 both Britain and France began to rearm in order to deter potential aggressors and to be able to defend their empire if it came to war. The British prime minister, Neville Chamberlain, and his French counterpart, Edouard Daladier, both knew that to defend the status quo they must argue from a position of strength. By 1939 the combined output of British and French tanks and aircraft exceeded that of Germany. Germany was seen in the West as the key to the international crisis, but Italy and Japan, if allied to her, constituted a formidable threat in the Mediterranean and Far East. Between 1936 and 1939 neither Britain nor France was yet in a position to face these multiple threats with any real force.

In early 1939 both the British and French governments came to realize that unless they could curb German expansion, both the postwar settlement (and the balance of power and their democratic way of life) were dangerously threatened. In February Britain committed herself to fighting alongside France, and the two military staffs began to plan for a possible war in 1939. On March 15th German troops occupied the rest of Czechoslovakia. On March 31st Chamberlain gave an unconditional guarantee to Poland of British help if Germany violated Polish sovereignty. Poland, with its large German minority, seemed likely to be Hitler's next ambition. In the event, the guarantee was given before Hitler had decided to attack Poland and tear up the last shreds of the Versailles Settlement.

On April 6th Hitler instructed his armed forces to prepare a brief campaign against Poland in the fall. He expected the conflict to be localized: he was convinced that Britain and France were too militarily weak and too politically spineless to oppose him seriously, despite the growing evidence to the contrary. To ensure western nonintervention Hitler made overtures to the Soviet Union for an agreement. On August 23rd the Nazi-Soviet Non-Aggression Pact was sealed in Moscow. Three days later Britain entered a formal military alliance with Poland. Throughout the summer Britain and France had given Hitler clear warnings of their intention to fight. Preparations for war were well advanced by August, though both Chamberlain and Daladier expected Hitler to stand back from war when he realized the risk. Deterrence failed. On September 1st German forces attacked on a broad front. Mussolini's last-minute attempt to mediate between the powers on September 2nd failed, and Britain and France declared war on Germany the following day.

2 the polish campaign plans, 1939

Polish forces

German forces

2 The Polish government in 1939 was the first to stand up to Hitler (map left). Foreign Minister Josef Beck argued that Germany was bluffing and its military strength exaggerated. Boosted by a guarantee of support from Britain and France, the Polish army drew up defense plans. Poland's 37 divisions and 200 aircraft would fight a brief holding action and then withdraw to central Poland to fight in front of Warsaw. They had few tanks, relying on cavalry for mobility. During August 1939 troops and arms were smuggled into Danzig by German forces in East Prussia. On the night of August 31st, SS units captured the city, and the following day German soldiers began the invasion of Poland.

The European war, which began in September 1939, became two years later a world war involving all the treaty powers. It was the most destructive war in history. This was "total war," fought against civilians as well as soldiers and waged across the globe, in which the mobilization of national resources reached unprecedented levels and at least 55 million people were killed. The war marked a watershed in world history. Both sides fought to promote their version of a new world order to replace that established in 1919. The involvement of the Soviet Union and the United States beginning 1941 ensured the final outcome would no longer be decided by the European powers. The postwar world, dominated by these two new superpowers, left little room for traditional European imperialism. With the defeat of the Italian, Japanese, and German empires in 1945, the age of imperialism was dead.

Fighting on the Eastern Front, June 1943

PART III **THE WORLD AT WAR**

axis conquests

At 4:45 on the morning of September 1, 1939, the German training ship *Schleswig-Holstein*, on a visit to Danzig, opened up its guns on Polish installations. SS units, smuggled into Danzig, overpowered Polish officials in the city. Within hours it was in German hands, the first stage in a campaign of conquest which, in two years, took German forces across Europe: to the Atlantic coast in the west and to Moscow and the Crimea in the east.

The seizure of Danzig prefaced a rapid assault on the whole of Poland. Against Poland's 30 divisions and 11 brigades of cavalry and her tiny air force, Germany mustered 55 divisions—including the six so-called "Panzer" divisions with large numbers of tanks and vehicles—and 1,929 aircraft. Using the tanks and aircraft together to outflank and demoralize the enemy, German forces quickly overran western Poland. Although the French high command had promised a campaign in the west after mobilization was complete, nothing was done to ease the pressure on Poland's armies. On September 17th Soviet forces began to occupy the almost undefended eastern areas of Poland, and on September 27th, following a fierce aerial bombardment, Warsaw surrendered to German forces. Poland was partitioned between Germany and the Soviet Union on lines agreed in Moscow on September 28, 1939.

Hitler's instinct was to strike at Britain and France while the iron was hot. But disagreements over the plan of operations and deteriorating weather conditions led to 29 postponements. The final date was fixed for May 10, 1940. The plan of campaign, devised by General von Manstein and approved by Hitler, was to attack with three army groups, one of which would contain most of the tanks and heavy vehicles designed to penetrate the enemy line north of the Maginot Line fortifications and to encircle Allied armies in northeast France and Belgium. While the final preparations were put in place, Hitler became increasingly anxious about possible British plans to occupy Scandinavia in order to threaten Germany's northern flank. Two operations were hastily improvised against Denmark and Norway. The former was occupied with little resistance on April 9-10. The attack on Norway on April 9th was resisted with British support. Norwegian forces did not surrender until June 7th.

On May 10th the long-awaited German attack in the west began. Against a total of 144 Allied divisions (French, British, Dutch, Belgian) the Germans mustered 141. The German air force had 4,020 operational aircraft, the Allies a little over 3,000. The gap in tank strength favored the Allies: 3,383 against 2,335. Yet in six weeks, and at a cost of only 30,000 dead, German forces conquered the Netherlands, Belgium, and Luxembourg, and on June 21st forced the capitulation of France. Spurred on by German success, Italy declared war on Britain and France on June 10th. The secret of German success was not vast numerical superiority, but effective operational planning and the fighting skills of its army. British forces were divided—much of the air force stayed at home to avert the bombing threat—while the French forces, tanks included, were parceled out along the Maginot Line. The Germans were concentrated for a short, sharp blow against the Allies in northeastern France.

While the French struggled to cope with Germany's mobile armies, British forces on the continent were evacuated. Some 370,000 troops (139,000 of them French) were shipped back to Britain in May and June 1940, with almost none of their equipment. For several weeks Hitler hesitated between offering terms to Britain and invading. In the end he decided to invade in the fall (Operation Sealion), as long as British air power could be neutralized. During August and September the "Battle of Britain" was fought across the skies of southern England. The failure to neutralize the British air force, whose number and organization had been seriously underestimated, dented Hitler's enthusiasm. In July he began to talk of possible war with the Soviet Union, his current ally. By December 1940 he had made up his mind to defeat Stalin first, before finishing Britain off at his leisure.

2 the battle of britain, 1940

HQ Fighter Command headquarters
G group headquarters
--- group boundaries
△ sector command post
▲ fighter bases
high-level radar station
low-level radar station
● observer centers
■ Luftflotte HQ
● Luftwaffe bomber base

The Blitz
✶ 1–5 major raids (100 tons+)
✱ 6–10 major raids
✸ more than 10 major raids

www.worldwar2history.info/war/Axis.html
The lead-up to WW2
www.raf.mod.uk/bob1940/bobhome.html
History and events of the Battle of Britain

1 Between September 1939 and April 1941, German and Italian forces conquered nine European states (map right). Germany dominated Europe, while Italy extended its power in the Mediterranean basin. While Germany was engaged in the war in the west against France and Britain, the Soviet Union extended its political sphere in eastern Europe. A short war with Finland (November to March 1940) gave the USSR control of the Karelian peninsula; in June 1940 Lithuania, Latvia, and Estonia were annexed; in the same month Romania was compelled to give up Bessarabia.

2 The air battle fought over England between the RAF and the German air force was vital for keeping Britain in the war (map left). British forces had the advantage of radar, which gave accurate readings of approaching German aircraft. German forces took high losses of pilots and aircraft between July 1940, when the German attacks began, and October 1940, when the battle ended.

1 the german advance, 1939–41

Axis territory, Sep.1, 1939	→	Axis advances, 1939
Axis co-belligerents	→	Axis advances, 1940
occupied by Axis after Sep. 1939	→	Axis advances, 1941
Vichy France and territories	⛵	Axis airborne landings
Soviet annexed territory, 1939–41	→	Allied forces
neutral powers	→	Soviet advances, 1939–40
frontiers, Sep. 1, 1939	⇢	Allied retreat and withdrawal
	🏭	major cities severely damaged by bombing

73

the **nazi-soviet** conflict

1941 Germany invades Russia (Operation Barbarossa); declares war on U.S.

1941 (July 12) Anglo-Soviet agreement of mutual assistance

1941 (July 27) Germans invade Ukraine

1941 (Sept. 8) German forces start the siege of Leningrad after failing to take the city

1941 (Oct. 25) first German offensive against Moscow fails

1941 (Nov. 16) second German offensive against Moscow

1941 (Dec. 2) Soviets launch counteroffensive against Germans

The operation against the Soviet Union was codenamed "Barbarossa" after the medieval German emperor, Frederick I, who led the Third Crusade. Hitler viewed the attack on the Soviet Union as a modern crusade—the forces of European culture against the heathen Slavs and their Marxist masters.

From the 1920s onward Hitler had looked to the east as an area for German conquest and colonization. The rich resources of western Russia were to give him the means to turn Germany into a superpower. The preparations were conducted in the strictest secrecy. The attack was scheduled for May to give a summer of good fighting weather for German tanks and aircraft. The pretence was maintained that Britain was still the object of the new campaign, but by late spring there was growing intelligence evidence that German forces were swinging to the east. Efforts to persuade Stalin that his ally was

about to betray him were brushed aside by the Soviet leader as Western propaganda. Then in April 1941 Hitler was diverted to the Balkans in response to the failure of the Italian attack on Greece and an anti-German coup in Yugoslavia. On April 6th Belgrade was bombed and after a brief campaign both Yugoslavia and Greece were defeated and occupied by a mixed Italian-German force.

The Balkan conflict meant the postponement of Barbarossa until June 22nd. Stalin considered the date too late for the onset of hostilities that year, and Soviet defenses were not alerted to any threat. Though Soviet forces outnumbered those of Germany—20,000 tanks to 3,350 and 10,000 aircraft to the Luftwaffe's 3,400—they were poorly organized and short of modern equipment. The German army of 146 divisions, organized into three army groups, North, Center, and South, and spearheaded by 29 Panzer and motorized divisions, achieved complete surprise when the orders were given to roll across the Soviet frontier on June 22nd.

The German forces achieved a series of spectacular victories against a poorly prepared and demoralized Red Army. Huge pincer movements by mobile forces enveloped Soviet armies: two million prisoners were taken in the first three months. By the fall almost all Soviet tanks and aircraft in the western areas had been destroyed, Leningrad and Moscow were threatened, and German armies in the south had penetrated deep into Ukraine, where food supplies and industrial production were concentrated.

In October 1941 Hitler returned from his headquarters behind the battle lines to Berlin, where he announced to an ecstatic crowd that the Soviet Union was on the point of complete defeat and the time had now come for Germany to begin the construction of a New Order in Europe. In the east the plan was to destroy the Soviet state and raze its major cities to the ground. The bulk of the Slavic population would be pushed back beyond the Urals. The rest of the Soviet Union was to be broken into colonial regions ruled by Nazi commissars and permanently settled and garrisoned by Germans. The rest of Europe was to be organized hierarchically: The more developed and racially superior areas would hold privileged positions within the German empire;

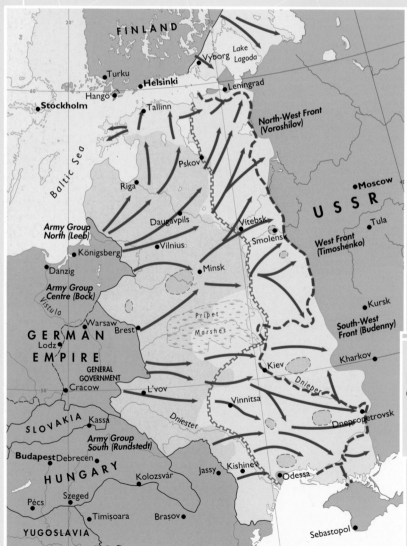

1 the german assault on the ussr, 1941

- Germany and her allies, June 22, 1939
- ᒍᒪᒍᒪ Stalin line
- → German attacks
- occupied by Germany and her allies by July 9, 1941
- - - - frontline, Sep. 1, 1941
- occupied by Germany and her allies by Sep. 30, 1941
- under Soviet control on Sep. 30, 1941
- ○ trapped Soviet pockets
- —— frontiers, early 1941

1 On June 22, 1941 Germany launched an attack against the Soviet Union on a front of almost 1,000 miles with three million troops (map left). In three months German armies, supported by troops from Romania, Finland, Hungary, and Italy, almost reached Moscow and Leningrad. By December the advance was halted and the Red Army began the counteroffensive that saved the Soviet capital.

those less developed and inhabited by Slav or Latin peoples would form a lower tier of poorer, rural states. At the center was to be the rich and industrialized Germany, dominating the continent as Rome had once done.

The declaration of the New Order proved premature. The German campaign in the east slowed with the onset of fall rains and high losses of equipment and men. Confident of a quick victory, little effort had gone into supplying equipment and clothing for winter fighting. Soviet forces fought fiercely when they stood their ground. In front of Moscow, whose outskirts were reached in December 1941, a young Soviet general, Georgiy Zhukov, organized a frantic but effective defense. Supported by fresh troops pouring in from the Soviet eastern provinces, equipped with winter clothing and weapons newly produced in the east, the Red Army inflicted the first reverses on German forces. Mobile warfare was replaced by two defensive lines that stretched for more than 1,000 miles deep into Soviet territory.

2 Germany and Italy both had ambitions in the 1930s to construct a new European order, dominated by the two fascist powers (map below). By 1942 most of Europe was under Axis control or was allied to or dependent on the Axis bloc. Hitler gave Mussolini a free hand in the Mediterranean area. The rest of Europe was the German sphere. The Versailles Settlement was turned on its head. Germany annexed neighboring areas to create "Greater Germany." The rest of occupied Europe was controlled by German plenipotentiaries or German puppet governments.

2 the axis new order 1939–43

- prewar borders
- frontiers, Nov. 1942
- Grossdeutsches Reich (Greater Germany)
- occupied by Germany
- occupied by Italy
- Axis satellites
- neutral
- Allied territory

RADOM German administrative areas
- ■ German civil administration
- ▲ German military administration

civil administrative areas
1 GENERAL GOVERNMENT
2 PROTECTORATE OF BOHEMIA-MORAVIA
3 DANZIG-WEST PRUSSIA
4 KATTOWITZ
5 WARTHELAND
6 CARINTHIA AND CARNIOLA
7 LOWER STYRIA
8 BIALYSTOK

regions
9 TRANSNISTRIA (to Romania 1941)
10 BESSARABIA (returned to Romania)
11 N. BUKOVINA (returned to Romania)
12 TRANSYLVANIA (to Hungary 1940)
13 SPIŠ (to Slovakia 1939)
14 BAČKA (to Hungary 1941)
15 MEDJIMURJE (to Hungary 1941)
16 PREKMURJE (to Hungary 1941)
17 LJUBLJANA (LUBIANA) (to Italy 1941)
18 ZICHENAU (to E. Prussia)
19 SUWALKI (Sudauen) (to E. Prussia)
20 KOSOVO (to Albania 1941)
21 THRACE (to Bulgaria 1941)

the **nazi-soviet** conflict

1942 (June 28) German offensive in southern Russia; Battle of Stalingrad

1942 (November) soviet counteroffensive, Operation Uranus

1943 German VI army surrenders at Stalingrad; Italian capitulation

1944 (June 22) Stalin ordered massive offensive, Operation Bagration

1944 Russian advance on Eastern Europe

1945 Yalta conference; defeat of Germany

1945 (April 30) suicide of Hitler

In the spring of 1942 Hitler was confident he could complete the defeat of the Soviet Union, which had eluded him in 1941. Against the advice of his generals, who were eager to capture Moscow, Hitler opted for a drive on the southern flank to secure Ukraine's rich resources and seize the oil of the Caucasus region. He hoped the Soviet front would be unhinged and that German forces could then wheel from the south to the rear of Moscow, encircling what remained of the Red Army.

On June 28th the southern "Operation Blue" was launched. Again German forces made remarkable gains. The Red Army was weaker in the south and withdrew in disorder toward the Volga and the Caucasus mountains. It stopped to fight on the mountain passes, which proved the limit of the southern advance toward the oil. Only the oil town of Maikop was captured, though following Soviet demolitions fewer than 70 tons of oil a day could be delivered. The Soviet forces also halted the German advance on the banks of the Volga at Stalingrad.

The city of Stalingrad was a major industrial center and the key to the flow of oil northward to the Soviet armies. Hitler ordered General Friedrich Paulus and his Sixth Army to seize the city from the retreating Soviet forces. A bitter battle ensued as the city was demolished street by street. The Soviet 62nd Army under General Chuikov was pressed back to the very edge of the river, where it fought with a fanatical tenacity. Both armies reached the very limits of endurance, driven on by Stalin and Hitler, who saw the contest as a symbol of the struggle between them. In November a Soviet counteroffensive, "Operation Uranus," broke the German front around Stalingrad and left Paulus and his army trapped. On January 31st he surrendered.

The Red Army drove the Germans back across the territory they had conquered in 1942 until, by the spring, poor weather and exhaustion brought a halt. In 1943 both sides prepared for what they saw as the decisive confrontation. Around the steppe city of Kursk lay a large Soviet salient in the German frontline. Here the German army concentrated almost one million men, 2,700 tanks, and 2,000 aircraft. Zhukov prepared a series of defensive lines to absorb the German attack, while he built up large reserves behind the battlefield for a massive blow against the German front. Soviet forces were transformed from the demoralized, ill-prepared troops of 1941. Improved technology and training, a clearer command structure, and the reorganization of mechanized and air forces in imitation of German practice all contributed to a narrowing of the gap in military effectiveness between the two sides. When the German assault began on July 5th against the 1.3 million men and 3,400 tanks of the Red Army it was blunted within a week. Zhukov then hurled his reserves into the battle. The German front broke, and German armies began the long grueling retreat back to the Reich.

By November 6th Soviet armies had reached Kiev. Early in January 1944 they crossed the old Polish border. Over the next six months German forces were cleared from the southern areas of the Soviet Union and from eastern Belorussia. On June 22, 1944, timed to coincide with the invasion of France by the western Allies, Stalin ordered a massive offensive—"Operation Bagration"—to clear German armies from Belarus, the Baltic States, and western Poland. By July the Red Army reached the Vistula opposite Warsaw. They inflicted 850,000 casualties on the defending German forces. The rapid Soviet advance brought the collapse of Germany's allies, Finland, Romania, and Bulgaria. Massively outnumbered in men and equipment, German armies fought a desperate rearguard defense until, in January 1945, their frontline protecting Germany finally broke. Within four months the Soviet armies swept to Berlin and Vienna. Rather than be captured, Hitler shot himself on April 30, 1945, as Soviet forces were storming the last streets of the German capital.

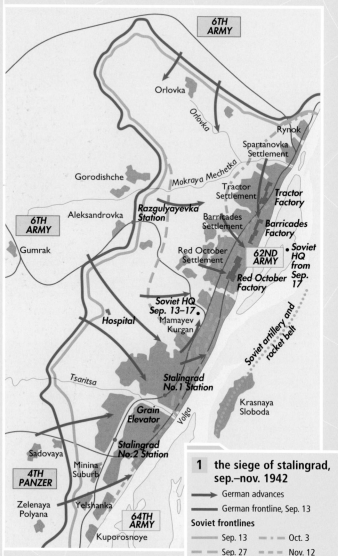

6TH ARMY

Orlovka

Orlovka

Rynok

Spartanovka Settlement

Gorodishche

Mokraya Mechetka

Tractor Settlement

Tractor Factory

Aleksandrovka

Razgulyayevka Station

Barricades Settlement

Barricades Factory

6TH ARMY

Gumrak

Red October Settlement

62ND ARMY

Soviet HQ from Sep. 17

Red October Factory

Soviet HQ Sep. 13–17 •
Mamayev Kurgan

Hospital

Soviet artillery and rocket belt

Tsaritsa

Stalingrad No.1 Station

Volga

Krasnaya Sloboda

Grain Elevator

Stalingrad No.2 Station

Sadovaya

Minina Suburb

4TH PANZER

Zelenaya Polyana

Yelshanka

64TH ARMY

Kuporosnoye

1 the siege of stalingrad, sep.–nov. 1942

→ German advances

— German frontline, Sep. 13

Soviet frontlines

— Sep. 13   —·— Oct. 3

--- Sep. 27   --- Nov. 12

1 In Stalingrad (map left), German armies drove the Soviet defenders to the very edge of the Volga River in the factory district and the city center. In November 1942, German forces were encircled and two months later capitulated with a total loss of 200,000 men.

www.militaryhistoryonline.com/wwii/stalingrad/blue.aspx
The battle of Stalingrad
www.stalingrad.net/
The battle of Stalingrad

2 **the defeat of germany, 1942–45**

— "Grossdeutches Reich" 1942

— maximum extent of Axis control, 1942

← Axis attacks

⇠ Axis withdrawals

← Allied attacks

cities under heavy air attack

partisan/resistance movements

major battle with date

2 Starting early in 1943 the Soviet army experienced an almost unbroken run of successes (map below), pushing the Germans back as far as Kiev in late 1943. 1944 saw the frontline move as far west as Warsaw, Romania, and Bulgaria. In 1945 the Red Army swept through eastern Germany. Berlin surrendered on May 2nd.

Norwegian Sea

North Sea

Baltic Sea

Feb.–Apr. 1945

NORWAY (neutral)

SWEDEN (neutral)

FINLAND

DENMARK

1940–44

Narvik

Trondheim

Bergen

Oslo

Gothenburg

Aarhus

Copenhagen

Malmö

Flensburg

1940–45

Lübeck

Hamburg

Bremen

Hanover

Amsterdam

Düsseldorf

Cologne

Bonn

Berlin

May 1945

Torgau

Dresden

Breslau

1941–44

Frankfurt

Mannheim

Metz

Nuremberg

May 1945

Stuttgart

Strassburg

Munich

Brünn

Prague

Cracow

GERMANY

Zurich

SWITZERLAND (neutral)

Berne

Innsbruck

AUSTRIA

Vienna

Apr. 1945

Bratislava

SLOVAKIA

1944

Kassa

Budapest

1944–45

HUNGARY

Szeged

Debrecen

Kolozsvár

Milan

Venice

Trieste

Turin

Genoa

MONACO

Livorno

Bologna

Rimini

Zara

Florence

Perugia

Spalato

Sarajevo

Mostar

MONTENEGRO

Kotor

1941–44

Zagreb

Pécs

Ujvidék

Belgrade

CROATIA

SERBIA

Nish

Danube

ROMANIA

Ploesti

Bucharest

Ruse

Varna

Burgas

Sofia

Plovdiv

Edirne

1944

BULGARIA

Skopije

Tirana

ALBANIA

Salonika

GREECE

Rome

Corsica

Sardinia

Naples

Bari

Taranto

ITALY

Turku

Helsinki

Viipuri

Lake Ladoga

1944

1944

Leningrad

Novgorod

1941–42

Narva

Tallinn

ESTONIA

Pskov

Riga

LATVIA

Daugavpils (Dünaburg)

Velikiye Luki

1942–43

Rzhev

Moscow Dec. 1941

Vyazma

1941–42

Tula

Orel

LITHUANIA

Kaunas

Vilnius

1944

Vitebsk

Königsberg

Danzig

E. PRUSSIA

POLAND

Bialystok

Minsk

June–Aug. 1944

Mogilev

Gomel

BELARUS

July–Aug. 1943

Kursk

1943–44

Stettin

Warsaw

1944–45

Brest

Lemberg

Tarnopol

Vinnitsa

Kiev Sep.–Oct. 1943

Dnieper

Kharkov

Voronezh

Don

Orel

UNION OF SOVIET SOCIALIST REPUBLICS

Gorkiy

Volga

Saratov

Stalingrad

Sept. 1940– Feb. 1943

Volga

Rostov

1942–43

1942–43

1942–43

Caucasus

UKRAINE

Transnistria

Dniester

Jassy

Krivoy Rog

Odessa

Crimea

Kerch

Sevastopol

Batum

Black Sea

Trabzon

Istanbul

Ankara

TURKEY (neutral)

Petsamo

Murmansk

1944

1944

1941–44

77

japanese conquests

- **1940** Japan begins occupation of French Indo-China
- **1941** Russo-Japanese neutrality pact
- **1941 (Dec. 7)** Japan attacks Pearl Harbor
- **1941 (Dec. 10–22)** Japanese landings in Philippines
- **1942 (Jan. 11)** Japanese take Kuala Lumpur
- **1942 (Jan. 20)** Japanese invade Burma
- **1942 (Feb. 15)** British surrender to Japanese at Singapore
- **1942** Battle of Midway

While Hitler's Germany was fighting to conquer Asia from the west, Japan was carving out an empire in the east. The conquest of eastern China, begun in July 1937, had sucked Japan into a long war of attrition against Chinese forces, both nationalist and communist. The Chinese war was seen in Tokyo as the key to the establishment of the Japanese New Order in Asia, but the military threat posed by an imperialist Japan involved her in increasing conflict with the Soviet Union and the United States.

Japanese leaders faced a dilemma. The army wanted to concentrate its efforts on the conquest of China and face the threat from a heavily armed Soviet Union on the Manchurian frontier: Two major battles were fought with the Red Army in 1938 and 1939 along the border, and Japan was defeated on both occasions. The navy meanwhile looked south to the rich resources of oil and other materials on which the future of any Japanese war effort depended. However, southern advance would bring Japan into conflict with the U.S., which was already giving aid to China and preparing to reinforce its possessions in the Pacific basin.

The war in Europe opened up new possibilities. The defeat of France encouraged Japan to look toward the vulnerable European colonies of South East Asia. In September 1940 Japan signed a Tripartite Pact with Germany and Italy on the redivision of the world into a New Order. The same month Japan occupied the northern part of French Indo-China, prompting the US to impose oil and steel sanctions. When the German-Soviet conflict in 1941 ended the threat from the north, the advance south was accelerated. In July 1941 the rest of Indo-China was occupied by 40,000 Japanese soldiers. In retaliation sanctions were tightened, depriving Japan of 80 percent of her overseas oil supplies. Rather than retreat, the expansionists argued for a campaign to secure a perimeter from Burma to Australia and the Pacific islands, defensible by Japanese naval and air power.

The plan was approved in September after much argument. The prime minister appointed in October, General Tojo, tried one more diplomatic offensive while Japanese forces moved into position for attack. While negotiations continued in Washington, Japanese aircraft launched an attack on the U.S. base at Pearl Harbor on the morning of December 7, 1941. The same day Japanese forces attacked Hong Kong, which surrendered on Christmas Day, and swept down the Malayan peninsula to Singapore, which surrendered on February 15, 1942. The U.S. possessions—Guam, Wake Island, the Philippines—all fell, one after the other. The heroic resistance of the U.S. garrison on Corregidor ended on May 6, 1942. In the west Japanese forces reached the Indian border at the end of May, when the offensive finally paused for breath.

The southward advance exceeded the wildest Japanese expectations. Well prepared operations against weaker, poorly armed forces, who had greatly underestimated Japanese fighting skills, brought rich dividends. Japan's military leaders decided to consolidate their position by seizing a further ring of islands, including Midway on the approaches to Hawaii. This time, forewarned by their radio intelligence, U.S. naval forces were deployed to intercept. The first wave of renewed attacks around the Coral Sea were repulsed on May 5–7. Against Midway the Japanese naval commander, Admiral Yamamoto, sent the bulk of the fleet and all four major aircraft carriers to destroy U.S. naval power in the Pacific. Vastly outnumbered, U.S. naval forces this time enjoyed the element of surprise. On June 3–6 U.S. naval aviators destroyed all the Japanese carriers. The Battle of Midway decisively halted Japanese expansion and shifted the initiative to the United States.

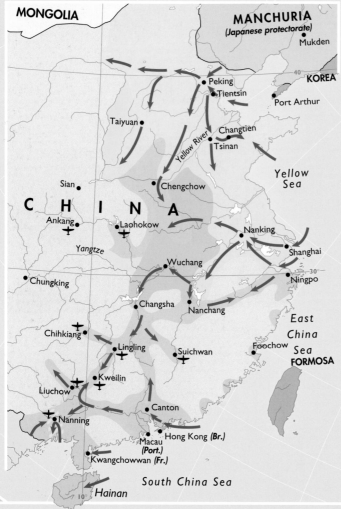

2 the japanese invasion of china, 1937–45

▨ Japanese empire and dependencies, 1937	occupied by Japan, July 1938–July 1939	occupied by Japan, Jan. 1942–Aug. 1945, mainly from Apr. 1944 as Operation Ichi-go
occupied by Japan, July 1937–July 1938	occupied by Japan, July 1939–Dec. 1941	

➤ Japanese advances
✈ US/Chinese air bases
— frontiers, 1936

2 Following the onset of war with China in July 1941, Japan occupied much of northern China (map left). A second assault on the Yangtse Valley in 1938 brought much of central China under Japanese control. Coastal areas were occupied in 1941.

www.worldwarihistory.info/WWII/Japan.html
Japanese Pacific and Asian conquests
www.history.navy.mil/photos/events/wwii-pac/pearlhbr/pearlhbr.htm
The Japanese raid on Pearl Harbor

1 Starting in December 1941, when Japanese naval pilots attacked the American base at Pearl Harbor, until 1942, when the Japanese army reached the India-Burma border, Japan greatly extended the areas of southern Asia and the Pacific under its control (map below).

Japan relied on naval air power to destroy enemy warships and on the navy to move men and supplies. Most of Japan's army remained in China fighting the Chinese and guarding the long Japanese-Soviet border.

1 the japanese advance, 1941–42

- – – Japanese empire, 1941
- → Japanese advance or strike
- ● Japanese base
- ■ Allied base
- ✕ battle

U S S R

Bering Sea

Sea of Okhotsk

Komandorski Is.

Aleutian Is.

Attu Kiska

Japanese perimeter July 1942

MANCHURIA (MANCHUKUO)

INNER MONGOLIA

Kurile Is.

Sea of Japan

JAPAN

Tokyo

Japanese forces repulsed June 3–6, 1942 ✕ Midway

Tsingtao

KOREA

East China Sea

CHINA

Yangtze

Nanking

Shanghai

Changsha

Volcano Is.

Bonin Is.

Hawaiian Is.

Pearl Harbor attack on Pearl Harbor Dec. 7, 1941 Oahu

Kunming

Pacific Ocean

Wake I.

Laokai

Hanoi

Formosa

BURMA

Hong Kong captured 1941

Hainan

Japanese take Rangoon Mar. 8, 1942 Imphal dalay

Japanese attack on Philippines Dec. 8, 1941

FRENCH INDO-CHINA

Rangoon

SIAM

Manila

Corregidor surrenders May 6, 1942

Philippine Is.

Saipan

Guam

Caroline Is.

Phnom Penh

Saigon

Gulf of Siam

Mindanao

Zamboanga

Palau

Truk

Kwajalein

MALAY STATES ng

Japanese land on Malay coast Dec. 8, 1941

dan

Kuala Lumpur

Singapore

Japanese take Singapore Feb. 15, 1942

Borneo

Halmahera

Admiralty Is.

Manus

Bismarck Arch.

New Ireland Green Is.

Bougainville

Makin

Gilbert Is.

Abemama

DUTCH EAST INDIES

Celebes

New Guinea

Rabaul

Ellice Is.

le of the Java Feb. 27, 1942; ccessful attempt alt Japanese sion of Java ✕

Macassar

Ceram

Banda Sea

Tanimbar Is.

Aru Is.

Solomon Is.

Sumatra

Batavia Java

Surabaya

Lombok

Sumba

Flores

Timor

Cape York

Port Moresby

Buna

Battle of the Coral Sea May 1942: Japanese forces repulsed ✕

Guadalcanal

Santa Cruz Is.

Espiritu Santo

New Hebrides

U.S. forces land Feb. 9, 1942

Fiji Is.

Japanese perimeter July 1942

Coral Sea

New Caledonia

U.S. forces land Mar. 12, 1942

AUSTRALIA

U.S. commit ground forces to defense of Australia starting in Feb. 1942

Sydney

Melbourne

79

the **defeat** of japan

The Battle of Midway may have ended Japanese expansion in the Pacific, but how to defeat Japan posed serious problems. The brunt of the war against Japan was borne by the United States, which had to supply its forces across 6,000 miles of ocean and balance these demands with other commitments in the Middle East and Europe. Furthermore the war with Japan was fought against an enemy that had no concept of surrender. Every island was defended with a fanatical determination which made progress slow, even when the material balance between the two sides so clearly favored the Allies.

The Pacific campaign was begun in August 1942 when American forces invaded Tulagi and Guadalcanal in the Solomon Islands. Responsibility was divided between the U.S. navy, under Admiral Chester Nimitz, and the U.S. army in the Pacific, under General Douglas Macarthur. The British had responsibility for the Indian Ocean and the Burma front, but with the defense of India their main priority they were only able to play a modest part in the campaign against Japan until enough forces could be spared from other theaters to renew the offensive in 1944 with U.S. and Chinese assistance. Burma was reconquered in 1945.

U.S. forces advanced across the Pacific under a strong air umbrella and a screen of fast aircraft carriers. Japanese defense was stubborn, but the island garrisons were gradually isolated by American air and submarine attacks on Japanese shipping, which made the supply of munitions and oil intermittent at best. The U.S. forces had radar, which most Japanese units did not; their intelligence supplied regular interceptions of Japanese intentions; and their aircraft were sturdier, more heavily armed and gave their pilots armored protection. Japanese aircraft were light and long-range, but only because they lacked adequate protection. Japanese pilots regarded armor as incompatible with the samurai tradition, but as a result lost more than 50 percent of their number each month by 1944.

In 1944 the U.S. was poised to retake the Philippines and attack the Mariana Islands as a potential jumping-off point for the offensive on the Japanese home islands. The attack on Saipan in June 1944 was treated by Japanese leaders as the decisive engagement of the war, and strong naval and air forces were sent to intercept. In the Battle of the Philippine Sea (June 19, 1944) the Japanese force was thoroughly defeated. In October 1944 the American invasion of Leyte Gulf provoked one final attempt by Japan to defend her new empire. A powerful three-pronged attack was directed at the superior American force, which again ended in complete disaster.

The way was now open to secure bases for a final attack on Japan. In February 1945 U.S. marines landed on Iwo Jima, where Japanese troops fought almost literally to the last man—20,700 were killed, and only 216 taken prisoner. The next target was Okinawa in the Ryukyu islands. The island took three months to conquer, from April to June 1945. By May 50,000 Japanese troops had been killed, and only 227 taken prisoner. Suicidal defense made the prospect of invasion of the Japanese home islands a bleak one. Instead the new bases allowed the latest American heavy bomber, the B–29 Superfortress, to reach targets within Japan. Japanese cities were reduced one by one to ash, and then on August 6, 1945 the first atomic bomb was exploded on Hiroshima. On August 15th Japan surrendered, after months of bitter argument in the cabinet. Many Japanese leaders had accepted Japan's failure long beforehand, but military domination of Japanese politics made peace negotiations impossible. The emperor's decision to surrender was taken in the face of military opposition to anything other than a fight to the death for the honor of Japan.

2 the allied bombing campaign against japan, 1944–45

— Allied air attack
- atomic bomb target
- the "Big Six" fire raid targets
- secondary fire raid targets
- coastal bombardment by U.S. forces

2 For the bombing of the Japanese home islands (map above) the U.S. air force developed the B-29 Superfortress bomber. Against weak defenses it was able to bomb in daylight using incendiaries to burn Japan's wooden cities.

3 The Allies planned "Operation Downfall" for the invasion of Japan (map right), and 14,000 aircraft and 100 aircraft carriers were assigned to the campaign. At least one million casualties were expected from fanatical Japanese resistance.

3 allied invasion plans for Japan, Aug. 1945

→ planned U.S. advances

www.asij.ac.jp/hslibrary/pathfinder/asia_ww2.htm#Allied%20Counterattack
The Allied counterattack on Japan
www.microworks.net/pacific/battles/midway.htm
The Battle of Midway, 4–6 June 1942

1 The tide of Japanese advance was finally halted in May 1942 (map below). The Allies stabilized the front and then began limited step-by-step offensives against Japanese garrisons until in 1945 they were close enough to Japan to finish the war from the air.

1 the allied counter-offensive against japan, 1942–45

→ Allied advance	● Japanese base	**Japanese perimeters**
┤ Allied air attack	◉ Japanese base bypassed or neutralized	······ March 1944
■ Allied base		—·—· October 1944
✳ atomic bomb target	✕ battle	— — August 1945

81

the **battle** of the **atlantic**

1939 to 1945

- **1939 (Sep. 30)** *Graf Spee* sinks first ship
- **1940 (June)** Allied shipping losses reach 585,000 tons in a month
- **1940 (Nov.)** Sunderland flying boat detects U-boat by using radar for first time
- **1941** U.S. Navy begins to patrol West Atlantic; *Bismarck* sunk (May 27)
- **1942** beginning of U.S. convoy system
- **1943 (March 5–20)** biggest convoy battle of war; 5 Allied ships sunk
- **1943 (April 28)** Battle of Convoy; 7 U-boats sunk
- **1943 (Nov. 15)** Germans abandon U-boat operations in Atlantic

2 The Atlantic was a battlefield between Western navies and aircraft and the German submarine force throughout the war (maps below). The battle was fought in a number of phases. In the early part of the war most losses were in and around the British Isles. Starting in January 1942, with American entry, submarines moved to the Caribbean and the American east coast. Through the winter of 1942–3 most victims were sunk in the "Atlantic Gap," outside Allied air cover. In May 1943 the submarine was defeated and only isolated sinkings continued away from the main convoy routes.

While the Japanese fought to control the sea routes of the Pacific, the Western Allies fought a prolonged struggle to maintain the sea links between the Old World and the New against the threat of German submarines. Victory in the Battle of the Atlantic was critical to the Western war effort, for only Allied naval power could secure the lifeline of military supplies, food, and materials for the campaigns in Europe.

In the early stages of the war this threat was not immediately apparent. The British and French navies vastly exceeded the German navy in weight and number of ships: the 22 battleships and 83 cruisers of the Western navies faced only three small "pocket" battleships and eight cruisers. But after the defeat of France the balance began to change. In 1940 Hitler ordered an air and submarine assault on British shipping to cut off British imports and starve Britain into submission.

The air attacks were immediately successful. In 1940 aircraft sank 580,000 tons of shipping; the following year they sank more than one million tons, more than Britain could make good from her dockyards. The submarine attack took longer to achieve results, but as a larger number of new submarines came into service, their commander, Admiral Karl Dönitz, ordered them to hunt in "wolf-packs" at night, where they would be undetected by current antisubmarine technology. In the first four months of 1941, two million tons of shipping were sunk. By the beginning of 1942 the number of German submarines had increased to 300 and German interception of British naval ciphers led the wolf-packs accurately to the convoy routes.

The loss of U.S. merchant ships brought the United States into the Atlantic battle even before the onset of hostilities with Germany on December 11, 1941. U.S. forces occupied Greenland and Iceland, where aircraft were stationed to give shore-based air cover; U.S. warships patroled the western Atlantic. When war broke out between the United States and Germany, Dönitz turned his attention to the American eastern seaboard, where ships still sailed with lights burning and radios on and without the use of a convoy system. Within months the U.S. navy learned its lesson and the area became too dangerous for the U-boats

to operate in strength. But there remained the "Atlantic Gap," the wide stretch of water in midocean out of range of aircraft. It was here that Dönitz concentrated his submarines in 1942 and early 1943. In 1942, 5.4 million tons of shipping were sunk. By 1943 the Royal Navy was down to just two months' supply of oil.

The Western navies turned to technology in their efforts to fight the submarine. Aircraft were converted for long-range patrols, fitted with new centimetric radar and powerful searchlights. They began to impose heavy loss rates on submarines returning to their bases on the French coast, where they could be attacked by day or night when they surfaced. In 1943 British intelligence began to break German signal ciphers regularly. In November 1942 the submariner, Admiral Max Horton, was appointed to command the Atlantic battle. It was his insistence on the use of very long-range aircraft over the Atlantic Gap and on the use of quick-response support groups made up of a powerful flotilla of antisubmarine warships that turned the tide. In March 1943 two large convoys, HX229 and SC122, were severely mauled by the waiting submarines. But in April and May the new tactics reduced sinkings sharply, and increased the destruction of submarines. In May, 41 were sunk; in June and July 54 more. On May 31st Dönitz recalled his boats from the Atlantic and the battle was over.

From May 1943 until the end of the war the submarine threat disappeared. In 1944 only 31 Allied ships were sunk in the Atlantic against a figure of 1,006 in 1942. Though German industry developed new long-range submarines capable of avoiding detection from the surface, they were not brought into service in time. Victory over the submarine made possible the buildup of forces for a land attack on Europe and ended the threat of blockade against Britain.

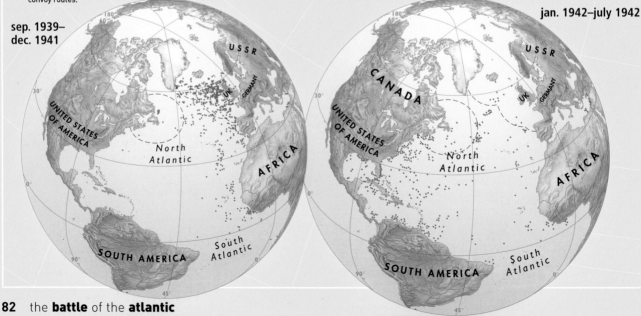

sep. 1939–dec. 1941

jan. 1942–july 1942

www.mariner.org/atlantic/
The Mariners' Museum guide to the Battle of the Atlantic
www.iwm.org.uk/online/atlantic/
Imperial War Museum guide to te Battle of the Atlantic

1 the pursuit of the *bismarck*, may 1941

Battleship routes

→ Bismarck
-- Prinz Eugen
-·- Hood
-·- Victorious
-·- King George V
-·- Rodney and Britannic
→ Task Force H
⚓ sinkings

1 By 1941 the first of a new generation of heavy German battleships was ready to attack convoy routes in the Atlantic. The *Bismarck* set out in May 1941 with the cruiser *Prinz Eugen* (map left). After sinking HMS *Hood* the German vessel was damaged by a torpedo aircraft. She was then immobilized by naval planes and sunk by British warships on May 27 with the loss of all but 115 of her 2,222 crew.

2 the battle of the atlantic (maps below)

· areas of merchant ship sinkings

-- maximum extent of air cover

Map labels (pursuit of Bismarck):

May 24 Hood sunk, Prince of Wales damaged
May 23, 1922
ICELAND
Hood, Prince of Wales and six destroyers
King George V, Victorious and two cruiser sqdns
May 24–25 Victorious attacks Bismarck
May 24
Shetland Is.
Orkney Is.
May 22 home fleet sails
May 23 Rodney and Britannic
May 18, 1941 Bismarck and Prinz Eugen set sail
Atlantic Ocean
1800 May 25
May 25 King George V turns north east in error
May 25
May 26 Bismarck sighted by RAF Catalina
0800 hrs, May 27 battleships attack the Bismarck
1036 hrs, May 27 Bismarck sunk
May 26 torpedo strike from Ark Royal cripples Bismarck
Prinz Eugen to Brest, arrives June 1
May 26 Force H Renown, Ark Royal, Sheffield sail from Gibraltar

Place names:
Narvik, NORWAY, SWEDEN, FINLAND, Trondheim, Bergen, Oslo, Stockholm, Baltic Sea, North Sea, DENMARK, Copenhagen, Danzig, Glasgow, Edinburgh, GREAT BRITAIN, Dublin, Manchester, NETHS., London, BEL., GERMANY, Berlin, Prague, Brest, Paris, Munich, Vienna, AUSTRIA, FRANCE, SWITZERLAND, Lyons, Milan, ITALY, Bay of Biscay, Marseilles, Corsica, Rome, Naples, Sardinia, Madrid, SPAIN, Lisbon, PORTUGAL, Palermo, Mediterranean Sea, Gibraltar (Br.), ALGERIA, Færoe Is.

Globe maps:
CANADA, USSR, UK, GERMANY, UNITED STATES OF AMERICA, North Atlantic, AFRICA, SOUTH AMERICA, South Atlantic, Azores

aug. 1942–may 1943   **june 1943–may 1945**

war in the **mediterranean**

1940 (June) Mussolini enters war as Axis partner

1940-1 Italians expelled from Somalia, Eritrea, and Abyssinia

1941 Germans and Italians conquer Cyrenaica; Greece

1942 Germans and Italians advance into Eygpt

1942 Battle of El Alamein; Italian/German defeat and retreat

1942 Anglo-American landings in Morocco and Algeria

1943 Capitulation of Axis forces in Tunisia

1944 (June 5) Rome falls to Allies

1 Following Mussolini's declaration of war in June 1940, British forces drove Italian armies back across Libya (map below). Over the next two years the campaign moved back and forth across the Libyan desert, until in November 1942 the Italian-German forces under Marshal Graziani were finally defeated at El Alamein.

During the first half of the war, Britain divided her efforts between the Battle of the Atlantic and the conflict in the Mediterranean, which had been opened up by Mussolini's decision to enter the war in June 1940. Britain had long regarded the Mediterranean as a lifeline to her eastern empire and a key element in her global strategic security and, despite fears of a German invasion, diverted troops to the Mediterranean immediately Mussolini declared war.

British Commonwealth forces were initially successful, defeating the Italians in Abyssinia and Eritrea. The bulk of the Italian army stationed on the Egyptian border in Libya was driven back by British Commonwealth forces in 1940 and early 1941, and hundreds of thousands of Italian prisoners taken. But in 1941 Hitler was reluctantly forced to intervene to save his Axis ally from defeat. In February 1941 a small German army and air force was sent to Libya. Two months later German troops were also sent to Greece, where an ill-judged Italian invasion was stoutly resisted by the Greek army, assisted by a small British expeditionary force. However, Greece was conquered in April, and the British driven out. Crete fell to a costly paratroop assault in May 1941. General Erwin Rommel, a tank commander and hero of the Battle of France, was sent to lead the assault in North Africa, where his Afrika Korps took Axis forces to the Egyptian frontier by June 1942.

In 1942 Britain faced a crisis. The sea lanes through the Mediterranean were subject to air and submarine attack; Malta and Gibraltar were at risk; and Axis forces in North Africa and the Caucasus threatened to sweep through the Middle East and secure the valuable oil resources and the key supply route to Britain's Far Eastern empire. All this contributed to Churchill's pressure on his American ally to consider an attack in 1942 by Anglo-American forces somewhere in the Mediterranean theater, rather than the strategy preferred by Roosevelt's chief of staff, General Marshall, of a direct attack on Hitler's Europe.

The lack of U.S. preparation for such an attack persuaded Roosevelt that the Mediterranean was the most expedient option. U.S. forces would be seen to be in action in Europe, and something decisive might be achieved with slim forces. The two allies planned an assault on North Africa codenamed Torch. In November heavy reinforcement of the Egyptian front produced a clear victory over Rommel and the Italian army at El Alamein. In the same month Allied forces landed in Morocco and Algeria. Axis forces were squeezed into a defensive pocket in Tunisia, where more than 230,000 surrendered on May 13, 1943.

Despite American misgiving, the argument for continuing the pursuit into Italy was strong. The Torch landings had made a cross-Channel invasion in 1943

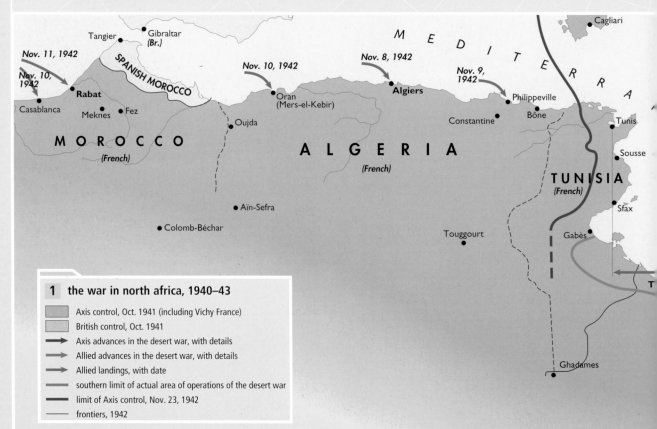

1 the war in north africa, 1940–43

- Axis control, Oct. 1941 (including Vichy France)
- British control, Oct. 1941
- → Axis advances in the desert war, with details
- → Allied advances in the desert war, with details
- → Allied landings, with date
- — southern limit of actual area of operations of the desert war
- ━ limit of Axis control, Nov. 23, 1942
- — frontiers, 1942

www.ibiblio.org/hyperwar/ETO/Med/index.html
The Mediterranean campaign
www.ez-zone.co.uk/ww2desert/index.htm
The north African desert campaigns

impossible. In July 1943 "Operation Husky" led to the capture of Sicily, and in early September Anglo-American forces crossed to Italy. On the evening of September 8th Italy surrendered. Allied forces expected the landings at Salerno the following day to be unopposed, but German forces almost drove the assault back into the sea. The Italian war turned into a long one of attrition between an Anglo-American force and a stubborn German defense. German forces retreated up the peninsula to prepared defensive lines, which proved difficult to penetrate despite overwhelming Allied air power. Churchill's vision of a hard blow at the soft Axis underbelly failed to materialize.

Allied forces under Field Marshal Alexander gradually found themselves taking a back seat to the preparations for the invasion of occupied France in 1944. Progress was painfully slow and losses high. Rome finally fell to the U.S. Fifth Army on June 5, 1944. German forces fell back on the so-called Gothic Line, running across the peninsula just north of Florence, which was not breached until September 1944. The Allied front stalemated over the winter of 1944–5. Only in April 1945 did the final Allied assault break German resistance and lead to capitulation on May 2. The campaign tied down more than 20 German divisions, and 35 more were caught up in the antipartisan war in the Balkans. Still, the Mediterranean campaign failed to achieve any decisive results. Victory in Europe was won only through direct attack on Germany.

2 In July 1943 (map right) Anglo-American forces invaded Sicily and launched a campaign to take Italy out of the war. Although Italy surrendered in September 1943, German armies fought a bitter retreat up the peninsula under the command of Field Marshal Albert Kesselring.

2 the italian campaign, 1943–45

→ Allied advance
- - - Allied frontlines

invasion from the west

1944 to 1945

- **1944 (June 6)** D-Day; Allied landings in Normandy: Operation Overlord
- **1944 (June 12)** beach heads are joined
- **1944 (July)** Caen falls to the Allies
- **1944 (Aug. 25)** liberation of Paris
- **1944 (Sept.)** Operation Market Garden
- **1944 (Dec.)** Battle of the Bulge
- **1945 (May 7)** unconditional surrender of all German forces to Allies

The arguments over whether to concentrate on defeating Germany by pushing north from the Mediterranean or invading across the English Channel were not finally resolved until the Teheran Conference in November 1943.

Stalin, with wholehearted support from the U.S., insisted that an invasion of France was the only way to defeat Germany. In January 1944 serious preparation began for "Operation Overlord." Eisenhower was named supreme commander, with British deputies for army, air, and naval forces. The plan was to attack on a narrow front in Normandy, initially deploying five divisions. Artificial "mulberry" harbors were to be towed into place on the invasion day so that the invasion beaches could be supplied rapidly with forces and equipment.

The critical issue was to keep the destination secret from the Germans. By keeping the enemy guessing, the German forces would be stretched out along the entire coast, rather than concentrated at the invasion point. A deception plan, "Operation Bodyguard," was mounted and succeeded against all reasonable expectation in persuading Hitler that the major target was the Pas de Calais. Although Germany had 58 divisions in France, there were only 14 facing the Normandy beaches. The second imperative was to use Allied air superiority to neutralize the German air force and to cut off the communications net in northern France to prevent German reinforcement. Both campaigns were successful. On invasion day—popularly known as D-Day—there were 12,000 Allied aircraft against 170 German aircraft, while reinforcements from Germany to the front took weeks to reach the fighting, so poor had communications become.

1 The invasion of Normandy on June 6, 1944 was the largest amphibious assault ever launched. 12,000 aircraft and over 7,000 ships of all sizes supported the operation. Five divisions were landed on a series of five invasion beaches. Paratroopers were sent in on both flanks during the night of June 5–6th. The initial beach heads were secured by June 7th, and positions established by June 11th. Progress thereafter was slow. Marshy ground, thick hedgerows, and determined German defense prevented a breakout and threatened to recreate the trench stalemate of the First World War.

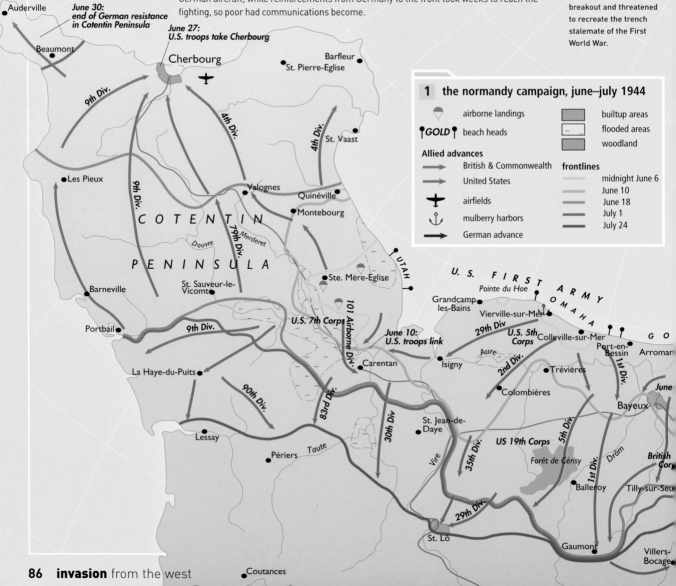

June 30: end of German resistance in Cotentin Peninsula

June 27: U.S. troops take Cherbourg

June 10: U.S. troops link

1 the normandy campaign, june–july 1944

- airborne landings
- **GOLD** beach heads

Allied advances
- British & Commonwealth
- United States
- airfields
- mulberry harbors
- German advance

- builtup areas
- flooded areas
- woodland

frontlines
- midnight June 6
- June 10
- June 18
- July 1
- July 24

www.ddaymuseum.co.uk/
Operation Overlord and D-Day
www.mm.com/user/jpk/battle.htm
The Battle of the Bulge (the German Ardennes offensive)

2 the allied advance through france, july–dec. 1944

→ Allied advances

╌╌╌ Allied frontlines and date

─── planned Allied frontlines

⊢─┴─ West Wall

2 On July 25, 1944 the American forces in Normandy launched "Operation Cobra" to force a breakout (map below). American air power and armor made remarkable strides. General Patton's Third Army pushed into Brittany and then wheeled east toward Paris as the Germans retreated. By September the Allies had crossed France, but the attempt to drive into Germany was defeated.

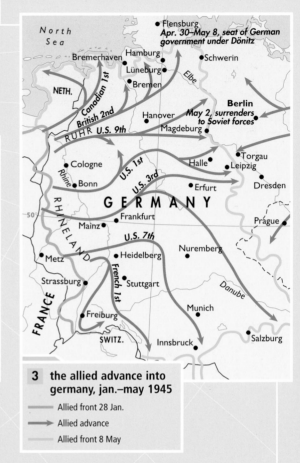

3 the allied advance into germany, jan.–may 1945

─── Allied front 28 Jan.

──→ Allied advance

─── Allied front 8 May

3 After the collapse of German resistance in France, the Western Allies stopped to regroup on Germany's borders and to allow the supply system to catch up with the armies (map above right). In December Hitler ordered a counteroffensive, the Ardennes Offensive, which failed to break the Allied line. The effort severely weakened forces already outnumbered. In February the Allies breached the West Wall fortifications and drove into the Rhineland. In three months they pushed across western and central Germany until they met with Soviet forces on the bridge over the Elbe at Torgau.

The invasion was set for June 5th. In the event bad weather meant it had to be postponed until the following morning. Paratroopers were sent in overnight to secure the flanks and ensure that initial positions were established successfully. German forces were divided and reinforcements were slow to arrive. Air power gave Allied forces—British, American, French, and Canadian—great advantages. The German commander, Field Marshal Rommel, hero of the fast-moving desert campaigns, found himself forced to fight a tough defensive campaign in hedgerows and fields.

The Allied plan was to force the German armies to concentrate on the eastern wing of the invasion front, while in the west the Cotentin Peninsula was cleared and American forces broke out into France toward Paris. Progress was slow, and in the east the city of Caen, fiercely defended by the Germans, took over a month to capture. But the constant attrition wore down the under-strength German forces. On July 25th General Omar Bradley broke out into the west and within days Bradley had swept up resistance and his forces were wheeling toward the Seine. A desperate counterattack at Mortain by remaining German armored forces was repulsed and a headlong retreat followed. By late August the Allies were across the Seine and by September stood on the German frontier.

While the Allied supply system caught up with the rapidly advancing air forces and armies, German forces were given time to regroup to defend the Reich. Montgomery, the British army commander, wanted to press on into Germany, but the assault by paratroopers at Arnhem on September 17th was bloodily repulsed. Allied forces paused during the winter, but on Christmas Day were surprised by a strong German counterthrust toward Antwerp. The "Battle of the Bulge" was won through rapid redeployment of Allied forces. By January the Western Allies had 25 armored divisions and 6,000 tanks massed against 1,000 German tanks. Montgomery pushed north into the Ruhr and toward Berlin, while American generals swung into southern Germany. Despite strong local resistance the final defeat of Germany was achieved by early May when German forces capitulated to Montgomery on Lüneburg Heath.

the **bombing** campaign

The bombing of enemy cities and industry—or strategic bombing—became a serious technical possibility only by the early 1940s. But strategic bombing did not become a significant force until 1944, and only in the war with Japan did bombing play a decisive part.

Strategic Allied bombing began in 1940 with the first British attacks on German targets, authorized by Churchill in May in retaliation for the German destruction of Rotterdam during the Battle of France. In September 1940 Hitler ordered the Luftwaffe to attack British cities in an attempt to drive Britain out of the war without a costly invasion. Although German attacks killed 42,000 in the winter of 1940–41, they had little effect on British war production and failed to bring the British government to the negotiating table. The Blitz showed Hitler that bombing could not achieve war-winning results and starting in 1941 the German air force concentrated on tactical air support over the battlefield.

1 the first hamburg raid, 24–25 July 1943

- residential areas
- industrial areas
- u-boat construction yards
- planned bombing area
- areas of total burnout, July 24–Aug. 3
- areas of total and heavy damage, July 24–Aug. 3

1 On the night of July 24-5th 1943 RAF Bomber Command undertook "Operation Gomorrah" (maps above and right)—the massive air attack on the German port of Hamburg. The city was hit by wave after wave of high explosive and incendiaries, and was attacked by day by the U.S. Eighth Air Force. Hamburg became the victim of the first firestorm, which killed more than 40,000 people.

www.rafmuseum.org.uk/milestones-of-flight/british_military/1945.html
Timelines of British military aviation
www.alien8.de/dd/page-1.html
Pictures of Dresden before and after the bombing campaigns of 1945

Britain maintained the bombing offensive for want of any other way of retaliating once her armies had been expelled from Europe. The early attacks achieved little and were shown by photo reconnaissance to be wildly inaccurate. British bombers attacked by night to avoid German fighters, which made it difficult to attack anything much smaller than a city. In February 1942 Bomber Command was ordered by the British chiefs of staff to concentrate on area attacks against German industrial cities. On May 31, 1942 the first 1,000-bomber raid was staged, against Cologne.

Starting in February 1942 Bomber Command was led by Air Marshal Arthur Harris. He introduced tactical changes—including a specialized Pathfinder Force to increase bombing accuracy—and benefited from the introduction of new technology: the Lancaster heavy bomber and improved naviga-tional aids. In 1942 Bomber Command was joined by the U.S. Eighth Air Force, which bombed by day, attacking specific industrial and military targets rather than whole cities. In 1943 the two forces were directed by the British and American combined chiefs of staff to undertake a combined bomber offensive against key targets—oil, aviation, submarines—as well as against the war-willingness of the German population.

During 1943 the combined offensive began to have real effects on German strategy. Extensive resources were put into air defense with the construction of the Kammhuber Line of antiaircraft guns, radar, and fighters. But by the winter of 1943-4 the bombing offensive was grinding to a halt because of mounting losses of men and planes. The campaign was saved by the introduction of long-range "strategic" fighters—in the main the P-51 Mustang, fitted with disposable fuel tanks, which won air superiority over Germany. Better navigational aids, improved training and much higher numbers of heavy bombers turned bombing into a real threat. The defeat of German air power in 1944 left the Reich open to attack. By 1945 both forces could roam over German air space without serious resistance. Some 83 percent of the 1.9 million tons of bombs dropped fell in 1944 and 1945.

Bombing did not defeat Germany on its own, but it had a devastating impact on the German war effort. Some 400,000 were killed, and the major German cities reduced to rubble. Eight million people were evacuated and two million Germans were tied to air defense and the effort to clear the destruction. By 1944 more than 54,000 guns were concentrated against the Allied bombing, and the defense effort used one-third of the output of optical and electrotechnical equipment and one-fifth of all ammunition. This vast diversion of effort was compounded with the loss in 1944 of one-third of the potential output of aircraft, tanks, and trucks. Bombing forced an expensive and time-consuming dispersal of industry and resulted in high levels of absenteeism. For ordinary Germans bombing was the dominant issue on the home front from 1943 onward. It was demoralizing for all who experienced it, producing not so much political protest as apathy and fear.

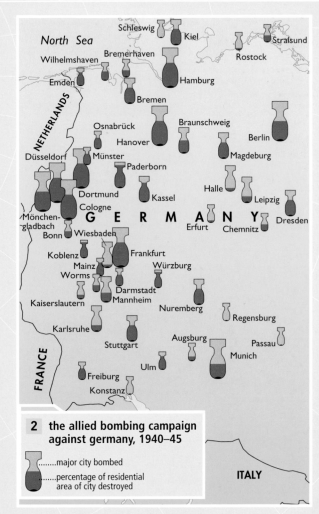

2 the allied bombing campaign against germany, 1940–45

........major city bombed

........percentage of residential area of city destroyed

2 From 1941 the RAF began to attack German industrial cities systematically (map above). The object was to reduce industrial output and to "de-house" the workforce. By 1945, 45 percent of the housing in Germany's major cities was destroyed and eight million Germans had been evacuated.

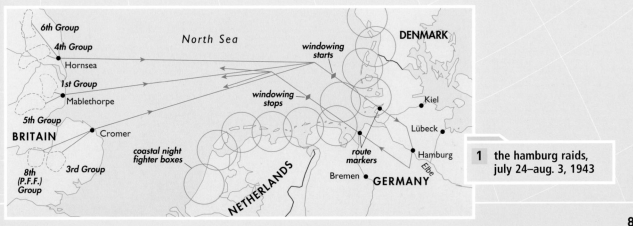

1 the hamburg raids, july 24–aug. 3, 1943

genocide in europe

- **1935** announcement of Nuremberg Laws
- **1938 (Nov. 9-10)** Kristallnacht; pogrom against German Jews
- **1939** Himmler begins official extermination of disabled
- **1942** German genocide of Jews begins in full (to 1945); Wannsee Conference; "The Final Solution"
- **1943 (April)** armed revolt in Warsaw ghetto
- **1942-45** as many as 6 million Jews die in Nazi death camps

The largest single body of civilian victims in the Second World War was Europe's Jewish population. They were systematically exterminated by the Hitler regime. By the end of the war only about 300,000 survived. Around six million perished.

Jewish genocide was the product of a state whose whole ideological outlook was rooted in racism. Hitler was a radical anti-Semite, who had preached a final showdown with the Jewish people since the early 1920s. But there were those around him who wanted anti-Semitism to be part of a general program of ethnic cleansing and racial hygiene. Medical and scientific opinion was mobilized to support the sterilization—and eventually the extermination—of the physically and mentally handicapped, the hereditarily ill, and those classified as "asocial." The search for a pure Germanic race was the obverse of the policies of discrimination and extermination directed at those regarded as un-German.

The formal persecution of the Jews began in September 1935 with the announcement of the Nuremberg Laws. These effectively denied Jews the same civil rights as other Germans. Over the next four years Jewish property was expropriated under a program of "Aryanization," and during this time half of Germany's Jewish population emigrated. A racist bureaucratic apparatus was developed under the head of the SS, Heinrich Himmler, which by 1939 began the official extermination of the disabled, euphemistically known as euthanasia.

1 The German persecution of the Jews moved from the discrimination against German Jews in the 1930s through the policy of isolation in ghettos in 1940 and 1941 to the final stage of physical extermination, aimed at the entire Jewish population of occupied and satellite Europe (map below).

www.holocaust-history.org/
The Holocaust History Project archive of documents, photographs, recordings, and essays
www.ushmm.org/outreach/nlaw.htm
The Nuremberg Race Laws

The war changed the situation. Emigration, which was Hitler's preferred option for the "Jewish question," was cut off by the Allied blockade. Millions of Polish Jews were also brought under German control. The regime decided on a policy of isolation. Jews and other "asocials" were rounded up and sent to designated ghettos, where they were denied adequate food and medical care. In the summer of 1940, after the defeat of France, Hitler toyed briefly with the idea of turning Madagascar into a vast tropical ghetto, but British control of the seas ruled it out.

In 1941 circumstances changed again. The war with the Soviet Union was defined by Hitler as a race war against Jewish-Bolshevism, and the armed forces and special SS death squads (the *Einsatzgruppen*) were instructed to murder Jews and communists indiscriminately. In the first two months of the campaign hundreds of thousands were killed with appalling brutality, some by native anti-Semites in the Baltic States and Ukraine, the large part by German soldiers, policemen, and Himmler's agents. The precise date of Hitler's decision to exterminate all Jews—the so-called "Final Solution"—is unknown, but by the middle of July 1941, at the height of German victories in the east, a change was evident. Orders were sent out to end the program of indiscriminate and public murders and to create a systematic killing program, based on extermination centers using poison gas.

By the end of 1941 the system was in operation. At eight extermination centers millions of Jews from all over Europe were gathered. The young and fit were used for slave labor until they died from overwork or disease. The rest, including 1.5 million children, were sent straight to the gas chambers and then cremated. Their hair, glasses, gold fillings, and shoes were collected and recycled for the war effort. Jewish property was seized by the state or stolen by the Nazi officials who ran the apparatus of death.

During the second half of the war Germany put pressure on its allies and satellites to release their Jewish populations. In Italy and Hungary this pressure was resisted until German occupation in 1943 and 1944. In the occupied zones the army and police were able to transport Jews to the eastern extermination centers with little resistance. In Warsaw in April 1943 the Jews in the ghetto rose in armed revolt, but the rising was brutally crushed. Those who survived the genocide did so by joining partisan groups, hiding with non-Jews or working as slave-laborers. Some of those who perpetrated the race program were shot or hanged after the war, but many have evaded justice to this day.

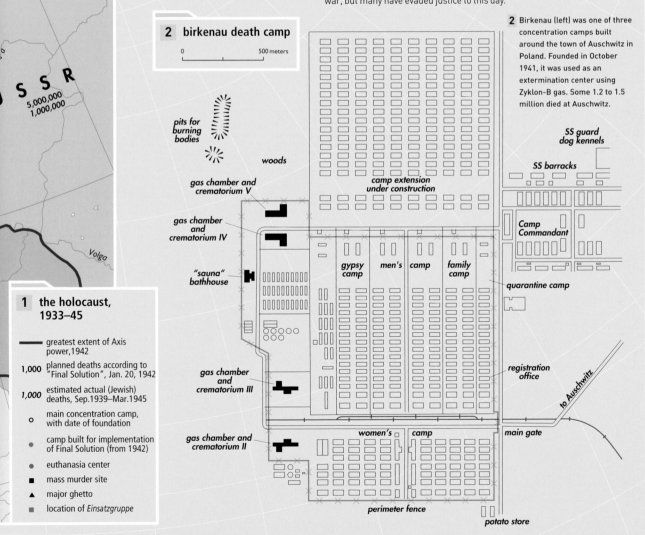

2 birkenau death camp

0 _____ 500 meters

2 Birkenau (left) was one of three concentration camps built around the town of Auschwitz in Poland. Founded in October 1941, it was used as an extermination center using Zyklon-B gas. Some 1.2 to 1.5 million died at Auschwitz.

pits for burning bodies

woods

gas chamber and crematorium V

gas chamber and crematorium IV

"sauna" bathhouse

gas chamber and crematorium III

gas chamber and crematorium II

camp extension under construction

gypsy camp

men's camp

family camp

quarantine camp

SS guard dog kennels

SS barracks

Camp Commandant

registration office

to Auschwitz

women's camp

main gate

perimeter fence

potato store

1 the holocaust, 1933–45

▬ greatest extent of Axis power,1942

1,000 planned deaths according to "Final Solution", Jan. 20, 1942

1,000 estimated actual (Jewish) deaths, Sep.1939–Mar.1945

○ main concentration camp, with date of foundation

● camp built for implementation of Final Solution (from 1942)

● euthanasia center

■ mass murder site

▲ major ghetto

■ location of *Einsatzgruppe*

S S S R

5,000,000
1,000,000

Volga

the **costs** of war

1942–45 as many as 6 million Jews die in Nazi death camps

1944 (22 July) Bretton Woods agreement; establishing parameters for post-war economy; established World Bank and International Monetary Fund (IMF)

1945 Nuremberg Trials; war criminals tried in International Military Tribunal; leading Nazis sentenced to death

1946 Military Tribunal for the Far East

German genocide was the most conspicuous and terrible cost of the Second World War. The conflict was fought on an exceptional scale and with extraordinary ferocity. It fulfilled all the worst expectations of total war. Civilians no longer had any immunity from the conflict. In the east they were defined by German leaders as race enemies, to be exterminated or exploited.

German and Japanese cities were blasted from the air on the grounds that the workers housed there sustained the fighting power of enemy forces at the front; Japanese soldiers were taught to regard the Chinese as racial inferiors. The laws of war, established over the previous half century by international agreement, were torn up. War became the instrument of a deeper ideological and racial conflict.

As well as the human cost, the war destroyed much of the physical and cultural environment in which it was fought. In the Soviet Union some 17,000 cities and 70,000 villages were destroyed. Half of Germany's housing stock in major cities was destroyed and much of the rest damaged. Italy lost one-third of its national wealth. European states under German rule paid out 150 billion marks—one-quarter of Germany's war expenditure—as tribute to sustain the German war effort. The cultural heritage of Europe was the victim of war damage, such as that inflicted on the monastery of Monte Cassino, or of deliberate destruction, such as the burning down of the ancient university library in Naples by retreating German troops. At the end of the war the Western Allies set up vast collecting centers for lost and looted art. In Wiesbaden alone more than 400,000 items were recovered, of which three-quarters remained unclaimed five years after the end of the war.

As well as the loss of physical resources through war damage and expropriation, the war made great demands on the productive economies of every warring state. Up to two-thirds of industrial output was devoted to war, and consumers everywhere, except in the United States, which had generous supplies of foodstuffs, were forced to eat rationed quan-

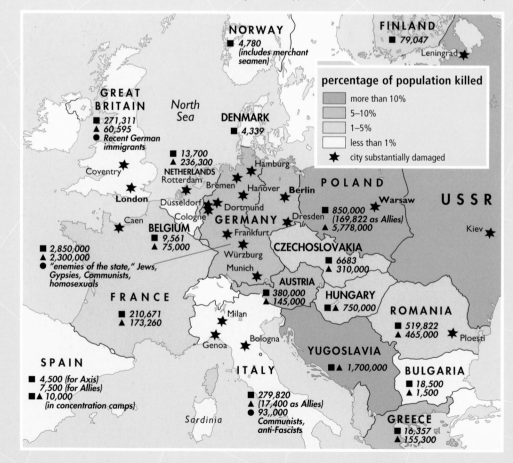

www.loc.gov/exhibits/wcf/wcf0001.html
Women journalists, photographers, and broadcasters of WW2
www2.sunysuffolk.edu/westn/effectww2.html
The effects of WW2 on the major world powers

tities of food and consumer goods. The greatest level of sacrifice was imposed in the Soviet Union, which lost half its meat and grain output with the occupation. The Soviet workforce consisted largely of women and young boys, forced to work long hours with poor food supplies, sometimes at the point of a gun. By 1944 half the native workforce in Germany consisted of women, many of them on German farms keeping up vital supplies of food. In Britain and the U.S. more than one-third of the workforce was female by the end of the war.

The war encouraged the development of new technologies, particularly in aeronautics, rocketry, and electronics. In Germany, rockets, jets, and nuclear power were already in the process of development at the start of the war. They failed to make an impact on Germany's war effort only because of the confused nature of the wartime administration and Hitler's arbitrary intervention in the German research program. Elsewhere the quality of weapons was often below that of Germany, but produced in much larger quantities using new mass-production techniques made possible by the flow of modern specialized machine tools from the U.S. In the Soviet Union spectacular improvements were achieved in the quality of weapons, which were produced in giant plants with relatively simple methods. The Soviet Union alone, despite wartime losses of industry and raw materials, outproduced Germany.

The war interrupted the normal development of the wider world economy. The United States was a net gainer. Here incomes rose by 75 percent. As European exports disappeared, the U.S. picked up a large proportion of world trade. European economies, by contrast, were set back years. In the fall of 1945 German industrial production was down to just 14 percent of its level in 1936. Britain, though a victor power, had large debts and a declining trade position and by 1947 was close to bankruptcy. The economic balance of power moved decisively to the United States as a result of the war. In 1944 at a meeting at Bretton Woods, New Jersey, U.S. officials got Allied powers to agree to a new economic order after the war, based on liberal trade and U.S.-backed monetary cooperation.

1 The Second World War was the costliest in history (maps below and left). Accurate figures on the number who died are hard to find and the total estimate of 55 million is subject to a wide margin of error. Civilians made up a high percentage of casualties, the victims of genocide, bombing, terror, hunger, and physical exploitation.

1 war casualties, 1939–45 (maps below and left)

- ■ military dead
- ▲ civilian dead
- ● large groups of civilian internees
- ★ city substantially damaged
- ▨ countries in which civilian population came under direct attack

NEW ZEALAND
■ 12,162

Solomon Is.
New Ireland
New Britain
New Guinea

AUSTRALIA
29,395 ■
● citizens of Japanese or Italian origin

JAPAN
■ 1,506,000
▲ 300,000
★ Tokyo
★ Kobe
Hiroshima ★★ Nagasaki
KOREA
MANCHURIA
★ Nanking
Formosa

PHILIPPINE IS.
BR. N. BORNEO   Borneo   Java
SARAWAK
DUTCH EAST INDIES
MALAYA   Sumatra

CHINA
■ 1,324,000
▲ up to 10,000,000

USA
■ 292,100
● citizens of Japanese origin

CANADA
■ 39,319

ARCTIC OCEAN

USSR
■ c. 14,500,000 (c. 9.5 million on Eastern Front including 3 million as prisoners of war; c. 2 million on Far Eastern Front)
▲ over 7 million
● "enemies of the state," population of recently acquired territories in Western Soviet Union

INDIA
■ 36,092

see inset left

★ Stalingrad
★ Kharkov
★ Sebastopol

IRAQ
SYRIA

DJIBOUTI
BRITISH SOMALILAND
EGYPT
ERITREA
ITALIAN SOMALILAND
ALGERIA   LIBYA
ETHIOPIA
MADAGASCAR

ATLANTIC OCEAN

BRAZIL
■ 943

UNION OF SOUTH AFRICA
■ 8,681

93

the **global impact**

The shift in the economic balance of power at the end of the Second World War in favor of the United States was matched by a corresponding shift in the political balance. In 1939 Europe was still thought to be the leading force in world affairs, and Hitler had ambitions to turn Germany into a global superpower.

By 1945 the United States and the Soviet Union, both of which had stood aside from Europe's quarrels in the interwar years, became major players in the world order as a result of their efforts to defeat the Axis powers. In 1939 the war was not a global one but consisted of a number of different conflicts: a German-Polish war; a war between Germany and the French and British empires; and a war between Japan and China. Over the next two years the various conflicts merged. In 1940 Italy declared war on Britain and France, bringing the whole Mediterranean and Middle East into the war sphere. In 1941 the Balkans were drawn in. When Germany attacked the Soviet Union in June 1941 and Japan attacked the U.S. in December, the war became genuinely global in extent, linked by the fact that the Axis faced a common enemy in the U.S. and Britain, stretching across three oceans.

The three Axis states, Germany, Italy, and Japan, had no formal military alliances. They collaborated poorly. Italy and Japan did not inform Germany of their attacks on Greece and Hawaii; Germany did not reveal the assault on the Soviet Union. When Italy surrendered in 1943 Germany treated the northern provinces as it treated the rest of occupied Europe. The Allies had no binding military alliance either, although Britain and the USSR signed a pact of mutual cooperation in May 1942. But the three major Allies were bound by an informal commitment to the unconditional surrender of the Axis, announced at the Casablanca Conference in January 1943 by President Roosevelt without prior consultation with his allies. They were also bound by the terms of the Atlantic Charter, first signed by Churchill and Roosevelt in August 1941, but signed subsequently by other states joining the Allied side.

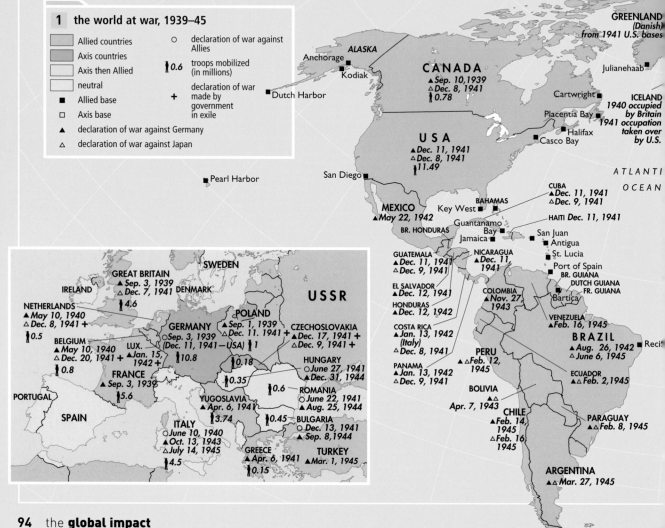

1 the world at war, 1939–45

- Allied countries
- Axis countries
- Axis then Allied
- neutral
- ■ Allied base
- □ Axis base
- ▲ declaration of war against Germany
- △ declaration of war against Japan
- ○ declaration of war against Allies
- ▮0.6 troops mobilized (in millions)
- + declaration of war made by government in exile

www.dickinson.edu/~rhyne/232/Casablanca.html
Casablanca Conference, 1943
www.britannia.com/history/docs/atlantic.html
The Atlantic Charter: Roosevelt and Churchill's mutual goals for the post-WW2 world.

The Atlantic Charter was a commitment to create a free world after the end of the war on the basis of the self-determination of peoples. It had a strong Wilsonian flavor, but after the failure of the First World War American leaders were committed to making the new postwar order work. Roosevelt referred to the Allied powers as the United Nations, a term first employed in January 1942. By the end of the war, 45 states, including the Soviet Union, had subscribed to the ideals of democratic freedom. In reality agreements were made between the three major Allies at a series of conferences—Teheran in November 1943, Yalta in February 1945, Potsdam in July of that year—which made a mockery of self-determination. Furthermore the Soviet Union was determined to safeguard its interests in Eastern Europe at the expense of popular nationalism, particularly in Poland.

Nonetheless the commitment to the principle of national independence had implications for the empires that Britain and France had gone to war in 1939 to defend. During the war the empires faced serious challenges. Nationalism, particularly in India, became a potent force in the face of British and French defeats. Japan and Germany encouraged independence movements or set up puppet regimes. Both the United States and the USSR were hostile to colonialism and keen to encourage decolonization. The moral authority of the remaining imperial states was blunted by the defeat of Italian, German, and Japanese imperialism, and the empires were gradually relinquished over the 30 years following the war.

The defeat of the Axis exposed the transformation of the world order. The Soviet Union dominated Eastern Europe. The United States was now both willing and able to take the lead in the Western world. In April 1945 a conference was convened at San Francisco to establish formally a United Nations organization. Disagreements between the U.S. and the USSR were resolved sufficiently for the new structure to be set up. The U.S., the USSR, China, Britain, and France became permanent members of a security council. By the time the conference ended in June, Germany was defeated. The prospect now lay open for the establishment of a new world order based on principles of peaceful cooperation and national independence.

1 During the Second World War almost the entire globe was drawn into the conflict (maps below) with the exception of four neutral states in Europe. The European empires drew on the resources and manpower of their overseas territories. Worldwide over 79 million men and women were mobilized in armed forces, and millions more drafted to war work.

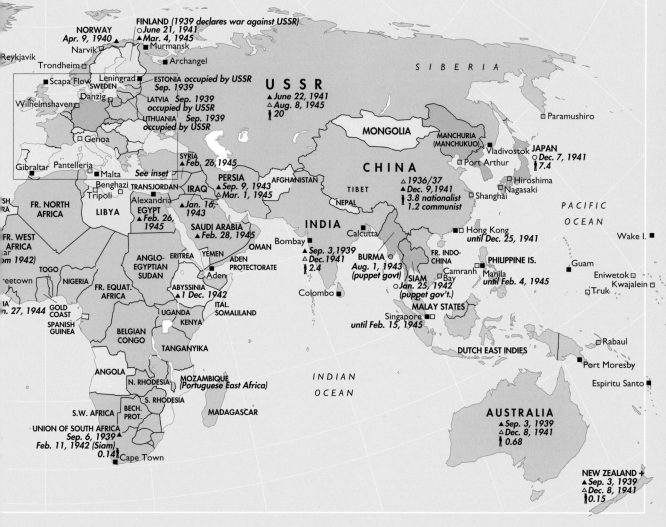

The end of the Second World War opened up a new era in world affairs. The dominant position enjoyed by western Europe for more than a century disappeared. It was replaced by a system based around a growing hostility between the two major victors of the war: the United States and the Soviet Union. By the 1950s a state of Cold War existed between the American-led western bloc of democratic capitalist states and the Soviet-led communist world, which now stretched from central Europe to the Far East. The confrontation lasted for 40 years, during which fear of the use of nuclear weapons held both sides back from the brink of major war. In the shadow of the nuclear threat both sides enjoyed the most prolonged and expansionary economic boom in history, which transformed standards of living and lifestyles in the developed world and hastened the pace of modernization, with all its costs, in every other region.

East German border guards, Berlin, August 14, 1961

PART IV   **THE COLD WAR WORLD**

the **roots** of the **cold war**

The defeat of the Axis states in 1945 depended on the survival of an unlikely alliance between two democratic Western states and the communist Soviet Union. They were united by a common hostility to Hitler but by little else. The long history of tension and mistrust between the Soviet Union and the Western world began to resurface as victory over Germany drew closer.

The most serious issue was the political future of the reconquered lands. Though the three major Allies had agreed not to reach a separate peace with any of the enemy states, Britain and the United States accepted Italian surrender in 1943 without Soviet involvement. Stalin took this as his excuse to act on his own in the liberated states of Eastern Europe. As they were occupied one by one by the Red Army, the Soviet Union excluded Western intervention and set out to create a system of satellite states friendly to Soviet interests.

Though the Western Allies recognized that there was little they could do to prevent Soviet domination, there were two states in whose fate they had a real political interest: Poland and Germany. Poland, for which Britain had ostensibly gone to war in 1939, was the subject of tense negotiation at the Teheran Conference in November 1943. It was agreed that Poland must relinquish the areas seized by the Soviet Union in 1939 and should be compensated instead with territory carved out of eastern Germany. The settlement was confirmed at the Potsdam Conference in July 1945, by which time a pro-Soviet government had been installed in Warsaw. Although the Soviet Union paid lip service to the idea of establishing a popular democracy in Poland, in practice Polish communism was ruthlessly promoted. Elections in 1947 returned a communist majority and Poland came firmly within the Soviet sphere.

The German question was equally delicate. The Allies had agreed in 1943 to divide Germany into Allied zones of occupation. The demarcation lines were scrupulously observed by both sides, even though their respective forces had arrived at somewhat different points by the end of the war. It was agreed not to impose a peace settlement as had been done in 1919. Reparations were seized, mainly by the Soviet Union, and German political and military leaders put on trial at Nuremberg in November 1945 before an international military tribunal composed of the four victor states. Germany was completely disarmed. There was no agreement, however, on the future political shape of Germany. Cooperation between the zones was limited, until in 1947 Britain and the United States created a joint area, known as Bizonia, which they began to see as the kernel of a new German state. With the Soviet Union vehemently opposed to a U.S.-dominated capitalist state in Central Europe, the German issue became a symbol of the wider conflict forming between communist East and capitalist West.

This conflict was clear by 1946. On March 5th, in Fulton, Missouri, Winston Churchill told an American audience that an "Iron Curtain" had descended across Europe, separating the democratic peoples of the West from the new communist bloc. The hopes which had been expressed by U.S. statesmen for "one world" after the war based on self-determination and economic freedom were replaced by fears of a new polarization, christened by the American journalist Walter Lippmann the "Cold War."

Soviet leaders were equally anxious about the new world order and saw U.S. ambitions as every bit as imperialist as those of European fascism. In 1946 Stalin ordered Western communist parties onto the political offensive. In Greece a civil war, which had begun during the Second World War, threatened a communist takeover. In 1946 the United States embarked on a strategy of "containment" aimed at restricting the further expansion of communism worldwide. The American president announced the Truman Doctrine, promising aid to any peoples resisting internal and external threats to democratic freedom. The first beneficiary was Greece, where U.S. aid in 1947 helped turn the tide against the communist guerrillas—a pattern to be repeated many times during the Cold War era.

1 germany and poland, 1945–49

- U.S.
- British
- French
- Soviet
- boundaries between zones of occupation
- jointly occupied cities

territories lost by Germany, Poland and Czechoslovakia

- lost by Germany to Poland
- lost by Germany to USSR
- lost by Poland to USSR
- lost by Czechoslovakia to USSR

frontiers from 1947

- Poland, 1947
- Federal Republic of Germany, 1949
- The Saar, 1949
- frontiers, 1947

www.ibiblio.org/expo/soviet.exhibit/coldwar.html
Cold War: Postwar estrangement and Soviet perspectives
www.trumanlibrary.org/whistlestop/study_collections/doctrine/large/doctrine.htm
Harry Truman and the Truman Doctrine

DENMARK

Bremerhaven
Hamburg
Bremen

Elbe

Oder
Potsdam Berlin

zones
onomically
united
in 1948

(German Democratic
Republic from 1949)

Leipzig

Dresden

kfurt
Iain

added to
economically
united zones
in 1949

Nuremberg

ctgart

Munich

MANY

Danube

Linz
Salzburg

AUSTRIA

ITALY

Graz

YUGOSLAVIA

Prague

CZECHOSLOVAKIA

Brno

Vienna

Bratislava

Szczecin
(Stettin)

WEST POMERANIA

EAST POMERANIA

Danzig Free State
ceded to Poland,
1947

Gdańsk

Liegnitz

Wrocław
(Breslau)

UPPER
SILESIA

POLAND

Poznan
(Posen)

Łodz

Warsaw

Vistula

Cracow

LITHUANIA

Vilnius

Kaliningrad
(Königsberg)

EAST PRUSSIA

UNION OF SOVIET SOCIALIST REPUBLICS

Brest-
Litovsk

L'vov
(Lwów)

Dniester

HUNGARY

Košice

ROMANIA

1 The Allies agreed to move Poland physically westward after the war (map
above). Poland obtained East Prussia and large parts of eastern Germany
but lost the eastern territories awarded at Versailles, which became part of
the Soviet Union. Some three million Germans and three million Poles
moved west with the frontiers.

2 In 1946 the Allies agreed to a limitation of industry plan for Germany, but the
extreme plans to agrarianize the economy were dropped. The onset of the
Cold War hastened the reformation of a German state divided between East
and West. Berlin was similarly partitioned into zones of occupation (map
right) and was physically divided by a guarded wall built in 1961.

2 berlin, 1945–90

American sector
British sector
French sector
Soviet sector
city borders
the Berlin Wall,
1961–89
Autobahn
international
railroad
⊕ airport
▪ headquarters
◻ allied HQ
→ air corridor

Bernau

Havel

REINICKENDORF

Falkensee

SPANDAU

Tegel
WEDDING

PANKOW

WEISSENSEE

Neuenhagen

TIERGARTEN
CHARLOTTENBURG

PRENZLEUER-
BERG
MITTE FRIEDRICHS-
HAIN

LICHTENBERG

Gatow

WILMERSDORF SCHÖNE-
BERG

KREUZBERG

Spree

Rüdersdorf

ZEHLENDORF

Tempelhof
TEMPELHOF

STEGLITZ

NEUKÖLLN

KÖPENICK

Potsdam

Schönefeld

Schmöckwitz

1947 European communists set up Cominform

1948 Communist takeover in Czechoslovakia and Hungary; Berlin airlift; Yugoslavia splits from Soviet bloc

1949 formation of NATO alliance and COMECON; West and East Germany created

1949 Communist victory in China

1953 (5 March) Death of Stalin

1953 East Berlin revolt crushed; Fidel Castro prominent in foiled Cuban rebellion

1955 Warsaw Pact signed

1961 East Germans build Berlin Wall; U.S. cuts links with Cuba—"Bay of Pigs" fiasco

1962 Cuban missile crisis

The Cold War was at its most dangerous in the years between 1947 and 1963. During this period both the major superpowers, the United States and the Soviet Union, struggled to gain the lead in an arms race based on nuclear weapons, while smaller powers—Britain, France, and China—developed nuclear weapons of their own.

The arms race underpinned the political confrontation between the two blocs. Until August 1949 the United States had a monopoly on the new weapon. With the explosion of a Soviet atomic bomb and the development in the following decade of thermonuclear bombs with ever greater destructive capacity, the strategic balance altered. The more anxious each side became about its security, the more effort was put into stockpiling weapons capable of obliterating a great part of the globe. With the development of rockets in preference to long-range bombers as the means to carry nuclear weapons, the Soviet Union was able to bring the threat to bear on distant American cities. Equally, by 1956 it was calculated that the U.S. nuclear arsenal could inflict 200 million casualties on the Soviet population.

In practice the Cold War was conducted at a lower level of confrontation, using conventional weapons, political pressure, and propaganda. During 1947 and 1948 the states of Eastern Europe—Poland, Hungary, Czechoslovakia, Romania, Bulgaria, and Yugoslavia—all became communist and pro-Soviet. In reaction to Western efforts to reform the German economy the Soviet Union attempted to blockade Berlin and force the West to abandon the city. Between June 1948 and May 1949, 275,000 flights were made to bring supplies to the Western zones of Berlin. The Soviet decision to end the blockade heralded a shift in the German policy of both sides. The Western states set up a German Federal Republic to replace their zones of occupation in September 1949, and in October the Soviet zone became the German Democratic Republic.

In response to the communist domination of one half of Europe, the Western states set up the North Atlantic Treaty Organization (NATO) in April 1949, which provided a framework for military cooperation in the face of a common enemy. U.S. forces and equipment, including nuclear weapons, were stationed in NATO countries. In an effort to strengthen the alliance and to provide a clear military frontier in Europe, the Federal Republic of Germany was admitted to the NATO alliance in 1955.

The first serious test of the new anticommunist alliance came outside Europe. In 1950 war broke out in Korea between communist north and democratic south, following a partition agreed in 1948 between the United States and the USSR (see pages 120–1). U.S. forces were dispatched to save the south and large-scale rearmament began. Under pressure the United States' allies within Europe, as well as other United Nations states, gave assistance. The war dragged newly communist China in on the side of North Korea, and a long war of attrition set in until 1953. In this case "containment" was shown to work and the Korean partition was reimposed.

2 The high point of the Cold War was reached in 1962 when the United States forced the Soviet Union to abandon its program to deploy missiles and nuclear warheads in Cuba (map right), where a procommunist revolution had occurred in 1959. In October 1962 the United States blockaded Cuba, and the Soviet Union, rather than risk all-out war, agreed on October 26 to withdraw its missiles.

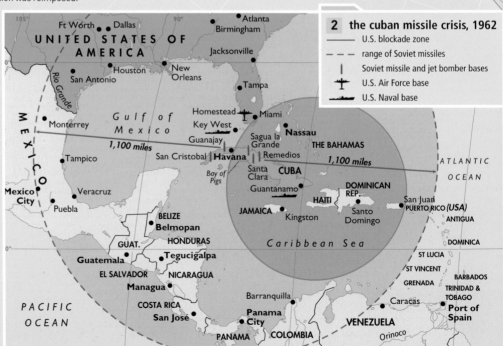

2 the cuban missile crisis, 1962

— U.S. blockade zone

-- range of Soviet missiles

Soviet missile and jet bomber bases

U.S. Air Force base

U.S. Naval base

www.historylearningsite.co.uk/coldwar.htm
History of the Cold War, 1945-80
www.cia.gov/csi/books/17240/index.html
Documents on the intelligence war in Berlin, 1946–61

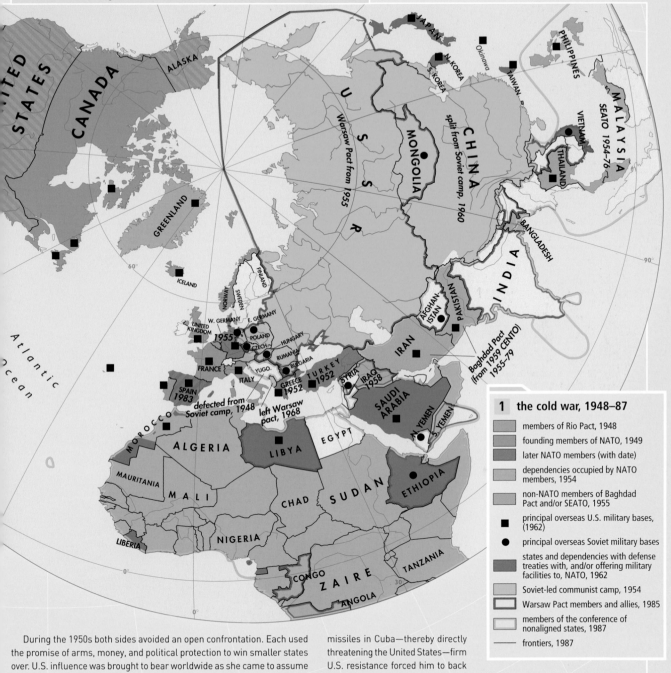

1 the cold war, 1948–87

- members of Rio Pact, 1948
- founding members of NATO, 1949
- later NATO members (with date)
- dependencies occupied by NATO members, 1954
- non-NATO members of Baghdad Pact and/or SEATO, 1955
- ■ principal overseas U.S. military bases, (1962)
- ● principal overseas Soviet military bases
- states and dependencies with defense treaties with, and/or offering military facilities to, NATO, 1962
- Soviet-led communist camp, 1954
- Warsaw Pact members and allies, 1985
- members of the conference of nonaligned states, 1987
- frontiers, 1987

During the 1950s both sides avoided an open confrontation. Each used the promise of arms, money, and political protection to win smaller states over. U.S. influence was brought to bear worldwide as she came to assume the role of the world's policeman. In the late 1950s, following the successful launch of the first space satellite (in 1957), Khrushchev, Soviet leader since 1956, embarked on a more aggressive strategy of expanding Soviet influence in the developing world. The strategy soon fell apart. The American fear of a "missile gap," prompted by the Soviet space program, provoked a massive increase in U.S. military procurement, which took the United States to a real lead in the arms race by the early 1960s.

The communist bloc was faced with its first serious crisis when China rejected Soviet collaboration in 1960. When Khrushchev tried to recover the Soviet position by putting pressure again on Berlin and later by placing missiles in Cuba—thereby directly threatening the United States—firm U.S. resistance forced him to back down. The Cuban crisis of 1962 marked a turning point in the Cold War. The following year the two sides agreed to a nuclear test-ban treaty, and the tension between the two blocs began to give way slowly to a mood of détente.

1 In the decade following the Second World War much of the world was divided into two armed camps (map above), one based around the Soviet Union and China, as the leading communist states, the other based around the United States, the most powerful and economically successful of the Western democracies. Both sides built up military alliance blocs and engaged in a long-term arms race.

In the 20 years following the Cuban missile crisis, the level of tension of the Cold War was reduced but by no means eradicated. The Sino-Soviet split and the economic revival of Europe created a more multipolar system and also forced the Soviet Union to adjust to two rival major powers rather than one.

The political and ideological conflict was shifted to Asia, Africa, and Latin America. In 1963 the U.S. committed its forces fully to the civil war in Vietnam (see page 120), and at its peak had well over half a million troops stationed in South East Asia. The U.S. also actively supported anticommunist forces throughout Latin America, intervening in Nicaragua, Chile, and, in 1983, the Caribbean island of Grenada. The USSR also increased its activities in the developing world, often by proxy. Soviet-backed Cuban forces participated in civil wars in the Horn of Africa and the former Portuguese colony of Angola.

There were, nonetheless, clear signs that the unstable superpower conflict of the 1950s was waning. In the United States and throughout the Western world there was strong hostility to U.S. involvement in Vietnam (and more muted hostility to the Soviet intervention in Czechoslovakia in 1968). The rise of an international peace movement challenged the ideological foundations of confrontation, which the postwar generation

2 intermediate-range land-based missiles in europe after 1973

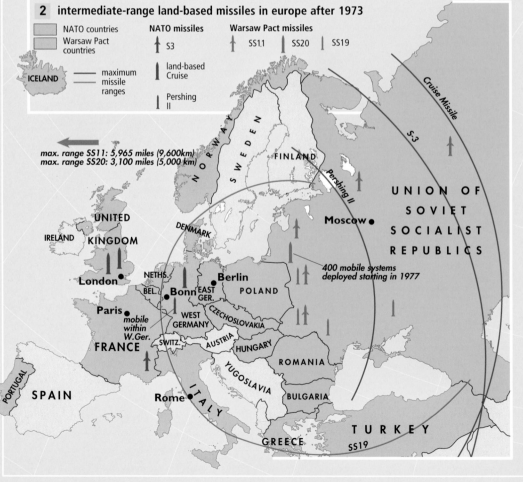

max. range SS11: 5,965 miles (9,600km)
max. range SS20: 3,100 miles (5,000 km)

400 mobile systems deployed starting in 1977

mobile within W.Ger.

2 Throughout the Cold War the USSR deployed a larger number of short- and medium-range than intercontinental missiles (map left). In 1979 the U.S. stationed theater nuclear weapons in Europe to face the Soviet challenge. This provoked strong resentment in Western Europe, which saw itself as the nuclear battlefield.

www.coldwar.org/museum/
Record of the people, places, and events of the Cold War
www.brook.edu/fp/research/areas/nmd/salt1.htm
Agreement of limitation of Strategic Offensive Arms between U.S. and USSR

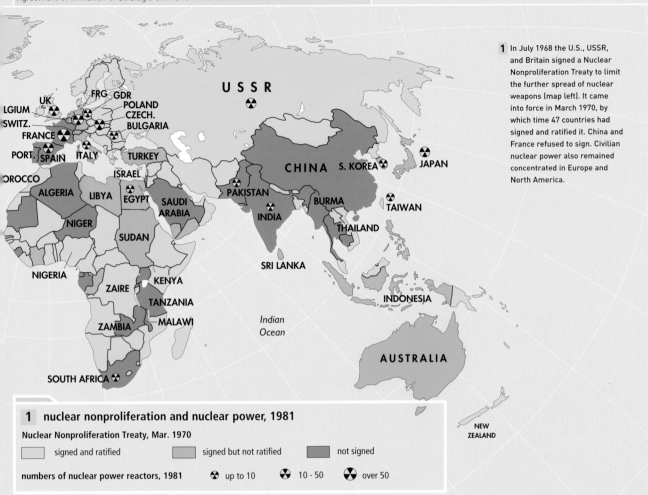

1 In July 1968 the U.S., USSR, and Britain signed a Nuclear Nonproliferation Treaty to limit the further spread of nuclear weapons (map left). It came into force in March 1970, by which time 47 countries had signed and ratified it. China and France refused to sign. Civilian nuclear power also remained concentrated in Europe and North America.

1 nuclear nonproliferation and nuclear power, 1981

Nuclear Nonproliferation Treaty, Mar. 1970

signed and ratified

signed but not ratified

not signed

numbers of nuclear power reactors, 1981   ☢ up to 10   ☢ 10 - 50   ☢ over 50

found difficult to understand. Links between the two opposing sides were also established. Arms limitation talks, begun in 1969, were successful in producing the first of a number of agreements on cutting back nuclear weapons development (SALT I). Also in 1969 the West German chancellor, Willy Brandt, launched closer links with the East German state, leading by 1971 to a Four-Power Agreement on Berlin and relaxing the harsh confrontation established there since the 1940s. The United States moved to mend its bridges with communist China. President Nixon signed an historic agreement with Mao's China during a visit to Peking in February 1972, which restored political and trade relations. Finally, in August 1975, after three years of negotiation on security and cooperation in Europe (CSCE), the Helsinki Accords were signed. Thirty-three European states, as well as Canada and the U.S., were party to the agreement, which recognized Europe's existing frontiers and committed all parties to observe human rights and improve communication between the power blocs.

Despite the sense that Helsinki had ushered in a new age of security, the Cold War had one last gasp. The administration of President Jimmy Carter (1977–80) produced a powerful mood of anticommunism, partly based on Democratic hostility to the Soviet human rights record, partly on renewed American fears that arms limitation had narrowed the gap dangerously between U.S. and Soviet military strength. Once again that

fear prompted a sharp increase in U.S. military spending, and the development of a new range of weapons—the neutron bomb, multiple warhead systems, Cruise missiles—which destabilized the military balance and aroused Soviet anxieties. Carter's hostility was also based on the Soviet decision to invade Afghanistan in 1979 (see page 114).

There followed a five-year period of U.S. posturing, first by Carter, then by his Republican successor, Ronald Reagan. Playing on U.S. uncertainties about its position in the world following defeat in Vietnam in 1973, Reagan returned to the rhetoric of the 1950s. The Soviet Union became the "evil empire"; arms spending doubled between 1980 and 1985; and work was begun on the Strategic Defense Initiative (SDI), a space-based defense system. Behind the scenes Reagan's United States was less flamboyantly hostile. The basis was laid for what in 1985 became a period of true détente and the final end of the Cold War.

europe: from reconstruction to union

1947 Marshall Plan for reconstruction in Europe

1948 Organization for European Economic Co-operation (OEEC) set up

1949 democracy restored in West Germany; Council of Europe set up

1951 European Coal and Steel Authority set up

1955 democracy restored in Austria

1957 Treaty of Rome; foundation of European Economic Community (EEC)

1959 Britain establishes European Free Trade Association (EFTA)

The Europe which helped generate the Cold War was a region of extraordinary desolation in 1945. More than 30 million people had been killed, and 16 million permanently resettled. Even a year after the war's end, industrial production was barely one-third of the pre-war level and food production only half. The war also left a legacy of deep bitterness: collaborators with fascism were imprisoned, murdered, or ostracized. In the ruins of war there were very real fears of social and economic collapse.

Revival depended on the U.S., the only state with the economic resources to invest in reconstruction. Through the United Nations Relief and Reconstruction Administration (UNRRA) and the International Bank for Reconstruction and Development (later the World Bank) the U.S. pumped $17 billion into the revival of European economies. In spring 1947 a further program was set up by the U.S. secretary of state, George Marshall, in an effort to stabilize European politics and stimulate industrial revival. The European Recovery Program provided $11.8 billion between 1948 and 1951 for the supply of raw materials, machinery and food and investment in recovery projects. In April 1948 the 16 nations receiving the assistance set up the Organization for European Economic Cooperation (OEEC) to coordinate the aid program. The USSR refused U.S. assistance and compelled the states of Eastern Europe under its control to do likewise. In 1947 and 1948 communist regimes were established throughout Eastern Europe and a program of Soviet-style economic modernization imposed (see page 124). Eastern Europe was effectively closed off from the economic and political influence of the Western world, its development dependent on the interests of the Soviet Union.

In the rest of Europe economic reconstruction was the key to political stabilization. By 1950 output of goods was 35 percent higher than in 1938; by 1964 it was 250 percent greater. Europe embarked on the longest and largest economic boom in its history, made possible by the liberalization

1 the marshall plan, 1947–51

applied for and received Marshall aid, with amounts (in U.S.$)

applied for Marshall aid but withdrew application

did not apply

14.0% net Marshall aid as percentage of national income 1948–49

1 In the spring of 1947 U.S. Secretary of State George Marshall put his name to a European Recovery Program backed by U.S. money. The Marshall Plan (map right) was designed to stabilize democratic governments in Europe and revive the European trade area. It was granted to 16 Western countries, but it was also offered to the Soviet-dominated states of Eastern Europe, where Stalin insisted on rejection. In all, some U.S.$11.8 billion was made available, in addition to funds offered under other recovery schemes. The scheme gave Europe access to foodstuffs, oil, and machinery at a time when they lacked the dollars to buy from the United States directly.

ICELAND
$24 m 5%

NORWAY
$236 m 5.8%

SWEDEN
$118 m 0.3%

FINLAND

DENMARK
$257 m 3.3%

IRELAND
$116 m 7.8%

UNITED KINGDOM
$2.825 bn 2.4%

NETH.
$979 m 10.8%

EAST GERMANY

POLAND

U.S.S.R

BELGIUM
$546 m 0.6%

WEST GERMANY

SAARLAND

GERMANY
$1.297 bn 2.9%

CZECHOSLOVAKIA

FRANCE
$2.445 bn 6.5%

LIECH.

SWITZ.

AUSTRIA
$560 m 14.0%

applied for Marshall aid but received nothing

HUNGARY

ROMANIA

PORTUGAL
$50 m

SPAIN

denied Marshall aid because of Franco's pro-Axis sympathies

ITALY
$1.314 bn 5.3%

YUGOSLAVIA

BULGARIA

ALBANIA

GREECE
$515 m

TUR
$152

www.loc.gov/exhibits/marshall/
The Marshall Plan
www.hri.org/docs/Rome57/
Treaty of Rome establishing the European Community

of trade and the greater degree of state economic management. After 1945 European governments adopted policies to stimulate economic growth along lines advocated by the British economist John Maynard Keynes. The state provided investment, gave subsidies for modernization, used tax policies to stimulate demand, and redistributed income through national welfare systems. The provision of welfare was designed to avoid the desperate poverty of the 1930s and to link socialist labor movements more closely with the prevailing capitalist system. The growth of "mixed economies" combining private enterprise with state regulation and the establishment of welfare states helped produce more effective parliamentary systems in Europe than had been possible before the war.

Democracy was restored in Italy in 1946, in West Germany in 1949, in Austria in 1955. There were widespread calls for political collaboration, even political unity. In 1949 a Council of Europe was set up under the leadership of the Belgian politician Paul-Henri Spaak, its ambition to create a politically united Europe. The only progress made in the 1950s was on economic integration. In 1952 a European Coal and Steel Community was established between France, Germany, Italy, and the Benelux countries to rationalize and coordinate their heavy industry. In 1957 they moved toward full economic union when they signed the Treaty of Rome establishing the European Economic Community. Britain stood aside because of her Commonwealth links. For the states that did join, the 1960s saw a boom in trade between them, and a decline in the national tensions that had brought war twice since 1900.

2 As the Cold War confrontation hardened after 1945, Europe was divided into two armed camps (map below). NATO was formed with the USA and Canada in 1949 as the centerpiece of Western security. In 1955 the Soviet Union created the Warsaw Pact, linking the states of the Communist bloc in a single defense pact. Economic union divided the continent along the same lines. In the west the EEC (1957) and EFTA (1960) created capitalist trading blocs matched by COMECON (1949) in the Soviet bloc.

2 european military and economic trading blocs, 1947–81

military partitions

Nato 1949– (including United States and Canada)

Warsaw Pact 1948–91

economic blocs

Benelux customs union, 1947

original European Economic Community (EEC) members, 1957

joined EEC, 1973

joined EEC, 1981

founder members of European Free Trade Association (EFTA), 1960

subsequent EFTA members

Council for Mutual Economic Assistance (COMECON) members, 1949

subsequent COMECON members

ICELAND
joined EFTA 1970

FINLAND
associate member of EFTA from 1961

NORWAY

SWEDEN

DENMARK
withdrew from EFTA Dec. 1972

IRELAND
joined EFTA 1970–2

UNITED KINGDOM
withdrew from EFTA Dec. 1972

NETH.

EAST GERMANY
member of COMECON 1950

POLAND

USSR

BELGIUM

LUX.

WEST GERMANY

CZECHOSLOVAKIA

FRANCE
left command structure of NATO 1966

SWITZ.

LIECH.

AUSTRIA

HUNGARY

ROMANIA

PORTUGAL

SPAIN

ANDORRA

MONACO

SAN MARINO

ITALY

YUGOSLAVIA
associate member of COMECON 1964

BULGARIA

ALBANIA
withdrew from Warsaw Pact 1968

GREECE

TURKEY

1959 to 1986

1963 France vetoes British entry into EEC; France withdraws from NATO (1966)

1968 student riots in France; spread across Western Europe

1972 EEC Paris summit pledges political union by 1980

1973 Britain, Ireland, and Denmark join EEC; Greece (1981); Spain and Portugal (1986)

1973 miners' strike in Britain brings 3-day week

1978-9 British Winter of Discontent

1986 single European Act heralds closer integration

www.nato.int/docu/update/index.htm
Up-to-date news on NATO activities and events
www.fordham.edu/halsall/mod/modsbook49.html
Western Europe since 1945

The reduction in international tension in Western Europe owed much to the rapprochement between France and Germany which was achieved in the mid-1950s and sustained by the European commitment of successive German and French leaders, from Konrad Adenauer and Charles de Gaulle in the late 1950s to Helmut Kohl and François Mitterand in the 1980s. Both states looked to build a strong European identity in the 1960s.

De Gaulle was hostile to American influence in Europe and to the survival of Britain's wartime "special relationship" with the U.S. When Britain applied for membership of the EEC in 1962 de Gaulle vetoed her entry, and in 1966 he withdrew French forces from NATO.

It took another ten years before further progress was made on European integration, and by this time Britain, like the other colonial powers, had shed much of her global empire (see page 122). De Gaulle retired in 1969 and the new generation of politicians in EEC states were keen to extend the principle of integration. In 1973 Britain, Ireland, and Denmark joined the EEC. After a period of growing economic crisis in the 1970s sparked by the increase in oil prices in 1973, and followed by rising unemployment and inflation, other states sought entry. Greece joined in 1981; Spain and Portugal joined five years later.

Despite the economic integration of Western Europe, little progress was made on political ties. Fears of losing sovereignty and arguments about currency reform and welfare policies divided the EEC members too sharply to fulfill the pledge made at the EEC Paris Summit in 1972 to produce political union by 1980. There also existed differences of opinion within the member states on the political future. While some groups favored a supranational Europe, there was an evident decline in the domestic consensus of the 1950s and 1960s that had sustained postwar welfare capitalism.

The crisis of national identity was in part a product of generational conflict. In the late 1960s Western Europe was hit by a wave of popular student-led protests against militarism and conservative values, much of which rejected the growth of consumerism and left-wing collaboration with capitalism. University reforms calmed down much of the student unrest, but in the 1970s terrorist groups emerged in Italy (the Red Brigades) and West Germany (the Baader-Meinhof gang), which waged a violent war against authority and the business community.

At the same time labor relations worsened as trade unions tried to retain the wage gains of the postwar period in an age of inflation. In a major strikewave between 1972-5 more than 150 million working days were lost in Britain, Italy, France, and West Germany. States which had grown used to high levels of employment and government spending found Keynesianism no longer capable of sustaining growth. In the early 1980s Europe again faced high levels of unemployment while governments began to cut spending growth and to leave the economy to market forces. The result was further industrial unrest in France and Britain, where in 1984 a prolonged coal strike was used as an opportunity to undermine union influence. If by the late 1980s Western Europe was richer, more secure, and more politically stable than it had been in the 1950s, there nevertheless remained underlying elements of crisis and uncertainty.

1   western europe:
      separatism and
      nationalism, 1945–85

—— territorial autonomy based on ethnic group, with date of autonomy

—— separate administration/ autonomy for other reasons

✊ linguistic minorities or other communities whose members have used violence in pursuit of greater autonomy or other change of political status, with areas inhabited

✗ devolution rejected by referendum, with date

✓ devolution approved by referendum, with date

● ethnic or other communal based party delegated to national parliament in 1985

1 Although the post-1945 settlement left fewer issues of self-determination and minority nationalism than the Versailles Settlement after 1919, there remained areas of conflict which war and reconstruction left untouched (map left). The issue of Irish nationalism remained alive. In Northern Ireland the Irish Republican Army agitated for a union of Northern Ireland with the Irish Republic, and in the late 1930s, the late 1950s and the period starting in 1972 and onward conducted a campaign of violence on the British mainland to pressurize the British government. In Spain the Basque separatist movement, ETA, kept up a terrorist campaign against the Franco government. In Cyprus the Turkish and Greek communities resorted to civil war in 1974, which led to the island's partition. The growth of multinational and supranational organizations in Europe has not eroded the force of regionalism and irredentism.

Where Europe faced the devastation of war in 1945, the United States emerged from the conflict richer, more united, and willing to play a full part in shaping the world economy and the international order. The wartime boom saw GNP grow by 50 percent and average incomes increase by 75 percent.

For the next 25 years the U.S. economy continued to boom, sustained by the application of science, a rapidly rising population, and world demand for food and machinery from U.S. producers. Americans were the world's richest consumers, enjoying a standard of living that was the envy of the rest of the world. The United States' new role brought its problems. The Cold War, widely regarded as a contest between good and evil, fed back into domestic politics. In 1950 the Wisconsin senator Joseph McCarthy began an official campaign to root out communists in American politics and culture. McCarthyism had support from the nationalist right in the U.S., which resented the loss of China in 1949 and feared a vast fifth column of Soviet spies and agents. In 1954-5 anticommunism reached a frenzied finale of purges directed at anyone suspected of liberal sympathies. It ended only when McCarthy turned against the army. President Dwight Eisenhower, a wartime army hero, called a halt.

Many of those who hated communists hated Blacks as well. For years the Southern Black community had put up with segregation and a denial of civil rights. The war moved many to the north and west of the country, and eroded racism in the armed forces. In 1948 Truman made the forces fully open to American Blacks. In 1954 the Supreme Court ruled that segregation in Southern schools should end. Across the South the nonblack community prepared to fight. White citizens' councils were set up which engaged in acts of violence and intimidation, reaching a notorious climax in Little Rock, Arkansas in 1957, when Black children tried to enrol in the high school. Civil rights acts in 1957 and 1960 did little to dent this discrimination.

3 civil rights and urban unrest, 1960–68

- civil rights demonstrations
- riots and urban unrest
- → civil rights marches

In 1960 Eisenhower was succeeded by a young Democrat, John F. Kennedy, who promised a "New Frontier" in U.S. politics. He symbolized the growing youth culture of the United States and the optimism of its prosperous classes. But he was also a strong Cold Warrior and did little for civil rights until his hand was forced by riots in Mississippi in 1963. That year Southern black groups launched a nationwide drive to end segregation, and 200,000 marched on Washington in August 1963 to meet the president. A new civil rights bill was drawn up, but three months later Kennedy was assassinated. Despite new civil rights legislation in 1964 and 1965, which at last gave Southern Blacks the vote, Black communities in the west and north, numbering in 1960 some 7.5 million, reacted violently against impoverishment and ghettoization. From 1965 to 1968 rioting, arson, and looting became familiar fare in America's cities.

In the 1970s the confident U.S. of the postwar years was hit first by economic crisis following the sharp increase in oil prices in 1973, then by political crisis sparked off by the corruption of the Nixon administration and the loss of the Vietnam War. The economic crisis was a profound psychological shock. The dollar was forced to float, in effect to be devalued, while the U.S. faced a widening trade gap and intense competition from those very states she had helped to reconstruct in the 1940s. Income growth began to stagnate, and poverty remained too large even for the world's richest state to solve.

The political crisis was sparked by election malpractices which led to Nixon's impeachment in 1974, but at root there were profound divisions in American society revealed by conflicts over the Vietnam War, conscription, and the rise of an alternative youth culture which rejected the American middle-class ideals of the 1950s. The mounting sense of uncertainty among the American public was reversed in the 1980s with the surprise victory of Ronald Reagan, who won a Republican landslide on the promise of a nationalist revival, tax cuts, and anti-Marxism. His presidency restored the battered morale of the American white middle classes and reversed economic stagnation, but the American consensus could not be restored. Blacks, Latinos, women, and gays organized in powerful, often radical, lobby groups hostile to mainstream America. In 1992 the Democrat Bill Clinton was elected with the support of many of these groups, but he focused on foreign policy issues at the expense of domestic reform. His successor, George W. Bush, faced further economic pressures and, like Clinton, external challenges which diverted attention away from domestic policy.

www.spartacus.schoolnet.co.uk/USAmccarthyism.htm
McCarthyism within the U.S.
www.spartacus.schoolnet.co.uk/USAcivilrights.htm
U.S. civil rights campaigners

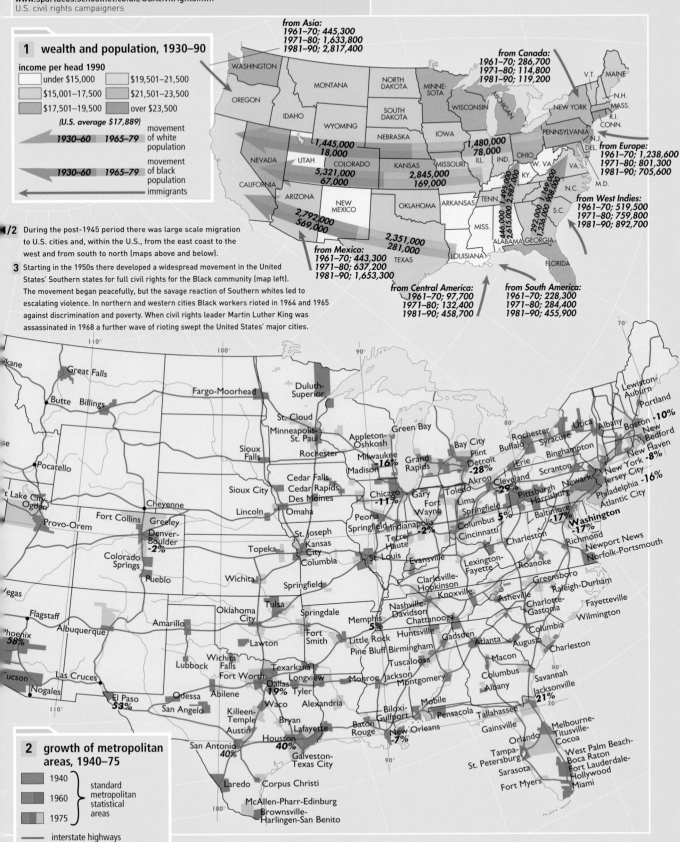

1 wealth and population, 1930–90

income per head 1990

- under $15,000
- $15,001–17,500
- $17,501–19,500
- $19,501–21,500
- $21,501–23,500
- over $23,500

(U.S. average $17,889)

movement of white population 1930–60 1965–79

movement of black population 1930–60 1965–79

immigrants

from Asia:
1961–70: 445,300
1971–80: 1,633,800
1981–90: 2,817,400

from Canada:
1961–70: 286,700
1971–80: 114,800
1981–90: 119,200

from Europe:
1961–70: 1,238,600
1971–80: 801,300
1981–90: 705,600

from West Indies:
1961–70: 519,500
1971–80: 759,800
1981–90: 892,700

from Mexico:
1961–70: 443,300
1971–80: 637,200
1981–90: 1,653,300

from Central America:
1961–70: 97,700
1971–80: 132,400
1981–90: 458,700

from South America:
1961–70: 228,300
1971–80: 284,400
1981–90: 455,900

/2 During the post-1945 period there was large scale migration to U.S. cities and, within the U.S., from the east coast to the west and from south to north (maps above and below).

3 Starting in the 1950s there developed a widespread movement in the United States' Southern states for full civil rights for the Black community (map left). The movement began peacefully, but the savage reaction of Southern whites led to escalating violence. In northern and western cities Black workers rioted in 1964 and 1965 against discrimination and poverty. When civil rights leader Martin Luther King was assassinated in 1968 a further wave of rioting swept the United States' major cities.

2 growth of metropolitan areas, 1940–75

- 1940
- 1960 } standard metropolitan statistical areas
- 1975

— interstate highways

109

the **superpowers**: **U.S.** foreign policy

At the dawn of the Cold War US statesmen were aware they would have to shoulder responsibilities in the international arena they had shunned before 1939. They hoped that the American new order would bring an age of international prosperity and collaboration. The first ambition proved easier to achieve than the second.

U.S. leaders in 1945 were determined not to return to the bad old days of protectionism and economic nationalism of the 1930s. They persuaded the noncommunist world to accept worldwide trade liberalization, which produced the General Agreement on Tariffs and Trade (GATT) in 1947. In Germany the U.S. insisted on decartelization and antitrust legislation, and the revived union organization was strongly influenced by the American desire to avoid a platform for labor radicalism. In Japan starting in 1948 the U.S. occupiers began an economic reform program to revive Japan's economy along Western capitalist lines with, in the end, remarkable results.

U.S. economic strength allowed the practice of "dollar diplomacy" worldwide. U.S. firms took the lead in all areas of modern technology, and in the 1950s and 1960s became household names: Boeing aircraft; IBM office equipment; General Electric household goods, which transformed lifestyles throughout the Western world. Americanization was exported

1 The United States after 1945 maintained a world presence through a network of military bases and defense pacts in Europe, the Middle East, and Asia (map below). The desire to contain the threat of communism forced America into the role of the world's policeman, intervening militarily on numerous occasions. Many states saw America's role as a new imperialism, replacing the defunct colonial empires of Europe. In Iran and Libya rejection of American influence led to popular anti-imperialist revolutions.

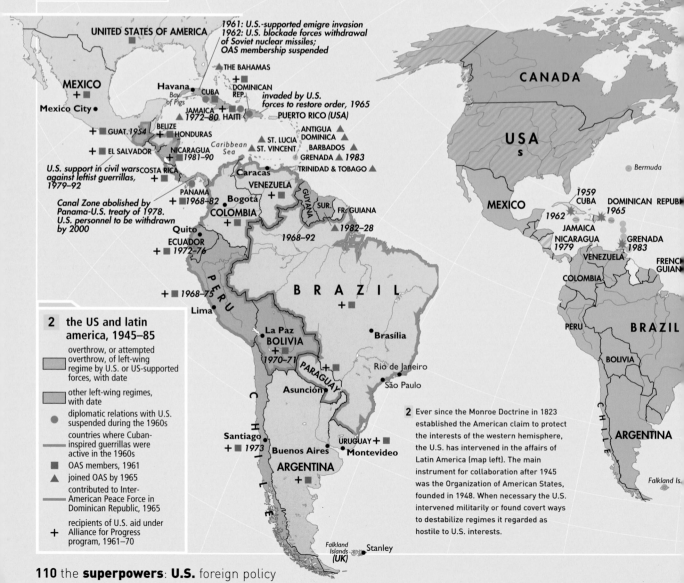

2 the US and latin america, 1945–85

- overthrow, or attempted overthrow, of left-wing regime by U.S. or US-supported forces, with date
- other left-wing regimes, with date
- ● diplomatic relations with U.S. suspended during the 1960s
- countries where Cuban-inspired guerrillas were active in the 1960s
- ■ OAS members, 1961
- ▲ joined OAS by 1965
- contributed to Inter-American Peace Force in Dominican Republic, 1965
- + recipients of U.S. aid under Alliance for Progress program, 1961–70

2 Ever since the Monroe Doctrine in 1823 established the American claim to protect the interests of the western hemisphere, the U.S. has intervened in the affairs of Latin America (map left). The main instrument for collaboration after 1945 was the Organization of American States, founded in 1948. When necessary the U.S. intervened militarily or found covert ways to destabilize regimes it regarded as hostile to U.S. interests.

www.state.gov/www/about_state/history/frus.html
Archive of U.S. foreign relations
www.zompist.com/latam.html
Chronology of U.S. interventions in Latin America

along with the dollar loans and American goods. American movie studios provided much of the world's output. American popular culture, from Coca-Cola to rock and roll, provided icons of modernity.

There was a harsher side to the United States' world role. The Cold War forced the U.S. to intervene militarily in Europe (Greece, 1947); Asia (Korea, 1950, Indo-China 1954-73); and the Middle East (Lebanon 1958), where in January 1958 the Eisenhower Doctrine was proclaimed, committing the U.S. to prevent the spread of communism in the region. To cement the American strategy of containing the Soviet and Chinese threat, the U.S. made numerous defensive pacts. A peace treaty was signed with Japan in San Francisco in 1951, committing the U.S. to defend Japan against her larger communist neighbors. Similar agreements were reached with Australia, New Zealand, the Philippines, South Korea, and Taiwan. These broadened out into the SEATO alliance in 1954—the Asian counterpart of NATO.

Containment in Latin America took a slightly different form. In 1947 all 21 American republics signed the Inter-American Treaty of Reciprocal Assistance. The United States used collaboration as a means to limit political radicalism

in the region, which it did by encouraging right-wing coups (Guatemala 1954, Chile 1973, Cuba—unsuccessfully—in 1961) or through direct intervention (Dominican Republic 1965, Grenada 1983). In 1960 Washington set up the Inter-American Development Bank to sweeten intervention with dollars.

In the 1980s and 1990s America's world position altered. The decline of communism and the eclipse of Soviet power after 1989 created a world order with the U.S. as the only real superpower. America began to play the role of the world's policeman despite misgivings at home about the costs and risks. In the Gulf War in 1991, Somalia in 1992, Bosnia in 1995, Kosovo in 1999, Afghanistan in 2001, and Iraq in 2003, American forces were committed on a wide scale. Under both Bill Clinton and George W. Bush, American foreign policy became more assertive. U.S. dependence on allies in NATO became less important as American military and political leaders accustomed themselves to the responsibilities of exceptional American power. On September 11, 2001 a massive terrorist attack on New York and Washington pushed the U.S. to the forefront in a global conflict with terrorism and with so-called "rogue states."

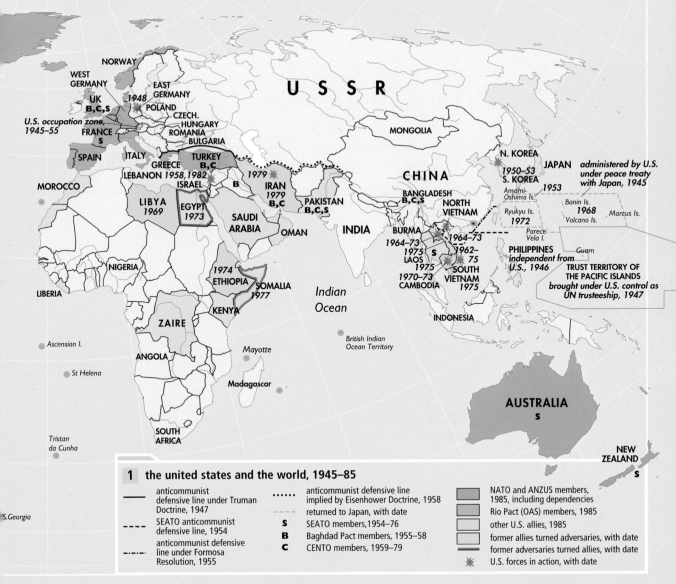

1 the united states and the world, 1945–85

— anticommunist defensive line under Truman Doctrine, 1947

---- SEATO anticommunist defensive line, 1954

-·-·- anticommunist defensive line under Formosa Resolution, 1955

······ anticommunist defensive line implied by Eisenhower Doctrine, 1958

-- -- returned to Japan, with date

S SEATO members, 1954–76

B Baghdad Pact members, 1955–58

C CENTO members, 1959–79

NATO and ANZUS members, 1985, including dependencies

Rio Pact (OAS) members, 1985

other U.S. allies, 1985

former allies turned adversaries, with date

former adversaries turned allies, with date

✳ U.S. forces in action, with date

1949 first Soviet Nuclear bomb test

1953 death of Stalin; East Berlin revolt crushed

1956 Khrushchev criticizes Stalinist regime; 8–9 million political prisoners released from prison camps

1964 Khrushchev announces new Party Program

1964 Brezhnev becomes Soviet leader; KGB restored to central role in stamping out dissent

1980 Soviet Union possesses nearly 10,000 nuclear warheads

The Soviet Union also emerged from the Second World War as a superpower, but its new status was won at the cost of exceptional sacrifice. Almost half of Soviet territory was utterly devastated: 20 million were killed; seven million horses and 17 million cattle lost; 98,000 collective farms and 4.7 million houses destroyed. The Soviet Union had to start again on the economic revolution begun in the 1930s.

First Stalin had some scores to settle. Any individual or group classified as traitors was liquidated or sent to the network of labor camps and penal colonies run by Stalin's notorious head of police, Lavrenti Beria. The victims included the entire Party leadership in Leningrad, which had withstood the 900 days of siege during the war. In the last period of Stalin's rule 100,000 were purged each year from the Communist Party. Stalin also took revenge on the Soviet peasantry, who had succeeded during the war in freeing themselves from the grip of the collective farm organization. In September 1946 Stalin began a renewed campaign against peasant "profiteering." Their savings were eliminated, thousands brought back into the collectives and 34,600,000 acres (14 million hectares) of land returned to state-run farms.

The nationalities of the Soviet Union, 1989

Russians 53.19%	Mordvins 0.42%	Bashkirs 0.53%
Latvians 0.54%	Turkmen 1.00%	Georgians 1.46%
Lithuanians 1.10%	Uzbeks 6.12%	Armenians 1.70%
Estonians 0.38%	Tajiks 1.55%	Azerbaijanis 2.49%
Belarussians 3.78%	Kazakhs 2.98%	Jews (scattered) 0.51%
Poles 0.41%	Kirghiz 0.93%	Germans (scattered) 0.75%
Moldavians 1.23%	Chuvash 0.31%	others 3.73%
Ukrainians 16.18%	Tatars 2.44%	

1 **principal ethnic groups of the soviet union, 1989**

- Slav
- Caucasian
- Moldavian
- Iranian
- Turkic
- Finno-Ugric
- Baltic
- others

ASSR autonomous Soviet Socialist Republic

SSR Soviet Socialist Republic

AO autonomous Okrug

AD autonomous district

1 The Soviet Union was a patchwork of different nationalities (map above). There were 22 ethnic groups with more than one million members in the 1980s, but at least 80 other smaller ones. Russians made up just more than half the population; Slavs (Russians, Ukrainians, and Belarussians) approximately three-quarters. Each major national area also had its own political organization as one of the constituent republics of the Soviet Union, though none enjoyed political independence from the center. The large disproportion of Russians and Ukrainians was reflected in the distribution of political power.

www.zum.de/whkmla/region/russia/cccp196485dom.html
Domestic policy under Leonid Brezhnev, 1964–85
www.robertcutler.org/modules/sdp-1791.htm
The domestic politics of the Soviet Union

While crushing peasant agriculture, Stalin launched a new era of state-directed industrial planning. The process of modernization continued its prewar trajectory. By 1980 rural workers made up only one-fifth of the labor force, where they had constituted more than half in 1945. The urban population was 69 million in 1950, but 186 million in 1988, by which time the rural population had fallen from 109 million in 1950 to 95 million. Priority went to heavy industry and the military at the expense of consumer goods.

The Soviet system underwent a minor revolution when, on March 5, 1953, Stalin died. There followed a period of collective leadership under Malenkov, Khrushchev, and Molotov, but by the time of the 20th Party Congress in 1956, at which Stalin and Stalinism were denounced from the platform, Khrushchev emerged as the leading figure. The era of de-Stalinization had important if limited effects. Some eight to nine million political prisoners were released from the labor camps. Censorship was relaxed and the ministry of the interior (home of the NKVD security police) closed down. Khrushchev attempted to reform agriculture and reverse peasant impoverishment, and to decentralize state economic planning in order to restore limited incentives to Soviet industry.

Chukchi AD

Koryak AD

Jewish AO

The results were disappointing. Economic decentralization produced chaos in both industry and agriculture. Wages stagnated, while expectations were raised. The relaxation of police terror opened up the issue of political dissidence and the extent to which the state could tolerate it and maintain communist ascendancy. In 1964 Khrushchev made one last attempt to secure change. At the 22nd Party Congress he announced a new Party Program, the first since 1919. He promised genuine communism in 20 years: ten years building the material base for it and ten years redistributing the new product. His colleagues were unimpressed. Following the climbdown over Cuba (see page 100), Khrushchev was the victim of a palace coup. In October 1964 he gave way to another period of collective leadership, which by 1966 led to the emergence of Leonid Brezhnev as Party leader.

The Brezhnev years reversed much of the liberalization. The interior ministry and a new security service, the KGB, were restored to their central role in stamping out dissent. Censorship was reimposed. Central state planning was reintroduced to ensure some level of economic growth. In the 1970s Brezhnev balanced coercion with an increase in the output of consumer goods, but there persisted a gap between the popular political and economic aspirations of ordinary Soviet citizens and the ability of the regime to satisfy them. Neither of Brezhnev's successors in the 1980s, Yuri Andropov (1982–84) and Konstantin Chernenko (1984–85), was willing to risk comprehensive reform. By the 1980s Soviet society had reached stalemate.

2 Following victory in the 1941–5 war the Soviet military became a central feature of the state (map below). One-fifth of the budget was devoted to military spending while between 1952 and 1976, 101 military leaders became full members of the Central Committee of the Communist Party. Striking progress was made following the first Soviet nuclear bomb test in 1949. In 1955 the Soviet Union possessed only 24 missiles and 324 nuclear warheads. In 1980 there were 3,017 land- and sea-based missiles and 9,653 nuclear warheads.

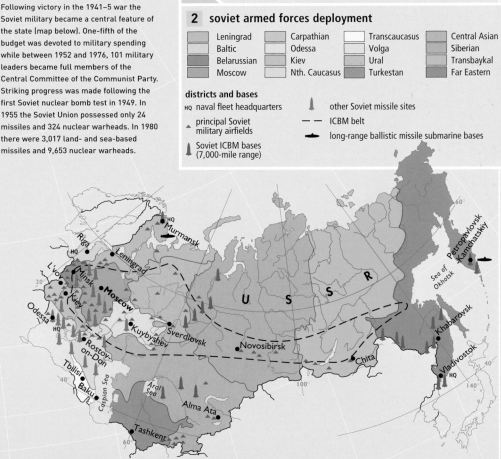

2 soviet armed forces deployment

Leningrad	Carpathian	Transcaucasus	Central Asian
Baltic	Odessa	Volga	Siberian
Belarussian	Kiev	Ural	Transbaykal
Moscow	Nth. Caucasus	Turkestan	Far Eastern

districts and bases
HQ naval fleet headquarters
▲ principal Soviet military airfields
▲ Soviet ICBM bases (7,000-mile range)
▲ other Soviet missile sites
- - - ICBM belt
⬤➤ long-range ballistic missile submarine bases

When Hitler's armies reached the suburbs of Moscow in December 1941, communism looked spent as a force in world politics. Soviet victory four years later was a triumph for Stalin's brand of communism, and the USSR sought to export its politics to the areas liberated by the Red Army. This was a process carried out step by step, building on the existence of large and popular communist parties in much of Eastern Europe.

A multiparty system was tolerated, but communist and socialist organizations were given special preference. In 1947 and 1948 political pluralism was eradicated and in Poland, Romania, Czechoslovakia, Albania, Bulgaria, and Hungary people's republics were declared, ruled by a single pro-Soviet party bloc. In September 1947 a communist international organization, Cominform, was set up, dominated from Moscow. In June 1948 Yugoslavia under Tito was expelled from this for refusing to toe the Moscow line, although by 1957 better relations were restored between Yugoslavia and the post-Stalinist USSR.

The triumph of communism in China in 1949, in North Korea, and in 1954, in Vietnam, enhanced the international prestige and influence of the USSR. Khrushchev hailed communism as the "wave of the future" and confidently expected it to triumph throughout the developing noncapitalist world. In the 1950s the USSR and the Soviet European bloc sought to

2 Between 1944 and 1948 a communist pro-Soviet bloc was created in Eastern Europe (map left). Soviet forces were stationed throughout the bloc, which was bound together by economic agreements (COMECON, 1949) and a military alliance (Warsaw Pact, 1955). In June 1948 Tito's Yugoslavia broke ties with Moscow. All other attempts to challenge Soviet domination in the 1950s and 1960s—in East Germany, in Hungary and in Czechoslovakia—were crushed.

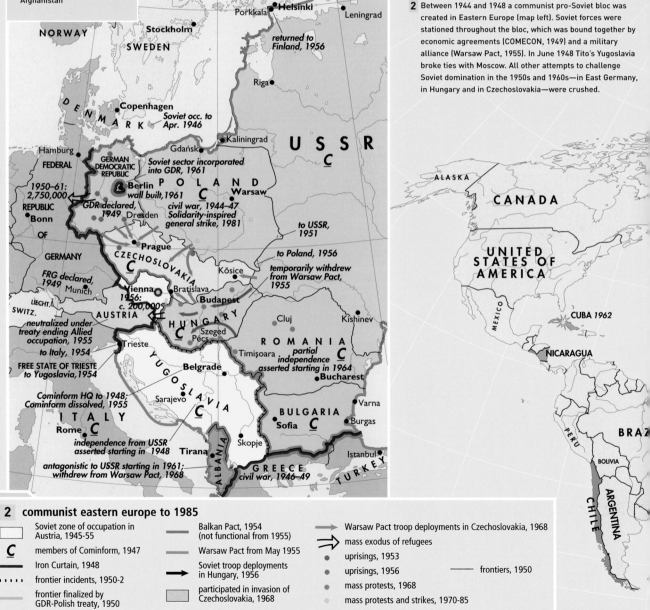

2 communist eastern europe to 1985

- Soviet zone of occupation in Austria, 1945-55
- **C** members of Cominform, 1947
- Iron Curtain, 1948
- ..... frontier incidents, 1950-2
- frontier finalized by GDR-Polish treaty, 1950
- Balkan Pact, 1954 (not functional from 1955)
- Warsaw Pact from May 1955
- Soviet troop deployments in Hungary, 1956
- participated in invasion of Czechoslovakia, 1968
- Warsaw Pact troop deployments in Czechoslovakia, 1968
- mass exodus of refugees
- uprisings, 1953
- uprisings, 1956
- mass protests, 1968
- mass protests and strikes, 1970-85
- frontiers, 1950

www.worldhistory.com/wiki/C/Cominform.htm
Cominform: Soviet-dominated organization of Communist parties
www.shsu.edu/~his_ncp/CMEA.html
The Council for Mutual Economic Assistance historical record

cement closer ties. In 1955 Egypt, under Colonel Nasser, obtained Soviet aid and technical assistance—a move that revolutionized the diplomacy of the region. There followed agreements with Afghanistan, Syria, Tunisia, and Yemen, though none of these turned the recipient state into a Soviet bloc member. Developing countries distrusted Soviet motives almost as much as American.

There were significant limits by the 1960s to the further extension of Soviet influence. There were political problems in Soviet-dominated Europe. In 1953 there were strikes and riots in Poland and East Germany. In 1956 a more serious insurrection took place in Hungary under the leadership of the liberal communist, Imre Nagy. He promised multiparty elections and withdrew Hungary from the military alliance with the USSR. In November 250,000 Soviet troops and 5,000 tanks reimposed Soviet power. Two years later the first splits appeared in relations with China, and in 1960 Mao declared the USSR guilty of "bourgeois deviation" and placed China at the head of the world communist revolutionary movement. In Albania, the Far East, and parts of Latin America communists followed China rather than the USSR. During the 1960s the European bloc states began to develop a more independent, nationalist form of development, which ended in 1968 with a further series of protests against Soviet hegemony and the Soviet invasion of Czechoslovakia.

Renewed efforts were made in the 1970s to curb Soviet influence. Cuba rallied to the side of the USSR after Castro's revolution in 1959. By the late 1970s there were an estimated 40,000 Cuban troops in Africa supporting communist regimes and guerrillas, and 8,000 Soviet military advisers. But elsewhere, in the Middle East, Latin America, and Asia, the Soviet Union, like the U.S., found itself the victim of popular local nationalism and the Islamic revival, symbolized by the Iranian revolution of 1979 and Muslim revolt in Afghanistan, which led to Soviet intervention there in 1979. Communism in much of the developing world was persecuted violently; in the developed states it withered as a major electoral force. In France the Communist Party was the major party of the left from 1945 down to the early 1980s, when it was eclipsed by moderate social democracy. In Italy the left was dominated by moderate communism until the 1980s, when the social democrats increased their share of the vote. The collapse of the Soviet bloc in 1989 (see pages 140–41) proved fatal for Western communism.

1 In the aftermath of the war the Soviet Union placed itself at the head of worldwide communism (map below). It engineered the transition to communist regimes in Eastern Europe, and tried to dominate Chinese and East Asian communism in the 1950s. A network of Soviet agents, military advisers, and technicians spread out across the developing world, particularly in Africa and the Middle East, where the Soviet Union established military bases for a brief period.

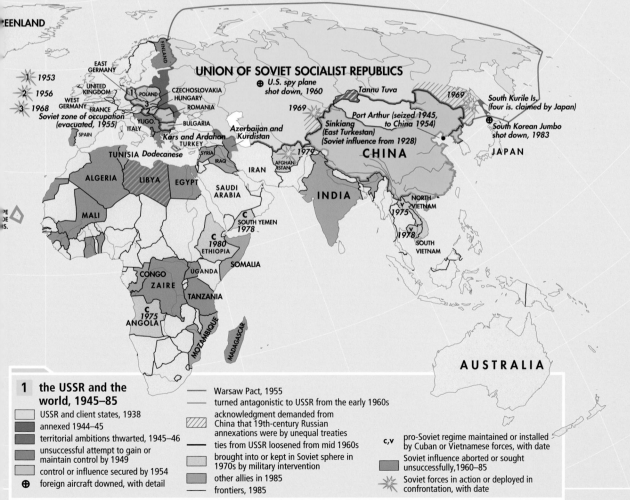

1 the USSR and the world, 1945–85

- USSR and client states, 1938
- annexed 1944–45
- territorial ambitions thwarted, 1945–46
- unsuccessful attempt to gain or maintain control by 1949
- control or influence secured by 1954
- ⊕ foreign aircraft downed, with detail

- ⎯ Warsaw Pact, 1955
- ⎯ turned antagonistic to USSR from the early 1960s
- ⧢ acknowledgment demanded from China that 19th-century Russian annexations were by unequal treaties
- ⎯ ties from USSR loosened from mid 1960s
- brought into or kept in Soviet sphere in 1970s by military intervention
- other allies in 1985
- ⎯ frontiers, 1985

- c,v pro-Soviet regime maintained or installed by Cuban or Vietnamese forces, with date
- Soviet influence aborted or sought unsuccessfully, 1960–85
- ✳ Soviet forces in action or deployed in confrontation, with date

the **long boom**

The Cold War struggle was carried out against a background of extraordinary economic revival from the devastation of the Second World War. From the 1940s to the early 1970s the world underwent the "Long Boom"—25 years of almost uninterrupted growth at rates higher than any yet recorded. In Europe income per head grew faster in 20 years than in the previous 150. Unemployment rates throughout the developed world were low, rarely rising above three percent. The business cycle was replaced by the economic miracle of almost continuous growth.

The boom had many causes. The war itself helped by creating boom conditions in the U.S., the world's largest economy. At the same time, European demand for food, materials, and weapons stimulated output in developing countries. The war also forced the U.S. to take the leading place in the world economy, a development isolationist sentiment had precluded before 1939. The U.S. became the world's major source of investment funds and aid. More significantly, U.S. statesmen were committed to reversing the prewar drift to protectionism and tariff wars by restoring a more open world market, with stable currencies.

The restoration of a healthy environment for trade was the single most important cause of the boom. In October 1947, 23 countries signed the General Agreement on Tariffs and Trade, which launched a round of negotiations on reducing protection. The first round covered 45,000 tariff items, produced 123 agreements and covered about one-half of world trade. By the mid-1950s the U.S. alone had reduced tariff levels by 50 percent, while a second major round in the early 1960s led to a further reduction of almost 50 percent in tariffs between developed economies. World trade grew at six percent a year between 1948 and 1960, and by nine percent between 1960 and 1973. Europe's trade between 1950 and 1970 grew from $18 billion to $129 billion.

The second cause was technical. After 1945 the application of modern science to industry and agriculture produced a wave of new products and production methods. Mechanization and modern plant biology created a so-called Second Agricultural Revolution, which stimulated food production in the less developed regions. Modern mass-production methods and rational factory organization, both stimulated by the war, were applied across the developed world, raising productivity remarkably and producing a boom in profits and in wages.

The third factor was political. States had begun to intervene more in regulating their economies before 1939 to cope with the recession. After the war there was a general desire to maintain regulation, or even to increase the level of planning and subsidy in order to avoid further slumps. State expenditure roughly doubled in the developed economies between the 1930s and the 1950s. State help was generally welcomed by firms keen to restore stability and by labor unions seeking to avoid high unemployment. By the early 1970s the noncommunist economies were typically "mixed economies," combining private enterprise and state regulation to maximize growth.

It was just at this point that the postwar boom turned sour. The rate of innovation and of profit and productivity growth slowed down sharply. Developed economies began to ossify, with large state sectors, expensive welfare programs, and high-cost workforces. The sudden increase in oil prices in 1973 turned a modest rate of world inflation into a price boom. Increased competition and new technology created high levels of unemployment. Low growth and high inflation—"stagflation"—pricked the bubble of seemingly endless expansion.

NORTH AMERICA

13,180 20,020 26,220 35,660 59,520

USA

6,697   10,977

7,540   9,240   9,950   12,670

SOUTH AMER

1 From the 1940s to the early 1970s the world economy experienced an exceptional period of expansion. World output doubled and world exports quadrupled. The developing areas received increasing quantities of aid from the richer economies, which helped sustain their economic modernization (map above). The boom meant employment and high prices for raw material producers.

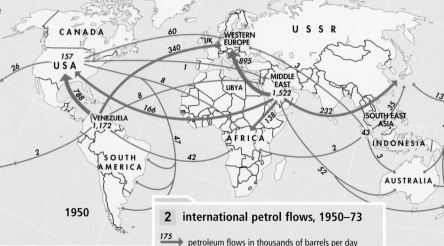

CANADA   60   UK   WESTERN EUROPE   U S S R

157   340   1   895
26   USA   8   3
788   8   MIDDLE EAST   232   35   13
VENEZUELA   166   LIBYA   1,522   SOUTH EAST ASIA   43   13
1,172   138   AFRICA   INDONESIA   2
2   47   42   3
SOUTH AMERICA   52   AUSTRALIA

1950

2 international petrol flows, 1950–73

175 → petroleum flows in thousands of barrels per day

www.ciesin.org/TG/PI/TRADE/gatt.html
General Agreement on Tariffs and Trade, from 1947
www.users.globalnet.co.uk/~semp/bdecline.htm
Britain's post-war economic decline

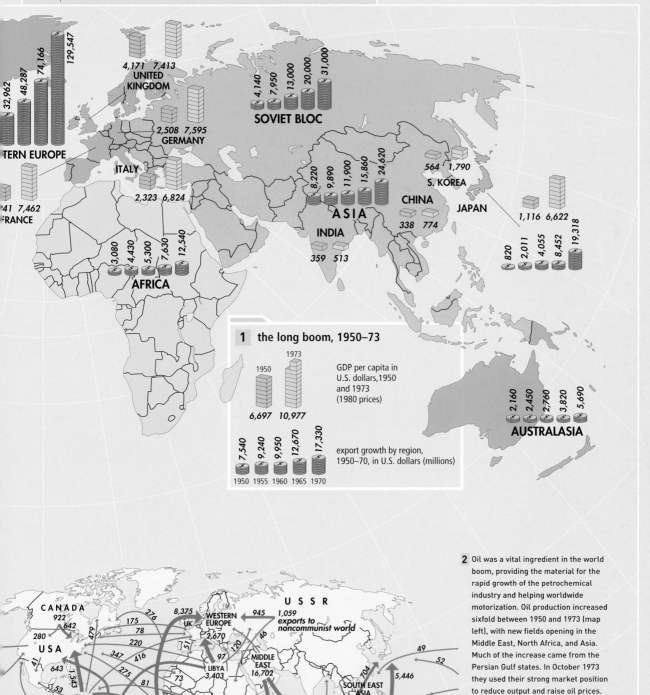

the long boom, 1950–73

GDP per capita in U.S. dollars, 1950 and 1973 (1980 prices)

1950: 6,697 1973: 10,977

export growth by region, 1950–70, in U.S. dollars (millions)

1950: 7,540 1955: 9,240 1960: 9,950 1965: 12,670 1970: 17,330

2 Oil was a vital ingredient in the world boom, providing the material for the rapid growth of the petrochemical industry and helping worldwide motorization. Oil production increased sixfold between 1950 and 1973 (map left), with new fields opening in the Middle East, North Africa, and Asia. Much of the increase came from the Persian Gulf states. In October 1973 they used their strong market position to reduce output and raise oil prices. Between 1970 and 1972 oil rose from $1.50 to $3.00, but at the end of 1973 Gulf oil fetched $18 a barrel. The price rise created havoc in the developed states and brought the long boom to an end. The temporary shortage of fuel was followed by sustained worldwide inflation.

117

china

Communism in postwar China had different roots from that in the Soviet bloc and followed a very different course. When in 1945 the war with Japan ended, U.S. negotiators tried to effect a reconciliation between the nationalist leader, Chiang Kai-shek, and the communist Mao Tse-tung. The following spring, when Soviet forces evacuated Manchuria, a full-scale civil war broke out between communists and nationalists.

Early victories persuaded Chiang that he could smash communism. In April 1948 he was appointed president by a new national assembly. The communists worked to achieve the support of the peasantry, and their army swelled in number. In late 1948 the nationalists were defeated in Manchuria, and by September 1949 the nationalist cause had collapsed. Mao Tse-tung became head of a new communist republic in October 1949. Chiang fled to Taiwan.

In 1949 the Communist Party set up a "democratic dictatorship" under Mao. Although other parties were tolerated, the communists dominated. The 4.5 million party members grew to 17.5 million in 1961 (and 46 million in 1988). The first priority was agriculture. In September 1950 an Agrarian Reform Law was announced, under which 300 million peasants benefited from the redistribution of 700 million *mou* (equal to one-sixth of an acre) of landlord estates. By 1957 the villages were collectivized, pooling resources but retaining private ownership. The slow pace of change encouraged Mao to gamble on what became known as the Great Leap Forward. Launched in February 1958, it was a program to modernize China in three years, based around the Maoist concept of the people's commune. By November 1958 the countryside was organized into 26,000 communes, each responsible for abolishing private ownership and charged with delivering

1 When the communists came to power in China the economy was badly damaged by 12 years of war and civil war. Mao initiated a forced state-led industrialization (map below), based on Five-Year Plans. The first from 1953-7 was overfulfilled; a second plan, even more ambitious, ran from 1958 to 1962. China's GNP doubled in the 1950s, and increased by one-third again in the 1960s. Growth slowed down as a result of the social upheavals of the 1960s. Steel output rose from 1.5 million tons in 1952 to 18.6 million tons in 1960, but by 1976 the figure was only 21 million. Not until after Mao's death did China begin a sustained period of economic development.

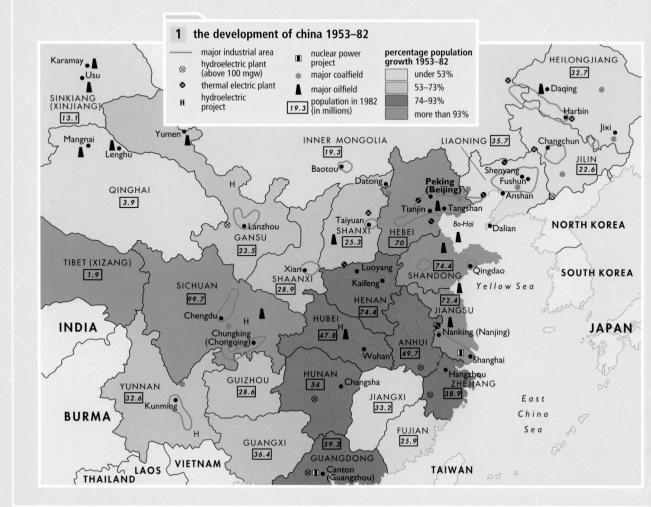

1 the development of china 1953–82

- —— major industrial area
- ⊗ hydroelectric plant (above 100 mgw)
- ⊗ thermal electric plant
- H hydroelectric project
- ▯ nuclear power project
- ● major coalfield
- ▲ major oilfield
- 19.3 population in 1982 (in millions)

percentage population growth 1953–82
- under 53%
- 53–73%
- 74–93%
- more than 93%

2 After the defeat of Japan the Chinese nationalists and the Chinese communists competed for the administration of the liberated areas (map below). The communists dominated Manchuria and the north. In 1947 full-scale civil war broke out between the two sides. Nationalist armies were defeated in Manchuria in 1948, and at Suchow from November 1948 to January 1949. In October 1949 a communist republic was proclaimed, and in May 1950 the nationalist remnants fled to Taiwan.

immense (and entirely unrealistic) increases in agricultural and industrial output. It was the age of the "backyard furnace," when 600,000 miniature blast furnaces were set up across China's villages and towns.

The Great Leap Forward was a grotesque failure: economic output declined sharply; a severe famine killed 20 million. Mao, who had stood down as chairman of the republic in 1959 to concentrate on developing his ideological input to the revolution, found himself isolated by moderate elements in the party, led by Liu Shao-ch'i, who wanted to replace Maoist utopias with socialist realism on the Soviet model. In 1961, despite Mao's fears that the Party was being taken over by a bureaucratic, revisionist elite, the Great Leap Forward was abandoned.

Undeterred, in 1966, in alliance with the army and its leader, Lin Piao, Mao introduced a second revolutionary wave. Supported by enthusiastic young communists who shared Mao's fear that the revolutionary tide was ebbing, and who faithfully followed The Thoughts of Chairman Mao (a collection of Mao's revolutionary beliefs, distributed by the million), Mao encouraged violent rooting out of deviationists. His wife, Chiang Ch'ing, led the Cultural Revolutionary Committee. It was responsible for imposing Maoist conformity and committed endless atrocities in the name of ideological purity.

In 1968 the violence was threatening the complete collapse of Chinese life. Lin Piao was called on by Mao to restore order. The following year a party congress unanimously elected Mao party chairman and The Thoughts of Chairman Mao were adopted as the official party line. Lin Piao was groomed as Mao's successor and the army came to play a prominent part in national politics. Once again Mao feared for his political position. In 1970 he isolated Lin politically, and in 1971 foiled an attempted military coup, which ended with Lin Piao's death in September in a plane crash in Outer Mongolia. Mao, now a sick man, was unable to prevent his young and ambitious wife and her allies on the Cultural Revolutionary Committee from continuing a radical Maoist course. When Mao died on September 9, 1976, Chiang and her "Gang of Four" tried to seize control of the state.

By 1976 the army and much of the elite had had enough of ultraleftism. Chiang and her coconspirators were arrested, tried, and expelled from the party. A more moderate leadership, keen to pursue economic modernization, emerged under Hua Guofeng. Thanks to détente with the U.S., which in October 1971 led to China's entry to the United Nations, China was able to base her modernization on closer links with the international community. In 1978 the Cultural Revolution was officially declared at an end. In the 1980s China began to unravel the legacy of Maoist oppression and economic mismanagement.

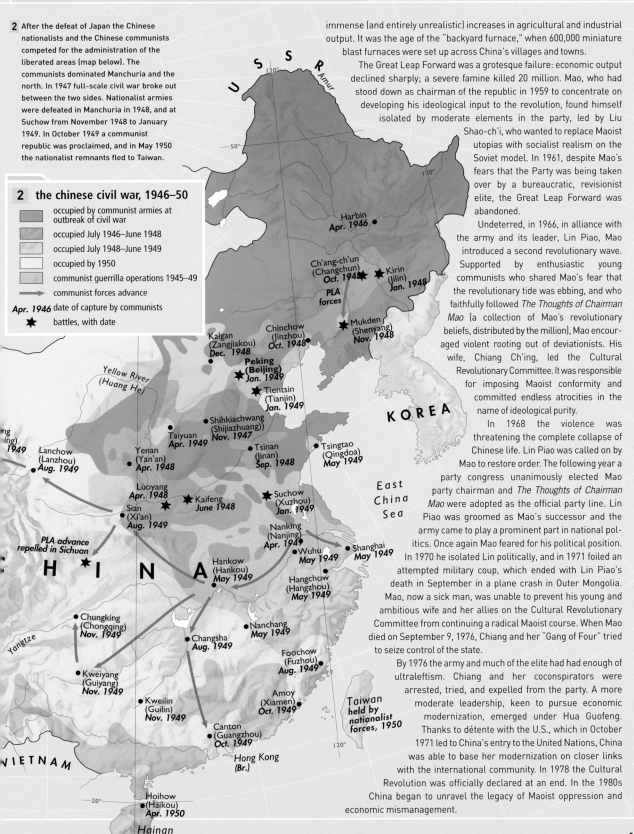

2 the chinese civil war, 1946–50

- occupied by communist armies at outbreak of civil war
- occupied July 1946–June 1948
- occupied July 1948–June 1949
- occupied by 1950
- communist guerrilla operations 1945–49
- communist forces advance
- Apr. 1946 date of capture by communists
- ★ battles, with date

119

the cold war in asia

1946 beginning of Vietnamese struggle against France

1950 Korean War begins (to 1953)

1954 Vietnam partitioned after French defeat

1955 Bandung Conference

1959 war between North and South Vietnam (to 1975)

1961 increasing U.S. involvement in Vietnam

1973 U.S. forces withdraw from South Vietnam

1975 communists take over Vietnam, Laos, and Cambodia

China was not the only area to come under communist control following the collapse of the Japanese empire. In Korea, which was divided in 1945 between Soviet and U.S. occupation forces, a communist regime was installed in the Soviet north in September 1948. In South East Asia, under the influence of Maoist theory on mobilizing the peasant masses, communism was established in northern Vietnam by 1954 and extended to the whole of Indo-China by 1975.

In June 1950, confident that the United States would not intervene after it had withdrawn its forces in June 1949, North Korea invaded the south. After early victories communist forces were driven back to the Chinese frontier by a United Nations force supplied from 20 states but largely made up of U.S. troops. A Chinese counterattack, which reached beyond Seoul by January 1951, threatened to turn the Korean conflict into a major war. When UN forces pushed the Chinese back to the original frontier between north and south, U.S. President Truman accepted a Soviet suggestion for talks. After two years an armistice was finally signed, leaving the two states where they had been in 1950 except for 1,500 square miles granted to the south.

In South East Asia Vietnam became the focus of communist activity. In 1946 Vietnamese communists under Ho Chi Minh (the Vietminh) declared a Democratic Republic of Vietnam, but the French were determined to reimpose colonial control. In November 1946 French forces bombarded Ho's capital, in Hanoi, killing 6,000 people. The Vietminh launched a guerrilla war against the French which ended in May 1954 in a spectacular French defeat at Dien Bien Phu. Under agreements reached in Geneva in July 1954, a communist state was established north of the 17th parallel, and a pro-American regime under Ngo Dinh Diem set up in the south with its capital at Saigon. Diem ignored the Geneva agreement and refused to hold elections in 1956. The north launched a guerrilla war in 1957, and in 1960, in reaction to the brutal Diem dictatorship, his South Vietnamese opponents set up the National Liberation Front, supported from Hanoi. The NLF, or Vietcong, controlled most of the countryside and were supplied with arms from the north. In 1963 Diem was assassinated by his own generals, and for the next 12 years South Vietnam suffered a harsh and destabilizing civil war.

In 1960 the United States stepped up its assistance to Vietnam, and its support of Laos and Cambodia, two royalist states which won independence from France in 1954. U.S. intervention provoked Hanoi. In 1964 North Vietnamese gunboats fired at U.S. destroyers in the Gulf of Tonking, and Congress passed a resolution which virtually amounted to a declaration of war. For nine years U.S. military help kept alive the feeble pro-Western regimes in South Vietnam, Laos, and Cambodia. When the U.S. finally withdrew the whole region fell to popular peasant-based communism. Vietnam was united in April 1975 following the fall of Saigon.

Cambodia (Kampuchea) came under the control of the communist Khmer Rouge, led by Pol Pot. Inspired by Mao's Cultural Revolution, he launched a campaign of extermination against enemies of the party. One-fifth of the population, mainly urban, was slaughtered. In December 1978 Vietnam, which was closely aligned with the Soviet Union, invaded Cambodia and drove Pol Pot from power. China, which disliked Soviet support for Vietnam and Hanoi's policy of discrimination against its Chinese minority, invaded Vietnam in January 1979, but was forced to retreat. Vietnamese communism predominated throughout Indo-China, but political and racial conflict persisted into the 1990s.

3 vietnam, 1966–68

areas of control, early 1966

- controlled by the Vietcong
- under Vietcong influence
- controlled by the South Vietnamese government
- under government influence
- heavily contested areas
- ✳ Tet offensive, 1968

7th U.S. fleet 1964

2 korea, 1950–53

2 After the defeat of Japan in 1945 Korea was occupied by Soviet and U.S. forces who divided the peninsula along the 38th parallel. In 1948 both sides established regimes sympathetic to their interests: a communist north under Kim Il Sung; and a pro-Western south under Syngman Rhee. In June 1950 the north launched a surprise attack on the south (map above). A United Nations force, composed chiefly of U.S. troops and aircraft, and led by General MacArthur, drove the communist forces back to the Chinese border, but were then attacked by a force of 200,000 Chinese troops in October 1950. U.S. forces lost 33,000 men. In June 1951 negotiations began, and two years later the old frontier on the 38th parallel was restored and a demilitarized zone created between the two states.

3 In 1954 agreement was reached in Geneva between the French government and Vietnamese insurgents on the independence of Vietnam. It was divided on the 17th parallel between a communist north and pro-Western south. From 1957 guerrilla war was waged in the south by communist forces, which led in 1960 to large-scale U.S. assistance. The South Vietnamese government controlled the urban areas, the guerrillas most of the countryside (map left). In 1968 the guerrillas launched the "Tet" offensive against the cities which prompted gradual U.S. withdrawal. In 1973 U.S. troops left Vietnam altogether and two years later the whole country was united under communist rule.

www.fact-index.com/d/di/division_of_korea.html
Background to the division of Korea in 1945
www.english.uiuc.edu/maps/vietnam/causes.htm
The causes of the Vietnam War

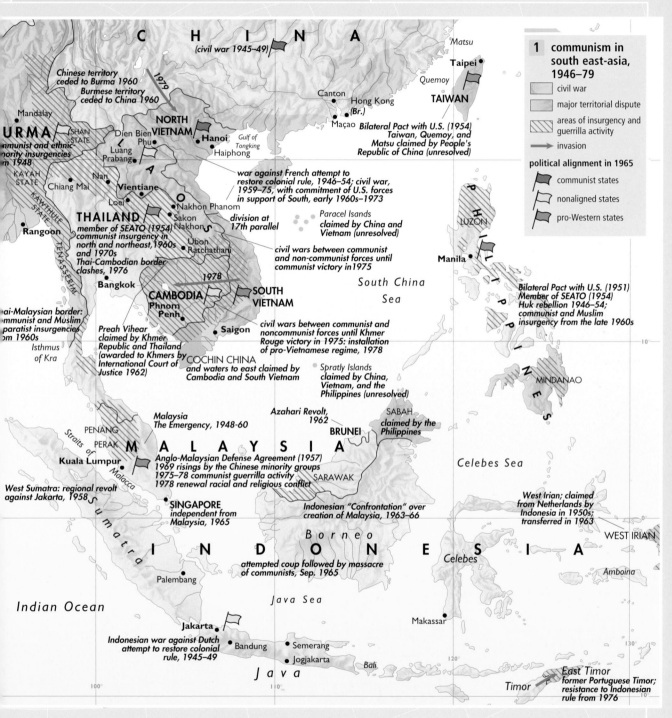

1 communism in south east-asia, 1946–79

- civil war
- major territorial dispute
- areas of insurgency and guerrilla activity
- → invasion

political alignment in 1965
- communist states
- nonaligned states
- pro-Western states

CHINA (civil war 1945–49)

Chinese territory ceded to Burma 1960
Burmese territory ceded to China 1960

1979

Mandalay

BURMA
communist and ethnic minority insurgencies from 1948

SHAN STATE

KAYAH STATE

KAWTHULE STATE

Chiang Mai

Nan

Loei

Rangoon

TENASSERIM

THAILAND
member of SEATO (1954)
communist insurgency in north and northeast, 1960s and 1970s
Thai-Cambodian border clashes, 1976

Isthmus of Kra

Thai-Malaysian border: communist and Muslim separatist insurgencies from 1960s

Bangkok

Dien Bien Phu

Luang Prabang

Vientiane

L A O S

Nakhon Phanom

Sakon Nakhon

Ubon Ratchathani

1978

CAMBODIA
Phnom Penh

Preah Vihear claimed by Khmer Republic and Thailand (awarded to Khmers by International Court of Justice 1962)

NORTH VIETNAM
Hanoi

Haiphong

Gulf of Tongking

war against French attempt to restore colonial rule, 1946–54; civil war, 1959–75, with commitment of U.S. forces in support of South, early 1960s–1973

division at 17th parallel

civil wars between communist and non-communist forces until communist victory in 1975

SOUTH VIETNAM

Saigon

COCHIN CHINA
and waters to east claimed by Cambodia and South Vietnam

civil wars between communist and noncommunist forces until Khmer Rouge victory in 1975: installation of pro-Vietnamese regime, 1978

Canton

Hong Kong (Br.)

Macao

Bilateral Pact with U.S. (1954) Taiwan, Quemoy, and Matsu claimed by People's Republic of China (unresolved)

Matsu

Taipei

Quemoy

TAIWAN

Paracel Isands claimed by China and Vietnam (unresolved)

South China Sea

Spratly Islands claimed by China, Vietnam, and the Philippines (unresolved)

P H I L I P P I N E S

LUZON

Manila

Bilateral Pact with U.S. (1951) Member of SEATO (1954) Huk rebellion 1946–54; communist and Muslim insurgency from the late 1960s

MINDANAO

Malaysia The Emergency, 1948-60

Azahari Revolt, 1962

BRUNEI

SABAH claimed by the Philippines

PENANG

PERAK

Straits of Malacca

M A L A Y S I A

Kuala Lumpur

Anglo-Malaysian Defense Agreement (1957)
1969 risings by the Chinese minority groups
1975–78 communist guerrilla activity
1978 renewal racial and religious conflict

SARAWAK

Indonesian "Confrontation" over creation of Malaysia, 1963–66

Celebes Sea

West Irian; claimed from Netherlands by Indonesia in 1950s; transferred in 1963

WEST IRIAN

West Sumatra: regional revolt against Jakarta, 1958

S u m a t r a

SINGAPORE independent from Malaysia, 1965

Palembang

B o r n e o

I N D O N E S I A

Celebes

Amboina

attempted coup followed by massacre of communists, Sep. 1965

Java Sea

Indian Ocean

Jakarta

Bandung

Semerang

Jogjakarta

Bali

J a v a

Makassar

Timor

East Timor former Portuguese Timor; resistance to Indonesian rule from 1976

Indonesian war against Dutch attempt to restore colonial rule, 1945–49

1 Throughout South East Asia native communist movements fought against the restoration of colonial rule after 1945 (map above). The communist guerrilla war was defeated in Malaya in 1960, and communism suppressed in Indonesia and the Philippines in the 1960s. In Indochina communism achieved power in North Vietnam in 1954, but it took until 1975 before the communists controlled South Vietnam. The same year communist guerrillas in Cambodia, the Khmer Rouge, seized control with Chinese backing, and in Laos the communist Pathet Lao movement overthrew a coalition government. Vietnam, with Soviet support, extended its influence first into Laos in July 1977, then invaded Cambodia (Kampuchea) in December 1978. The United States tried to contain communism in Cambodia by heavy bombing of its capital, Phnomh Penh in 1973 (above). After U.S. withdrawal government troops proved unable to resist the Khmer guerrillas, who were drawn largely from the Cambodian peasantry. The Khmer Rouge defeated the pro-American regime in April 1975 and imposed a savage rule.

the **retreat** from **empire**

The Second World War created opportunities for communism, but it sounded the death knell for colonialism. By 1945 the Italian, Japanese, and German empires were destroyed.

The colonies of East Asia had been overrun by the Japanese and local nationalists were unwilling to return to colonial dependence. Neither the United States nor the Soviet Union was willing to tolerate the survival of an unreformed imperialism. Only the British empire, one of the major victors in 1945, survived relatively intact, and it was here, paradoxically, that the greatest concessions were extracted in the first postwar decade.

In India the war years ended the brief experiment in partial self-government begun in 1937. The nationalist Congress refused to participate in the war effort on the grounds that they had not been consulted about India's declaration of war on Germany. Members began a "Quit India"

campaign which led to their arrest and imprisonment. By the end of the war it was clear to the British that they could not hold onto India on prewar terms. A broad Muslim movement, backed by a 1940 League of Nations resolution approving a separate state for India's Islamic population, called for partition. Congress reluctantly agreed and two states—India and Pakistan—were granted independence on August 15, 1947.

In Britain's other Asian possessions there was a threat from nationalists and communists, inspired by Mao's example in China. In Malaya a long counterinsurgency war defeated the communists but brought the more moderate nationalist elements independence in 1957. In Burma, which had

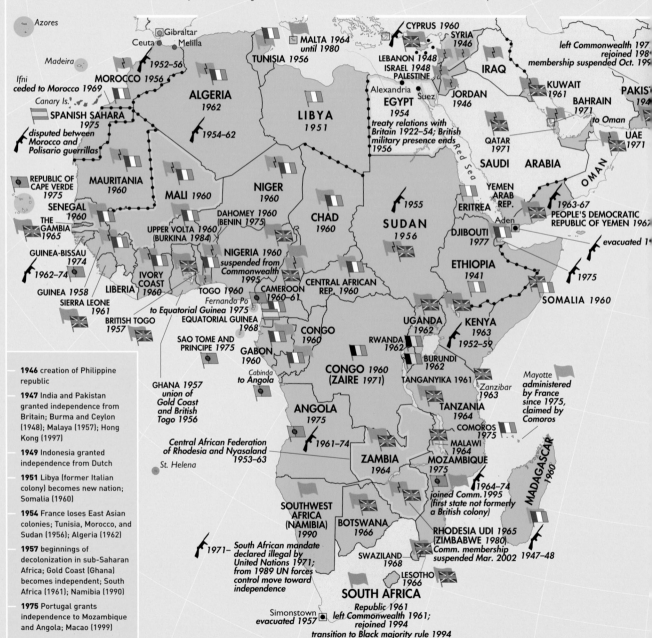

- **1946** creation of Philippine republic
- **1947** India and Pakistan granted independence from Britain; Burma and Ceylon (1948); Malaya (1957); Hong Kong (1997)
- **1949** Indonesia granted independence from Dutch
- **1951** Libya (former Italian colony) becomes new nation; Somalia (1960)
- **1954** France loses East Asian colonies; Tunisia, Morocco, and Sudan (1956); Algeria (1962)
- **1957** beginnings of decolonization in sub-Saharan Africa; Gold Coast (Ghana) becomes independent; South Africa (1961); Namibia (1990)
- **1975** Portugal grants independence to Mozambique and Angola; Macao (1999)

www.fordham.edu/halsall/mod/modsbook51.html
Decolonization from 1945
www.hyperhistory.net/apwh/essays/comp/cw31decolonizationafricasamerica.htm
Decolonization in Latin America and Africa

been occupied by the Japanese and granted a puppet government, British rule was violently rejected and independence was granted in 1948. The French and Dutch faced the same problems in the Far East. The Netherlands never regained control of the Dutch Indies after the Japanese left and independence was formally achieved in 1949. France attempted to pursue a strategy of assimilation with the metropolitan power, or the granting of associated status, to remove the stigma of colonial control. French rule was nonetheless rejected in Indo-China. The restored administration in Vietnam found itself in head-on confrontation with a mass communist and nationalist movement. Military defeat in 1954 at Dien Bien Phu (see page 120) persuaded French leaders to abandon the Far Eastern empire altogether.

The occupation of French North African colonies by British and American forces during the war also created problems when French rule was restored. Tunisia and Morocco were given independence in 1956. After eight years of brutal civil war between French settlers, Algerian nationalists and Islamic insurgents, and the French army, the French president, Charles de Gaulle, ended the conflict in 1962 by granting Algeria full independence rather than risk civil war at home. Italy's former possessions were placed under the United Nations: Libya became a new nation in 1951, Somalia in 1960. In the Middle East Britain abandoned Palestine, which formed the core of the new State of Israel set up in 1948. Civil wars in Cyprus and Aden precipitated British withdrawal in 1960 and 1967. In 1968 the British government announced the end of a British presence east of Suez.

In sub-Saharan Africa there were fewer challenges to European rule. Economic problems in Europe encouraged a vigorous exploitation of African resources, while in eastern and southern Africa there were large white settler communities anxious to obstruct the black independence movements. But here too violence forced the hand of the colonial powers. The Gold Coast was freed in 1957, Nigeria in 1960. The bloody Mau-Mau rebellion in Kenya was followed by independence for Kenya and Tanganyika by 1964 and, in central Africa, for Nyasaland (Malawi) and northern Rhodesia (Zambia). Belgium withdrew from the Congo in 1960, and France from its tropical African possessions between 1958 and 1960. Portugal was the last state to abandon empire. After a bitter guerrilla war Angola and Mozambique freed themselves from Portuguese rule by 1975. With the loss of the most significant colonial areas empire was at an end, leaving in its wake a legacy of political instability, religious and tribal conflict, impoverishment and oppression. Only a few of the new states were untouched by violence.

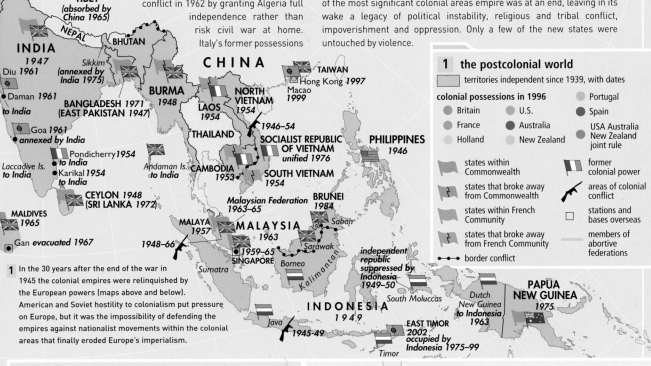

1 the postcolonial world

☐ territories independent since 1939, with dates

colonial possessions in 1996
- ● Britain
- ○ France
- ○ Holland
- ● U.S.
- ● Australia
- ○ New Zealand
- ● Portugal
- ● Spain
- ● USA Australia New Zealand joint rule

- states within Commonwealth
- states that broke away from Commonwealth
- states within French Community
- states that broke away from French Community
- ●–●–● border conflict
- former colonial power
- areas of colonial conflict
- ☐ stations and bases overseas
- members of abortive federations

1 In the 30 years after the end of the war in 1945 the colonial empires were relinquished by the European powers (maps above and below). American and Soviet hostility to colonialism put pressure on Europe, but it was the impossibility of defending the empires against nationalist movements within the colonial areas that finally eroded Europe's imperialism.

1945 to 1967

- **1946** Syria gains independence from France
- **1948** Britain abandons mandate in Palestine; establishment of state of Israel; first Arab-Israeli war
- **1951** Mossadeq nationalizes oil in Iran; military coup (1953)
- **1952** military revolt in Egypt; proclamation of republic (1953)
- **1954** Egyptian King Farouk overthrown; Nasser becomes prime minister
- **1956** Suez crisis; Anglo-French invasion of Canal Zone; Second Arab-Israeli war
- **1958** U.S. forces intervene in Lebanon; United Arab Republic founded (Syria and Egypt); Kassem overthrows republic in Iraq
- **1964** Palestinian Liberation Organization set up

The Middle East was the most unstable of the postimperial regions after 1945. Ever since the collapse of Ottoman power in the early part of the century, the ambition of the Arab peoples had been to create new Arab nation-states.

Arab nationalism produced an independent Iraq in 1932, and in 1936 an Egyptian state was established, although with a continued British military presence. The same year the French agreed to relinquish their mandate over Syria within three years. These gains were consolidated after 1945: Syria and Lebanon won full independence in 1945 and 1946; Transjordan was granted independence in March 1946; Libya in 1951. In 1951 Egypt abandoned the 1936 treaty with Britain and a schedule for the withdrawal of British troops was agreed. Despite efforts to keep a European military presence in an area of strategic concern to the West, by 1956 the Arab region was genuinely independent of European power.

The most intractable issue of all was the future of the Palestine mandate, granted to Britain by the League of Nations in 1920. Arab nationalists saw this as Arab land, and demanded its independence. But in November 1917 the British politician Arthur Balfour had published a declaration committing Britain to provide the Jewish people with a homeland in the Palestine region. The world Zionist organization, set up in the 1890s, wanted Britain to honor this pledge. As a result, in the 1930s the British administration found itself caught between a militant Arab nationalism, inspired by the idea of *jihad*, or holy war, and Jewish demands for a homeland. In 1937 Jewish activists set up Irgun Zvai Leumi (National Military Organization). In 1940 Abraham Stern founded the Fighters for the Freedom of Israel. Both groups undertook acts of terrorism against Arab and British targets. By 1945 there were 100,000 British troops in Palestine to resist the threat.

Reviled by both sides, the British struggled to maintain order. In July 1946 the King David Hotel in Jerusalem was blown up by Jewish terrorists and 91 killed. Public opinion in Britain turned against maintaining the mandate. In 1947 Britain asked the UN to resolve the issue, and on November 29, 1947 a UN resolution divided Palestine into a Jewish and an Arab state. Britain withdrew in haste in May 1948, as Jewish militia laid siege to Jaffa and Jerusalem. On May 14th, David Ben-Gurion declared the foundation of the State of Israel and became its first prime minister, with Chaim Weizmann, leader of the world Zionist movement, as Israel's first president.

The following day the new state was invaded from Syria, Transjordan, and Egypt, and by an Arab volunteer force. After fierce fighting a ceasefire was arranged early in 1949. Between 600,000 and 750,000 Palestinians became refugees, crowded into the Gaza Strip and the West Bank. Transjordan annexed the West Bank and the Arab state of Palestine disappeared. An uneasy truce followed. The Arab states were never reconciled to Israel's survival, which owed a good deal to American support. Terrorist attacks on Israel continued until in October 1956, with British and French support, Israel invaded the Sinai Peninsula and defeated the Egyptian forces there. Under strong international pressure Israel withdrew, but the peninsula was placed under a UN force and demilitarized.

There followed a decade of uneasy peace. Israel's Arab neighbors embarked on programs of economic modernization or political reform. Egypt and Syria established a United Arab Republic in 1958 as the core of a broader Arabist movement, but Arab unity proved skin-deep. The Republic broke up in 1961. A radical regime established in Iraq in 1958 under Abdel-karim Kassem threatened the independence of Kuwait in 1961 until restrained by the other Arab states. In Yemen a civil war between monarchists and republicans divided the Arab camp still more. Saudi Arabia backed the monarchists, Egypt the republicans. Nasser's attempt to place himself at the head of a broader Arab movement foundered on local nationalism and division between the royalist regimes (Saudi Arabia, Jordan, Libya) and more radical republican movements.

Nasser made one last attempt to revive the Pan-Arabist movement. Egypt and Syria cultivated close ties with the Soviet Union in the late 1960s, which furnished them with military advice and modern weaponry. Nasser hoped to use the relationship as a lever to complete the extinction of Israel, but instead he prompted strong American military assistance to Israel and the anti-Soviet Arab states, and yet further divisions in the Arab camp. In May 1967 Nasser demanded the removal of the UN peacekeeping force in Sinai, which soon followed. He then cut Israel off from sea routes to the Gulf of Aqaba. The absence of an Israeli response was interpreted as a sign of weakness. Nasser called for a final reckoning with Zionism.

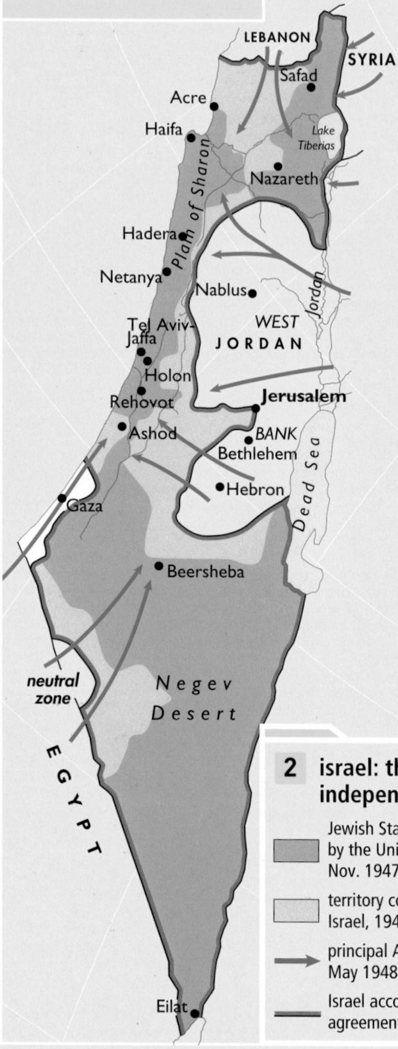

2 israel: the war of independence, 1948

- Jewish State as proposed by the United Nations, Nov. 1947
- territory conquered by Israel, 1948–49
- principal Arab attacks, May 1948
- Israel according to armistice agreements, 1949

2 Following the declaration of an independent Jewish State of Israel on May 14, 1948, forces from the surrounding Arab states invaded former Palestine to reestablish Arab claims to the area (map left). After seven months of war, a ceasefire was agreed with the Palestinians. Subsequent agreements left Israel with 21 percent more land than she had controlled in 1948.

1 Between the 1930s and the 1960s the Middle East and North Africa freed themselves from European rule and established independent Arab states (map right), with the exception of the Jewish State of Israel, founded in 1948. The region has been constantly unstable, first because of anti-European and anti-Israeli conflicts, later because of the importance of Arab oil and the rise of militant Islamic movements throughout the region.

www.mideastweb.org/mandate.htm
The Palestine Mandate of the League of Nations
www.globalsecurity.org/military/world/war/israel-inde.htm
The Israeli war of independence

1 the middle east starting in 1945

→ invasion   ✊ guerrilla activity
✴ major conflicts

1969 Increase in Palestinian guerrilla activity
1975 Lebanese civil war breaks out
1976 Syrian invasion
1978 Israeli invasion
1982 Attack on Beirut by Israel
1985 Formal withdrawal of Israeli troops
1992 Christians boycott first elections for 20 years
2002 Israeli forces withdraw from buffer zone in South Lebanon

1963–74 Intermittent intercommunal clashes
1974 Turkish invasion and occupation of northern part of island

1946 Withdrawal of French troops
1958–61 Union with Egypt (United Arab Republic)
1963 Ba'th Party seizes power
1967 Six Day War; Syria loses Golan Heights
1970 General Hafiz al-Assad seizes power
1973 October (Yom Kippur) War; Syria and Egypt attack Israel; Syrian forces expelled from Golan Heights and Israeli forces occupy Syrian territory
1976 Syrian forces intervene in Lebanese civil war
1980 Treaty of Friendship and Cooperation with USSR
1991 Peace made with Lebanon
2000 Death of President Hafiz al-Asad, succeeded by his son Bashir al-Asad

1955 Anti-Soviet Baghdad Pact
1958 Hashemite dynasty overthrown in military coup power seized by General Abdel-karim Kassem
1963 Kassem overthrown in military coup
1968 Ba'th Party seizes power
1972–75 Intermittent fighting between Kurds and government
1974–75 Iraq-Iran War; Iran withdraws support from Kurds; Kurdish rebellion collapses
1979 Saddam Hussein becomes president
1980–88 Iran-Iraq War
1990 Invasion of Kuwait by Iraq
1991 UN coalition expels Iraqi army from Kuwait; Shia and Kurdish rebels attempt overthrow of Saddam; massive reprisals ordered by Saddam; Western sanctions imposed; de facto independent Kurdish state established in north
1991–98 Western sanctions remain in place. UN weapons inspectors seek to locate and neutralize Iraqi weapons of mass destruction
1998 UN weapons inspectors withdraw. Operation "Desert Fox": large-scale airstrikes against Iraq
2002 UN weapons inspectors return to Iraq
2003 U.S.-led forces invade and overthrow Saddam
2003–04 Continuing insurgency against U.S. coalition forces

TURKEY

● Aleppo
Hama ●
SYRIA
Euphrates
Beirut ●
CYPRUS
LEBANON
Damascus ●
ISRAEL
Jerusalem ●   ● Amman
Cairo ●
EGYPT
JORDAN

IRAQ
Baghdad ●
Tigris

● Teheran
I R A N

1941 Abdication of Shah Reza Pahlavi following Anglo-Russian occupation of Iran; his son Mohammed Reza Pahlavi becomes Shah
1951 Nationalization of oil industry; deterioration in relations with UK
1953–54 Prime Minister Mossadeq becomes de facto ruler; the Shah flees but is later reinstated by royalist military forces with covert U.S. support; oil dispute settled
1961 Shah declares "White Revolution"
1975 Algiers Agreement with Iraq acknowledges Iran's supremacy in Gulf
1978–79 Revolution; the Shah is exiled; Ayatollah Khomeini returns from exile; Iran becomes an Islamic Republic
1980–88 Iran-Iraq War
1989 Khomeini dies, Rafsanjani president
1995 U.S. imposes economic sanctions
1997 Moderate Khatami elected president
2001 Khatami reelected president
2004 Reformists defeated in parliamentary elections

1952 Accession of King Hussein
1970 Attempted destruction of PLO by Jordanian Army (Black September)
1990 King Hussein refuses to join coalition against Iraq
1994 Peace accord and full diplomatic relations with Israel
1999 Death of King Hussein

Kuwait ●
KUWAIT

1990 Invaded by Iraq; Gulf Crisis
1991 Liberated by UN coalition forces

Persian Gulf

BAHRAIN   **QATAR**
Doha ●
Abu Dhabi ●
UAE
● Muscat

1971 Created from former British-protected Trucial States after British evacuation

48 Leads Arab coalition against Israel
52 Monarchy overthrown; military ~~g~~overnment led by Nasser after 1952
56 Nationalization of Suez Canal ~~Co~~mpany; tripartite invasion by Britain, ~~Fra~~nce, Israel
58–61 Union with Syria (United Arab Republic)
67,1973 Wars with Israel
70 Nasser dies; Sadat becomes president
79 Egyptian-Israeli peace treaty
81 Sadat assassination; Mubarak becomes ~~pre~~sident
89 Egypt readmitted to Arab League
90 Egypt sends troops to anti-Iraq coalition

Nile

SAUDI ARABIA
● Riyadh
Medina ●

1951 Mutual Defence Assistance Agreement with U.S.
1960 Organization of Petroleum Exporting Countries formed
1981 Gulf Cooperation Council formed (with Bahrain, Kuwait, Oman, Qatar, and UAE)
1973 Saudi Arabia embargos oil exports to U.S.; oil price soars
1990 Base for UN Coalition attacks against Iraq
1992 Tentative steps toward political openess
1996 King Fahd temporarily steps down

Red Sea
● Mecca

OMAN

1965–75 Marxist insurgency by People's Democratic Republic of Yemen defeated with British and Iranian help
1970 Accession of Sultan Qaboos
1999 "Basic Statues of the State" promulgated; Oman's first written constitution

S U D A N

53 Anglo-Egyptian agreement on ending British ~~co~~ndominium of 1899
56 Sudan gains independence
58 Coup by General Ibrahim Abboud
63–72 Civil war between Arab Muslim rulers in north ~~an~~d Christian and animist Africans in south
69 Abboud deposed; Colonel Gaafar Mohammed Nimeiri seizes power
83 Civil war reerupts; food shortages increase
85 Military coup ousts Nimeiri
89 Military coup; National Islamic Front effective control
90–91 Famine worsens; reports military aid from Iran
94–95 Ceasefire between feuding southern ~~an~~ti-government forces
98 U.S. attack suspected chemical weapons plant
99–2001 Parliament suspended
01 Arrest of Hassan al-Turabi, speaker of ~~pa~~rliament and founder of National Islamic Front
03– Civil war continues in Darfur and other ~~we~~stern regions; widespread famine

YEMEN ARAB REPUBLIC
1962–69 Civil war
1972–79 Intermittent war with Aden
San'a ●
● Aden

PEOPLE'S DEMOCRATIC REPUBLIC OF YEMEN
1967 Coup by National Liberation Front; civil war; Britain withdraws troops from Aden
1968 Ali Nasar Muhammad overthrown as president by Haidar al Attas

YEMEN

1948 Assassination of Imam Yahya; his son takes power
1959 Creation of the Arab Emirates of the South (later the Federation of South Arabia)
1962 Civil war and revolution in San'a; Yemen Arab Republic (North Yemen) established
1967 Withdrawal of British forces; declaration of People's Democratic Republic of Yemen (South Yemen)
1990 YAR and PDRY united
1994 Civil war breaks out: Democratic Republic of Yemen declares secession (supressed July)
1999 First direct Presidential elections held; Ali Abdallah Salih elected

40°   30°   50°   60°

125

the middle east

1967 Third Arab-Israeli war (Six Day War)

1968 Saddam Hussein takes power in Iraq

1970 Assad takes power in Syria

1973 Fourth Arab-Israeli war (Yom Kippur); OPEC crisis

1975 civil war in Lebanon; Syria invades (1976)

1977 Egypt-Israeli peace talks (Camp David peace treaty 1978)

1979 fall of Shah of Iran; establishment of Islamic republic under Ayatollah Khomeini

In June 1967 war broke out between Israel and her Arab neighbors but not the war Nasser had expected. Instead the Israeli government, nervous at Nasser's escalation, ordered a preemptive strike. On June 5 the Israeli air force attacked and destroyed the Egyptian air force on the ground. The army occupied the Gaza strip and the Sinai Peninsula in three days. Jordan, Iraq, and Syria rallied to Egypt's support, but their forces were routed in a further three days of fighting.

The West Bank and the Arab half of Jerusalem were seized by Israel from Jordan. The Golan Heights on the Israeli-Syrian border were occupied by Israel on June 10, though not officially annexed until 1982. The war precipitated a new and more serious Palestinian problem. Israel now had almost one million Arabs under her direct rule. Up to 250,000 fled from the West Bank into Jordan. Four hundred thousand refugees lived in Lebanon. In the camps young Palestinians formed armed guerrilla movements dedicated to winning back the areas lost in 1967. The Palestine Liberation Organization (PLO), founded in 1964, assumed leadership of the struggle, and used the camps as a base for a campaign of terrorism directed against Israel.

Within five years the Egyptian threat revived as well. Nasser's successor in 1970, Anwar Sadat, had ambitions to avenge Egypt's humiliation in 1967. In November 1972 he decided to attack Israel, again in collaboration with Syria.

After 11 months of preparation they attacked on October 6, 1973, the Jewish holy day of Yom Kippur. After initial Arab gains in Sinai and on the Golan Heights, Israel successfully counterattacked. An armistice was agreed on October 24th under American and Soviet pressure. Egypt bowed to reality. Agreement was reached with Israel in 1974 and 1975 on

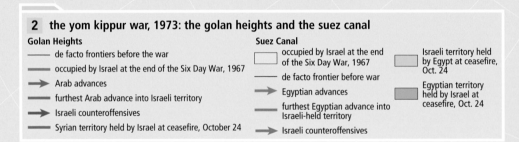

2 the yom kippur war, 1973: the golan heights and the suez canal

Golan Heights

—— de facto frontiers before the war

—— occupied by Israel at the end of the Six Day War, 1967

→ Arab advances

→ furthest Arab advance into Israeli territory

→ Israeli counteroffensives

—— Syrian territory held by Israel at ceasefire, October 24

Suez Canal

☐ occupied by Israel at the end of the Six Day War, 1967

—— de facto frontier before war

→ Egyptian advances

→ furthest Egyptian advance into Israeli-held territory

→ Israeli counteroffensives

☐ Israeli territory held by Egypt at ceasefire, Oct. 24

☐ Egyptian territory held by Israel at ceasefire, Oct. 24

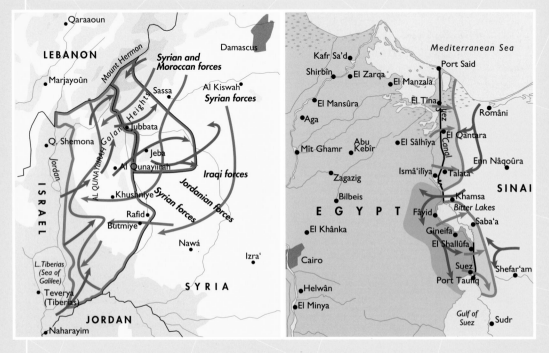

2 The Yom Kippur War, in October 1973, hit Israeli forces with almost complete surprise when Egypt and Syria launched an attack on Israeli-held territory (maps left). The Israeli air force restored the position in the Golan Heights and extended the territory under its military control. When Egyptian forces moved into Sinai away from their missiles' defense system, Israeli air-ground cooperation broke the Egyptian line and brought Israel's army to within 50 miles of Cairo. On October 24th a ceasefire came into operation after the U.S. put its forces on nuclear alert.

www.fsmitha.com/h2/ch28isl.html
A history of Muslim-Israeli conflict to the 1967 War
www.mideastweb.org/briefhistory.htm
A history Israel and Palestine

the disengagement of forces in Sinai and in 1977, despite widespread hostility from the rest of the Arab world, Sadat finally sought a peace settlement. On November 19th he flew to Israel, whose parliament was dominated by the hardline Likud bloc led by Menachem Begin, where he offered to recognize Israel and sign a peace treaty. In September 1978 the two sides met in the U.S. at Camp David, where, in the presence of President Jimmy Carter, Sadat and Begin agreed to peace between their states.

Sadat's move provoked outrage in the Arab world. Egypt was thrown out of the Arab League and exposed to a political and economic boycott. In practice this division simply added one more conflict to an Arab world that was anything but united. Civil war broke out in Jordan in 1970 between Palestinians and King Hussein's army. Despite Syrian assistance for the refugees, hundreds were forcibly expelled. During the 1970s violence briefly flared between Egypt and Libya, between Iran and Iraq, and between Iraq and Syria. In Lebanon divisions between Christians and Muslims, between Lebanese and Palestinians and between Sunni and Shia forms of Islam created a microcosm of the wider tensions in the Arab world. In April 1975 full-scale civil war broke out in Lebanon, and in 1976, anxious about Israeli reaction, Syria occupied Lebanon and introduced an Arab peace-keeping force. In 1978 Israel invaded the south in retaliation against PLO incursions and Lebanon was effectively partitioned.

The Lebanese crisis highlighted a new development in the Middle East: the rise of revolutionary Islam. By the 1970s the Cold War tension between conservative and radical Arab states gave way to a new tension between secular Arab nationalism and Islamic fundamentalism. The Islamic movement dated back to the foundation of the Muslim Brotherhood in 1928, but it was given new life by the failures against Israel in 1967 and 1973. Radical movements spread throughout the Arab world: in 1974 in Lebanon, Imam Musa al-Sadr founded Amal, committed to the violent defence of Shia Islam; in November 1979 a group led by a self-styled Mahdi (messiah) seized the Grand Mosque in Mecca and held it until expelled by Saudi police. Militant Muslims declared a *jihad* (holy war) against Arab secularists and Westernizers and Western "cultural imperialism."

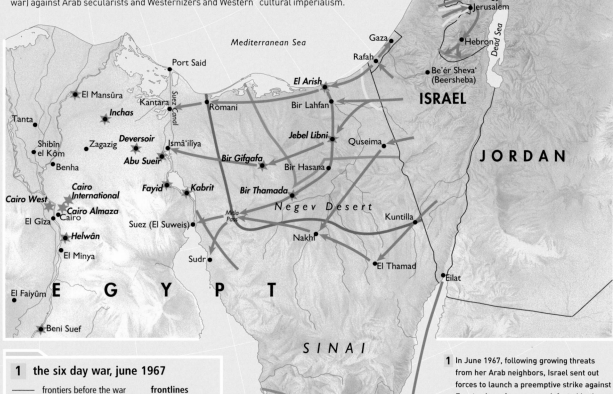

1 the six day war, june 1967

— frontiers before the war
★ Israeli air strikes
→ Israeli advances
⚐ airborne landings

frontlines
June 5
June 6
June 7
June 8
June 9–10

1 In June 1967, following growing threats from her Arab neighbors, Israel sent out forces to launch a preemptive strike against Egypt, whose forces were defeated in three days. Attempts by Syria, Jordan, and Iraq to help Egypt led to the rapid defeat of their forces (map above), and a fivefold increase in the territory under Israeli control.

africa after independence

1965 Rhodesia declares UDI

1967–70 civil war in Nigeria (secession of Biafra)

1971 Mogadishu declaration

1971 Amin seizes power in Uganda

1977 Bokassa proclaims "Central American Empire"; Bokassa falls (1979)

1979 Tanzanian forces invade Uganda and expel President Amin

1980 Black majority rule established in Zimbabwe (Rhodesia)

1984 famine in Sahel and Ethiopia; continuing war against secession

Most countries in Africa were independent by 1965, but a handful of colonies survived, mainly in southern Africa, where they were dominated by white minority regimes, which held political and economic power. The Portuguese dictatorship regarded its African colonies of Angola, Mozambique, and Guinea-Bissau as integral overseas provinces of the state. The resources of the colonies helped enrich Portugal's weak economy and several hundred thousand Portuguese had settled in Angola and Mozambique. In 1974 a coup in Lisbon overthrew the dictatorship and in the following year the colonies were given their independence. However, in Angola and Mozambique, the nationalist armies fought each other in bitter civil wars.

In 1965 the small white population of Southern Rhodesia, led by Ian Smith, issued a Unilateral Declaration of Independence in the face of opposition from the British government and leaders of the Black majority. A guerrilla war developed which led in 1980 to the abandonment of white rule and the establishment of an independent state led by the Marxist nationalist Robert Mugabe. Namibia (former South West Africa) was occupied by South Africa in defiance of the United Nations. Attacks by nationalist guerrillas from Angola, supported by Cuban troops, dragged South Africa into a border war. Namibia finally gained its independence in 1990.

In South Africa, the most economically developed sub-Saharan state, a policy of separate development (apartheid) had been steadily imposed by the white minority government since 1948. African political activity was repressed and parties such as the African National Congress (ANC) were banned and forced into exile. However, African opposition continued, especially in the expanding urban areas. Opposition also came from the newly independent "Front-line states" and in order to preserve itself the South African regime attacked its northern neighbors in an attempt to destabilize governments and economies. The white regime was faced with growing internal unrest, economic difficulties, and international hostility, which made the maintenance of the system increasingly difficult.

Most new African states inherited weak economies and hastily created parliamentary systems of government. Many were soon subverted by military coups or the creation of one-party or one-man dictatorships. Ethnic and political strife was endemic in the Horn of Africa, in Mozambique, and Angola, but it has punctuated the history of many other African countries since the 1950s: the Congo between 1960 and 1965; Nigeria from 1967 to 1970; the southern Sudan since 1956; and Uganda between 1971 and 1980. Wars and severe drought and famine resulted in large numbers of refugees. These conflicts often became the focus of Cold War rivalries and external intervention.

Compared to the economies of Asia and Latin American countries in the 1970s and 1980s, those of most African states were fragile. They suffered from all the indices of low levels of human well-being: rapid population growth, high infant mortality rates, low levels of life expectancy, and what Julius Nyerere, president of Tanzania, called "poverty, ignorance, and disease." They relied on the export of one or more primary products the demand and price for which were determined in foreign capitals. They were also largely dependent on foreign countries for most of their capital, skills, and manufactured goods. The Cold War states of East and West could use external aid to gain leverage in Africa. This had the unfortunate consequence of mortgaging Africa's economic development to the shifting forces of world politics. In attempts at greater economic and political independence many African states pursued socialist state-directed policies, which invariably failed.

1976 Morocco occupied northern half, and 1979 occupied all W. Sahara 1976–79 Mauritania occupied southern half

Canary Is (Sp.)

WESTERN SAHARA

1963–74 armed resistance to Portuguese rule

MAURITANIA ● Nouakchott

CAPE VERDE ISLANDS `1975`

THE G IS

Senegal

Dakar ● **SENEGAL** `1960`

Banjul **GUINEA-BISSAU** `1974`

Ban

● Bissau

GUINE `19`

Conakry ● Freetown **SIERRA LEONE** `1961`

LIB

Monrovia ● `n/c`

1958 only French colony to vote "Non" in de Gaulle's referendum on independence 1958–84 ruled by Sekou Touré

1980 President Tolbert overthrown by Master Sergeant Doe

1957 first sub-Saharan colony to gain independence 1966 Nkrumah deposed

CENTRAL AFRICAN REPUBLIC
SUDAN

BAMONGO

● Paulis
ORIENTALE · BANGALA
BANGALA
● Stanleyville
EQUATEUR
● Coquilhatville
BAMONGO
UGANDA
Z A I R E
RWANDA
● Kindu
BATETELA · BALUBA (KASAI) · KIVU
BURUNDI
KASAI · BAKUSU
Brazzaville ●
BAKONGO · Léopoldville
LÉOPOLDVILLE
Lake Tanganyika
● Matadi
● Gungu · BENALULA · BASONG
● Albertville
● Luluabourg
BAPENDE
BALUBA (KATANGA) · KATANGA
TANGANYIKA
BALUNDA
● Kamina
BATSHOKWE · BALUNDA
NORTHERN RHODESIA (Zambia 1964)
● Elisabethville

1 africa from independence to 1985 (right)

`1951` date of independence
● coup d'etat
✳ violent insurrection and war
✊ organized guerrilla activity
⚔ border disputes
🏃 refugee movements
— southern limit of Muslim predominance

2 the congo crisis, 1960–65

▢ area of Katanga secession 1960–63
▢ maximum area of rebel advance, 1964
BAKUSU main ethnic groups
● UN troop bases
— railroads
▪ Belgian intervention
✊ centers of 1963–64 rebellion
▽ Belgian paratroop intervention 1964
---- state borders

2 The Congo (Zaire) dissolved into conflict following independence in June 1960 (map left), and a breakaway state of Katanga was set up until UN intervention in 1963. A second revolt in 1964 was suppressed and in 1965 the army seized power.

www.bbc.co.uk/worldservice/africa/features/storyofafrica/index.shtml
All apects of African history
www-sul.stanford.edu/depts/ssrg/africa/history.html
All apects of Africa south of the Sahara

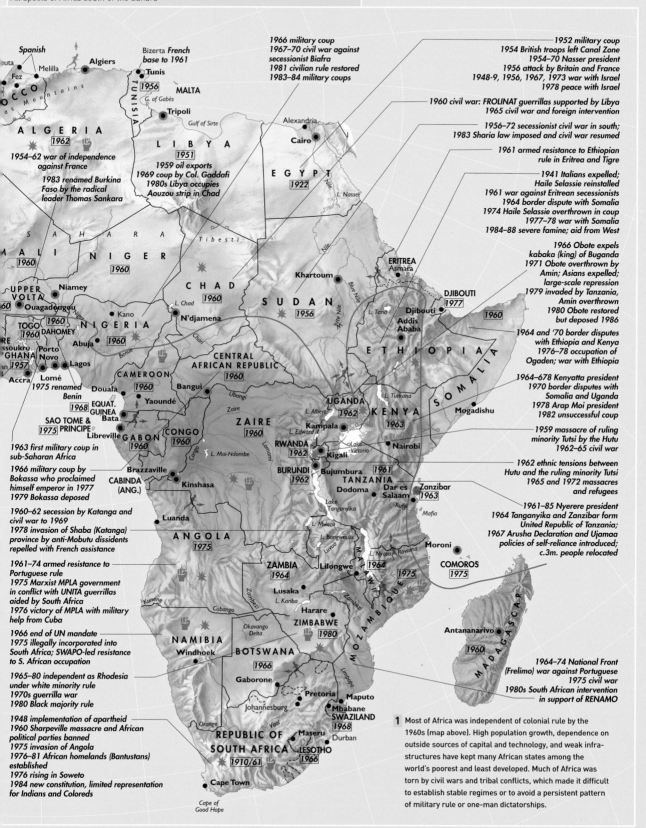

1966 military coup
1967–70 civil war against secessionist Biafra
1981 civilian rule restored
1983–84 military coups

1952 military coup
1954 British troops left Canal Zone
1954–70 Nasser president
1956 attack by Britain and France
1948-9, 1956, 1967, 1973 war with Israel
1978 peace with Israel

1960 civil war: FROLINAT guerrillas supported by Libya
1965 civil war and foreign intervention

1956–72 secessionist civil war in south;
1983 Sharia law imposed and civil war resumed

1961 armed resistance to Ethiopian rule in Eritrea and Tigre

1941 Italians expelled;
Haile Selassie reinstalled
1961 war against Eritrean secessionists
1964 border dispute with Somalia
1974 Haile Selassie overthrown in coup
1977–78 war with Somalia
1984–88 severe famine; aid from West

1966 Obote expels kabaka (king) of Buganda
1971 Obote overthrown by Amin; Asians expelled; large-scale repression
1979 invaded by Tanzania, Amin overthrown
1980 Obote restored but deposed 1986

1964 and '70 border disputes with Ethiopia and Kenya
1976–78 occupation of Ogaden; war with Ethiopia

1964–678 Kenyatta president
1970 border disputes with Somalia and Uganda
1978 Arap Moi president
1982 unsuccessful coup

1959 massacre of ruling minority Tutsi by the Hutu
1962–65 civil war

1962 ethnic tensions between Hutu and the ruling minority Tutsi
1965 and 1972 massacres and refugees

1961–85 Nyerere president
1964 Tanganyika and Zanzibar form United Republic of Tanzania;
1967 Arusha Declaration and Ujamaa policies of self-reliance introduced; c.3m. people relocated

1954–62 war of independence against France

1983 renamed Burkina Faso by the radical leader Thomas Sankara

1951
1959 oil exports
1969 coup by Col. Gaddafi
1980s Libya occupies Aouzou strip in Chad

Bizerta French base to 1961

1975 renamed Benin

1963 first military coup in sub-Saharan Africa

1966 military coup by Bokassa who proclaimed himself emperor in 1977
1979 Bokassa deposed

1960–62 secession by Katanga and civil war to 1969
1978 invasion of Shaba (Katanga) province by anti-Mobutu dissidents repelled with French assistance

1961–74 armed resistance to Portuguese rule
1975 Marxist MPLA government in conflict with UNITA guerrillas aided by South Africa
1976 victory of MPLA with military help from Cuba

1966 end of UN mandate
1975 illegally incorporated into South Africa; SWAPO-led resistance to S. African occupation

1965–80 independent as Rhodesia under white minority rule
1970s guerrilla war
1980 Black majority rule

1948 implementation of apartheid
1960 Sharpeville massacre and African political parties banned
1975 invasion of Angola
1976–81 African homelands (Bantustans) established
1976 rising in Soweto
1984 new constitution, limited representation for Indians and Coloreds

1964–74 National Front (Frelimo) war against Portuguese
1975 civil war
1980s South African intervention in support of RENAMO

1 Most of Africa was independent of colonial rule by the 1960s (map above). High population growth, dependence on outside sources of capital and technology, and weak infra-structures have kept many African states among the world's poorest and least developed. Much of Africa was torn by civil wars and tribal conflicts, which made it difficult to establish stable regimes or to avoid a persistent pattern of military rule or one-man dictatorships.

129

1947 India and Pakistan become independent amid widespread rioting; 500,000 die

1948 Ghandi assassinated; Indo-Pakistan dispute over Kashmir

1956 Pakistan declared Islamic state

1965 Indo-Pakistan war

1971 breakaway of East Pakistan (Bangladesh)

1977 military coup ends democratic rule in Pakistan; General Zia ruler (1978)

1979 Afghanistan invaded by USSR

1984 Indira Ghandi assassinated; renewed Indo-Pakistan conflict over Kashmir

South Asia, like Africa, was faced with the same problems of constructing new modern nation-states when the imperial presence ended in the 1940s. When India and a separate Muslim Pakistan were established as independent states in August 1947, the national frontiers had not even been clearly defined.

The subsequent settlement led to the transfer of as many as 15 million people from one state to the other, and religious conflict between Muslims, Hindus, and Sikhs that may have cost the lives of as many as 500,000 people. The resettlement of the refugees was a major burden on the infant states, and tensions between resident and immigrant communities still persist. In India the new state also had to define the role of the 600 small princely states that survived on the subcontinent. Most joined either India or Pakistan, but the Muslim Nizam of Hyderabad had to be forcibly absorbed into India in 1948. In Kashmir, which was predominantly Muslim but was ruled by Hindus, the two new states fought a war from October 1947 to December 1948, when the UN imposed a ceasefire and divided the area between India and Pakistan. The solution pleased neither side, and a second war in 1965 was also fought on the issue of the frontier, following efforts by Pakistan to infiltrate troops into the Indian-held parts of Kashmir. A peace settlement restoring the status quo was reached in Tashkent, but the Kashmiri region remains an area of friction.

Even within the new states ethnic, religious, and linguistic disputes persisted. In India around ten percent of the postpartition population was Muslim. India also contained 23 major linguistic groups, with Hindi-speakers making up 40 percent of the whole. The Nehru government's attempt to make Hindi the national language was resisted in the Dravidian south. In 1956 the states of India were reorganized along linguistic lines. In the northeast the tribal peoples, led by the Nagas and Mizos, pressed for separate statehood. In the Punjab the rise of militant Sikhism led to demands in the 1980s for an independent Sikh state of Khalistan.

Tensions between the western and eastern halves of Pakistan, brought about by Bengali resentment at their economic and political subordination and their dislike of the military dictatorship imposed in 1958 by General Ayub Khan, led to their partition into two separate states in 1971. In Ceylon, the growing domination of the Buddhist majority provoked hostility from the Hindu Tamils of the north of the island. Though the island was a democracy, 800,000 Tamil laborers were nonetheless disenfranchised as descendants of Indian migrants. During the 1980s Tamil militants sought a separate Tamil state, Eelam, and fought a terrorist war against the Sinhalese authorities, which prompted Indian intervention from 1987 to 1990. In Burma democracy gave way to a socialist military revolution in 1962, and military rule became the norm.

The economic development of the region has been hampered by high population growth, low incomes, and dependence on external sources of capital, technology, and financial aid. Under Nehru India embarked on a series of Five-Year Plans, which helped create a small industrial core but most Indians remained in peasant agriculture or traditional crafts and trades.

1 India and Pakistan embarked on a period of rapid economic modernization and high growth (map right), aided by new crops which made them self-sufficient in basic foodstuffs. Growth has been compromised by rising levels of population and by the presence of deeply held religious and ethnic differences.

3 Two days after Indian and Pakistani independence on August 15, 1947, a Boundary Commission reported on the partition of the Punjab (map below left), recommending a division that forced 6 million Muslims to cross into Pakistan and 4.5 million Sikhs and Hindus to seek refuge in India.

4 The modern state of Bangladesh, formed in 1972 from the eastern half of Pakistan, was the product of the division of Bengal in 1947 (map below right). The largely Muslim province was the home of the Muslim League, set up in 1906 to fight for a separate Muslim identity. Division led to the transfer of 1.6 million Hindus into India, and approximately 1.2 million Muslims from Calcutta and eastern India into East Bengal.

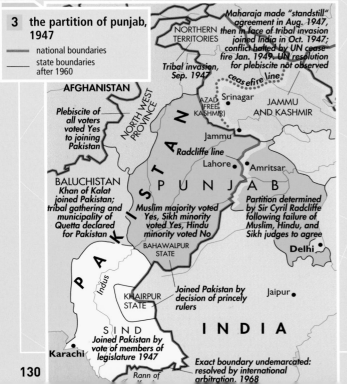

3 the partition of punjab, 1947

— national boundaries
— state boundaries after 1960

Maharaja made "standstill" agreement in Aug. 1947, then in face of tribal invasion joined India in Oct. 1947; conflict halted by UN cease fire Jan. 1949. UN resolution for plebiscite not observed

Tribal invasion, Sep. 1947

NORTHERN TERRITORIES

ceasefire line

Srinagar

AZAD (FREE KASHMIR)

JAMMU AND KASHMIR

AFGHANISTAN

NORTH WEST PROVINCE

Plebiscite of all voters voted Yes to joining Pakistan

Jammu

Radcliffe line

Lahore

Amritsar

BALUCHISTAN
Khan of Kalat joined Pakistan; tribal gathering and municipality of Quetta declared for Pakistan

P U N J A B

Muslim majority voted Yes, Sikh minority voted Yes, Hindu minority voted No

Partition determined by Sir Cyril Radcliffe following failure of Muslim, Hindu, and Sikh judges to agree

BAHAWALPUR STATE

Delhi

P A K I S T A N

Indus

KHAIRPUR STATE

Joined Pakistan by decision of princely rulers

Jaipur

SIND
Joined Pakistan by vote of members of legislature 1947

I N D I A

Karachi

Exact boundary undemarcated: resolved by international arbitration, 1968

Rann of

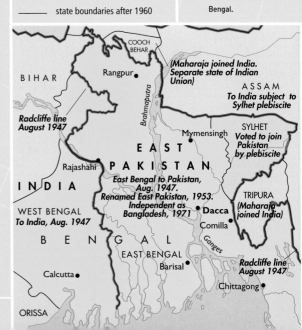

4 east pakistan, 1947–71

— national boundaries
— state boundaries after 1960

COOCH BEHAR

BIHAR

Rangpur

(Maharaja joined India. Separate state of Indian Union)

Brahmaputra

ASSAM
To India subject to Sylhet plebiscite

Radcliffe line August 1947

E A S T P A K I S T A N

Mymensingh

SYLHET
Voted to join Pakistan by plebiscite

Rajashahi

I N D I A

East Bengal to Pakistan, Aug. 1947. Renamed East Pakistan, 1953. Independent as Bangladesh, 1971

Dacca

Comilla

TRIPURA
(Maharaja joined India)

WEST BENGAL
To India, Aug. 1947

B E N G A L

EAST BENGAL

Ganges

Barisal

Calcutta

Radcliffe line August 1947

ORISSA

Chittagong

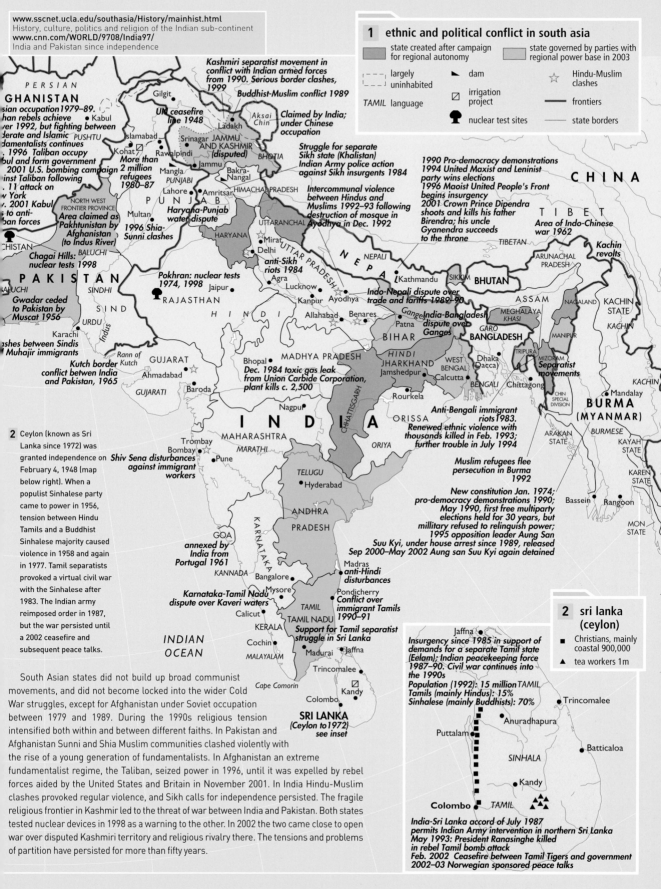

www.sscnet.ucla.edu/southasia/History/mainhist.html
History, culture, politics and religion of the Indian sub-continent
www.cnn.com/WORLD/9708/India97/
India and Pakistan since independence

1 ethnic and political conflict in south asia

- state created after campaign for regional autonomy
- state governed by parties with regional power base in 2003
- - - - largely uninhabited
- TAMIL language
- ◣ dam
- ▨ irrigation project
- ♣ nuclear test sites
- ☆ Hindu-Muslim clashes
- frontiers
- state borders

Kashmiri separatist movement in conflict with Indian armed forces from 1990. Serious border clashes, 1999

Buddhist-Muslim conflict 1989

UN ceasefire line 1948

Claimed by India; under Chinese occupation

Struggle for separate Sikh state (Khalistan) Indian Army police action against Sikh insurgents 1984

Intercommunal violence between Hindus and Muslims 1992–93 following destruction of mosque in Ayodhya in Dec. 1992

1990 Pro-democracy demonstrations
1994 United Maxist and Leninist party wins elections
1996 Maoist United People's Front begins insurgency
2001 Crown Prince Dipendra shoots and kills his father Birendra; his uncle Gyanendra succeeds to the throne

Area of Indo-Chinese war 1962

Kachin revolts

AFGHANISTAN
...sian occupation 1979–89.
...han rebels achieve ...ver 1992, but fighting between ...derate and Islamic ...damentalists continues
...1996 Taliban occupy ...bul and form government
...2001 U.S. bombing campaign ...inst Taliban following ...11 attack on ...w York ...y 2001 Kabul ...s to anti-...ban forces

Chagai Hills: nuclear tests 1998

PAKISTAN

Gwadar ceded to Pakistan by Muscat 1956

...ashes between Sindis ...Muhajir immigrants

Kutch border conflict betwen India and Pakistan, 1965

Area claimed as Pakhtunistan by Afghanistan (to Indus River)

1996 Shia-Sunni clashes

Haryana-Punjab water dispute

More than 2 million refugees 1980–87

anti-Sikh riots 1984

Pokhran: nuclear tests 1974, 1998

Dec. 1984 toxic gas leak from Union Carbide Corporation, plant kills c. 2,500

Indo-Nepali dispute over trade and tariffs 1989–90

India-Bangladesh dispute over Ganges

Anti-Bengali immigrant riots 1983. Renewed ethnic violence with thousands killed in Feb. 1993; further trouble in July 1994

Muslim refugees flee persecution in Burma 1992

Separatist movements

New constitution Jan. 1974; pro-democracy demonstrations 1990; May 1990, first free multiparty elections held for 30 years, but military refused to relinquish power; 1995 opposition leader Aung San Suu Kyi, under house arrest since 1989, released Sep 2000–May 2002 Aung san Suu Kyi again detained

Shiv Sena disturbances against immigrant workers

GOA annexed by India from Portugal 1961

Madras anti-Hindi disturbances

Pondicherry Conflict over immigrant Tamils 1990–91

Karnataka-Tamil Nadu dispute over Kaveri waters

Support for Tamil separatist struggle in Sri Lanka

2 Ceylon (known as Sri Lanka since 1972) was granted independence on February 4, 1948 (map below right). When a populist Sinhalese party came to power in 1956, tension between Hindu Tamils and a Buddhist Sinhalese majority caused violence in 1958 and again in 1977. Tamil separatists provoked a virtual civil war with the Sinhalese after 1983. The Indian army reimposed order in 1987, but the war persisted until a 2002 ceasefire and subsequent peace talks.

SRI LANKA (Ceylon to 1972) see inset

2 sri lanka (ceylon)
- ■ Christians, mainly coastal 900,000
- ▲ tea workers 1m

Insurgency since 1985 in support of demands for a separate Tamil state (Eelam); Indian peacekeeping force 1987–90. Civil war continues into the 1990s
Population (1992): 15 million
Tamils (mainly Hindus): 15%
Sinhalese (mainly Buddhists): 70%

India-Sri Lanka accord of July 1987 permits Indian Army intervention in northern Sri Lanka
May 1993: President Ranasinghe killed in rebel Tamil bomb attack
Feb. 2002 Ceasefire between Tamil Tigers and government
2002–03 Norwegian sponsored peace talks

South Asian states did not build up broad communist movements, and did not become locked into the wider Cold War struggles, except for Afghanistan under Soviet occupation between 1979 and 1989. During the 1990s religious tension intensified both within and between different faiths. In Pakistan and Afghanistan Sunni and Shia Muslim communities clashed violently with the rise of a young generation of fundamentalists. In Afghanistan an extreme fundamentalist regime, the Taliban, seized power in 1996, until it was expelled by rebel forces aided by the United States and Britain in November 2001. In India Hindu-Muslim clashes provoked regular violence, and Sikh calls for independence persisted. The fragile religious frontier in Kashmir led to the threat of war between India and Pakistan. Both states tested nuclear devices in 1998 as a warning to the other. In 2002 the two came close to open war over disputed Kashmiri territory and religious rivalry there. The tensions and problems of partition have persisted for more than fifty years.

latin america

1943 military coup in Argentina: Peron comes to power (1946–55)

1959 Cuban revolution; follows foiled rebellion in 1953

1964 military coup in Brazil

1973 president of Chile assassinated; General Pinochet becomes dictator (to 1988)

1976 military junta takes power in Argentina (to 1982)

1979 civil war in Nicaragua (to 1990) and El Salvador (to 1992)

1983 democracy restored in Argentina following Falklands war (1982)

1983 coup in Grenada; U.S. invades

1985 democracy restored in Brazil and Uruguay

1989–90 U.S. military intervention in Panama; arrest and extradition of Noriega

1992 leader of Peruvian "Shining Path" captured

1994 U.S. invasion of Haiti; exiled leader Aristide returns

2001 start of Argentina's worst ever economic crisis

Latin America after 1945, unaffected by decolonization, pursued its own course. The major issue for all Latin American countries was the drive to industrialize. But where other developing areas became integrated with the long boom in the industrialized world, Latin American states continued the policies of economic nationalism—tariffs, import substitution, state economic management—inherited from the 1930s.

The desire to industrialize presented both economic and political difficulties. Latin American economies had long depended on the export of food and raw material. By shifting to domestic industrialization the regimes tried to limit that traditional export dependence, alienating the rich agrarian elites who controlled the commodity trade. In Colombia a virtual civil war—La Violencia—which left more than 200,000 dead was fought from the 1940s to the 1960s between industrial modernizers and agrarian conservatives. The buildup of industry also needed a strong domestic market, but more than two-thirds of the Latin American population were poor rural workers. Efforts were made starting in the 1940s to redistribute land or to reform agricultural practices, but this generated conflict with the rural elites and in Chile and Peru led to a fall in agricultural output. Millions of peasants moved into the cities, where poor living conditions and soaring unemployment created yet another set of problems.

In the 1960s the high rates of industrial expansion suddenly fell away. State preference for industry led to a decline in export earnings from the traditional commodity trade. Between 1948 and 1960 Latin America's share of world trade fell from 10.3 to 4.8 percent. In 1961 the Kennedy administration launched an Alliance for Progress with Latin America to encourage economic restructuring and social reform, but with escalating inflation (over 46 percent a year in Brazil between 1960 and 1970), high unemployment, and growing class conflict, little was achieved. Rapid urban growth and village decay created the conditions for the spread of communism, which had been a tiny force until the 1960s. Communist reformers, inspired by Castro's revolution in Cuba in 1959, offered an alternative model of state-directed growth and social transformation. Under the twin pressures of economic crisis and revolutionary threat many Latin American states faced political collapse. The limited constitutionalism practiced since 1945 gave way to military rule in Brazil (1964–85), Argentina (1966–84), Peru (1968–80), Chile (1973–89), and Uruguay (1973–85). Where the military did not rule directly, they conducted campaigns against communist guerrillas—including the Argentine "Che" Guevara, killed in Bolivia in 1967—or helped prop up authoritarian party systems. By 1975 only Colombia, Venezuela, and Costa Rica had elected governments.

Harsh rule did little to alleviate the problems. During the 1970s Latin American regimes survived on accumulating massive debts with the developed world. Like the states of Eastern Europe, Latin America built inefficient state-dominated economies and controlled the consequences with large bureaucracies and police oppression. In the 1980s the decaying system collapsed. In 1982 Mexico defaulted on its international debt, which totaled more than $85 billion. All the other debtor states declared insolvency. Wealthy Latin Americans, fearing financial collapse, sent their money abroad, making a bad situation worse. The creditor states insisted on rescheduling payments and on financial stringency. Governments cut spending programs: living standards fell sharply. By 1987 Latin America had paid back $121 billion at the cost of impoverishing the continent.

The result was political crisis. Without economic growth to support them the dictatorships had nothing to offer. They toppled one by one as popular reformist movements, backed by new urban classes demanded, and won, free elections. The new generation of politicians rejected the strategy of state-backed industrialization and autarky practiced since the 1930s, and looked to market reforms and liberalization to bring Latin America back into the wider world system. Between 1988 and 1990 new governments committed to democracy and economic reform appeared in Mexico, Argentina, Chile, Brazil, Uruguay, and Peru, but continued economic crisis, inflation, political corruption, and civil conflict left a mixed political legacy throughout the continent.

UNITED STATES OF AMERICA

U.S. intervention

Dominican Republic 1916–24 1965–66

Grenada 1983

Cuba 1921–23, 1933, 1961

Haiti 1915–34, 1944, 1994

Panama 1903–18 1989

Nicaragua 1912–33

Guatemala 1954

Mexico 1914

1 For much of the period from 1945 Latin American states were ruled by military dictatorships or forms of single-party rule. During the 1960s communism emerged as the major political opposition (map left), backed by the Soviet bloc or by China, and assisted by the one communist state in the region, Fidel Castro's Cuba. As popular movements confronted repressive elites throughout the continent, aid programs were seen as a way of increasing communist influence and trade. Starting in the 1970s, however, substantial strides have been made toward greater democracy, notably in Chile, Brazil, and Argentina.

MEXICO 5,000
Mexico City
Puebla Veracruz

☐ *Mexican revolution 1910–40*
◇ *Zapatista revolt, 1994*

BELIZE
GUAT. 300
HONDURAS M
750 M
Guatemala City
Tegucigalpa

☐ *Guatemalan revolution 1944–54*

EL SALVADOR
NICARAGUA 100 M
Managua
125 M
San José
COSTA RICA

▽ ◇ *Military Junta 1979*

☐ ○ *Sandinista revolution 1979–90; democratization 1990*

○ *Figueres 1948*

○ *Liberal-Conservative Pact, 1957*

▽ *Intermittent militarism to 1978*
○ *Election of reformist government 1978*

Havana **CUBA** 125,000 M

Cuban-inspired guerrilla movements 1959–68

1,400
DOMINICAN REP.
PUERTO RICO (USA)

HAITI n/a M

Caribbean Sea

1,000 M
PANAMA 500 M
Panama City
Cartagena

GRENADA
Port of Spain

Caracas
VENEZUELA 8,000 M

Georgetown
GUYANA 100 M SUR.
Paramaribo
Cayenne
FR. GUIANA

Bogotá
COLOMBIA 11,000 M/P

Quito
ECUADOR 1,200 M/P
Guayaquil

Piura

3,500 M/P
Trujillo
PERU
Huánuco
Callao
Lima Cuzco

Macapá
Amazon
Manaus Belém

B R A Z I L

Fortaleza

Recife

Salvador (Bahía)

Cuban revolution 1959 ☐

Rómulo Betancourt 1945–48, 1959–64; Carlos Andrés Pérez 1974–79 ○

Rafael Caldera 1969–74; Luis Herrera Campins 1979; Jaime Lusinchi 1984 Hugo Chavez 1998– ◇ ☆

Getulio Vargas 1930–45; 1950–54; João Goulart 1961–64 ○

Modernizing militarism 1964 ▽

Civilian rule 1985; democratization 1986 ○

1 latin america since 1945

political change in Latin America since 1945

☐ *Social revolution* Fundamental change (attempted or achieved) in economic and social structure by nationalist or Marxist movements

○ *Reformism* Moderate socio-economic change or modernization for democratic or other process

☆ *Populism* Interventionist state based on multiclass alliance for policy of development

◇ *Christian Democracy* Radical socioeconomic change by Christian Democratic parties

▽ *Unreformed militarism* Military dictatorship of the right without social or modernizing program

◇ *Indigenous guerrilla movements* Urban guerrillas starting in late 1960s following failure of Cuban-inspired rural guerrillas

communism in Latin America, 1974

70,000 communist party membership

M/P loyalty (Moscow/Peking)

communist party status

☐ in power
☐ legal opposition
☐ illegal

☆ *Radical militarism 1968*
☐ *Sendero Luminoso from 1980*
○ *Return to civil rule 1980 President Fujimori suspends constitution 1992*

☐ *Bolivian revolution 1952–64*
☐ *Che Guevara (killed 1967) Military 1980; democratization 1982*
▽

◇ *Eduardo Frei 1964–70*
☐ *Salvador Allende (Popular Unity) 1970–73*
▽ *Pinochet 1973–88*
○ *Democratization 1989*

La Paz
BOLIVIA
Sucre 3,200 M/P
Arequipa

7,000 M/P

Brasília

Belo Horizonte
Rio de Janeiro
São Paulo
Santos

Antofagasta
Copiapó
120,000 M
Tucumán
Córdoba
Santa Fé
Valparaíso
Santiago Mendoza
Concepción
Valdivia
Osorno
Rawson

C H I L E

PARAGUAY
Asunción

Uruguay
Fray Bentos
Rio Grande
URUGUAY 22,000 M
Montevideo

Florianópolis
Porto Alegre

Military dictatorship Stroessner 1954 Rodriguez 1989 ▽

Batllismo 1903–33 ○
Military 1973 ▽
Tupamaros ◇
Civilian rule 1985; democratization 1986 ○
Montoneros ◇

Buenos Aires
ARGENTINA 70,000 M
Bahía Blanca

Comodoro Rivadavia

Santa Cruz

Stanley

Tierra del Fuego

Juan Domingo Perón 1943–55, 1973–74 ☆
Military 1976–83 ▽
Democratization and civilian rule 1984 ○

Falkland Islands (Islas Malvinas) occupied by Argentina 1982: occupation ended by UK Task Force June 1982

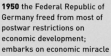

2 Labor shortages in the 1960s produced a flood of migrant workers, reaching more than 3 million by the early 1970s. With rising unemployment in the 1980s, many returned home (map below), but the *gastarbeiter* remained a permanent feature of German society, prompting race attacks and nationalist hostility with echos of the 1930s.

Few people in 1945 would have predicted how rapidly Germany was to recover from the disastrous economic effects of the Second World War. In the year of defeat, industrial production sank to one-third of the prewar level. The German currency once again experienced high inflation. Germany was occupied and divided by states determined to extract reparation and to limit the German industrial revival. In 1946 the victor states agreed a "Level of Industry Plan" designed to reduce German steel production to eight million tons (one-quarter of its wartime level), to restrict trade, and to prohibit the output of a range of modern products.

Germany's economic future depended on political developments outside German control. The onset of the Cold War produced a territorial division of Germany into two states: a Federal Republic (West Germany) set up in cooperation with the Western Allies; and a much smaller rump German state set up under Soviet domination, the German Democratic Republic (East Germany). The Western state, set up in 1949, was soon integrated with the wider capitalist economy. In 1950 the Federal Republic (FRG) was freed from most of the post-war restrictions on economic development, and embarked on the "Economic Miracle." Eastern Germany (the GDR) adopted the Stalinist model. Development there was in general above the standard for the rest of the Soviet bloc, but far below the economic achievements of the West.

In the 1950s and 1960s the Federal economy was dominated by the theory, usually associated with Economics Minister Ludwig Erhard, of the social market economy. This was an economy committed to avoiding too much state direction while building up an effective welfare state. Economic revival became the central ambition of German society. Freed from 30 years of war and peacetime restrictions, the German peoples enthusiastically embraced the rush for growth. The achievement was remarkable. The national product grew almost fourfold in 20 years. In the 1950s, the West German economy was catching up lost ground after defeat and occupations. From the 1960s to the 1980s, West Germany became a wealthy country, overtaking other European states. The most successful regions more than quadrupled output. The German Central Bank began storing large quantities of capital, supporting the IMF,

and acting as the central industrial economy in the EC. In 1986 Germany became the world's largest exporter.

Foreign trade was key to German success. In the 1950s reconstruction set up a vigorous demand for just the goods in which Germany specialized—high-quality engineering products, chemicals, electro-technical goods, vehicles. The state gave the export industries tax and investment concessions, while German industry concentrated on effective marketing and after-sales service to compete with well established rivals. Starting in 1951 the balance of trade remained in permanent surplus. Thanks to steady productivity growth, German prices were kept at competitive levels despite regular revaluations of the Mark since 1961.

Low inflation was also a central plank in Federal economic policy. Wage growth was modest in the 1950s and 1960s as workers accepted the need for growth and employment as a greater priority than high levels of consumption. Memories of the hyperinflation of 1923 ran deep in German society. Financial stability was accepted as an essential element in the state's economic strategy. Inflation remained low, and German goods enjoyed a permanent advantage on world markets as a result.

In 1990 the Federal economy faced a new challenge. The GDR collapsed and was brought into the Western state. The Eastern provinces were poor by Federal standards, their industries uncompetitive. The costs of the transition were expressed in high unemployment rates and rising state debt. By the early 2000s corruption, political radicalism and violence against immigrants revived in Germany and the consensus that underlay the "economic miracle" gave way to new uncertainties about the German future.

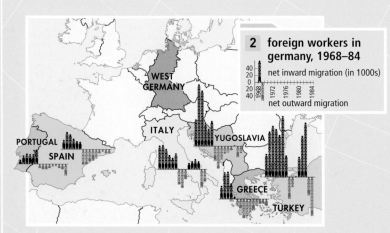

2 foreign workers in germany, 1968–84

net inward migration (in 1000s)

net outward migration

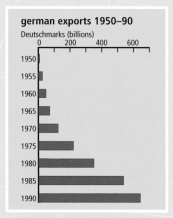

german exports 1950–90

Deutschmarks (billions)

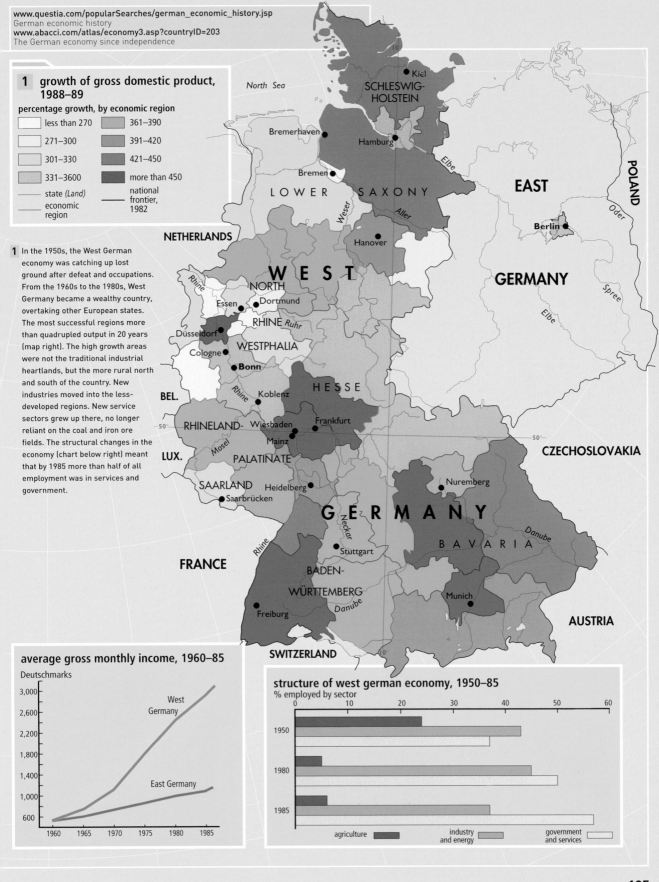

1 growth of gross domestic product, 1988–89

percentage growth, by economic region

less than 270	361–390
271–300	391–420
301–330	421–450
331–3600	more than 450

— state (Land)
— economic region
— national frontier, 1982

1 In the 1950s, the West German economy was catching up lost ground after defeat and occupations. From the 1960s to the 1980s, West Germany became a wealthy country, overtaking other European states. The most successful regions more than quadrupled output in 20 years (map right). The high growth areas were not the traditional industrial heartlands, but the more rural north and south of the country. New industries moved into the less-developed regions. New service sectors grew up there, no longer reliant on the coal and iron ore fields. The structural changes in the economy (chart below right) meant that by 1985 more than half of all employment was in services and government.

average gross monthly income, 1960–85

Deutschmarks

structure of west german economy, 1950–85

% employed by sector

agriculture · industry and energy · government and services

the new **economic superpowers**: japan

1945 to 2000

1952 U.S. ends occupation of Japan

1955 Japan launches "Five-Year Plan" for economic growth

1956 Japan joins UN

1969 Japanese engineers produce first factory robots

1970s Japanese fight for leading share in new computer market

1978 Sino-Japanese Treaty of Friendship

1980s Japanese economic miracle

1998 financial crisis in Asia. Currencies fall sharply in value. Japan begins 10 years of decline and deflation

EUROPE **33,500** NETH. 800
8,424 34,710
WEST GERMANY 400
2,500
UK 6,576
1,800 LUX.
FRANCE 330
SOVIET BLOC
860 2,288
62
U S S R
SOUTH KOREA 4,868
JAPAN
650
ASIA **404,700**
CHINA 1,200
15,565 57,239
TAIWAN 370
1,413
HONG KONG 1,100
MIDDLE EAST **12,000**
54
THAILAND 250
MALAYSIA 160
AFRICA **27,100**
SAUDI ARABIA
272
LIBERIA 267 4,162 4,244
SINGAPORE 500
INDONESIA 550
OCEANIA **26,400**
2,163 6,30
AUSTRALIA 1,200

1/2

During the 1970s and 1980s Japan's economic presence abroad expanded dramatically (maps above and left). By 1987 overseas investments were worth $139 billion, three-quarters of it placed in the 1980s. Foreign trade totaled only seven billion Yen in 1970, but was 40 billion by 1993. The U.S. trade deficit with Japan reached a yawning $60 billion by 1987, more than one-third of the total trade deficit. The great bulk of Japanese exports, more than 75 percent in the middle of the 1980s, was made up of machinery and equipment.

SOVIET UNION
MONGOLIA
Sea of Okhotsk
Peking
N. KOREA
S. KOREA Seoul 606
CHINA 438
Shanghai Osaka Tokyo
Canton
Hanoi
Chiangmai
Rangoon
Taipei TAIWAN 494
Bonin Is.
BURMA
THAILAND
Hong Kong 1,898
1,276
Bangkok 1978
1979 Pen-ang
MALAYSIA 673
PHILIPPINES 202
Caroline Is.
Phnom Penh
Kota Kinabulu
Medan 1978
Johor Bahru 1982
BRUNEI
PACIFIC OCEAN
SINGAPORE 1,902
Borneo
Celebes 631
KIRIBATI
Kuala Lumpur
Sumatra
Jakarta Java Bali
I N D O N E S I A
New Guinea
PAPUA NEW GUINEA
Bismarck Arch.
TUVALU
Timor
Cape York
Timor Sea
Darwin
Coral Sea
Santa Cruz Is.
VANUATU
FIJI
Port Moresby
SOLOMON IS.
New Caledonia
Townsville
AUSTRALIA
Brisbane
New Zealand
Perth
Adelaide Sydney Auckland
Melbourne
Wellington
NEW ZEALAND
Hobart
Christchurch

2 japan, australia, and asia to 1989

631 Japanese direct investment, 1989 (U.S.$ million)

Bangkok 1978 major Japanese transportation/infrastructure project, with date

▲ pilot Japanese transportation/infrastruc projects

✈ major international airports

— principal air routes

//// development corridors

www.fsmitha.com/h2/ch27jp.htm
Japanese economic recovery since 1945
www.japan-guide.com/e/e644.html
Present day guide to the Japanese economy

1 japanese investment overseas, 1970–89

15,565 57,239	trade with region, 1970–74 and 1985–89 (billion Yen)
6,576 →	Japanese direct foreign investment in region, 1987 (U.S.$ million)
1,200	Japanese direct foreign investment in country, 1987 (U.S.$ million)
404,700	workers in Japanese affiliated companies, 1980

CANADA
650

NORTH AMERICA
83,900

USA
14,700

15,357

17,170 75,190

4,814

BAHAMAS
730

CAYMAN ISLANDS 1,200

PANAMA
2,300

LATIN AMERICA
128,100

BRAZIL
230

2,024 2,372

Japan found herself in much the same position as Germany at the end of the Second World War. Not only had her major cities been burned down during the bombing offensive, her home islands were occupied by American forces, her economy was in ruins, and the Allies intended Japan to pay reparations to the countries she had occupied during the war.

The United States wanted to prevent the revival of a strong Japanese industrial economy, and to keep Japan disarmed. Forty years later Japan was one of the world's new economic superpowers and had the fourth-largest armed forces in the world. The American occupiers contributed significantly to this revival. On March 6, 1946 Japan was forced to accept a new constitution, which permitted free labor unions, created a genuine parliamentary system, and excluded war as an option in settling disputes. The enforced modernization of Japanese society and politics was accompanied by generous aid to revive the economy. With the Korean War, the United States changed tack and began to encourage the rebuilding of Japanese industry to supply the war effort. Reparations were shelved, a peace treaty was signed in San Francisco in 1951, and Japan was hailed as the Asian capitalist bulwark against the march of Asian communism.

The Japanese authorities seized the opportunity. During the 1950s they pursued a conscious policy of "catching up" with the West. In 1955 Prime Minister Ichiro Hatoyama launched a "Five-Year Plan for Economic Self-Reliance," which was masterminded, as was all subsequent expansion, by the Ministry of International Trade and Industry (MITI). The industrial strategy was based on priority for selected growth areas in heavy industry and high-technology sectors. Development aid, subsidies, export bounties, and tariffs were all used to secure high domestic growth and a vigorous export performance. Free labor unions, initially run by Japanese communists, gave way to "enterprise unions," which created close bonds between management and workforce and helped to achieve remarkable

growth in productivity. Japan's output grew at 9.5 percent a year in the 1950s and at 10.5 percent a year in the 1960s.

Japanese society exhibited a number of features favorable to high postwar growth. Great emphasis was placed on technical education. In 1974 Japan had 330,000 engineering students at university, one-fifth of all students. In Britain in the same year there were just 24,000. The ethos of the large enterprise discouraged individualism and encouraged loyalty to the firm and effective collaboration to achieve growth targets. The level of strike activity was tiny. Workers accepted low wages and rigid work discipline. Economic achievement became one of the defining features of postwar Japanese politics.

When Japan was hit by the oil crisis of 1973 these strengths enabled her to adapt quickly. In 1971 MITI produced "Visions for the 1970s," which formed the basis for the reorientation of the economy away from heavy industry and mass consumer products toward the sunrise sectors. In 1969 Japanese engineers produced the first factory robots; in the 1970s they fought tenaciously for a leading share in the new computer market. By the late 1970s Japanese output and exports had been restructured. Steel, ships, and chemicals gave way to high-quality technology—machinery and electronic equipment—which brought a second "economic miracle" in the 1980s. In the 1990s Japan's problems have been those of success: high expectations from her workforce; the ossification of the business elite; and competition from the Asian economies she stimulated in the 1980s. By the later 1990s Japan's long economic success story had effectively come to an end.

The 1980s and early 1990s witnessed fundamental changes in world politics and in the balance of economic power. The Cold War confrontation disappeared with the collapse of the Soviet bloc from 1989 and the eclipse of Soviet communism. At least partly as a result, popular democracy made strides in many parts of the world: in the former Soviet republics themselves; in Latin America; and in southern Africa. As important, the economic balance of power began to shift. In China and around the Pacific Rim, new economic powers emerged to challenge the long-held monopoly of the developed industrial world beginning the reversal of one of the central features of the century: Western economic imperialism. At the same time, two contrary pressures in world affairs developed. On the one hand, there was a move toward greater globalization: in communications, in finance, in manufacturing, and, through the activities of the UN and other international organizations, in politics, too. On the other hand, political fragmentation and conflict accelerated. The revival of nationalism, the growth of religious fundamentalism, and the spread of terrorism and corruption have all contributed to a more violent, less stable world.

The fall of the Berlin Wall, November 10–11, 1989

since 1989

1980 death of Marshal Tito

1980 creation of independent Polish Trade Union, Solidarity; Marshall Law (1981)

1985 Gorbachev becomes leader of USSR (to 1991)

1989 Poland and Hungary move toward political pluralism; popular protest topples communist regimes in East Germany, Czechoslovakia, Bulgaria, and Romania (Ceauçescu executed); Berlin Wall demolished

1990 reunification of Germany

by 1990 multiparty elections take place throughout former Soviet bloc

1999 Czech Republic, Hungary, and Poland join NATO

2004 Czech Republic, Hungary, Slovakia, the Baltic States, and Poland join European Union

In March 1985 Mikhail Gorbachev became leader of the Soviet Union. A young and popular member of the communist Politburo, he saw clearly that the Soviet bloc had reached a critical turning point. Over the following five years he tried to modernize socialism through a package of economic and political reforms. The result was the collapse of the USSR and the disappearance of the Soviet bloc in Europe.

The Soviet system in the 1980s faced critical choices. The escalating cost of modern defense systems made it difficult to keep up in the arms race without reducing domestic living standards, which had stagnated in much of the Soviet bloc. Gorbachev seized the initiative in 1985 in the face of hard-line opposition. He sought to establish serious disarmament talks so that the Soviet Union could run down its massive military commitment without risking its security. The resources this freed were intended to satisfy the population's demands for economic reform and improved living standards. Disarmament was not an immediate success. In October 1986 Gorbachev met President Reagan in Reykjavik, but final agreement on arms control was only achieved in Washington on December 8, 1987. The treaty removed one-fifth of existing nuclear weapons, including most intermediate-range nuclear weapons. Further cuts in the long-range nuclear arsenal were announced by both sides in 1988. The program of economic reform could not be achieved without a measure of political reform. In 1988 the Soviet system became a limited democracy.

Gorbachev's plans profoundly affected the rest of the Eastern bloc. Gorbachev regarded the other communist states as a drain on the Soviet economy. He encouraged them to think about economic and political reform in order to reduce their dependence on the Soviet Union. The change in Soviet attitudes came at a difficult time for the other Eastern bloc states, whose economic development had been adversely affected by recession in the West and by reductions in trade and aid resulting from renewed Cold War pressures. Economic modernization slowed in the 1980s, and provoked growing popular unrest, particularly in Poland. There a military dictatorship was set up in 1981 to suppress the democracy movement and to forestall possible Soviet military intervention. In Romania the isolated and impoverished regime of Nicolae Ceauçescu became yet more extravagantly repressive. In East Germany the *Stasi* (security police) clamped down on any signs of dissent.

There was little popular opposition in the 1980s, but there was limited enthusiasm for the regimes even among elements in the communist movements. In Czechoslovakia Václav Havel's Charter 77 kept alive the struggle for civil rights. In Poland the outlawed Solidarity Union maintained a network of Catholic and working-class opposition. When in 1989 Gorbachev put pressure on his communist partners to grasp the nettle of reform, popular protest grew rapidly. Without Soviet backing and generally unwilling to provoke civil war, the communist regimes crumbled one by one: opposition parties were legalized in Hungary in January 1989; in August 1989 Poland established the first noncommunist government since 1948. Demonstrations ended communist rule in Czechoslovakia in November 1989 and in East Germany in October. In Romania, Ceauçescu fought to the end using his *Securitate* agents to stamp out resistance until he was shot by an army firing squad on Christmas Day 1989 and replaced by a National Salvation Front government, composed largely of former communists.

By 1990 multiparty elections brought to power coalition governments with a shared commitment to economic liberalization and democratic reform. Many former communists remained in politics, and both political and economic change proved to be slower and more problematic than had been hoped. But by 2004 change was sufficiently advanced to secure the entry of 7 former eastern bloc states into the EU, recognition that the historic east-west divide opened up by the Cold War was finally bridged.

0

Sep. 1989: mass exodus of refugees reach the West via Communist leadership in cris Oct.–Nov. 1989: widespread demonstrations against lead Nov. 9, 1989: Berlin Wall breached DE *Mar. 1990: free elections July 1990: currency union wi West Germany Oct. 1990: reunified with West Germany*

NETHERLANDS

BELGIUM

GERM

● Bonn

Dec. 1989: economic war between Belgrade governme and Slovenia Apr. 1990: free elections June 1991: independence de Yugoslav army attempts to r control of Slovenia July 1991: Brioni Agreement fighting in Slovenia; Yugosla withdraws

SWITZ.

Apr.–May 1990: free election Dec. 1990: Serb-inhabited a declare independence June 1991: independence declared; fighting in Slovenic spreads to Croatia as Serbs to extend territory in Croatia Bosnia

1987: mass strikes against w freeze and falling living stan growing Serb militancy agai minorities July 1990: provincial autonom abolished 1990–91: increasing tension Belgrade government and Slovenia an Jan.–May 1990: democratic initiated by leadership Mar. 1991: free elections

10

1 Between 1989 and 1991 the Soviet bloc was transformed from a monolithic communist empire into a patchwork of independent states, most of which became multiparty democracies (map below). The process began in Poland and Hungary in January 1989, when talks began with noncommunist opposition parties, but accelerated in September with the flight of thousands of East Germans to Hungary, Poland, and Czechoslovakia. Between October and December communist regimes were replaced in East Germany, Czechoslovakia, Bulgaria, and Romania. The Soviet Union broke up into its constituent parts during 1991 and was officially dissolved on December 31, 1991.

1 the collapse of communism, 1985–91

- Soviet-dominated eastern Europe to 1989
- Soviet Union to 1991
- Yugoslavia to 1991
- united with the Federal Republic of Germany, 1990
- achieved independence, 1991
- other former communist states, 1991
- de facto independent states, late 1991, on former territory of the Soviet Union, internationally unrecognized
- overrun by Yugoslav army, July–Dec. 1991
- borders, 1991

SWEDEN

1985: Solidarity leads [oppo]sition to communism 1989: partially free [electi]ons 1989: Solidarity-led [gove]rnment takes office 1990: Communist [party] dissolved 1991: free elections

FINLAND

Baltic Sea

Tallinn
ESTONIA

Mar. 1990: Congress of Estonia formed, declares Soviet rule illegal Mar. 1991: referendum endorses independence Aug. 1991: independence declared Sep. 1991: independence recognized by USSR

Riga
LATVIA

1989: mass anti-Communist demonstrations Mar. 1991: referendum endorses independence Aug. 1991: independence declared Sep. 1991: independence recognized by USSR

LITHUANIA
Vilnius

1989: mass anti-Communist demonstrations Mar. 1991: independence declared Apr.–June 1990: economic embargo imposed by USSR Sep. 1991: independence recognized by USSR

Moscow

RUSSIAN FED.

TATARSTAN

POLAND

Warsaw

Minsk
BELARUS

June 1989: Popular Front founded Aug. 1991: independence declared Dec. 1991: founder member of Commonwealth of Independent States

RUSSIAN FEDERATION

Prague

[CZECHO]CHOSLOVAKIA

Bratislava
[AUS]TRIA

Budapest
HUNGARY

starting in 1988: antigovernment demonstrations Nov. 1989: mass demonstrations end Communist rule Apr. 1990: new constitution adopted; becomes a federation June 1990: free elections

Kiev

UKRAINE

1989: opposition mass-movements emerge Aug. 1991: independence declared Dec. 1991: referendum endorses independence; founder member of Commonwealth of Independent States

Mar. 1985: Mikhail Gorbachev becomes leader of Communist Party; initiates perestroika and glasnost, loosens Soviet control of satellite states June 1991: Boris Yeltsin elected president of Russian Federation Aug. 1991: hard-line Communist coup against Gorbachev fails Nov. 1991: Communist Party declared illegal Dec. 1991: USSR dissolved

from 1987: Communist regime relaxes control Sep. 1989: allows East Germans to travel to the West Oct. 1990: Communist rule ends peacefully Mar.–Apr. 1990: free elections

MOLDOVA

TRANSNISTRIA

June 1989: Popular Front wins 75% of votes in election Aug. 1991: independence declared

GAGAUZIA

Jan. 1990: state of emergency declared; Soviet troops intervene Oct. 1991: independence declared

Nov. 1991: independence declared

Belgrade

ROMANIA

Bucharest

YUGOSLAVIA
Sarajevo

KOSOVO

Tirana
ALBANIA

Skopje

BULGARIA

Sofia

Dec. 1989: mass demonstrations lead to armed uprisings and overthrow of Ceauçescu regime June 1991: free elections Nov. 1991: new constitution adopted

Nov. 1989: President Zhivkov removed from office June 1990: free elections July 1991: fresh elections following adoption of new constitution

Nov. 1988: mass demonstrations against Russification Mar. 1991: referendum endorses independence Apr. 1991: independence declared

Sep. 1989: economic embargo imposed by Azerbaijan Sep. 1991: referendum endorses independence; independence declared

CHECHENIA
Grozny

GEORGIA

Sep. 1991: independence declared

ARMENIA

AZERBAIJAN

NAGORNO-KARABAKH

the **collapse** of the **soviet union**

since 1988

1988 Party Conference decides to replace Supreme Soviet with Congress of People's Deputies

1990 military element of Warsaw Pact scrapped; Pact as a whole wound up (July 1, 1991)

1991 Russian troops sent into Baltic States and the Caucasus

1991 (19 August) hard-line communists attempt a coup in Moscow

1991 (December) Ukraine votes for independence

1991 (31 December) USSR dissolved; Boris Yeltsin becomes president of Russia

1999 former KGB official Vladimir Putin becomes president of Russia

2004 Beslan school massacre

The tidal wave that swept away the communist regimes of Eastern Europe was the direct consequence of the forces of change inspired by Mikhail Gorbachev's leadership of the Soviet Union. Within two years the wave engulfed both Gorbachev and the system he had tried to reform.

Gorbachev did not set out to destroy the system but to make it work better. He pinned his faith on *glasnost* (openness) and *perestroika* (restructuring). The apparatus that ran the Soviet Union proved resistant to both, but more particularly to Gorbachev's plans to decentralize the economy and encourage more economic individualism. This resistance led Gorbachev in 1988 to rally reformist elements in the party. At the Party Congress in June the decision was taken to replace the Supreme Soviet with a Congress of People's Deputies, two-thirds of whom would be popularly elected. The Congress then elected a 450-strong parliament in May 1989 and Gorbachev became president. The system was far from fully democratic, but it excited expectations of more fundamental change.

Arguments about the pace of reform and growing economic uncertainty led to a downturn in economic growth in 1990. There was growing nationalist unrest as the Russian-dominated republics of the USSR sensed the opportunity to emulate the Eastern European states' assertion of independence. In 1991 Gorbachev dithered between more radical reform and a return to old-fashioned authority. Russian troops were sent into the Baltic States and the Caucasus to hold the crumbling structure together.

The crisis could not be reversed. In April 1990 the military element of the Warsaw Pact had been scrapped, and on July 1, 1991 the Warsaw Pact as a whole was wound up. The COMECON trade bloc was ended in June 1991. Meanwhile, the president of the Russian Republic, Boris Yeltsin, elected in May 1990, urged Gorbachev to give the Soviet republics

1 During 1991 the former USSR began to disintegrate under the impact of Gorbachev's economic and political reforms. The Soviet republics which had made up the Moscow-dominated USSR took greater responsibility for local affairs. The Baltic States and Ukraine began to demand genuine independence, which was achieved by the end of 1991. In December 1991 the republics met at Alma Alta in Kazakhstan and set up the Commonwealth of Independent States. Within the Commonwealth the Russian authorities set up a Russian Federation composed of 21 republican and 69 other defined areas (map below). Since then, Tatarstan has won effective independence, while Chechenya sought to break away entirely, fighting bloody wars against Russian forces from 1994 to 1996 and again from 1999.

1 the russian federation, 1991–96

― the Russian Federation

constituent republics within the Russian Federation, Mar. 1992 (in national languages)

united with Russia by treaty, Feb. 15, 1994

independence declared, Nov. 1991; at war with Russia from Dec. 1994

entered into close political and economic union with Russia, Apr. 2, 1996 (Commonwealth of Independent States, CIS)

entered into close economic union with Russia, Mar. 30, 1996

other members of the CIS

60% percentage of Russians in other members of the Russian Federation

a KARACHAY-CHERKESSIA *42%*
b KABARDINO-BALKARIA *39%*
c NORTH-OSSETIA *30%*
d CHECHEN-INGUSHETIA *23%*

www.fsmitha.com/h2/ch33.htm
The events leading up to and including the disintegration of the Soviet Union
www.bbc.co.uk/history/war/coldwar/soviet_end_01.shtml
An essay on the end of the Soviet state

more independence. A reactionary backlash was not long coming. On August 19, 1991 a group of hard-line communists put Gorbachev under house arrest in the Crimea and attempted a coup in Moscow. Yeltsin suppressed the revolt, but the collapse of the coup signaled the end of the existing order. The non-Russian republics declared their independence. When Ukraine staged a referendum in December 1991 that resulted in an overwhelming vote for independence, Gorbachev bowed to reality. The USSR was dissolved on December 31st, to be replaced by a Commonwealth of Independent States (the CIS), cooperating on military and economic issues but no longer controlled from Moscow.

With no country left to rule, Gorbachev slipped into obscurity. Russia embraced a form of presidential democracy, with Yeltsin as its first president. Some republics—Belarus, Uzbekistan, Kazakhstan, Turkmenistan—maintained reformed communist governments; the others adopted some form of democracy. In Russia democracy gave rise to a fragmented collection of small political parties. In the parliamentary elections of 1993, Yeltsin's supporters controlled only a fraction of the new house. The largest share of the vote went to the extreme right-winger Vladimir Zhirinovsky. By 1999 he had faded, and the recently discredited Communist Party, led by Gennady Zyuganov, was once again a political force.

The revival of communism in Russia was a response to the years of crisis since 1991. Market economics, introduced throughout the former Soviet bloc, brought with them unemployment, low wages, a decline in welfare, and a wave of economic crime and corruption. The fragmentation of the USSR gave rise to numerous crises in the "Near Abroad," the circle of states once part of the Union. Arguments between Russia and Ukraine over the Soviet Black Sea Fleet and the nuclear arsenal on non-Russian soil were resolved peacefully. But in the Caucasus conflict has been endemic since 1988. Russia has established an uneasy coalition with its non-Russian neighbors under first Boris Yeltsin, then his successor since 1999, the former KGB official Vladimir Putin. He embarked on efforts to tackle organized crime and the black economy, and to make Russia a more effective player in world affairs. Russia's economic and environmental problems have remained to haunt all efforts to produce an effective and prosperous successor state.,

2 the successor states of the ussr to 1999

——	major concentrations of Russian minorities
30%	percentage of Russian population
——	autonomous areas
71	estimated level of real GDP, 1997 (1989=100)
5.8%	inflation, 1996
★	conflicts between states
▨	civil wars
●	unsuccessful assertion of independence
✊	ethnic conflicts
⚊	states with nuclear weapons, 1991
⊥⊥⊥	Russian troops deployed as border guards
●	Russian troops involved in conflicts or deployed as peacekeepers
○	contributed to Russian-led CIS force on government side in Tajik civil war, 1992
○	member of GUUAM group, 1999
▢	independent 1991, founder member of CIS (Dec. 8, 1991)
▢	independent 1991, joined CIS late Dec. 1991
▢	independent 1991, joined CIS 1993
▢	independent 1991
▢	de facto independent 1991

2 With the collapse of the USSR, around 25 million ethnic Russians were left outside the Russian Federation, formed in March 1992 (map above). They found themselves the victims of discrimination once they no longer had the direct protection of Russia. Ethnic conflict in Moldova, the Baltic States, the Caucasus, and Kazakhstan contributed to the instability of the new states. Increasingly, the new countries sought to break their dependence on Russia through cooperation agreements such as GUUAM.

civil war in yugoslavia

since 1991

1987 Slobodan Milosevic becomes leader of Serbia; promotes aggressive nationalism

1991 disintegration of Yugoslavia; Slovenia and Croatia declare independence

1992 civil war in Bosnia-Herzegovina: Bosnian Serbs fight Muslims and Croats

1995 agreement signed to end civil war in Bosnia

1997 Albanian government toppled following serious violence

1998 fighting erupts in Kosovo

1999 NATO bombing campaign against Serbia. Refugee crisis in Kosovo. NATO troops enter Kosovo

2000 federal elections formally end autocratic rule of Slobodan Milosevic: in 2001 he is handed over to UN War Crimes Tribunal in the Hague to face charges of crimes against humanity and genocide

The greatest casualty of the collapse of the communist bloc was Yugoslavia. A federation of six republics (Serbia, Croatia, Macedonia, Bosnia-Herzegovina, Slovenia, and Montenegro), it was held together by an overarching communist apparatus. As long as Tito, the founder of communist Yugoslavia, was alive, the federation seemed to work well. After his death in 1980, internal divisions began to appear.

In the 1980s, the economy was in decline, burdened by $18 billion of international debt and rising inflation and unemployment. The trigger for conflict was the emergence of aggressive nationalism. In 1987, following the choice of Slobodan Milosevic as leader of Serbia, tensions between the republics grew stronger. He suppressed the Albanian minority in Kosovo, and then set out to expand Serbia's influence in the federation as a whole, where there were large Serb minorities. Slovenia and Croatia moved toward separatism, and communist influence evaporated. In 1990 multiparty elections were held in all the republics, which brought nationalists to the fore in Slovenia and Croatia and paved the way for their simultaneous declaration of independence on June 25, 1991. By then ethnic conflict had already broken out between Croats and the Serb minority in Krajina, who were anxious for their future under the new Croat leader Franjo Tudjman. There followed a brief war in Slovenia in late June and early July 1991, and then a prolonged conflict between Croats and Serbs, which was brought to a halt in January 1992 following American diplomatic intervention. By then UN peacekeepers were in Croatia, and its independent existence was internationally recognized. On April 27, 1992 Serbia and Montenegro formed a new Federal Republic of Yugoslavia while in Bosnia-Herzegovina full-scale civil war broke out.

Bosnia was ruled by a fragile multi-ethnic government, led by Alija Izetbegovic. The collapse of Yugoslavia destabilized this most ethnically diverse of the republics. Bosnian Serbs, led by Radovan Karadzic, wanted to remain in a union with Belgrade, while the Bosnian Muslims and

Croats pushed for independence. International recognition in April 1992 led to civil war fought with a ferocious savagery as each ethnic group sought to "cleanse" the areas under its control of the opposing group's population. The Muslims were caught between the Croats, who had ambitions to create a state of Herceg-Bosnia in the Croat areas of Bosnia, and the Serbs, who set up a Serb Republika Srpska, intending to partition Bosnia altogether. By 1993 the Serbs controlled around 70 percent of Bosnia and the Muslims around 10 percent, mainly in the cities. From 1992 to November 1995 the Bosnian Serbs besieged the capital, Sarajevo, held by the Muslim-led government, but the Muslim enclave resisted, short of food and weapons and suffering high losses.

Against the odds, Bosnia survived. In 1992 international intervention by the European Community and the UN kept open a life-line to Bosnia. During much of 1993 and 1994 talks were held intermittently in an attempt to find a solution. In Serbia itself arguments developed between the political leaders over the future of Bosnia, and the expense of the war, while the weak state of the Serb economy made it difficult to complete the task of dividing Bosnia. In March 1994 President Clinton succeeded in getting Bosnian Muslims and Croats to form a federation. The same month the Russians put pressure on Serbia and Croatia to terminate hostilities. The Bosnian Serbs refused all compromise. In the summer of 1995 their military commander, Ratko Mladic, began one last assault on the Muslim enclaves. His spectacular success provoked, in August 1995, the armed intervention of NATO, accompanied by an

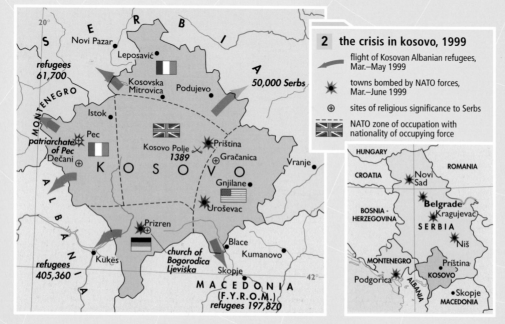

2 the crisis in kosovo, 1999

flight of Kosovan Albanian refugees, Mar.–May 1999

towns bombed by NATO forces, Mar.–June 1999

sites of religious significance to Serbs

NATO zone of occupation with nationality of occupying force

2 In 1990 the government of Slobodan Milosevic canceled the autonomy which Kosovo had within Serbia. Pressure for its restoration grew. In 1998 a low-level guerrilla war between the Albanian KLA and Serb security forces escalated sharply. At peace in 1998–9 the Albanian side accepted and the Serbs repudiated peace terms. As massacres of Albanians continued, pressure for NATO action mounted. On March 24 NATO bombers attacked Serbia, beginning an 11-week campaign (maps left). Yugoslav security forces responded by forcing Albanians from their homes, looting and killing. In early June Milosevic capitulated: his forces left Kosovo, and 40,000 NATO peacekeeping troops took over.

www.lib.msu.edu/sowards/balkan/
Lectures on modern Balkan history
www.balkan-archive.org.yu/politics/chronology/
A chronology of the Yugoslav crisis, 1990–95

1 The former Yugoslav federal republic of Bosnia and Herzegovina declared its independence in March 1992. There followed three and a half years of civil war between the Muslim, Serb, and Croat populations (map below right), with interventions from Croatia and Serbia. In 1992 the United Nations sent peacekeeping forces, and in November 1995 NATO intervened to keep the warring peoples apart and impose a peace settlement.

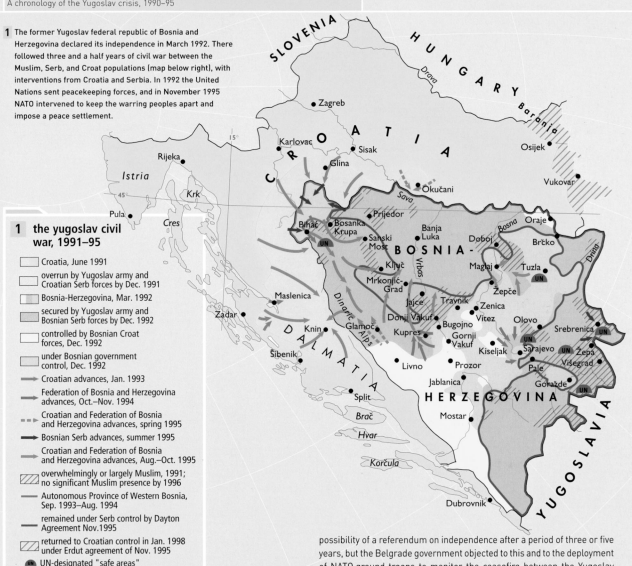

1 the yugoslav civil war, 1991–95

- Croatia, June 1991
- overrun by Yugoslav army and Croatian Serb forces by Dec. 1991
- Bosnia-Herzegovina, Mar. 1992
- secured by Yugoslav army and Bosnian Serb forces by Dec. 1992
- controlled by Bosnian Croat forces, Dec. 1992
- under Bosnian government control, Dec. 1992
- → Croatian advances, Jan. 1993
- → Federation of Bosnia and Herzegovina advances, Oct.–Nov. 1994
- ⇢ Croatian and Federation of Bosnia and Herzegovina advances, spring 1995
- → Bosnian Serb advances, summer 1995
- → Croatian and Federation of Bosnia and Herzegovina advances, Aug.–Oct. 1995
- overwhelmingly or largely Muslim, 1991; no significant Muslim presence by 1996
- Autonomous Province of Western Bosnia, Sep. 1993–Aug. 1994
- remained under Serb control by Dayton Agreement Nov.1995
- returned to Croatian control in Jan. 1998 under Erdut agreement of Nov. 1995
- UN-designated "safe areas"

offensive by Croatian ground troops (who retook the Serb Krajina region). In November, facing military defeat, and no longer fully supported by Milosevic, the Bosnian Serbs bowed to American-backed pressure to accept a settlement, leaving a fragile Bosnian state divided between the three ethnic groups and utterly devastated by four years of war. Despite international efforts, Bosnia remains fragile. The electorate still votes along ethnic lines, as the elections of 1996 and 1998 showed. Nikola Poplasen, a nationalist and the elected president of the Bosnian Serb Republic, was dismissed in March 1999 by Carlos Westendorp, the UN High Representative for Bosnia, and at the same time the disputed town of Brøko was declared a neutral zone. Both decisions further alienated the Bosnian Serbs, while tensions between the Bosnian Croats and the government in Sarajevo rose again.

After more than a year of sporadic fighting between Serb security forces and the Kosovo Liberation Army (KLA) the conflict escalated sharply in Serbia's province of Kosovo. Talks in Rambouillet and Paris in the winter of 1998–99 offered the Kosovo Albanians full autonomy within Serbia, with the possibility of a referendum on independence after a period of three or five years, but the Belgrade government objected to this and to the deployment of NATO ground troops to monitor the ceasefire between the Yugoslav forces and the KLA. NATO's response was to launch air strikes against Yugoslavia on March 24, 1999. The strikes aimed to force Belgrade to sign the peace agreement, to stop the repression of Kosovo Albanians, and to weaken the Yugoslav president Slobodan Milosevic. The Serbian security forces instead accelerated a program of "ethnic cleansing" against Kosovo's Albanians. As many as 600,000 fled the country and many more were displaced within the province. Villages were looted and burned. After more than two months of NATO bombing—with the Serbian government isolated internationally and the economy badly damaged—Milosevic caved in and agreed in early June 1999 to a peace plan which incorporated most of NATO's demands. A NATO-led peace implementation force (Kfor) entered the province, all Yugoslav forces left and the KLA was to be disarmed. After the war popular Serb resentment at the costs of Milosevic's dictatorship led to his downfall; in 2001 he was handed over to stand trial in The Hague on war crimes. Under a new prime minister, Zoran Djindjic, Serbia and Montenegro became, in 2003, virtually independent states. In March 2003 Djindjic was assassinated by a Belgrade mafia gang, highlighting the continued violence and corruption of Serbian politics.

europe in the age of monetary union

1987 Single European Act ratified; heralds closer European integration

1989 Margaret Thatcher wins exemption for British from social policy clauses of Single European Act

1991 Maastrict Treaty on European integration

1993 Britain ratifies Maastrict Treaty

1995 European Union (EU) established; Austria, Sweden, and Finland join EU

1999 European single currency launched

2002 European currency starts circulation in 12 European Union nations

2004 European Constitution published

While the Soviet bloc disintegrated after 1989, Western Europe moved toward greater integration. In the early 1980s the expanded European Economic Community was stagnating. In the attempt to reform it the ideal of full economic and political union, first championed in the 1940s, came closer to realization.

The impulse to reform came from the economic crises of the 1970s and early 1980s: growth rates in the EEC were only half the levels of the 1957–73 period. To cope with the crisis member states had introduced new restrictions on trade and capital movements, which challenged the very nature of the market. Doubts about the effectiveness of Community institutions grew.

In July 1981 the European Parliament set up an Institutional Committee, headed by Altiero Spinelli, which recommended a new treaty for the community to supplement the founding of the Rome Treaty. The proposals in the draft treaty were discussed at an Intergovernmental Conference in Luxembourg at the end of 1985 and formed the basis of the Single European Act, which was ratified by the member states in 1987. The Act paved the way for a full European Union in which remaining economic barriers would be removed, steps taken toward political union and foreign and defense policies merged. Two new commissions were established, one, under the energetic Community president, Jacques Delors, to work out the basis for European monetary union, the second to establish a framework for political union.

The proposals provoked strong argument, particularly on the prospect of creating a genuine monetary union and on the Social Chapter, a proposal to merge the welfare provisions of the member states into a single format. In 1989 Margaret Thatcher won exemption for Britain from the social policy clauses of the Single European Act. By the end of 1991 the work of the two commissions was finished, and on December 9, 1991 the heads of government met in the Dutch city of Maastricht to draw up a Treaty on European Union. More than 300 individual pieces of legislation were necessary to complete economic union. The date for the end of economic frontiers was set for December 31, 1992, but Britain continued to stall on monetary union and a final summit in Edinburgh was needed to win over the waverers. Britain ratified the Treaty in June 1993.

The prospects for political union were less fruitful. Although the European Union (as it became in 1995) expanded to 15 states, with another 13 applying for membership, there remained strong reservations about political merger. The problems of creating a common defense and foreign policy were exposed by the breakup of Yugoslavia, when Germany unilaterally

1 During the period 1986–99 the European Economic Community (from 1995 the European Union) expanded beyond Western Europe to create a continent-wide structure of full and associated members (map right). The accession, in 2004, of 10 further countries will lead to greater difficulties in reaching consensus in the Union's decision-making bodies.

1 the expansion of the european union, 1981–2004

- members of the EEC, Jan. 1981
- joined Jan. 1986
- admitted Oct. 1990
- joined Jan. 1995
- joined in 2004, with date of application
- countries scheduled for EU accession in 2007, with date of application
- other countries applying for membership

The European Economic Area (EEA)
- members of the EEA, June 1996

www.historiasiglo20.org/europe/acta.htm
The Single European Act and the Treaty of the European Union, 1986–92
www.ex.ac.uk/~RDavies/arian/euro.html
Viewpoints on European monetary union

recognized an independent Croatia and Slovenia, and then by the civil wars in Bosnia in 1992–95 and Kosovo in 1998–9. Both crises showed the extent to which Europe still relied on America even in policing its own problems. NATO, not the EU, provided the instrument for resolving both disputes. In 2003 the American decision to attack Iraq exposed further damaging divisions in Europe over the extent of support for American foreign policy.

The EU faced internal problems too. In 1999 the Commission had to resign because of evidence of widespread corruption, and the low turnout in elections that year exposed dwindling public interest. In 2002 former French President Giscard D'Estaing chaired a commission to draw up a constitution for the enlarged EU, but the crisis of the Iraq war and continued British opposition to a fuller role in Europe left the vision promoted at Maastricht in disarray.

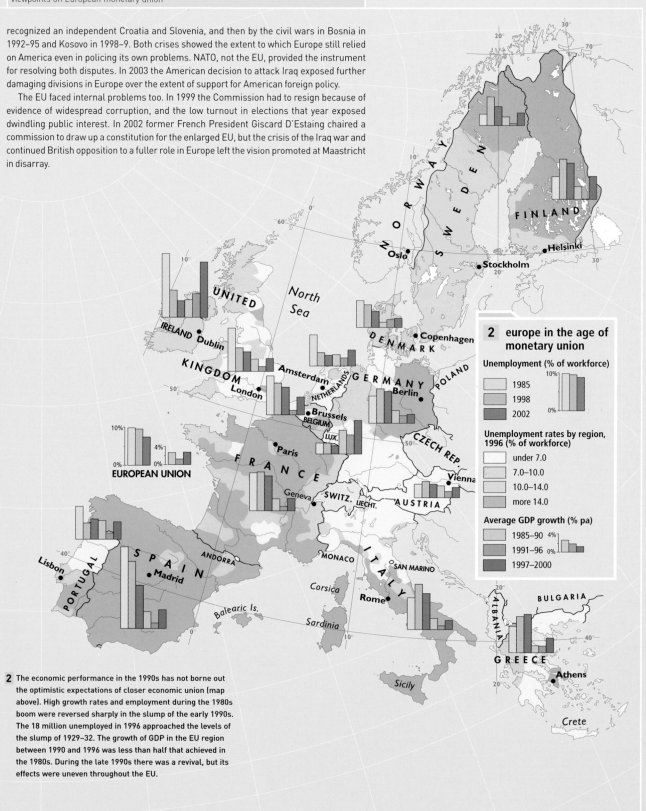

2 europe in the age of monetary union

Unemployment (% of workforce)
- 1985
- 1998
- 2002

Unemployment rates by region, 1996 (% of workforce)
- under 7.0
- 7.0–10.0
- 10.0–14.0
- more 14.0

Average GDP growth (% pa)
- 1985–90
- 1991–96
- 1997–2000

2 The economic performance in the 1990s has not borne out the optimistic expectations of closer economic union (map above). High growth rates and employment during the 1980s boom were reversed sharply in the slump of the early 1990s. The 18 million unemployed in 1996 approached the levels of the slump of 1929–32. The growth of GDP in the EU region between 1990 and 1996 was less than half that achieved in the 1980s. During the late 1990s there was a revival, but its effects were uneven throughout the EU.

china after mao

since 1979

1977 Den Xiaoping begins modernization drive

1979 "Democracy Wall" movement in China; collectively owned land parceled out on 20-year leases

1980 government creates four Special Economic Zones

1984 Sino-British agreement over Hong Kong (China to take over in 1997)

1989 student pro-democracy demonstration crushed in Beijing's Tiananmen Square

1996 China attempts military intimidation of Taiwan as islands hold first free elections in Chinese history

1997 death of Den Xiaoping; Jiang Zemin Chinese leader

2004 China fastest-growing economy in the world

Following the death of Mao in 1979, China embarked on economic reforms. Initially intended as modest changes to the command economy inherited from the Maoist era, these have in time turned into a transition to a market economy.

Ushered in by Deng Xiaoping, within the first five years the reforms accomplished a complete decollectivization of the rural economy, the opening wide of China to foreign trade and investment and the beginnings of a radical transformation of the state industrial sector. In 1980 the government created four Special Economic Zones (SEZ) close to Hong Kong, Macao and Taiwan (Hainan became the fifth in 1988). The SEZs are special administrative zones offering a package of inducements to attract foreign direct investment. Between 1978 and 1998 China's annual GNP growth rate averaged above 9.5 percent. Exports grew 19 times from 9.8 billion in 1978 to $182.7 billion in 1997, making China the tenth-largest trading country.In the countryside, collectively owned land was parceled out starting in 1979 to households on 15- to 20-year leases, which have since been renewed. By 1984 almost all land was farmed by households and within six years farm output had grown by 52.6 percent. The reform of the state industrial sector began in 1984, and, in contrast to that of the rural economy, has been tortuous and remains to be finished. State enterprises remain important, but Chinese industry is now diverse in terms of ownership and China is in effect no longer a planned economy. Notwithstanding its successes, the Chinese economy faces major problems of loss-making state enterprises, rising urban unemployment, the need to provide jobs for surplus rural laborers, and large regional disparities in wealth.

1 Starting in the 1970s communist China normalized relations with the outside world after years of isolation. Japan recognized China in 1972 and formal diplomatic relations were renewed with the United States in 1979. Agreement was reached over the transfer of Hong Kong and Macao to Chinese sovereignty. In December 1978 an "Open Door" policy was launched, to give China access to science, technology, and capital from the West to boost her modernization drive in the 1980s. The Open Door also admitted the ideas and culture of the West, and led to growing unrest which peaked in 1989 (map below).

1 china, 1976–99

— communist countries at end 1978

☐ allies of USSR, 1976

▨ pro-Soviet regime installed by conquest

☐ states friendly to China, 1976

← punitive Chinese attack, Feb.–Mar.1979

— sovereignty disputed with neighboring states

1987 frontier treaty signed (with date)

▨ claimed as part of national territory

● countries having improved relations with China by 1996

● Democracy Wall movement, 1979

● student demonstrations, 1986

☐ region or province experiencing demonstrations by national or religious minority

☐ provinces experiencing significant social unrest

www.chinatown-online.co.uk/pages/culture/history/
Chinese history, politics and culture
www.china.org.cn/e-china/openingup/sez.htm
Economic zones and the opening of coastal cities to overseas investment

Political reform, although not absent, has lagged behind economic reform. Formally the one-party state remains intact but under pressure from social changes. The period since 1979 has alternated between a loosening and a tightening of political control and the ideological straitjacket. With the passing of the Maoist era, 1978–9 saw the emergence of demands for a "Fifth Modernization"—democracy—to accompany the Four Modernizations of the economy and science and technology. The "Democracy Wall" with posters of uncensored expressions was shut down and its leader Wei Jinsheng sentenced to 15 years in prison. Following a loosening of political control and the criticism of the Party by the astrophysicist Fang Lizhi, in 1986 there were demonstrations in 15 major Chinese cities demanding greater democracy. Deng Xiaoping, who earlier talked about political reforms, responded by clamping down hard. The party secretary general, Hu Yaobang, was sacked for his liberal views. The conservatives in the party launched an "Anti Spiritual Pollution" campaign to counter the seeping effects of "bourgeois" liberalism. Hu Yaobang's death in April 1989 acted as the catalyst for demonstrations against corruption and for political reform. Supported by the general public, students occupied Tiananmen square. Demonstrations ended with the sending in of the army in Peking on June 4th and led to the dismissal of the then general secretary of the party, Zhao Ziyang, and the appointment of Jiang Zemin. In the runup to the 10th anniversary in 1999, the nervous leadership arrested dissidents who tried to register new political parties.

Following Tiananmen, economic reforms came to a halt. Fearing a reversal of economic reforms, in 1992 Deng Xiaoping launched a fresh round of economic liberalization which by accelerating the growth rate outflanked the conservative critics of liberalization. In its 1997 congress, the party adopted the transition to a market economy, thus jettisoning once and for all the out-moded planned economy. Recent years have seen a number of campaigns against corruption. The National People's Congress (China's Parliament), previously a rubber stamp, has grown in stature and begun to play a role in the formulation of laws while direct elections have been held for the choice of village leaders. China has begun to play a larger role in Asia. In 2002 the first efforts were made to reestablish relations with nationalist Taiwan. In 2003 China was the first major state to condemn the war against Iraq. Unlike Russia, China is a superpower with a flourishing economy and well organized armed forces, which may come to play a much larger part in world affairs.

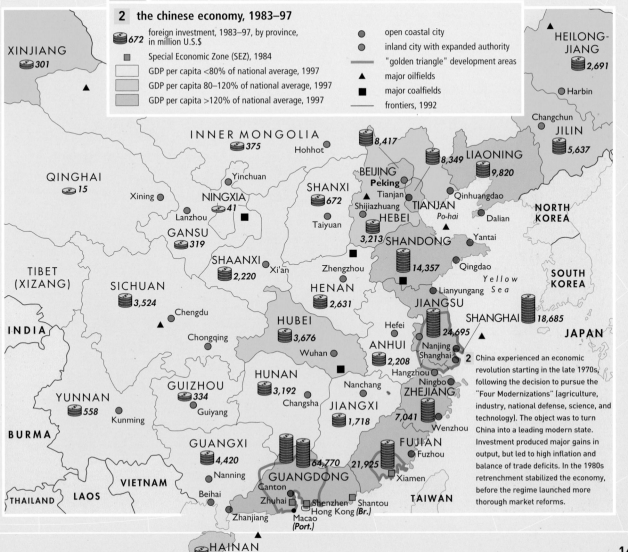

2 the chinese economy, 1983–97

672 foreign investment, 1983–97, by province, in million U.S.$

■ Special Economic Zone (SEZ), 1984

GDP per capita <80% of national average, 1997

GDP per capita 80–120% of national average, 1997

GDP per capita >120% of national average, 1997

● open coastal city

● inland city with expanded authority

— "golden triangle" development areas

▲ major oilfields

■ major coalfields

— frontiers, 1992

China experienced an economic revolution starting in the late 1970s, following the decision to pursue the "Four Modernizations" (agriculture, industry, national defense, science, and technology). The object was to turn China into a leading modern state. Investment produced major gains in output, but led to high inflation and balance of trade deficits. In the 1980s retrenchment stabilized the economy, before the regime launched more thorough market reforms.

XINJIANG 301

HEILONG-JIANG 2,691
Harbin

INNER MONGOLIA 375
Hohhot

QINGHAI 15
Xining

NINGXIA 41
Yinchuan
Lanzhou

GANSU 319

SHANXI 672
Taiyuan

BEIJING
Peking
Tianjan
Shijiazhuang
TIANJAN
Po-hai
8,417
8,349

LIAONING 9,820
Qinhuangdao
Dalian

Changchun

JILIN 5,637

NORTH KOREA

HEBEI 3,213

SHANDONG 14,357
Yantai
Qingdao

SHAANXI 2,220
Xi'an

Zhengzhou

HENAN 2,631

Lianyungang

Yellow Sea

SOUTH KOREA

TIBET (XIZANG)

SICHUAN 3,524
Chengdu
Chongqing

HUBEI 3,676
Wuhan

Hefei

JIANGSU 24,695
Nanjing
Shanghai

SHANGHAI 18,685

JAPAN

INDIA

ANHUI 2,208
Hangzhou

HUNAN 3,192
Changsha

Nanchang

ZHEJIANG 7,041
Ningbo
Wenzhou

YUNNAN 558
Kunming

GUIZHOU 334
Guiyang

JIANGXI 1,718

FUJIAN 21,925
Fuzhou
Xiamen

BURMA

GUANGXI 4,420
Nanning
Beihai

GUANGDONG 64,770
Canton
Zhuhai
Shenzhen Shantou
Hong Kong (Br.)
Macao (Port.)
Zhanjiang

VIETNAM

THAILAND LAOS

TAIWAN

HAINAN 5,237

economic revolution in **asia**: the **pacific rim**

since 1980

by 1976 Japan and the Four Dragons produce 60 percent of world's manufacturing exports

1978 Sino-Japanese Treaty of Friendship

1980s communist China and Vietnam begin to modernize their economies

1990s economic revolution in Asia alters balance of world economies

1997 Hong Kong returned to Chinese rule

1998 financial crisis in Asia. Currencies fall sharply in value

1999 Thailand, Malaysia, and South Korea begin to rebound

2003 Japan shows signs of emerging from 10 years of deflation

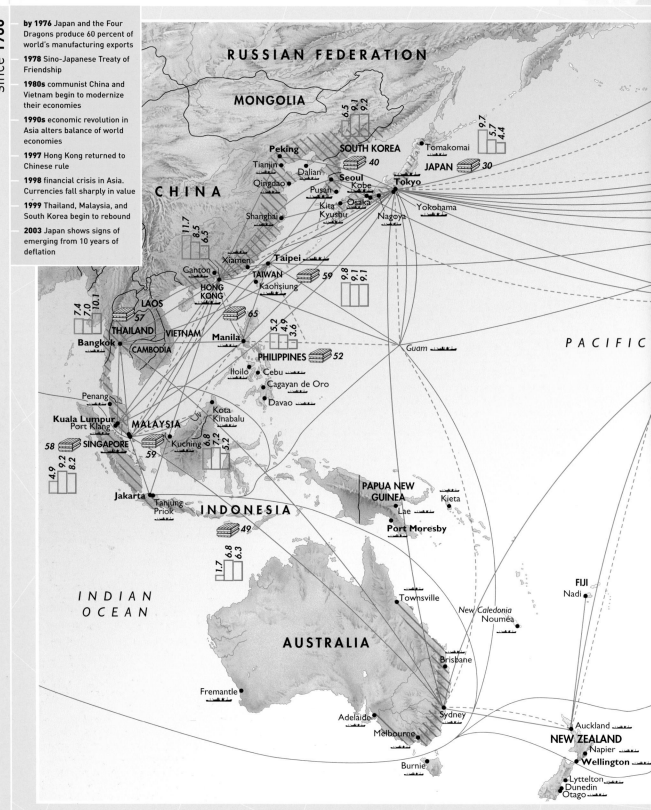

1 the pacific rim

- - - -   fibre-optic links

———   major air connections

▬▬▬   major container ports

———   major container-shipping routes

▨   development corridors

5.2 4.9 3.6   average growth rates
1960–65 1965–85 1985–92

52   proportion of imports from other
Pacific Rim producers, 1992

1 The Pacific Rim area was the fastest-growing economic region in the world during the 1980s and early 1990s (map left). Based on a complex and modern communications network and high-growth urban centers, the region is one of high investment, large-scale manufacturing output, and aggregate growth rates well above those of the rest of the developed world. The global crisis of 1997 hit the economies of South East Asia particularly hard, but by 1999 signs of recovery were seen in most areas, although Hong Kong's economy remained mired in recession and in Indonesia growth, although positive, remained sluggish.

Japan and China have been the two largest players in the transformation of the Asian Pacific Rim from an economic backwater in the 1950s to the hub of the world trading economy in the 1990s.

The east Asian region quadrupled its per capita income in 25 years, a record unparalleled in economic history. In 1997 Hong Kong and Singapore ranked among the ten richest states in the world per capita, ahead of France and Britain.

The economy of the Pacific Rim developed in a number of waves. Japan launched Asian prosperity in the 1950s. Spurred by her example, the so-called "Four Dragons" of the region—South Korea, Hong Kong, Singapore, and Taiwan—began a second wave of expansion. All four states lacked the advantages necessary for the normal path of industrialization. They were short of capital, they were overpopulated, and they possessed little arable land and few raw material reserves. They opted instead to concentrate on export-led growth, using cheap labor and borrowed capital to undercut established textile and light consumer goods producers. Their success was phenomenal. By 1976 Japan and the Four Dragons produced 60 percent of the world's manufacturing exports.

When the growth of the developed world slowed down in the 1970s, Japan and the Four Dragons began to invest heavily in the developing states of South East Asia—Malaysia, Thailand, Indonesia, and the Philippines—which were rich in raw materials and food supplies. These states, organized in the Association of South East Asian Nations (ASEAN) from 1967, then embarked on their own version of the Asian economic miracle, emulating their richer neighbors to the north by producing low-price exports in huge volumes. The region developed an increasingly integrated economy: Japan and the Four Dragons produced high-quality, high-cost manufactures; ASEAN produced more of the low-price consumer goods aimed at Asian and U.S. markets. The states of the Pacific Rim became each others' best markets. When communist China and Vietnam began to expand and modernize their economies in the 1980s, further huge new markets opened up. The rest of the Pacific Rim—Australia, New Zealand, western Canada and the U.S.—were drawn in as consumers and suppliers for the world's fastest-growing economic arena.

The success of the new industrial giants in Asia owed something to favorable economic circumstances. The emergence of rich overseas markets in the developed world and the globalization of trade and finance created a healthy framework for rapid export growth. Modern electronic technology was easily transferred between states, and products based around the microchip were particularly suitable for economies that lacked a heavy industrial base. There were also important advantages enjoyed by many Asian societies. They began with a cheap labor force, willing to work long hours for low pay and flexible in the face of new technologies. The cultural ethic, with its emphasis on frugality, group loyalty, respect for hierarchy, and for educational achievement, has been a stimulus for high savings and low labor unrest. Governments spent less on welfare and infrastructure and more on education and export subsidy. In the 1990s, 80 percent of 18-year olds in Taiwan and 85 percent in South Korea were still in full-time education. Literacy rates throughout the Pacific Rim were considerably higher than those in South Asia, Africa, or Latin America.

By the early 1990s the economic revolution in East Asia had altered the balance of the world economy, which for much of the century was dominated by the United States and Europe. But starting in the summer of 1997 most of the East Asian economies succumbed to the contagion of an unprecedented financial crisis. The once-booming economies of Thailand, South Korea, Indonesia, and Malaysia saw their currencies collapse in value and their national incomes drop sharply. Even Singapore and Hong Kong, with their robust financial systems, did not escape. Beginning in early 1999 three of the four worst-affected economies (Thailand, Malaysia, and South Korea) began to rebound. The political and economic prospects for Indonesia remain uncertain. A full recovery from the financial crisis may take some years.

1986 U.S. bomb Libya in retaliation for terrorist activities

1991 outbreak of civil war in Sierra Leone

1992 U.S. forces intervene to end Somalia's famine and civil war

1992 Algeria cancels election results after fundamentalist successes; bloody civil war erupts

1994 ethnic strife in Rwanda

1995 Nigeria expelled from Commonwealth for repeated human rights abuses

1997 Mobutu overthrown in Zaire; Laurent Kabila president of renamed Democratic Republic of Congo; Anti-Kabila rebellion (1998)

1998–99 war between Eritrea and Ethiopia

1999 seizures of white-owned farms by "war veterans" in Zimbabwe begin; Zimbabwe pulls out of Commonweath (2003)

2002 Jonas Savimbi killled; end of Angolan Civil War

2002 Northern Sudan institutes Shariah Law

2004 Libya renounces weapons of mass destruction and agrees to cooperate with West

Poverty and military conflict has been the lot of much of Africa since 1985. The collapse of the Soviet Union in 1989 and the end of the Cold War meant that Africa's significance in international affairs diminished.

The end of Soviet power also contributed to the pace of change in South Africa and to the final dismantling of the apartheid system. The South African government could no longer play on Western fears of communist-inspired revolution in southern Africa. Nelson Mandela, the leader of the African National Congress, was freed from prison and his party won the elections of 1994 (see pages 154–5). On the African stage, Mandela's political stature enabled him to act as a peace broker for various conflicts throughout the continent.

Relative to most nonindustrial countries elsewhere in the world, Africa's poverty increased in the 1980s and 1990s. Population continued to grow, towns to expand, and dependence on foreign supplies of foodstuffs to increase. African governments were also heavily indebted to Western countries. As elsewhere in the developing world, Western loans have initiated a vicious circle of debt, which has grown heavier since the 1970s. Much of the money was supplied from the IMF and World Bank, which used debt default as an instrument to compel economic changes through its structural adjustment

1 Savage civil wars have been fought throughout the Horn of Africa (map below). Military rule came to Somalia in 1970, to Ethiopia in 1974, and to the Sudan in 1969. In Ethiopia the Marxist-Leninist regime of Mengistu Haile Mariam fought a long war against the Eritrean and Tigrean independence movements until his overthrow in 1991, as well as a war with Somalia over the Ogaden region. In 1998–9 Ethiopia fought a war against the newly independent state of Eritrea for control of disputed border areas. By 1999 the central Somali state had effectively ceased to exist, with the northwest breaking away as "Somaliland" and the south divided between competing warlords.

1 ethiopia, somalia, and sudan 1985–2000

Ethiopia
- provinces claimed by Somalia, 1977–88
- held by Eritrean People's Liberation Front, 1986
- captured by EPLF by Mar. 1988
- secured by Tigre People's Liberation Front, Apr. 1988

Somalia
- controlled by competing tribes, clans, and factions, from 1989
- Siad Barre's base, Feb. 1991–Apr. 1992
- de facto independent, Mar. 1991

Sudan
- southern Sudan (non-Muslim, non-Arab), limited autonomy from 1972
- non-Arab populations in northern Sudan
- main areas of operation of South Sudan People's Liberation Army from 1984

others
- Eritrean war, 1998–2000

- government counterattacks, June 1988
- captured by TPLF, early 1989
- captured by EPLF, Feb. 1990
- advance of antigovernment forces, Apr. 1991
- de facto independent Apr. 1991, independence declared May 1993
- Siad Barre's last attempt to regain power, Apr. 1992
- controlled by Aidid, June 1992
- areas of most intense fighting
- under SPLA attacks, Aug. 1986
- SPLA attacks, Nov. 1987 and May 1989
- areas of intense fighting, 1990
- frontier claimed by Egypt
- refugees and refugee movements

Map labels: EGYPT, L. Nasser, Halaib Area, Nuba, Nile, Bedzha, SUDAN, 1993, 1995: Islamic Jihad infiltration, ERITREA, Nakfa, Afabet, Massawa, Asmara, Khartoum Apr. 1985: Numeiri deposed, Tigre, Blue Nile, White Nile, Gondar, Assab, L. Tana, DJIBOUTI, Djibouti, Berbera, Kurmuk, Hargeysa, Burao, SOMALILAND, Bentiu, Malakal, BAHR EL GHAZAL, acute famine in southern Sudan 1999, Apr. 1991: Addis Ababa, Mengistu flees, Horn of Africa, Wau, UPPER NILE, ETHIOPIA, Ogaden, Rumbek, CENTRAL AFRICAN REP., EQUATORIA, administered by Kenya, Juba, Belet Huen, Dec. 1992: occupied by UN (to Mar. 1995), Yei, Torit, UGANDA, Apr. 1992: Siad Barre flees, Garba Harre, Johar, SOMALIA, to July 1992: HQ of Garang's faction of SPLA when captured by government forces, Bardera, Jan. 1991: Siad Barre flees, Mogadishu, Merca, continued fighting to 1999, KENYA, Somali claims to Kenyan territory, Kismayu, Red Sea

www.globalsecurity.org/military/world/war/sudan.htm
The Sudanese civil war
www.globalpolicy.org/socecon/develop/indexafr.htm
Poverty and development in Africa

2 Independent Africa experienced sustained economic growth in the 1960s and early 1970s. The rate declined in the late 1970s and 1980s. In the 1990s (map right) many African states remain heavily reliant on the export of a handful of commodities and are burdened by huge external debts. Funds from the World Bank and IMF to assist African economies now tend to come with stringent economic austerity conditions attached.

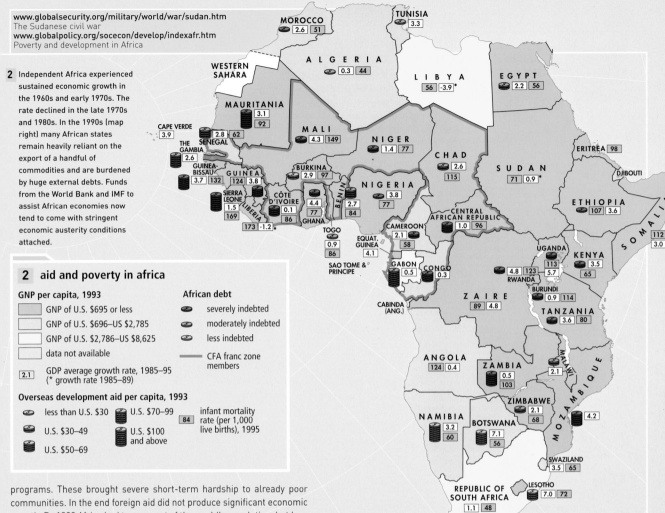

2   aid and poverty in africa

GNP per capita, 1993

- GNP of U.S. $695 or less
- GNP of U.S. $696–US $2,785
- GNP of U.S. $2,786–US $8,625
- data not available

[2.1] GDP average growth rate, 1985–95 (* growth rate 1985–89)

Overseas development aid per capita, 1993

- less than U.S. $30
- U.S. $30–49
- U.S. $50–69
- U.S. $70–99
- U.S. $100 and above

[84] infant mortality rate (per 1,000 live births), 1995

African debt

- severely indebted
- moderately indebted
- less indebted
- CFA franc zone members

programs. These brought severe short-term hardship to already poor communities. In the end foreign aid did not produce significant economic growth. By 1998 Africa had ten percent of the world's population, but less than one percent of its industrial output; and only nine out of the continent's 48 states had a per capita income of more than U.S.$1,000 a year. Poverty is directly related to exceptionally high rates of population growth, which have continued to average more than 2.5 percent a year in the years since 1985. Urban growth was also rapid and most states had to import food to feed their populations; child malnutrition levels varied between 25 and 50 percent in much of sub-Saharan Africa. HIV/AIDS infection is high, particularly in parts of east, central, and southern Africa. Arguments over this shrinking economic cake have been the root cause of much of the continent's political instability and violence since independence.

The ethnic unrest and war in the Horn of Africa continued after 1985. In the southern Sudan the long war between the Islamic north and the peoples of the south remained unresolved. The Marxist regime in Ethiopia collapsed in 1991 and Eritrea became the first African state to gain independence from another African state. In neighboring Somalia civil war broke out in the early 1990s and left the country politically divided and impoverished. The worst ethnic violence occurred in Rwanda in 1994 where militiamen from the the majority Hutu population massacred the minority Tutsi people. Up to a million people were killed, while as many as two million fled the country. In Zaire in 1996 a rebellion brought an end to the long and corrupt rule of President Mobutu. Within months Laurent Kabila, the new president of the Democratic Republic of Congo, was faced with a fresh revolt in the east of the country, again by ethnic Tutsis dissatisfied with his policies. His rule was only upheld by troops from other African states, while by early 1999 he had lost control of some 60 percent of the country.

The state in many African countries had grown weak and increasingly corrupt in the 1980s. Some were run as large "criminal" enterprises with ruling elites and factions siphoning off the national wealth. In Angola, Liberia, and Sierra Leone, armed rivals struggled to control the areas rich in diamonds, oil, and minerals. As a result thousands of people died, while others fled, and the economies were ruined. However, the long-running civil war in Mozambique, fueled by South African policies of destabilization, came to an end with the fall of apartheid. As a result of war—and conflict often exacerbates food shortages and famine—Africa has proportionately more refugees than any other continent. The problem of displaced people has been most serious in the Horn of Africa and southern Sudan.

In many states during the late 1980s and 1990s opposition to corrupt single party and military rule increased, particularly from people in urban areas and from church leaders. Generally rule by one-party or one-man dictatorship was abandoned in many African states, and the system of government was replaced with multiparty electoral politics. However, "democratization" did not necessarily mean a real change in the rulers, the means or the methods by which countries were run. Arbitrary governments still widely disregarded human rights. Religious rivalries between Muslims and Christians contributed to the violence in southern Sudan and in other states astride the Muslim-Christian boundary. Both Islam and Christianity gained many adherents in the 1980s and 1990s, with great increases in the number of Protestants in southern Ghana and Nigeria and in areas of East and Central Africa.

southern africa

2 the angolan civil wars, 1975–91, 1993–99

- Bakongo ethnic area
- Bambundu ethnic area
- Ovimbundu ethnic area

held in February 1975 by
- FNLA (Bakongo based, pro-Western)
- MPLA (Bambundu based, pro-Soviet)
- UNITA (Ovimbundu based, pro-Chinese then pro-Western)

- advance of FNLA-UNITA forces, 1975
- area secured by MPLA, mid-1976
- MPLA-supported incursions
- northwestern limit of UNITA activity, 1976 to May 1991 ceasefire
- MPLA attack on UNITA, 1990
- UNITA attacks 1998–99
- zones of intense fighting from 1992 elections to Lusaka peace accord, 1994
- northern limit of South African incursions, 1976–88
- ◊ diamonds
- ✎ gold ▲ oil

Nowhere has democracy been harder to establish than in sub-Saharan Africa. A concept belatedly imported by the colonial powers, the European model of parliamentary rule often meant little in the context of ethnic, linguistic, and religious conflict which the independent states of Africa inherited.

The one exception, South Africa, contained a large white minority community of British and Dutch (Afrikaner) origin, in which parliamentary government for whites was fully established by 1930. In this unlikely setting democracy made its most significant gain in Africa when in 1994 its 30-million Black population was admitted to the parliamentary system. The struggle for emancipation of the nonwhite population dated to early in the century, but gathered momentum with the election of the Afrikaner National Party government in 1948. The NP adopted the ideology of separate racial development apartheid. Economic, political, and military power was concentrated in white hands. African "bantustans" were set up: these fragmented, overpopulated, and impoverished black ethnic states were destined for "independence."

Starting in the 1970s, when the policy of separate development reached its climax, the white regime faced growing pressures. Popular protest grew in the African townships, backed by a campaign of violence waged by the ANC and the Pan-African Congress. The independence of Angola and Mozambique and the transfer to African rule in Zimbabwe presented South Africa with hostile frontiers across which guerrillas could operate, and drew the regime into brutal counterinsurgency wars. In the 1980s

the government of P.W. Botha became increasingly militaristic and dictatorial in the fight against internal and external enemies. Foreign opinion hardened against the regime's human rights abuses and in 1986 economic sanctions were imposed by the U.S. and EC. The resulting economic isolation damaged the South African economy just when the tide of violent protest was rising to a level the security forces could barely contain.

The result was a slow move toward reform and stabilization. The Colored and Asian communities were given a share in power in 1984, although the white regime was intent on maintaining control. In 1988 Botha agreed to negotiate a settlement of the antiguerrilla wars in Angola and Namibia. In September 1989 Botha was succeeded by F.W. de Klerk, who, with the backing of important sections of the white community, opened the door to reform. In 1990 the banned opposition parties were legalized and the ANC leader Nelson Mandela freed from prison. Sanctions were lifted abroad and the ANC abandoned violence. A referendum in 1991 among the white population gave de Klerk a two-to-one majority in favor of a new democratic constitution. The following year a Convention for a Democratic South Africa drafted a transitional constitution and power passed to a multiracial Executive Council. The whole process was rejected by the extreme Afrikaner parties, and by the large Zulu minority led by Chief Mangosuthu Buthelezi, whose people feared for their ethnic identity in a state dominated by non-Zulus. Buthelezi was persuaded to rejoin the democratic process but not before an estimated 15,000 people had died in interethnic clashes.

In April 1994 multiracial and multiparty elections gave Mandela's ANC 63 percent of the vote, the National Party 20 percent, and Buthelezi's Inkatha Freedom Party 10 percent. Mandela became president and de Klerk vice-president (until the withdrawal of the National Party from the coalition in 1996). A state of near civil war between supporters of the ANC and IFP continued in Zululand-Natal. A Truth and Reconciliation Commission, chaired by Archbishop Tutu, reported in 1998. It sought to make public and to reconcile all those who had been involved in the bitter conflict of the past decades.

The ANC government's status gained from President Mandela's international standing, but it faced serious economic and social problems and after its election was forced to retreat from its socialist agenda and embrace market ideas. Mandela stepped down after the election of June 1999 in which the ANC won an increased majority. He was succeeded by Thabo Mbeki.

Map labels

Briefly overrun by FLEC secessionists, Sep. 1992

MPLA aid to Kabila gov't. in Democratic Republic of Congo 1998–99

Cabinda

ZAIRE/CONGO

Soyo

300,000 Portuguese flee, 1975

Uige

Negage

Kafunfo

1977, 1978

Cuban forces, Soviet equipment 1975

Luanda

Malanje

Saurimo

Cuanza

People's Republic of Angola declared by MPLA, Nov. 11, 1975

A N G O L A

Bié Plateau

Luena

Lobito

Huambo

People's Democratic Republic of Angola declared by FNLA-UNITA, Nov. 11, 1975

Benguela

Lubango

Menongue

Cuando

Namibe

Cuito

Cunjamba HQ of UNITA, Oct. 1976

ZAMBIA

Cunene

Cubango

HQ of SWAPO forces until Namibian independence

SWAPO guerrillas, to 1988

N A M I B I A

2 Following Angola's independence the Marxist MPLA took over power (map left), while the South African-backed UNITA movement, led by Jonas Savimbi, waged a guerrilla campaign against them. A temporary truce in 1991 and a general election in 1992 did not prevent the resumption of civil war. In 1998–99 severe fighting continued with UNITA forces in control of 60 percent of Angola. Only Savimbi's death in 2002 effectively ended the war.

www.pbs.org/wgbh/pages/frontline/shows/mandela/
The life of Nelson Mandela
www-cs-students.stanford.edu/~cale/cs201/apartheid.hist.html
The history of apartheid in South Africa

In the national elections, the ANC won 252 seats (63% of the vote), the NP 82 seats (20%), the IFP 43 seats (10%), and other parties 23 seats (7%)

NORTHERN TRANSVAAL
ANC _38_ 95%
others _2_ 5%

ANC _50_ 58%
NP _21_ 25%
others _15_ 17%

ANC _26_ 87%
others _4_ 13%

GAUTENG
Pretoria
Johannesburg
NORTH WEST

MPUMALANGA
ANC _25_ 83%
NP _3_ 10%
others _2_ 7%

KWAZULU/ NATAL
IFP _41_ 51%
ANC _26_ 32%
others _14_ 17%
Durban

FREE STATE
ANC _24_ 80%
others _6_ 20%
Bloemfontein

Springbok
NORTHERN CAPE
ANC _15_ 50%
NP _12_ 40%
others _3_ 10%

EASTERN CAPE
ANC _48_ 86%
NP _6_ 11%
others _2_ 3%
East London

Cape Town
WESTERN CAPE
NP _23_ 55%
ANC _14_ 33%
others _5_ 12%

1 **south africa: national and provincial elections, 1994**

parties with control of Provincial Assemblies

☐ African National Congress (ANC)
☐ National Party (NP)
☐ Inkatha Freedom Party (IFP)

_50_ seats held
_50%_ percentage of vote

1 South Africa was transformed during the 1990s from rule by a white minority to a multiracial democracy (maps left and below). From 1948 the ruling Afrikaner National Party, representing the Dutch settler communities, established the policy of apartheid, or separate development for the different races. In 1959 black "homelands" or bantustans were created, four of which were granted "independence" starting in the late 1970s, but not recognized internationally. Widespread economic and political protests in the 1970s were violently suppressed, but in the 1980s, in the face of international sanctions and domestic criticism, some of the apartheid system was relaxed. In 1984 the Asian and Colored (mixed-race) communities were given separate parliamentary assemblies and responsibility for their affairs. In 1990 the ban on parties was lifted and the African National Congress, led by Nelson Mandela, and Chief Buthelezi's Inkatha Freedom Party (representing the Zulus of Natal), collaborated with the white government on a new multiracial constitution. In 1994 the ANC won an overwhelming electoral victory, marred by persistent violence between ANC and IFP activists. In 1999 and again in 2004 the ANC was the victor in general elections, but did not win the two-thirds majority necessary to amend the constitution.

1989: F.W. de Klerk succeeds P.W. Botha as president
1990: ban on ANC, PAC, and Communist Party lifted
1991: remaining apartheid legislation repealed. Convention for Democratic South Africa (CODESA) talks between government, ANC, IFP, and others (to 1992)
Apr. 1994: first universal suffrage elections
1994–96: coalition gov't led by President Mandela; ANC retreated from its socialist program
1998: Truth and Reconciliation Commission report on apartheid years
1999: general election; ANC won 66% vote. Thabo Mbeki president
2004: ANC again win general election

Mar. 1994: Homeland president, supported by armed white extremists, refuses to participate in elections; deposed by South African government

ZIMBABWE
MOZAMBIQUE
VENDA
resistance movement (RENAMO) received South African assistance
Pietersburg
Limpopo

TRANSVAAL
1956: mass demonstration by women, the culmination of a Defiance Campaign against apartheid from 1952

BOTS.

BOPHUTHATSWANA
Pretoria
Krugersdorp
Soweto
Johannesburg
Sharpeville
Kuruman

SWAZ.
1960: Sharpeville shootings, leading to further protest and to state of emergency. ANC and PAC banned.

NAMIBIA
guerrilla warfare between South African occupying forces and nationalist SWAPO
1990: South African withdrawal and Namibian independence

1976: Soweto uprising; hundreds of protestors shot mid-1980s: Vaal uprising

Kroonstad

Mar. 1994: violence between IFP and ANC leads to declaration of state of emergency. Virtual "civil war" continues through 1990s
KWAZULU

CAPE
REPUBLIC
OF
PROVINCE
SOUTH AFRICA

Orange
Springbok

Kimberley
Bloemfontein

ORANGE FREE STATE
1986–89: conflict between Inkatha and United Democratic Front

LESOTHO
Pietermaritzburg
Durban
NATAL

1973–75: widespread strikes
1975: Chief Buthelezi founds Inkatha
1985: township disturbances
1992: conflict between ANC and IFP

June 1998 South African military intervention in Lesotho

De Aar

1949: conflict between Africans and Indians
1959: Cato Manor beerhall protests
1985: conflict between Africans and Indians

1 **apartheid and democracy in south africa to 1995**

☐ "independent" bantustans

1959: legislation provides for the eventual creation of black "homelands" or bantustans. Four (Transkei, 1976; Bophuthatswana, 1977; Venda, 1979; Ciskei, 1981) were declared "independent," but were not recognized internationally

Drakensberg
TRANSKEI

Feb. 1960: Harold Macmillan's "wind of change" speech
1960: PAC demonstration against pass laws

1973-5: widespread strikes
1985: unrest in townships leads to state of emergency

CISKEI
East London

Cape Town

Port Elizabeth

the **middle east**

In the Middle East war, civil conflict and repression persisted just as they did in Africa. The major cause was no longer the Arab-Israeli conflict, which had produced four wars in a generation, but the threat posed to the whole region by revolution in Iran.

In the 1970s Iran was ruled by Shah Reza Pahlavi, whose politically corrupt regime was kept in power by Western support and the SAVAK secret police. He was opposed by communists and by Islamic Shia fundamentalists. One of their leaders, Grand Ayatollah Ruhollah Khomeini, called in public from his exile in Iraq for the faithful to rise up in revolution. Hostility to the shah reached boiling point in 1978, and on January 16, 1979 he left Iran. In February Khomeini declared Iran an Islamic Republic and imposed a militant Islamic regime. The revolutionary wave produced widespread killings and imprisonment of political opponents and Westernizers, and the imposition of a harsh Koranic law.

According to Khomeini's theology, the revolution had to be exported. Rather than a world of nation-states, he sought a broader Islamic religious community, or *umma*: Iran had a sacred duty to lead the worldwide struggle to disseminate the message of Islam. During the 1980s, Iran destabilized the whole of the Middle East in pursuit of this goal. Terrorism and subversion were aimed at Bahrain and Kuwait in the early 1980s. In Syria support for militant Islamic opponents of the regime of Hafez al-Assad led to the massacre of 15–20,000 fundamentalists in the city of Hama in 1982. In Lebanon Iran backed the Party of God (Hezbollah), founded in 1983 to wage terrorist war on Israel.

The greatest efforts were reserved for Iran's immediate neighbor Iraq, where there was a sizeable Shia community ruled by Saddam Hussein and the pan-Arabist Ba'ath

movement. Rather than risk an internal Islamic revolution, Hussein invaded Iran on September 23, 1980. Khomeini called the faithful to battle and thousands of poorly armed and trained Islamic militia—*Basij*—swarmed to the call. A long war of attrition, in which neither side made anysubstantial gains, ended in the summer of 1988 from mutual exhaustion. Hussein saw himself as the defender of the Arab world against Iranian extremism, playing the role Nasser had occupied in the 1950s as leader of the Arab cause.

The war with Iran had, however, bankrupted Iraq. In 1988 there was an $80 billion foreign debt and vast reconstruction costs. Hussein turned to his tiny oil-rich neighbor, Kuwait. An ultimatum was sent, asking Kuwait to give Iraq a gift of $30 billion and an annual $10 billion subsidy, to stop using Iraqi-claimed oilfields and to launch an Arab "Marshall Plan" for Iraq. When Kuwait refused, on August 2, 1990 Iraq invaded and annexed the emirate and its vast wealth. Although the West had supported Iraq in its war against Iran, the invasion of Kuwait posed a serious crisis in a region where the West had large oil interests. On the day of the invasion the UN passed Resolution 660 calling on Iraq to withdraw immediately from Kuwait or face military force.

Saddam Hussein refused to abandon Kuwait, partly because he did not believe that the UN could unite sufficiently to wage all-out war, partly because he could not risk the loss of face and consequent domestic political crisis. On January 16, 1991 a coalition of forces, including a number of Arab states, launched the operation to remove Iraqi forces from Kuwait. After a month of air strikes, the coalition began a ground offensive. Between February 24th and 27th Kuwait City was recaptured with the loss of 150 coalition soldiers. Iraqi losses were estimated at more than

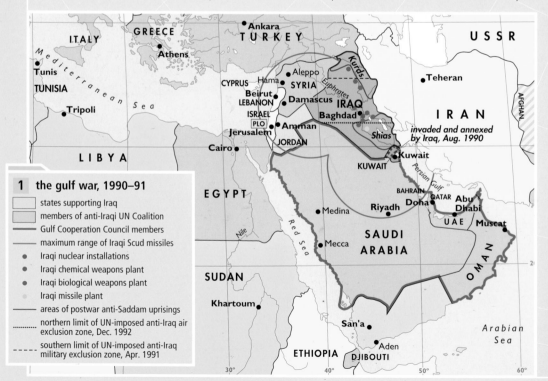

1 On August 2, 1990 Iraq invaded the oil state of Kuwait and on August 8th proclaimed the union of the two states. Following condemnation of Iraq's action by the UN, a coalition of states undertook Operation Desert Storm in January and February 1991 to drive Iraqi armies out of Kuwait (map left). The bulk of the military forces taking part in the operation were provided by the US. On February 28th Iraq withdrew unconditionally.

other UN coalition members:
Argentina / Netherlands
Australia / New Zealand
Bangladesh / Niger
Belgium / Norway
Canada / Poland
Czechoslov. / Romania
Denmark / Senegal
France / Spain
Germany / UK
Hungary / USA

1 the gulf war, 1990–91
- states supporting Iraq
- members of anti-Iraqi UN Coalition
- Gulf Cooperation Council members
- maximum range of Iraqi Scud missiles
- Iraqi nuclear installations
- Iraqi chemical weapons plant
- Iraqi biological weapons plant
- Iraqi missile plant
- areas of postwar anti-Saddam uprisings
- northern limit of UN-imposed anti-Iraq air exclusion zone, Dec. 1992
- southern limit of UN-imposed anti-Iraq military exclusion zone, Apr. 1991

www.merip.org/
Research and information on the Middle East
www.mideastweb.org/iraq.htm
History of the conflict between Iraq and the U.S./UN

2 the iran-iraq war, 1980–88

nonbelligerent countries supporting Iraq
nonbelligerent countries supporting Iran
Iraqi penetration, Dec. 1980–June 1982
southern limit of maritime exclusion zone declared by Iraq, Aug. 1982

Iranian penetration, with dates
★ bombed or attacked by missiles
Ⱥ centers of oil industry
frontline at ceasefire, July 1988
Kurdish ethnic areas
Arab ethnic areas in Iran
Shia-inhabited territory in Iraq

2 In September 1980 Iraq invaded Iran and sparked an eight-year war of attrition (map left), which ended in July 1988 when Iran sought an armistice. The war cost an estimated 400,000 dead and 750,000 wounded, and burdened both states with massive debts. The contested area was small and the outcome inconclusive.

200,000. Iraq was compelled to accept humiliating armistice terms. An estimated $170 billion of damage was done to Iraqi targets destroyed by coalition aircraft. The war split the Arab world, with Egypt, Syria, Saudi Arabia, and Morocco sending troops to help the UN Coalition, and Jordan, Yemen, Libya, Sudan, Algeria, Tunisia, and the PLO giving moral support, but no military help, to Iraq. Saddam Hussein survived the postwar crisis at home and remained in power over an impoverished and isolated state. His attempts to halt Islamic fundamentalism and then to pose as the new pan-Arab leader failed. During the 1990s Iraq was subject to strict UN regulations on weapons and military installations. In 2002, failure to comply with UN sanctions brought demands from the U.S. and Britain for immediate Iraqi disarmament and the following spring a predominantly Anglo-American expeditionary force invaded Iraq, without explicit UN support, and overthrew the Hussein regime.

Map 2 labels

Tabriz
L. Urmia
Caspian Sea
Rasht
Mar. 1987
Mosul
Rawandiz
Arbil
Teheran
Kirkuk
held by Iraq, May–July 1986
Feb. 1986
Kifri
Hamadan
Apr. 1987
Qom
Baquba
Bakhtaran
Nahavand
Borujerd
Tigris
Baghdad
Mehran
Khorramabad
Euphrates
evacuated by Iraq after ceasefire
IRAQ
Al Kut
Dehloran
Dezful
Isfahan
An Najaf
Masjed Soleyman
Feb. 1984–Mar. 1985
Susangerd
Ahvaz
Ramhormoz
IRAN
Majnun Island
Khorramshahr
Jan. 1987
Basra
Bandar Khomeini
Umm Qasr
Abadan
Feb. 1986
Faw
KUWAIT
Kharg Island
Shiraz
Kuwait
Bushehr
May 1987: Iraqi missile fired accidentally kills 37 US marines on USS Stark
1986–87: Iran and Iraq attack merchant shipping
May 1988: USS Vincennes mistakenly downs Iranian airliner
from 1987: Western warships protect international shipping
SAUDI ARABIA
Manama
BAHRAIN
Sirri Island
QATAR
Doha
The Gulf
UAE
Riyadh

3 Saddam Hussein was allowed to survive the 1991 Gulf War, but without international consensus on further action against his regime. In 2002 the U.S. accused Iraq of being in "material breech" of UN resolutions on weapons of mass destruction. A U.S.-led coalition invaded Iraq in 2003 (map right) and brought about the downfall of the Hussein regime.

Map 3 labels

TURKEY
secured, Apr. 11
Mar. 26 U.S. 173rd Airborne Brigade
36° N (Northern nofly zone, prewar)
Mosul
Arbil
secured, Apr. 9
Coalition special forces active before Mar. 19 and throughout conflict
Kirkuk
Mar. 31: destroyed by US and Kurdish forces
Turkey blocks entry of U.S. ground forces, Feb. 2003
Sulaymaniyah
Halabja
SYRIA
Tigris
IRAN
Tikrit
secured, Apr. 16
Samarra
Mar. 19: 1st air attack
Apr. 3: city reached by ground forces
Apr. 9: city falls
Beirut
Ar Ramadi
Euphrates
LEBANON
Damascus
2002–03: Increased U.S. diplomatic pressure; agrees to close terrorist organization offices, 2003
Karbala bypassed, 1 Apr.
Baghdad
ISRAEL
33° N (Southern no-fly zone)
B-52 bombers from UK
Amman
Karbala
Kut
B-52, B-1, B-2 bombers from Diego Garcia, Indian Ocean
Jerusalem
Special forces seize airfield; used by Coalition Mar. 26
Najaf
IRAQ
Samawah
JORDAN
Coalition special forces active before Mar. 119 and throughout conflict
Nasiriyah
secured, Apr. 7
slowed by sandstorm (Mar. 25–27)
Basra
Umm Qasr
U.S. 3rd Infantry Div. spearhead bypasses cities; 101st Air Assault later enters
Kuwait
Coalition amphibious landings
SAUDI ARABIA
U.S. and UK combat aircraft from Kuwait and UAE
U.S. Patriot anti-missile defences
KUWAIT

3 iraq, 2003

U.S. ground force advance
UK ground force advance
Kurdish and Coalition special forces advance
Coalition airstrikes
U.S. Navy carriers and Tomahawk-launching ships and submarines, based in the Mediterranean, Gulf, and Red Sea
☠ Ansar-al-Islam and terrorist camps

the search for peace in the **middle east**

since 1979

1979 Eygpt recognizes State of Israel

1987 beginning of Intefada in Gaza Strip

1988 PLO recognizes Palestinian and Jewish States in Israel

1992 PLO and Israeli government sign a Declaration of Principles on Interim self-government for the Gaza Strip and the West Bank

1994 King Hussein reaches peace settlement with Israel

1995 Oslo Accords

1995 Jewish extremist assassinates Israeli Prime Minister Rabin

1996 Israelis elect right-wing Likud government; Jewish settlements are built in occupied areas

2001 Israel begins new wave of military intervention into Palestinian areas

2003 "Road Map" for Middle East settlement published

2004 Death of Yasser Arafat

As the Iranian crisis grew in the 1980s, Israel's position in the politics of the Middle East began to alter. The decision by Egypt to recognize Israel in the peace settlement reached between them in 1979, although it initially provoked an Arab boycott of Egypt, created a framework that permitted the gradual easing of tension between Israel and the Arab states around her.

Jordan restored relations with Egypt in 1983, while in Amman in November 1987 most of the other Arab states were persuaded to do likewise. Formal recognition of Israel took longer, but in July 1994 King Hussein of Jordan ended the long-running state of war and reached a comprehensive peace settlement that September. Syria, which had led the campaign against Egyptian recognition of Israel throughout the 1980s, finally restored relations with Cairo in December 1989 and agreed in 1995 to talks with Israel.

The most significant breakthrough came with the recognition by the PLO in November 1988 of two states in Palestine, one Jewish, one Arab. In early 1989 exploratory talks began in Tunis on a Palestinian settlement. The reasons for the revolution in the PLO position lay in its declining fortunes. In 1982 Israel occupied southern Lebanon in an effort to end Palestinian attacks across her borders. The military defeat led to the transfer of the PLO to a base in Tunisia, remote from the seat of the conflict. The PLO failure also alienated many younger Palestinians, who began to turn to more radical groups—Hezbollah, Hamas, and Islamic Jihad—all of which remained focused on the physical destruction of Israel. The weakness of the PLO also encouraged the Palestinians in Gaza and the West Bank to take the political conflict into their own hands. In December 1987 violent clashes between Arabs and Israeli forces in the Gaza Strip launched the Inifada, a popular and often violent rebellion in the occupied areas against the Israeli occupation. The PLO claim that a Palestinian state and a Jewish state could live side by side was part of a concerted effort by Yasser Arafat and the PLO leadership not to lose touch with the grass roots of the liberation movement.

2 The issue of independence for the Kurds goes back to the unredeemed promise of an independent home-land made by the Treaty of Sèvres in 1920. Since 1961 the Kurds, supported by Kurdish minorities in Iran and Turkey, have fought against the Iraqi regime for national independence (map below). After the 1991 Gulf War millions became refugees from Saddam Hussein, but the Kurds succeeded thereafter in setting up an autonomous area in the north of Iraq.

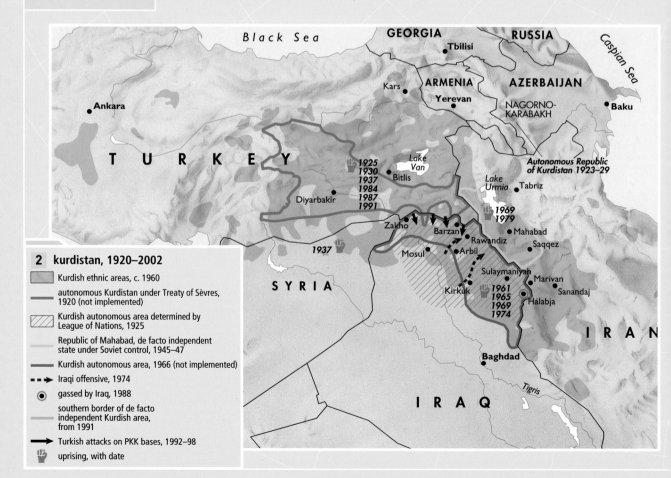

2 kurdistan, 1920–2002

- Kurdish ethnic areas, c. 1960
- autonomous Kurdistan under Treaty of Sèvres, 1920 (not implemented)
- Kurdish autonomous area determined by League of Nations, 1925
- Republic of Mahabad, de facto independent state under Soviet control, 1945–47
- Kurdish autonomous area, 1966 (not implemented)
- ▪▪▪▶ Iraqi offensive, 1974
- ◉ gassed by Iraq, 1988
- southern border of de facto independent Kurdish area, from 1991
- ▶ Turkish attacks on PKK bases, 1992–98
- ✊ uprising, with date

Little progress was made between the PLO and Israel, not because there were not circles in Israel willing to tackle the Palestine issue but because the Israeli government of Yitzhak Shamir was opposed to any idea of losing control over the occupied areas. In October 1991 President George Bush succeeded in setting up a summit in Madrid that brought the parties in the conflict together, including the PLO, which was represented by the Gaza politician Haydar al-Shafi. Progress accelerated when Shamir was replaced by the Labor prime minister, Yitzhak Rabin, in July 1992. In the spring of 1993 the PLO and the Israeli government met secretly to agree a basis for a settlement. In September both sides signed a Declaration of Principles on interim self-government for the Gaza Strip and the West Bank. In May 1994 Israel withdrew from Jericho and the Gaza Strip, and the Palestinian National Authority, with Arafat at its head, took over the running of these areas. Repeated terrorist attacks aimed at disrupting the peace process derailed the second stage of the Oslo Accords, which were not agreed until September 1995, but which led to the Israeli withdrawal from some areas of the West Bank and the extension of limited Palestinian self-rule until 1999.

The agreements met with bitter opposition from several quarters. Hamas, Islamic Jihad, and Hezbollah kept up a campaign of terror. Even moderate Palestinians were divided over Arafat's change of heart. Jewish fundamentalists were also profoundly hostile. The Gush Emunim (Bloc of the Faithful), set up after the 1973 war, remained implacably opposed to any loss of territory in the sacred land of Israel. An ultranationalist gunman was responsible for the murder of 29 Muslims at prayer in Hebron in February 1994. Rabin himself was the victim of a Jewish extremist in November 1995. The issues of Jewish settlement on the West Bank and the future of Jerusalem were not settled at Oslo and became major stumbling blocks following the election in May 1996 of a right-wing Likud government under Binyamin Netanyahu.

Under Netanyahu relations with the Palestinian leadership became strained. The Wye Agreement on further Israeli withdrawal from the West Bank, signed in the USA in October 1998, was never implemented. Efforts by his successor Ehud Barak, elected in 1999, to revive the peace process came to nothing. Under Ariel Sharon, elected in 2001, Israel began a new wave of military interventions in the Palestinian areas. In 2004 the Hamas spiritual leader Sheikh Yassim was murdered by Israeli forces, provoking a further wave of violence in the long Middle Eastern War.

1 In 1993 the Israeli government and the PLO agreed in Oslo to limited Palestinian self-rule and a phased Israeli withdrawal from Gaza and the West Bank (map right). Following a brief period of limited self-rule, continued violence brought the Israeli army to intervene in both areas. In 2003 the government of Sharon began to construct a security fence to separate Arab and Jewish settlements on the West Bank. In 2004 violence once again escalated between the two sides.

1 the israeli-palestinian agreement, 1993–2004

- under full Palestinian control starting in May 1994
- under full Palestinian control starting in 1995–97
- under Palestinian administrative control starting in 1995
- ■ Jewish settlements in occupied territories
- patrolled by the Israeli military
- patrolled by joint Israeli-Palestinian forces
- ☆ Israeli police posts
- ■ coordination offices
- East Jerusalem
- Completed sections of security fence, April 2004
- Projected sections of security fence, April 2004
- ● Palestinian villages behind security fence

Throughout the years of crisis in the Middle East the United Nations has played a prominent part, from the Arab-Israeli wars of 1948 through to the problems of Lebanon and Palestine in the 1990s. The UN has not succeeded in preventing wars in the region, but it has succeeded in the Middle East and elsewhere in containing violence and monitoring its aftermath.

The roots of the United Nations Organization lie in the Second World War. Roosevelt's secretary of state, Cordell Hull, who was later awarded the Nobel Peace Prize for his efforts, worked behind the scenes to turn the wartime anti-Axis coalition into a permanent world organization. In Dumbarton Oaks, Washington, in August 1944 the major powers drew up a preliminary charter for an organization that Roosevelt insisted should be called the United Nations.

The founding conference of the UN was held in San Francisco in April 1945. It was agreed that the organization should have a general assembly, a smaller security council with permanent Great Power membership, and a permanent secretariat. It differed little in structure from the League of Nations, which cooperated in the development of its successor. After two months the charter was agreed. The American millionaire John D. Rockefeller offered a free site in New York for a UN building, and the permanent headquarters was established there as a sign of American commitment to world peace. Membership was to be open to all, but exceptions soon emerged. Switzerland remained neutral and did not join; Japan and Italy were admitted after US pressure on the USSR in 1955; the two German states did not join until 1975. The two Korean states refused to join, since each claimed the other's territory. Taiwan kept its membership as the Republic of China following the Chinese revolution, but in 1971 communist China took its place and Taiwan was formally expelled.

The UN's primary purpose was to keep the peace. It was almost immediately involved in the Greek civil war (1947) and in 1948 in the war between Israel and its Arab neighbors. The monitoring organization set up—UNTSO—is still there, 50 years later. The greatest test came in 1950 when North Korea invaded the South. The Security Council immediately voted to take military action, but without the presence of the Soviet delegate. The USSR declared the UN intervention illegal, but rather than risk an open breach remained in the UN system. Since Korea the UN has been actively involved in most conflicts and has played some part in resolving them, its success dependent on the goodwill of those involved rather than on military strength.

The key element in the activity of the UN was support from the USA, which contributed disproportionately to the UN budget. American governments worked closely with the UN in the 1950s, but during the secretaryship of U Thant (1961–71) and the Austrian Kurt Waldheim (1971–81) the U.S. distanced itself from the UN, ignoring its resolutions and tending to act unilaterally. This change in attitude stemmed from strong UN criticism of American involvement in Vietnam, coupled with the shifting balance in the General Assembly toward the developing world and its problems. In the mid-1980s Congress moved to cut the U.S. budget contribution, creating a serious crisis for the new secretary-general, the Peruvian Javier Pérez de Cuellar. In 1988 President Reagan finally gave a new endorsement to the UN, following its successes in Afghanistan, in terminating the Iran-Iraq war, and in winning independence for Namibia. In the 1990s under Boutros Boutros Ghali and his successor as secretary-general, Kofi Annan, the UN found itself playing a larger political role in key areas of crisis. In the Balkans, Afghanistan and the Middle East it was UN resolutions that served as the basis of U.S.-led actions to end civil wars or to promote disarmament.

UNPROFOR
UN
Mar. 1992–
Dec. 1995
(FORMER YUGOSLAVIA)

UNCRO
UN
Mar. 1995–
Jan. 1996
(CROATIA)

UNTAES
UN
Jan. 1996–
Jan. 1998
(CROATIA)

UNPSG
UN
Jan 1998–
Oct. 1998
(CROATIA)

UNM
UN
Dec.
Dec. 2
(BOSNI

CANADA
198

MINUGUA
UN
Jan.–
May. 1997
(GUATEMALA)

USA

ONUSAL
UN
July 1991–
Apr. 1995
(EL SALVADOR)

UNMIH
UN
Sep. 1993–
June 1996

UNSMIH
UN
July 1996–
July 1997

UNTMIH
UN
Aug.–
Nov. 1997

MIPON
UN
Dec. 19
284

MEXICO

HAITI
HONDURAS
NICARAGUA
DOMINICAN
REPUBLIC

VENEZUELA

COLOMBIA

DOMR
UN
May 1
Oct. 1

UNOM
(SIERRA L
UN
July 1
Oct. 1

BRAZIL

ONUCA
UN
Nov. 1989–
Jan. 1992

BOLIVIA
204

UNAM
UN
Oct. 1
17,500

CHILE
URUGUAY
1,591

UNOM
UN
Sep. 1
Sep. 1

ARGENTINA
463

www.un.org/Depts/dpko/dpko/home.shtml
UN peacekeeping operations
www.mapleleafweb.com/features/military/peace_keeping/history.html
A chronology of UN peacekeeping missions

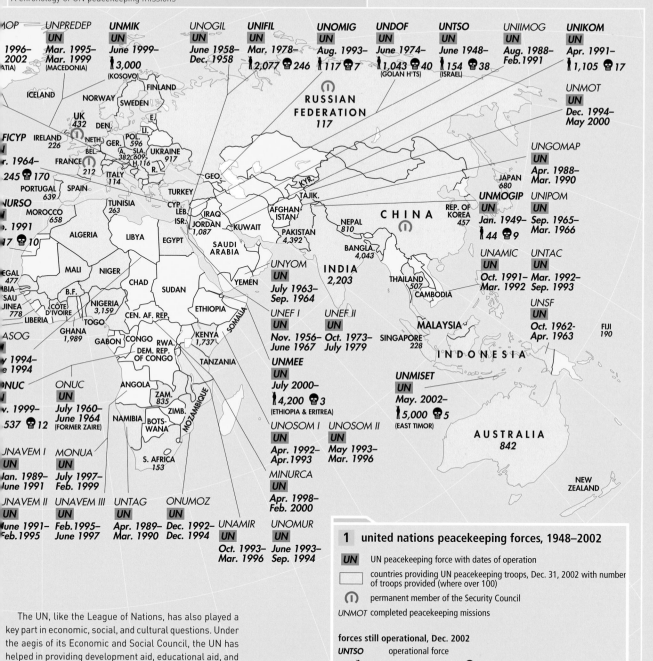

The UN, like the League of Nations, has also played a key part in economic, social, and cultural questions. Under the aegis of its Economic and Social Council, the UN has helped in providing development aid, educational aid, and cultural collaboration, and has taken initiatives on human rights, refugee problems and issues of drugs, health, and the environment. It is preeminently in these areas of global concern, on which eight percent of its budget is spent, that the UN has succeeded in becoming an indispensable inhabitant of the global village.

1 united nations peacekeeping forces, 1948–2002

UN   UN peacekeeping force with dates of operation

☐   countries providing UN peacekeeping troops, Dec. 31, 2002 with number of troops provided (where over 100)

◉   permanent member of the Security Council

UNMOT   completed peacekeeping missions

forces still operational, Dec. 2002

UNTSO   operational force

♦ (figure)   size of force   ☠   UN fatalities suffered to 2002

1   The United Nations was involved in keeping the peace from the start of its formal life. In January 1946 at the first Security Council meeting Iran asked the UN to compel the USSR to remove its forces stationed there during the war, which it successfully did. The UN has since been involved in keeping the peace across the world (map above). Its efforts have been mixed, since its powers to deploy force have been used sparingly. Though having stronger powers on paper, it has depended, like the League of Nations, on the goodwill of the major players in the international system to be effective. Peacekeeping has been expensive. The UN action in Yugoslavia in 1994 cost $1.6 billion.

the **world** in the **21st century**

2001 Al-Qaeda attacks New York and Washington

2002 Taliban overthrown in Afghanistan; common European currency; Bali terrorist bombing; Indian-Pakistani crisis over Khasmir

2003 U.S.-led coalition topples Saddam Hussein

2004 Huge increase in Islamic terrorism in Middle East; Madrid terrorist bombings; Beslan massacre

2004 (December 26) A giant tsunami strikes SE Asia, killing well over 150,000 people mainly from Indonesia, Sri Lanka, Thailand, India, and the Andaman and Nicobar Islands

2 With the revival, by the 1960s, of the major religious denominations, have come renewed conflicts (map below), directed both against secular governments and other religious groups. Many of these wars took on a nationalistic tone. The combination of religious fundamentalism and nationalism promises to be a potent danger in the 21st century.

Since 1990 the world has lived free of the shadow of the Cold War. Russia has declined rapidly as a military power. Former communist states in eastern Europe have become members of NATO. In place of the old conflict the growing confidence and colossal armed power of the United States has created a monopolar system.

The hope in the 1980s that Europe would become a "third force" between the United States and the Soviet bloc evaporated. The crises in Kosovo in 1999, Afghanistan in 2001, and Iraq in 2003 exposed growing divisions within Europe over American foreign policy. China and Russia have begun to play a larger part in trying to restrain American behavior. The American decision to conduct a global war against international "terrorism" highlighted the changing nature of the threats to the world order.

The new world order that has slowly emerged in the decade since the collapse of Soviet communism has seen a paradoxical contrast between increased economic and cultural globalization on the one hand, and a trend toward economic bloc-building and regional conflict on the other. The hopes that the collapse of communism would usher in the worldwide triumph of capitalism have only been partially realized. The rich industrialized world remains as economically privileged as ever, while economic dislocation, even decline, have been experienced in Russia and eastern Europe, throughout Africa, and even in the fast-growing "tiger" economies of eastern Asia.

Economic crisis has been accompanied by a revival of deep ethnic and religious conflicts, which have punctuated the years since 1990 with terrorist violence, civil war, and insurrection. In Chechenya in southern Russia a long and brutal war was fought to win independence for Chechens from Russian rule; in Israel the struggle between Israelis and Palestinians sharpened again. Efforts to reach agreement in both regions broke down in the 21st century and provoked a renewed wave of terrorist attacks and savage reprisals. In the former Yugoslavia, ethnic divisions and religious animosities produced three years of barbarous civil war between Muslim and Christian Serbs, and between Serbs and Croats. Ended in 1995 by NATO forces, violence erupted again in Serbia itself when Albanian Kosovans tried to break away. NATO again intervened to impose peace in 1999. The Kosovan campaign saw the largest deployment of forces in Europe since 1945.

Other conflicts surfaced in the Middle East, fueled by a resurgence of Islamic fundamentalism. Throughout the 1990s religious revival played a conspicuous part in many conflicts, based on a rejection of traditional religious values. In Afghanistan the Taliban imposed a harsh rendering of Koranic law, but movements for Islamic revival have emerged in areas from Morocco through to Indonesia. In India conflicts between Hindus, Muslims, and Sikhs have a

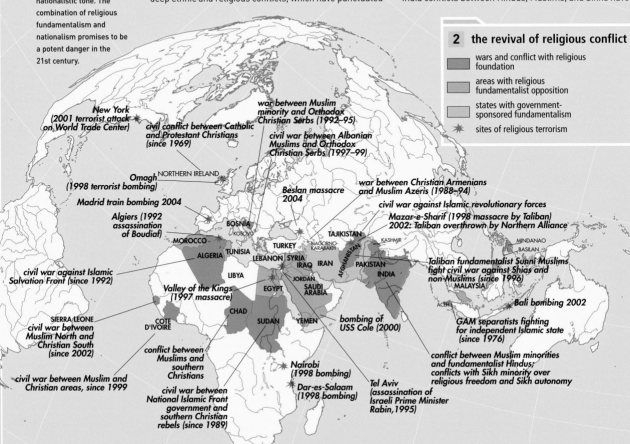

2 **the revival of religious conflict**

- wars and conflict with religious foundation
- areas with religious fundamentalist opposition
- states with government-sponsored fundamentalism
- ✳ sites of religious terrorism

New York (2001 terrorist attack on World Trade Center)

civil conflict between Catholic and Protestant Christians (since 1969)

war between Muslim minority and Orthodox Christian Serbs (1992–95)

civil war between Albanian Muslims and Orthodox Christian Serbs (1997–99)

Omagh (1998 terrorist bombing)
NORTHERN IRELAND

Beslan massacre 2004

war between Christian Armenians and Muslim Azeris (1988–94)

Madrid train bombing 2004

civil war against Islamic revolutionary forces
Mazar-e-Sharif (1998 massacre by Taliban) 2002: Taliban overthrown by Northern Alliance

Algiers (1992 assassination of Boudiaf)

BOSNIA
KOSOVO

TURKEY
NAGORNO-KARABAKH
TAJIKISTAN

KASHMIR

MINDANAO
BASILAN

MOROCCO
ALGERIA   TUNISIA
LEBANON SYRIA
IRAQ   IRAN
AFGHANISTAN
PAKISTAN
INDIA

civil war against Islamic Salvation Front (since 1992)

LIBYA
JORDAN
SAUDI ARABIA
EGYPT

Taliban fundamentalist Sunni Muslims fight civil war against Shias and non-Muslims (since 1996)
MALAYSIA

Valley of the Kings (1997 massacre)

SIERRA LEONE
civil war between Muslim North and Christian South (since 2002)

COTE D'IVOIRE

CHAD
SUDAN
YEMEN

ACEH

Bali bombing 2002

GAM separatists fighting for independent Islamic state (since 1976)

conflict between Muslims and southern Christians

bombing of USS Cole (2000)

civil war between Muslim and Christian areas, since 1999

Nairobi (1998 bombing)

Dar-es-Salaam (1998 bombing)

conflict between Muslim minorities and fundamentalist Hindus; conflicts with Sikh minority over religious freedom and Sikh autonomy

civil war between National Islamic Front government and southern Christian rebels (since 1989)

Tel Aviv (assassination of Israeli Prime Minister Rabin,1995)

www.incore.ulst.ac.uk/services/cds/themes/religion.html#news
Links covering religious conflict and reconciliation
www.globalisationguide.org/
Key questions on globalization

fundamentally religious core. In 1999 Indian and Pakistani forces found themselves fighting again in Kashmir along this key religious faultline between Islam and Hinduism. The revival of Islam has prompted a growing reaction from Christian communities in the West. Fundamentalist Christianity in America has come to see the conflict in terms which echo the medieval crusades.

Much of the violence worldwide has been fueled by a great expansion in the production and supply of armaments from the richer developed states. In the Middle East and east and south Asia large new markets have been found to compensate for the decline in military forces in Europe and the U.S. The collapse of the former Soviet bloc also resulted in a large, often illicit, trade in the latest technology. The ease with which sophisticated weapons can be procured has encouraged local warlordism and terrorism. There are fears in the West of terrorist attack with nuclear, biological, or chemical weapons, many of which were paradoxically produced and sold from western markets.

The combination of growing economic inequalities, religious conflict, and easy access to weapons promises a lethal cocktail for the new century. Political instability in Russia and growing nationalism in China mean that the world is a potentially more dangerous and disordered place than it ever was during the Cold War. While the rich states get richer, unpredictable and violent forces may yet overturn the prosperity and security enjoyed by the world's privileged minority.

1 After the end of the Cold War there was growing concern that weapons of mass destruction (map below) would begin to spread more widely with the sale of technical data or nuclear weapons technology. In fact 98 percent of the world's nuclear warheads are still held by just five powers, while the U.S. and Russia account between them for 92 percent, or 33,000 active or reserve warheads. This is more than enough to destroy the planet.

1 weapons of mass destruction

nuclear weapons

- nuclear states under the Non-Proliferation Treaty
- non-NPT with nuclear capability
- NPT states believed to have nuclear weapons programs
- states abandoning nuclear programs, with date
- warheads for bombers
- warheads for missiles
- submarine-launched warheads
- tactical warheads
- defense warheads
- missile and air-launched warheads (estimate only)

chemical weapons

- states who have not signed Chemical Weapons Convention
- states who have signed but not ratified Chemical Weapons Convention

163

The 20th century has witnessed a revolution in the lives of ordinary people. Improvements in health, in land and air communications, in telecommunications, and in education have produced a larger, more literate, and more informed population. In 1900 most people lived on the land. By the year 2000 a majority of people will live in cities, with all the problems of amenity, overcrowding, and pollution that cities generate. The costs of social and industrial transformation have to be weighed against gains in wealth and opportunity, which have been unevenly spread between the developed and the developing areas of the world. The United States in 1995 boasted one million millionaires. In Africa, South Asia, and Latin America millions still live at a bare level of subsistence, their traditional ways of life disrupted or torn up by relentless modernization. Rapid change, and the management of that change, are the hallmarks of 20th-century life.

Astronaut John Young of Apollo 16 salutes the American flag on the lunar surface

PART VI   THE REVOLUTIONARY CENTURY: THEMES

population explosion, wealth, and poverty

since 1900

1900 world population at 1.65 billion

1973 oil crisis sparks global economic recession

1978 China declares "Open Door" policy

1991 Russia begins program of economic reform

1995 EEC becomes the European Union

1997–8 financial crisis rocks east Asian economies

2004 37.2 million adults and 2.2 million children are HIV infected

2005 world population at 6.42 billion

1 The population boom which began in the 1960s showed some sign of slowing in the 1990s (map below). It is now expected that by the middle of the next century world population will stabilize at around 9 billion. The slow-down has been caused partly by improved contraception and efforts by states to restrict family size. Disease and famine have also played their part, especially in Africa. Smaller family sizes will also produce stable population growth.

The 20th century is the century of population increase. It is a century of extremes in wealth and poverty. At its start the global population was 1.6 billion. At its close it is more than six billion. This increase is rooted partly in growing agricultural efficiency and partly in the opening up of new areas of cultivation.

Such developments have combined with changes in medical provision to increase life expectancy and, particularly, to lower infant mortality. Life expectancy increased first in the prosperous countries of North America and western Europe, then in eastern and southern Europe, and finally in the less developed countries. Population growth placed increasing pressure on the land and encouraged peasants to go to the cities in search of work. Such migrations then further stimulated economic growth and set the cycle of population increase to work again.

However, demographic growth has not been universal or uniform. Population increase is usually linked to particular social circumstances. Societies in which people expect to be dependent on their children in old age encourage large families. So do rapidly industrializing countries, in which there is a strong demand for labor, especially child labor. Land inheritance systems may play a large part in influencing choices about the size of families. In France, legislation ensured land was divided equally among all heirs. Peasants had to limit the size of families to avoid their land being divided into plots too small to support them. Partly as a result, the population of France

hovered at just under 40 million throughout the period from 1870 to 1940. In contrast, laborers on the great estates of southern Italy, Spain, or Hungary had no land and consequently no incentive to limit population. Most striking of all, Russian peasants had a positive incentive to have large families because communal land was distributed among them according to the number of children that they had to work it: the Russian population increased by more than 50 percent between 1880 and 1910.

Control over the size of families was exercised by various means. In many countries unmarried women kept house for their brothers or were packed off into convents. Deliberate birth control became easier in the 20th century with the use of condoms and the contraceptive pill. A variety of agencies interested themselves in the control of population. The Catholic Church opposed birth control and succeeded in having its views enshrined in legislation in countries such as Ireland and Italy. States that were preoccupied with the military uses of a large population sometimes sought to prevent birth control.

Sometimes bids were made to raise birth rates among certain parts of the population while lowering them among others. Eugenicists from the early part of the century onward believed that the strength of the "race" was being undermined by the fact that the poorest, and therefore "least fit," were having the most children. The government of Nazi Germany institutionalized such thinking, encouraging high birth rates among the "racially fit" and abortion and sterilization among those that it regarded as least desirable. After 1945, as concerns focused more on economics, states began to seek low birth rates. The Chinese government tried to dissuade its citizens from having more than a single child. Efforts to influence population size are now linked to the problems of securing adequate economic and social development, which became a principal theme at the 1995 UN Cairo summit on population.

Los Angeles 13.2(14.5)
CANADA
USA 3(3)
MEXICO (11)
Mexico City 18.1(20.4)
New York 16.7(17.9)
DENMARK -0.9
SWEDEN -1.8
FINLAND -4.6
GERMANY 11(21) -3.8
CZECH REP. -16.7
POLAND -14.7
SLOVAKIA -8.2
ESTONIA -1.1% -2.0% -51.9
LATVIA -0.9% -1.5% -43.9
LITHUANIA 0.6% -27.8
SLOVENIA 0.8% -21.1
UNITED KINGDOM 19(26)
-0.3 BELGIUM
FRANCE (28)
-19.0 SWITZERLAND
-9.0 AUSTRIA
-0.8% ITALY
20 -22.0
BELARUS 0.5% -25.0
HUNGARY 0.5% -24.2
ROMANIA -19.6
UKRAINE 0.8% -1.1% -36.1
MOLDOVA -16.4
BULGARIA -0.9% -1.0% -35.1
GEORGIA 0.9% -1.2% -34.0
RUSSIA 6(18) 0.6% -0.9% -30.3
KAZAKHSTAN -10.9
JAPAN 9(15) -13.6
Tokyo 26.4(27.2)
Osaka 11.0(11.0)
S. KOREA -0.9
Beijing 10.8(11.7)
Tianjin(10.3)
Shanghai 12.9(13.6)
CHINA 1(2)
CUBA -10.1
PUERTO RICO -2.4
COLOMBIA (25)
TRINIDAD -5.3
GUYANA -33.2
-8.4 SPAIN
-9.9 PORTUGAL
-10.4 -0.8% BOSNIA
CROATIA -19.3
SERBIA -11.2
GREECE -10.0
Istanbul (11.4)
TURKEY 14(19)
ARMENIA 0.5% -1.1% -25.0
NEPAL (34)
IRAN 16(16)
AFGHANISTAN 3.9% (23)
Delhi 12.4(20.9)
Dhaka 12.5(22.8)
Manila 10.0(12.9)
PHILIPPINES 13(13)
BURMA (27)
VIETNAM 12(14)
THAILAND 18(22)
46.7 1.7% GUINEA BISSAU
BRAZIL 5(8)
3.8% SIERRA LEONE
46.6 4.1% 1.5% LIBERIA
48.9 1.8% BURKINA FASO
MALI 49.1 1.8%
NIGER 3.6% 49.8 (32)
CHAD 46.5
Lagos (16.0)
BENIN 46.2
Cairo (11.5)
EGYPT 15(12)
KUWAIT 3.5%
SAUDI ARABIA (31)
IRAQ (30)
PAKISTAN 7(4)
Karachi 10.0(16.2)
Calcutta 13.1(16.7)
INDIA 2(1)
Mumbai 16.1(22.6)
BANGLADESH 8(7)
YEMEN 3.5% 2.2% 49.1 (20)
SUDAN (29)
ETHIOPIA 17(9) 45.9
ERITREA 3.7% 45.8
SOMALIA 4.2% 2.1% 47.8
UGANDA 3.2% 2.0% 49.9 (17)
TANZANIA 45.8 (24)
RWANDA 45.4
BURUNDI 1.5% 48.0
MALAWI 45.6
MAURITIUS
NIGERIA 45.0 10(6)
CONGO 46.4
DEM. REP. OF CONGO (10) 46.8
ANGOLA 47.3 1.7%
46.3 ZAMBIA
INDONESIA 4(5)
Jakarta 11.0(17.3)
AUSTRALIA
ZEAL
Sao Paulo 18.0(21.2)
Rio de Janeiro 10.7(11.5)
ARGENTINA (33)
Buenos Aires 12.0(13.2)
BOTSWANA -20.0
SWAZILAND -9.2
SOUTH AFRICA -8.5
LESOTHO -22.9

www.oecd.org/home/
Organization for Economic Cooperation and Development
www.unfpa.org/issues/
An overview of global population issues

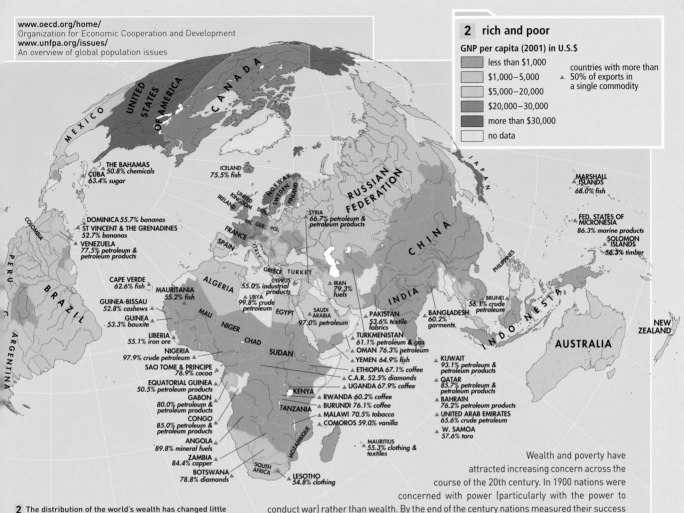

2 rich and poor

GNP per capita (2001) in U.S.$

- less than $1,000
- $1,000–5,000
- $5,000–20,000
- $20,000–30,000
- more than $30,000
- no data

▲ countries with more than 50% of exports in a single commodity

Map labels:

THE BAHAMAS 50.8% chemicals
CUBA 63.4% sugar
ICELAND 75.5% fish
MARSHALL ISLANDS 68.0% fish
DOMINICA 55.7% bananas
ST VINCENT & THE GRENADINES 52.7% bananas
VENEZUELA 77.5% petroleum & petroleum products
FED. STATES OF MICRONESIA 86.3% marine products
SOLOMON ISLANDS 56.3% timber
SYRIA 66.7% petroleum & petroleum products
CAPE VERDE 62.6% fish
MAURITANIA 55.2% fish
GUINEA-BISSAU 52.8% cashews
GUINEA 53.3% bauxite
LIBERIA 55.1% iron ore
NIGERIA 97.9% crude petroleum
SAO TOME & PRINCIPE 76.9% cocoa
EQUATORIAL GUINEA 50.5% petroleum products
GABON 80.0% petroleum & petroleum products
CONGO 85.0% petroleum & petroleum products
ANGOLA 89.8% mineral fuels
ZAMBIA 84.4% copper
BOTSWANA 78.8% diamonds
CYPRUS 55.0% industrial products
LIBYA 99.8% crude petroleum
SAUDI ARABIA 97.0% petroleum
IRAN 79.3% fuels
PAKISTAN 53.6% textile fabrics
TURKMENISTAN 61.1% petroleum & gas
OMAN 76.3% petroleum
YEMEN 64.9% fish
ETHIOPIA 67.1% coffee
C.A.R. 52.5% diamonds
UGANDA 67.9% coffee
RWANDA 60.2% coffee
BURUNDI 76.1% coffee
MALAWI 70.5% tobacco
COMOROS 59.0% vanilla
MAURITIUS 55.3% clothing & textiles
LESOTHO 54.8% clothing
BANGLADESH 60.2% garments
BRUNEI 56.1% crude petroleum
KUWAIT 93.1% petroleum & petroleum products
QATAR 85.7% petroleum & petroleum products
BAHRAIN 76.2% petroleum products
UNITED ARAB EMIRATES 65.6% crude petroleum
W. SAMOA 57.6% taro

2 The distribution of the world's wealth has changed little during the long period of boom since the Second World War, though Asia now takes a larger slice than it did thanks to the rapid growth of the Pacific Rim states (map above). The developed world has smaller populations, higher per capita incomes, and more diverse economies. Many developing economies depend on trading a single commodity for their survivals.

1 world population toward the millennium (left)

Family size and population growth

- very rapid growth (more than 5 children per family)
- intermediate growth (2.1–5 children per family)
- slow growth (fewer than 2.1 children per family)

Fastest-growing populations (% per annum)		Slowest-growing populations (% per annum)	
4.5%	2000–05	-4.5%	2000–05
4.0%	2045–50 (projection)	-4.0%	2045–50 (projection)
48.6	% of population under 15		

JAPAN 9 — countries with population of 50 million or more in 2000, in ranking order

JAPAN (15) — countries with population of 50 million or more in 2050 (projection), in ranking order

JAPAN -13.6 — countries with projected population decrease 2000–50, with percentage

Tokyo 26.4 ● — cities with populations over 10 million in 2000 (with population)

Tokyo (27.2) ● — cities with populations over 10 million in 2050 (with projected population)

Wealth and poverty have attracted increasing concern across the course of the 20th century. In 1900 nations were concerned with power (particularly with the power to conduct war) rather than wealth. By the end of the century nations measured their success in almost entirely economic terms. A military superpower like Russia was obliged to humble itself before the might of the International Monetary Fund while a state with almost no military ambitions—Japan—was widely seen as successful.

Similar changes occurred in the way people thought about wealth. At the beginning of the century, status, rank, and caste (concepts that were often linked to the military power) were more important. By the end of the century this had changed for a growing enthusiasm of the measurement of wealth. The debate about reparations after the First World War encouraged many nations to calculate their worth with a new zeal. Discussion of the international distribution of wealth was changed by the decolonizations of the 1960s. Newly created states in Africa were usually very poor, and membership of institutions such as the United Nations gave them some capacity to get their plight recocognized. Interest was also focused on gulfs between rich and poor within nations. Mobilization of resources during the two world wars obliged the wealthy states to take an interest in the diet and accommodation of their poorest citizens if only to ensure that they had effective soldiers. The interest in wealth and poverty that has marked recent history has not produced any consensus about how such conditions are defined. Infant mortality and calorie intake may provide some kind of indication of living standards in the Third World. However, infant mortality may also be high in an area such as the South Bronx in New York.

Most significantly assessment of wealth and poverty is almost always a matter of relativity. Outside sub-Saharan Africa few have experienced an absolute decline in their fortunes. Rapid economic growth after the Second World War masked issues of relative deprivation because almost everyone derived benefits from increasing prosperity. Slower economic growth since the oil crisis of 1973 has meant that awareness of, and conflicts over, distribution of wealth have become more intense. The globalization of the economy has created empires of wealth which stretch across frontiers. The rich in the U.S., Japan, and Germany have much in common; the poor of Ethiopia and of Europe almost nothing.

refugees

1920 Comintern set up in Moscow

by 1921 some 800,000 refugees flee the Soviet Union

1922-23 150,000+ Muslim refugees flee into Turkey

from 1933 racial persecution in Germany causes wave of refugees

1960s/70s vast number of refugees from Indo-China following communist takeover

1990–95 United Nations figures show more than 11 million refugees repatriated

1992 "ethnic cleansing" in Bosnia-Herzegovina creates waves of Muslim refugees

2 After the Russian Revolution thousands of former imperial subjects fled abroad. In 1922 (map below) there were an estimated 863,000 refugees, the largest number in Germany, Russia's former enemy. Some became naturalized citizens of the countries they fled to, but by 1937 there were still an estimated 450,000 unassimilated Russian refugees, making them the largest refugee population of the pre-1939 world. The decision to establish a League of Nations High Commissioner for Refugees owed a great deal to the Russian diaspora, which actively campaigned for the new category of "refugee" to enjoy a special legal status.

The distinction between refugees fleeing political persecution and migrants seeking to improve their standard of living is hard to make. The poem by Emma Lazarus that accompanied the Statue of Liberty spoke of "huddled masses yearning to breathe free," but most of those who entered the United States in the period before 1914 seem to have been primarily concerned with bettering themselves economically.

The most obvious refugees during this period were East European Jews who fled from anti-Semitism in the czarist empire and Romania. However, even they sometimes returned to their native land after having saved money working abroad. The Balkan wars and their aftermath marked the beginning of a large-scale refugee problem in Europe. In 1922 and 1923 177,000 Muslim refugees fled into Turkey; at the same stage more than a million Greek refugees poured into Greece from western and northern Turkey. The First World War and the Russian Revolution created further refugees, especially in Eastern Europe: by 1921 there were some 800,000 refugees from the Soviet Union alone. In this year the Norwegian explorer Fridtjof Nansen was made League of Nations High Commissioner for Refugees from Russia. The awareness of a specific "refugee problem" was exacerbated by two factors. First, economic conditions no longer permitted the absorption of large numbers of foreign workers that had still seemed possible in many countries before 1914. Second, the increasing emphasis on official identification of nationality through passports and identity cards accentuated the distinction between refugees and citizens.

The political and racial persecutions in Nazi Germany after 1933 created further waves of refugees and European governments responded to this with growing panic. By the late 1930s even the traditionally tolerant French government was beginning to incarcerate political refugees in specially created camps. Refugees came to make up important elements in the anti-Nazi resistance during the Second World War: defeated Spanish Republicans played an important part in the French Resistance.

The Second World War and its aftermath created the high point of the refugee problem in Europe. Millions of Europeans had fled their homes or were liberated from prison camps at a time when their families, their communities, or perhaps their entire countries had ceased to exist. However, in the long run postwar Europe did not suffer a refugee crisis comparable to that which had afflicted it before the war. Rapid growth in the Western European economies allowed refugees to be absorbed into employment. Indeed, the millions of ethnic Germans from Eastern Europe who fled to West Germany after 1945 and the million or so European "pieds noirs" who fled Algeria after it was granted independence in 1962 almost certainly benefited their host economies: they alleviated labor shortages while their desire to rebuild shattered prosperity often made them entrepreneurial and dynamic. West European governments were further helped by the closing of the frontiers between Eastern and Western Europe, which limited the numbers of refugees who were able to seek freedom in the West.

ALASKA

CANADA

UNITED STATES OF AMERICA

MEXICO

1960–80: 900,000 Cubans

1970–80: 500,000 Salvadoreans, Guatemalans and Nicaraguans

CUBA

BELIZE

GUATEMALA · EL SALVADOR

NICARAGUA

1 Not all refugees remain permanently in their place of asylum. The chart (bottom left) shows the significant number of returnees, many of whom encounter grave problems rebuilding their lives in the face of shattered infrastructure, famine, and continued political instability. Nearly three million refugees returned to Afghanistan alone after the Soviet withdrawal in 1989, but renewed violence has created a further wave of Afghan refugees (chart bottom right). The need for long-term aid to these groups is as significant as that to refugees themselves.

2 russian refugees from the revolution, 1922

Peking

Far East

145,000

10,000

17,000

55,000

Moscow

FINLAND and BALTIC STATES

240,000

175,000

140,000

10,000

Berlin

POLAND

Istanbul

GREAT BRITAIN

GERMANY

TURKEY BALKANS

London

Paris

70,000

I T A L Y

FRANCE

60

major refugee repatriations, 2002

Origin	Countries of asylum	Numbers
Afghanistan	Pakistan/Iran	26,100
Bosnia & Herzegovina	Yugoslavia/Croatia/ Germany	18,700
Burundi	Tanzania	27,900
East Timor	Indonesia	18,200
Eritrea	Sudan	32,700
FYR Macedonia	Yugoslavia/Albania	90,000
Rwanda	D.R. Congo/Tanzania	21,000
Sierra Leone	Guinea/Liberia	92,300
Somalia	Ethiopia	51,300
Yugoslavia	Germany/Bosnia & Herzegovina/ FYR Macedonia	25,600

origin of major refugee populations, 2002

Country of origin	Number of refugees
Afghanistan	3,809,600
Angola	470,600
Bosnia & Herzegovina	426,000
Burundi	554,000
D.R. Congo	392,100
Eritrea	333,100
Iraq	530,100
Somalia	439,900
Sudan	489,500
Vietnam	353,200

www.unhcr.ch/cgi-bin/texis/vtx/home
The UN refugee agency
www.ecre.org/
European Council on Refugees and Exiles

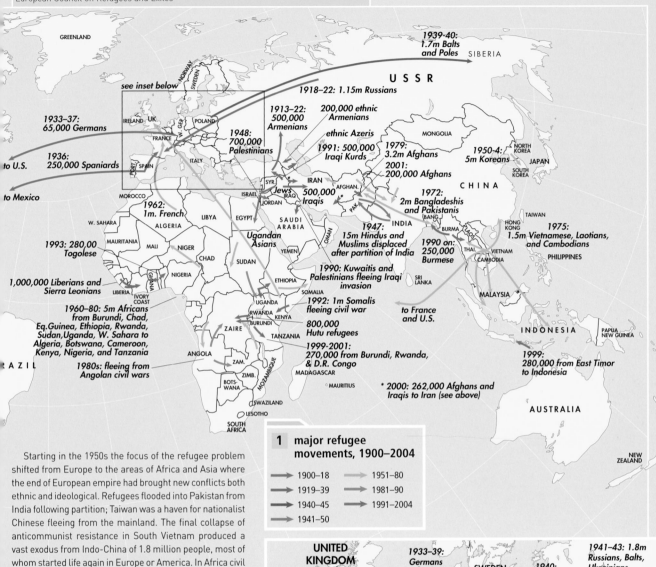

1 major refugee movements, 1900–2004

→ 1900–18	→ 1951–80
→ 1919–39	→ 1981–90
→ 1940–45	→ 1991–2004
→ 1941–50	

Starting in the 1950s the focus of the refugee problem shifted from Europe to the areas of Africa and Asia where the end of European empire had brought new conflicts both ethnic and ideological. Refugees flooded into Pakistan from India following partition; Taiwan was a haven for nationalist Chinese fleeing from the mainland. The final collapse of anticommunist resistance in South Vietnam produced a vast exodus from Indo-China of 1.8 million people, most of whom started life again in Europe or America. In Africa civil war has produced a chronic refugee problem. By 1991 there were around five million refugees, mostly living in rough settlements and camps, supported by international relief agencies because the host nations could simply not afford the burden. In Sudan, Ethiopia, and Somalia a whole generation has grown up knowing only life in the hundreds of makeshift refugee camps produced by years of civil strife.

Not all refugees remain permanently in a political no-man's lands. Millions of refugees in the past 20 years have been repatriated, some voluntarily, others (for example the Vietnamese "boat people") by force. According to UN figures more than 11 million refugees were repatriated between 1990 and 1995. During the Kosovo crisis, where more than 700,000 Albanians fled to camps in surrounding states, the aim of the international community was the repatriation of the refugees. Western states no longer take in large numbers of refugees; instead they have tried in the 1990s to alter the political circumstances that produce refugee crises.

UNITED KINGDOM
IRELAND
SWEDEN
DENMARK
NETH.
BELGIUM
E. GERM.
W. GERM.
POLAND
USSR
CZECH.
FRANCE
SWITZ.
AUSTRIA
HUNGARY
ROMANIA
YUGOSLAVIA
ITALY
BULGARIA
ALBANIA
GREECE
TURKEY
SPAIN

1933–39: Germans
1940: 750,000 Germans
1941–43: 1.8m Russians, Balts, Ukrainians
1945: 4m Germans
1919: 120,000 Germans
1941: 9m Poles, Ukrainians, Jews
1918–25: 2m Poles
1945: 1.8m Czechs and Slovaks
1945: 4m Germans
1919: 40,000 Germans
1956: 250,000 Hungarians
350,000 refugees from Bosnian civil war
160,000 refugees from Bosnian civil war
1995–96 550,000 Krajina Serbs
1999: over 700,000 Kosovan Albanians
1922–23: 177,000 Muslims
1922–23: 1.2m Greeks

169

health and disease

1919 League of Nations sets up permanent health organization in Geneva

1948 WHO (World Health Organization) created

1977 last case of smallpox in Somalia

1980s WHO institutes comprehensive program of immunization

1981 AIDS identified

1986 BSE (bovine spongiform encephalopathy—mad cow disease) first identified

2003 SARS (Severe Acute Respiratory Syndrome) spreads from China

1 In 1967 a world program was launched to eradicate smallpox, which was endemic in much of Africa and southern Asia. Within a decade the disease was virtually wiped out (maps far right). Samples were kept in laboratories in case the disease returned, but they are to be destroyed in 1999.

2 The incidence of poliomyelitis has been hugely reduced by the drive to provide effective immunization since the 1960s (map below). Cases of the disease have declined by around 85 percent since a World Health Organization campaign began in 1988. During 1995, more than 300 million children were immunized in 51 countries. Polio has disappeared entirely from the Americas, with the last reported case in Peru in 1991. The Indian subcontinent has more than two-thirds of all cases, with Africa and the Middle East accounting for most of the rest.

Health is an issue closely bound up with economic development. Improvements in health and healthcare over the century have depended on improvements in the general level of prosperity and on the breakthroughs in medical science made possible by expensive programs of advanced research. Throughout the century the level of general health and the prospects of survival have accordingly been higher in the developed regions of the world.

At the beginning of the century there was little international cooperation on health issues, many of which had not yet been properly identified or understood. In 1907 an Inter-national Office of Public Hygiene was established in Paris to discuss and advise on public health questions, and in 1919 the League of Nations set up a permanent Health Organization in Geneva. When the UN conference convened in San Francisco in 1945, Brazil proposed the creation of an autonomous international health body, which on April 7, 1948—now celebrated as World Health Day—became the World Health Organization (WHO). Its function was to monitor world health trends, advise on health care provision, and coordinate national efforts to promote health and eradicate disease. The main fruit of its early work was the publication in 1969 of International Health Regulations, which member states were supposed to observe.

Achievements outside the developed world were modest by the 1970s. In 1973 the role of the WHO was strengthened to allow it to act as a full partner in establishing effective healthcare in deprived regions. The organization took the lead in challenging major epidemic diseases. Its most conspicuous success was the eradication of smallpox between 1967 and 1977, when the last recorded case occurred in Somalia.

In 1977 the WHO launched the "Health for All by the Year 2000" program, which aimed to raise the level of primary healthcare globally. The aim of the campaign was not only to eradicate disease but to tackle the basic causes of poor health and hygiene through education, environmental improvements, and development economics. The WHO also pledged greater help for the identification and treatment of mental illness, which was estimated to affect more than 50 million people worldwide. In the 1980s this program was pursued through a comprehensive Program on Immunization, first launched in 1974 and aimed primarily at the established killers: tuberculosis, measles, and polio. The inoculation rate in the developing world quadrupled in ten years. There were remarkable results. In India and Indonesia the rate of the measles/TB inoculation was 0.1 percent in 1980–2. In 1987–90 it had risen to 86 percent. The exception to this improvement was in the Soviet Union, where immunization levels declined from 95 percent to 68 percent over the same period. Simultaneously the 1980s was declared the "International Drinking Water Supply and Sanitation Decade." Within ten years 1.59 billion people in the developing world were provided with safe water—a coverage of 68 percent compared with 29 percent in 1980. In 1988 the WHO embarked on a further fight against six major infections, including polio, leprosy, and tetanus, which affected more than 30 million people. The aim was to eradicate them by the year 2000.

The overall impact of improved healthcare has been to raise life expectancy levels sharply in 40 years. In the developing areas average life expectancy was almost 60 years in 1990, as against 41 years in 1948. Marked differences in health opportunities between the developed and developing world still remain. The costs of healthcare have risen steeply, and even within developed states there are differences in the levels of provision. Out of the 17 million healthcare personnel worldwide in 1990, 11.5 million were employed in Europe and North America.

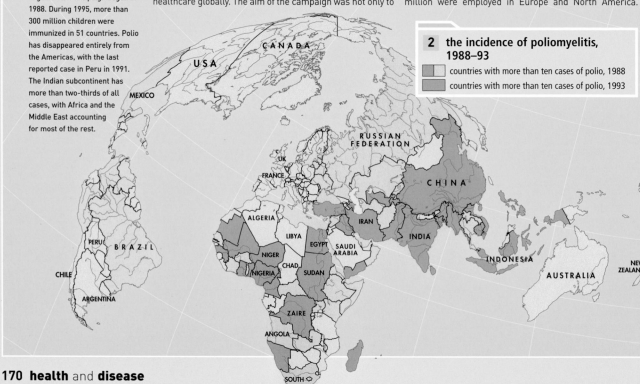

2 the incidence of poliomyelitis, 1988–93

countries with more than ten cases of polio, 1988

countries with more than ten cases of polio, 1993

www.who.int/en/
World Health Organization website
www.unaids.org/en/default.asp
Joint UN program on HIV/AIDS

Health expenditure in developing states in 1988 totaled four percent of GNP; in the developed economies the figure was 12.6 percent. In these circumstances "Health for All" by the millennium, in spite of remarkable gains in controlling deadly and debilitating infections, will still fall short of its ambition in what has otherwise been a remarkable century of medical progress.

The healthcare revolution which the WHO has led since the 1970s has been involved not only with eradicating long-established diseases but with fighting a crop of new epidemics, some the product of mutations in the stock of viruses and bacteria, some, more dangerously, the consequence of growing immunity to the spectrum of antibiotics used to contain infection.

New microbial strains have been responsible for the reemergence of cholera and diphtheria. The cholera outbreak in southern India in 1992 spread northward into most of China and South East Asia. Diphtheria developed in the former Soviet bloc, where immunization programs and effective disease screening declined with the breakup of the communist state systems.

New diseases with exceptionally high death rates and no known cure appeared alongside the resistant strains of bacteria in the 1980s. The Ebola virus, which first appeared in Zaire in 1977, returned to southern Zaire in 1995, but the rapid response of the local authorities and the WHO restricted the outbreak to just 316 cases, of whom 245 died.

Of the new viruses by far the most deadly and widely spread was the human immunodeficiency virus (HIV), which reduces the human body's resistance to infection and can lead to the fatal condition of acquired immunodeficiency syndrome (AIDS). HIV was first identified in 1981 on the basis of isolated cases in the 1970s. The virus spread rapidly. In 1990 an estimated five million were infected; in 1991, nine million; by 1996, 24 million. Most of them were in sub-Saharan Africa. The epidemic spread across the United States and Europe in the 1980s, and provoked extensive research and health education programs, which have had the effect of reducing the rate of growth of the disease. In the developed world HIV was closely linked to lifestyle. In the U.S. in 1988, 89 percent of those infected with AIDS came from the male homosexual or drug-using communities.

AIDS was not the only disease in the developed world whose spread was closely related to social behavior. Low levels of death from infectious diseases highlighted other major causes of premature death, such as smoking, alcohol consumption, and poor diet. In Russia life expectancy for males actually fell from 65 in 1986 to 59 in 1993, due in large part to a sharp increase in alcohol consumption and a doubling of the rate of homicide. By the year 2020 smoking is expected to kill ten million people annually.

3 Thirty infectious diseases have been identified since 1973, many of which have no known cure, and are difficult to control or prevent (map right).

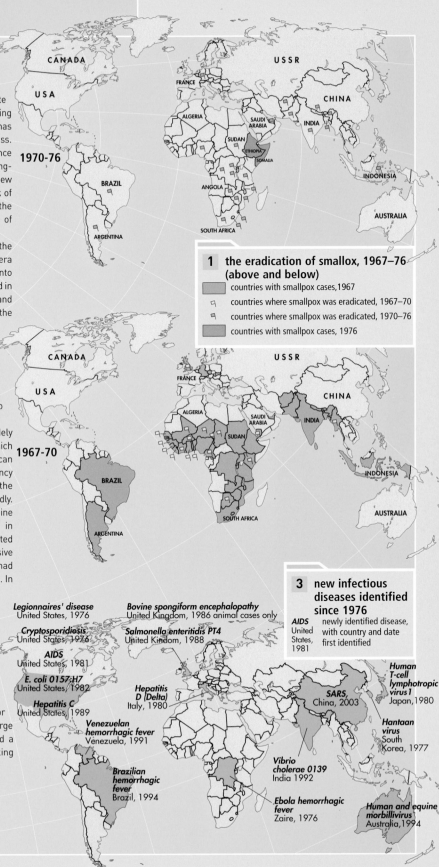

1970-76

1 the eradication of smallox, 1967–76 (above and below)
- countries with smallpox cases, 1967
- countries where smallpox was eradicated, 1967–70
- countries where smallpox was eradicated, 1970–76
- countries with smallpox cases, 1976

1967-70

3 new infectious diseases identified since 1976

AIDS United States, 1981 — newly identified disease, with country and date first identified

Legionnaires' disease
United States, 1976

Cryptosporidiosis
United States, 1976

AIDS
United States, 1981

E. coli 0157:H7
United States, 1982

Hepatitis C
United States, 1989

Venezuelan hemorrhagic fever
Venezuela, 1991

Brazilian hemorrhagic fever
Brazil, 1994

Bovine spongiform encephalopathy
United Kingdom, 1986 animal cases only

Salmonella enteritidis PT4
United Kindom, 1988

Hepatitis D (Delta)
Italy, 1980

Vibrio cholerae 0139
India 1992

Ebola hemorrhagic fever
Zaire, 1976

SARS,
China, 2003

Human T-cell lymphotropic virus 1
Japan, 1980

Hantaan virus
South Korea, 1977

Human and equine morbillivirus
Australia, 1994

communications

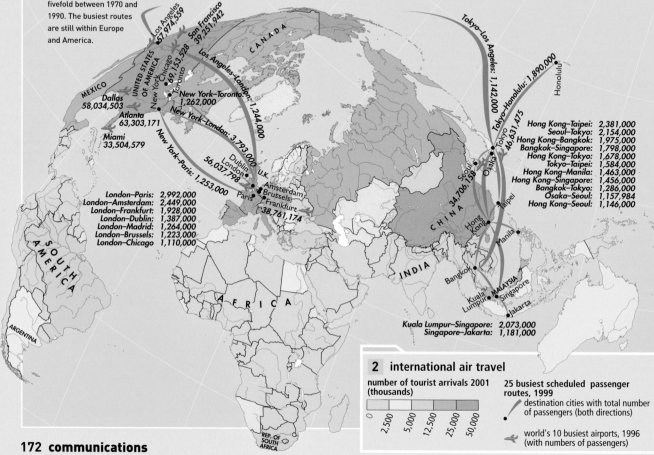

2 Organized air transportation began first in America and Europe, and by 1939 there was a network of routes around the world. The coming of jet airliners in the 1950s transformed the industry. Cheap and reliable air travel grew rapidly from the 1960s (map below). Passenger miles flown in America increased fivefold between 1970 and 1990. The busiest routes are still within Europe and America.

The 20th century has witnessed a profound revolution in communication of every kind. Motor vehicles and airplanes have made the whole globe accessible, molding the modern high-growth economy and transforming social life and leisure. The age of mass electronic communications has opened up possibilities undreamed of a century ago.

This revolution in communication has transformed practically every aspect of daily life. The changes were the fruit of a remarkable cluster of scientific breakthroughs in the 40 years before the First World War: the telephone, invented by Alexander Bell in 1876; the first cars powered by the internal combustion engine, pioneered by Karl Benz and Gottlieb Daimler in the 1880s; the radio transmitter, developed by Guglielmo Marconi in 1896; the discovery of the electron in 1897 by Joseph Thomson; and the development of powered flight, begun by the Wright brothers in 1903. The development of the silicon microchip in the late 1950s completed this scientific foundation.

The development of motorized transportation was dependent on the development of a sufficiently powerful and efficient engine. The internal combustion engine, fueled by refined oil, provided the key. Improvements in engine technology then made possible the evolution of mass-motoring and high-performance aircraft. Motor vehicles and airplanes gave transportation a flexibility and speed unattainable by railroads and horses.

Motorization began before the First World War in Europe and America. Henry Ford established his motor company in 1903, and within a decade had become the world's most successful mass producer of motor cars. The greater spread of wealth in the U.S. encouraged high levels of car ownership and by 1939 the majority of the world's motor vehicles were produced there. Rising incomes after 1945 fueled growing demand worldwide. By 1959 there were 119 million vehicles in use; by 1974 the figure was 303 million. Motor transportation transformed industry and commerce, produced a sharp change in social patterns and broke down the isolation of rural areas. Motorization also made possible mass leisure and mass tourism.

In 1919 the first primitive airlines opened in Europe using the experience of the war years in producing larger and safer aircraft. The first modern multi-engined monoplane airliners were developed in the 1930s by the Boeing and Douglas companies in America, and in 1939 the first successful passenger services were opened across the Atlantic Ocean. Air travel expanded rapidly from the 1950s thanks to the development of a new generation of high-performance wide-bodied jet aircraft. The first jet airliner, the British Comet, flew in 1952, but world airliner markets were subsequently dominated by a succession of Boeing models.

www.centennialofflight.gov/essay/Social/impact/SH3.htm
U.S. Centennial Flight Commission
www.webbconsult.com/history.html
Telecommunications history

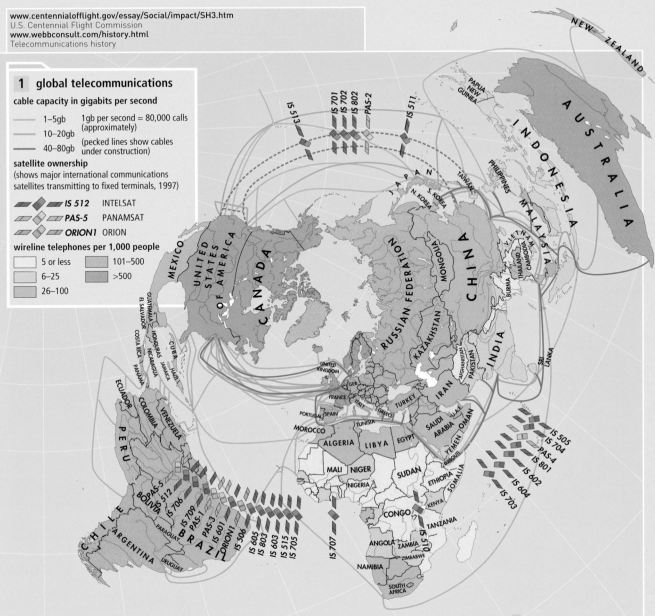

1 global telecommunications

cable capacity in gigabits per second

1–5gb	1gb per second = 80,000 calls (approximately)
10–20gb	(pecked lines show cables
40–80gb	under construction)

satellite ownership
(shows major international communications satellites transmitting to fixed terminals, 1997)

IS 512	INTELSAT
PAS-5	PANAMSAT
ORION1	ORION

wireline telephones per 1,000 people

5 or less	101–500
6–25	>500
26–100	

Aircraft have made the world a smaller place. Journeys that took months in the 19th century now take less than a day. For the populations of the richer developed states global travel is taken for granted. Meanwhile, many poorer states now depend on tourism as their primary source of income. The shrinking of the globe has led to the emergence of a common global culture. The exotic may be within reach, but modern communication and consumerism is challenging its very survival.

Telecommunications have changed faster than any other form of communication. The use of telephones expanded rapidly from the 1880s—there were just 50 million globally in 1930, but 350 million by 1975. Meanwhile in the 1920s television was developed, and the first public broadcasts followed in the 1930s. The development of the space program after the Second World War drove the search for new forms of electronic communication. The microchip opened up a new world of advanced communication. It allowed the development of small and increasingly efficient computer systems, and a modern global telephone network. In 1962 the first of many telecommunications satellites entered service. By the 1990s satellite communications were widely used for computer, television, and telephone communication. In the early 1990s the growth of the Internet opened up a world of instant electronic information for its millions of users.

The electronic revolution has shrunk the worlds of finance, commerce, and education. Billions of dollars or yen can be transferred at the press of a button. Information can be made instantly available. The pace of innovation shows no sign of slackening. The 21st century will see more changes in lifestyle and work as microchips perform work previously done by routine human labor.

1 The development of satellite communications since the 1960s and the revolution in microchip technology starting in the 1970s have created a global web of electronic communications by telephone, fax, television, and computer (map above). In the 1990s the growth of the Internet made possible instant communication worldwide via computer. The spread has been very uneven, however, with most electronic equipment concentrated in the world's most developed states.

173

religion

- **1947–56** discovery of Dead Sea Scrolls

- **1948** assassination of Mahatma Gandhi

- **1959** along with some 100,000 Tibetans, the 14th Dalai Lama flees the Chinese occupation of Tibet, and establishes an exile community in India. Chinese destroy nearly all Tibetan monasteries, and persecute Buddhist practitioners.

- **1962** Second Vatican Council begins, the most significant council since Trent, to promote new attitudes and practices in Catholicism.

- **1975–79** ccommunists under Pol Pot attempt to destroy Buddhism in Cambodia. By 1978 nearly every monk or religious intellectual had been either murdered or driven into exile, and nearly every temple and library had been destroyed.

In 1900 it seemed reasonable to assume that religion was losing the power that it had previously exercised. Liberal, educated opinion in much of the world had moved significantly against the primacy of religion, especially its traditional influence over the conduct of public affairs. Religion seemed arrayed against powerful forces of progress and rationality. The competition between progressive forces and the Roman Catholic Church was particularly acute. The declaration of Papal Infallibility (1870) seemed to have pitted the Church against tolerance and sKepticism. This struggle acquired dimensions of gender and social class with the most enthusiastically religious seen as uneducated and backward.

The struggle between religious and secular power manifested itself across the globe. It took place in France, where Church and state were separated in 1905, and in Spain in 1932, where disestablishment of the Catholic Church helped fuel the crisis that led to civil war. It was seen in Turkey, where Atatürk secularized the state during the 1920s, and in the Middle East since the 1940s.

However, the 20th century has not ended with a secularized world. In some countries religion continues to have a formal place alongside the state, despite falling church attendances. In Britain the Anglican Church—though attracting little devotion from its members—remains formally at the center of public life: the head of state is also head of the church. In the United States, religious attendance remains high despite the fact that there is no formal role for religion alongside the state. In India politics now revolve around religious issues as the Hindu nationalist BJP party overtakes the more secular Congress group. Most importantly, Muslim fundamentalism has gained a presence in many parts of the world, provoking fears in the secularized world that the division between Islam and the West may prove as damaging as that in the Cold War between communism and capitalism.

Religion has remained important for several reasons. First of all, the very upheavals of the 20th century often created a new need for religious structures. Those migrating to cities, or even to new countries, often clung to their religion as something to provide them with a sense of belonging. Catholic priests have done much to organize Irish, Polish, and Italian communities in North America; radical Islam has found a ready audience among the uprooted second generation Muslim immigrants of Great Britain and France. Secondly, religion has often blended into broader secular structures. In areas such as Brittany and Ireland, nationalism has been seen, in part, as a conflict between local Catholicism and the domination of a Protestant or secular state. In Eastern Europe religious and ethnic divisions coincided and reinforced each other. Poles flocked to Catholic churches because these seemed to symbolize resistance to communist rule, even though statistics on matters like abortion suggest that few Poles accept all the teachings of a conservative Polish Pope; the secularized Muslims of Bosnia were forced to accept help from Iranian Islamic militants in order to defend themselves against their Serbian Orthodox neighbors.

Religion also ties in with nationalism in many parts of the Third World. The most prominent leader of Indian nationalism, Gandhi, sought to exploit a complicated blend of Hindu traditionalism, anticaste modernization, and nationalism. His own subsequent assassination, by a Hindu extremist, and the importance religion assumed in underwriting

CANADA

Catholic

USA

Protestant

Catholic

Waco
(Branch Davidians, 1993)

North Atlantic Ocean

Jonestown
(People's Temple, 1978)

BRAZIL

Catholic

Catholic

Catholic

1 world religions from 1900

	Buddhist in 1900
	zone of coexistence of Buddhism with traditional systems of belief
	Christian in 1900
	divide between Orthodox and other Christian denominations
	Hindu in 1900
	Muslim in 1900
	divide between Shia and other Muslims
	tribal beliefs in 1900
	zones of substantial Christian advances
	zones of substantial Islamic retreats
→	Muslim advances
o	states with significant Muslim immigrant communities,1996
+	state under Muslim religious law
	atheist control for part of the century
●	atheist governments, 1996
	areas where Protestant Evangelism made significant gains from Catholicism after 1975
	areas where Armenian Christians were largely exterminated during World War One
	areas where Jews were largely exterminated during World War Two
o	significant Jewish minority, 1996
	partitioned on the basis of religion, with details
	civil war with interreligious conflict, with date
	civil war in which religion was an important component, with date
	war/independence movement with religious component, with details
●	religious cult activities leading to violence, with details

1 The map (above) shows changes in the influence of world religions across the 20th century. These changes have sometimes been the result of conversion. However, they have also been linked to migration (taking Islam into Western Europe); extermination (driving Judaism out of Central Europe); different birth rates (favoring Muslims over Christians and Catholics over Protestants); and politically motivated campaigns (seeking to eliminate religious practice in communist countries).

en.wikipedia.org/wiki/List_of_Christian_denominations
List of Christian denominations
www.palestinecenter.org/palestine/islamic.html
The rise of Islamic fundamentalism

political conflict in India suggests that he did not succeed in controlling the forces that he unleashed.

Party politics was another area that proved inseparable from religion. Christian Democrat parties became the dominant force in Italy and Germany after 1945. The influence of religion was less explicit, though perhaps even more effective, in the politics of the United States. Here a powerful religious lobby made up of Catholics and bornagain Protestants endorsed candidates who would defend school prayers and attack the right to abortion. A century that had begun with many assuming that the diffusion of Darwin's ideas would undermine religious belief ended with some parents in the U.S. insisting that children should be taught a strict Biblical view of the creation of the world. Secularism is in retreat. Religions have more adherents than a century ago and religious enthusiasm, particularly Islamic fundamentalism, has echoes of the religious confrontations of the Middle Ages.

2 Within each of the world's religions there are variations between denominations or sects (chart right). Roman Catholics make up 59 percent of all the world's Christians, while the Anglican (Episcopalian) Church, which still commands a degree of cultural and political influence, accounts for only three percent of Christians.

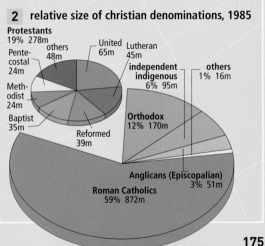

2 relative size of christian denominations, 1985

Protestants
19% 278m
Pentecostal 24m
others 48m
Methodist 24m
Baptist 35m
Reformed 39m
United 65m
Lutheran 45m
independent indigenous
6% 95m
others 1% 16m
Orthodox 12% 170m
Anglicans (Episcopalian) 3% 51m
Roman Catholics 59% 872m

education

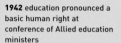

since 1900

1942 education pronounced a basic human right at conference of Allied education ministers

1945 UNESCO (United Nations Educational, Scientific, and Cultural Organization) created

1954 Free and Compulsory Education Project begun by UN

1960 UN adopts global program for provision of primary education

1990 International Literacy Year

1992 1.2 million students study abroad

2 Great strides have been made in the provision of primary education over the last 30 years (map below), though in parts of the world attendance, particularly for girls, is still low. The total for the world in 1995–6 was 83.6 percent of all boys and 75.5 percent of all girls. Improvements in education in the developing world have come about despite low levels of funding for schools.

Few aspects of the revolutionary century have touched more people than the spread of educational opportunity. Although there remain almost one billion illiterates worldwide, there has been a remarkable growth in the numbers receiving full-time education at every level in the second half of the century.

Early in the century most of the world's population was illiterate or nearly so, and formal long-term education for whole populations was confined to Europe and areas of European settlement. Even here most children left school after receiving only basic instruction. The numbers going onto secondary and then to higher education were tiny. In colonial regions education was provided by the imperial power, most of it by Christian organizations who saw education, as they did in Europe or America, as a means of moral instruction.

Not until the Second World War did the idea of education as a right, valuable in itself, become more generally accepted. The League of Nations established a Committee on Intellectual Cooperation in 1922, chaired by the French philosopher Henri Bergson, but its work was centered on Europe, where the provision of higher levels of instruction made substantial progress before 1939, at least for boys. A new agenda emerged from the war. In 1942 the British minister of education, Richard Butler, called a conference of Allied education ministers at which education was pronounced a basic human right to be promoted for its own sake. Butler's group laid the foundation for what, in November 1945, became the United Nations Educational, Scientific and Cultural Organization (UNESCO), whose first director-general was the British scientist Julian Huxley.

In 1947 UNESCO published the report, Fundamental Education, which laid the grounds for the postwar campaign against illiteracy and educational discrimination. Nine years later the UN adopted the Free and Compulsory Education Project, which laid down the principle that everyone was entitled to education regardless of race, sex, or religion for a minimum period of six years. The project was piloted in Latin America, where it made substantial progress. In Karachi in 1960 the UN endorsed a global program for the provision of primary education, and the following year produced the first comprehensive survey of global illiteracy. The survey showed that two-fifths of the world's adult population was illiterate, and that in some states almost the entire female population could neither read nor write. Since there was widespread agreement that education was a central explanation for differing levels of success in economic development—a fact highlighted by the attention lavished on education in the high-growth Pacific Rim—the UN established the fight against illiteracy as the central educational ambition.

The literacy drive had mixed results. In 1970 one-third of adults were still illiterate and the absolute number was growing rather than falling. The most striking gains were made only after 1980, when international funding rose sharply and economic success was no longer confined to the wealthy north. The aim of the UN in International Literacy Year (1990) was to eradicate illiteracy by the year 2000, particularly in what it called the "Least Developed Economies," where fewer than 50 percent of adults were literate. In some respects the gap between the developed and developing world has narrowed in the last ten years. Technology and information is easily transferred between

2 pupils in primary school

1998 or latest figures

- above 90%
- 70–90%
- 50–69%
- 30–49%
- below 30%
- no data

www.unesco.org/
United Nations Educational, Scientific, and Cultural Organization
www.literacyonline.org/explorer/overview.html
Literacy and international development

1 world illiteracy rates, 2001

proportion of population aged 15–24 illiterate

- below 1 %
- 1–5 %
- 5–10 %
- 10–20%
- 20–40 %
- 40–60 %
- above 60 %
- no data

Illiteracy has slowly retreated worldwide, but there remained an estimated 814 million illiterate in 1990 (map above and chart below right). In 1995 one billion children were enrolled worldwide (20 percent of the world's population) against a figure of 300 million (ten percent) in 1953. There has been a marked increase in the enrolment of pupils in secondary and higher education. The output of books has grown rapidly with improvements in education and rising prosperity (chart right).

regions: in 1992 1.2 million students studied abroad, mainly in Europe and the U.S. The numbers enrolled in secondary and tertiary education have risen dramatically in the developing regions, and those countries' expenditure on research and development, though still lagging significantly behind levels in Europe and the United States, has broken the near monopoly the latter enjoyed until the 1980s.

Where the gap still matters is in educational expenditure. Between 1980 and 1992 world spending on education rose from $526 billion to $1,196 billion. But by 1992 the developed world accounted for $927 billion of this, and the Least Developed Economies for just $4 billion. Expenditure per pupil in the developed world was $2,419 in 1990, in sub-Saharan Africa it was $58 and in East Asia $76. Spending on this scale has helped to maintain the knowledge gap between north and south and the gap in economic achievement. The focus for the future is no longer on the problem of illiteracy but on other skills and opportunities which literacy makes possible.

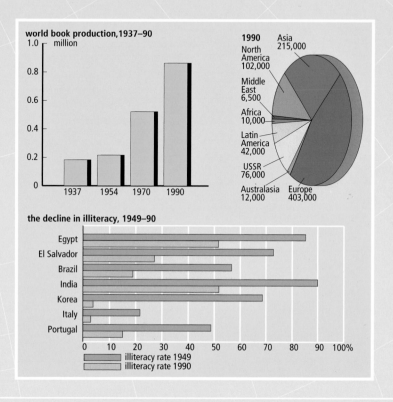

world book production, 1937–90

1990
- Asia 215,000
- North America 102,000
- Middle East 6,500
- Africa 10,000
- Latin America 42,000
- USSR 76,000
- Australasia 12,000
- Europe 403,000

the decline in illiteracy, 1949–90

- illiteracy rate 1949
- illiteracy rate 1990

177

the **environment**: pollution

since 1900

1970 U.S. Clean Air Act

1973 Oil price rise prompts worldwide crisis

1983 Green Party gains more than 5 percent of vote in German elections

1985 hole in ozone layer discovered over Antarctica

1986 Chernobyl nuclear accident

1987 Montreal Protocol on CFC emissions

1997 Smog from forest fires envelops Indonesia

2002 *Prestige* oil tanker disaster off northwestern Spain

The idea that the environment is something to be cherished is comparatively new. The growth of industrial cities in the 19th century began to create an awareness of the problems of pollution. Cities were seen as unhealthy, while the technological developments that made them so also made the countryside more accessible and more tolerable.

With the growth of private motor cars, rural living seemed like an escape rather than an imprisonment. The decline of rural industries made the countryside in developed countries seem more unspoiled than it had done for centuries. The rapid economic growth of the period after the Second World War saw the human impact on the environment at its most dramatic. Factories produced emissions that lowered air quality and sometimes produced "acid rain," which poisoned forests, rivers, and lakes. Environmental damage by industry was particularly bad in Eastern Europe. In the late 1980s, Czechoslovakia, with a population of 18 million, produced sulfur dioxide emissions that were twice as great as those of West Germany, with a population of 60 million. Sometimes Western companies moved production to countries where environmental regulations were less onerous.

Private motor cars were the second great source of environmental damage. Car usage increased vastly, especially in North America. Motor cars caused direct damage (through exhaust emission) and ensured that ever larger areas of the country were taken up by new roads. Developments in agriculture and forestry also caused great environmental damage. Forests throughout the world were cut down to provide timber. The use of pesticides and

1 Water pollution has become increasingly common and reflects once again the difficulty of containing pollution within national frontiers (map below). The map shows the impact of spillage by damaged oil tankers and industrial discharges into the world's seas and rivers. Areas of water bounded by industrial regions are particularly vulnerable to pollution.

1 environmental pollution

deforestation: rain forests under threat

- tropical rain forest
- edge of rain forest undergoing the most rapid deforestation
- ★ threatened area with large concentrations of endemic species

www.greenpeace.org/international_en/
Greenpeace; international environmental conservation group
www.epa.gov/air/oaq_caa.html/
The Clean Air Act

fertilizers to increase production in agriculture meant increasing quantities of harmful nitrates entered the soil and rivers. Environmental damage even became a weapon of war during the late 20th century: American forces used defoliants to strip away the jungle that provided cover for communist forces in the Vietnam war. In the Gulf War of 1991 Saddam Hussein turned to "environmental terrorism" by setting fire to Kuwaiti oil wells.

Concern for the environment became an increasing focus for political activity during the late 20th century. At first this concern came mainly from the political right. Conservatives lauded the countryside as the repository of real virtue and contrasted it with the degeneracy and political radicalism of the cities. "Peasant" often became a political label under which conservatives chose to present themselves: even urban conservatives took up the rhetoric of ruralism and in the 1940s "peasant" candidates won parliamentary elections in western Paris and gained places on the Budapest municipal council. In contrast, the left usually identified itself with technological progress, urbanization, and the need to expand the industrial working class. The upheavals emerging from the student demonstrations of 1968 changed all this. Young radicals who rejected the perspectives of the old left began to doubt whether unlimited economic growth was a possible or desirable aim. New "Green" parties were established and achieved particular success in West Germany, where they gained more than five percent of the vote and 27 seats in the 1983 elections. Greens argued that conventional politics was distorted by an emphasis on short-term material benefits. By 1998 they won enough support in Germany to share in government. By the 1980s a concerted international effort was finally underway to control some of the worst effects of environmental pollution. At the "Earth Summit" held in Rio de Janeiro in 1992 the first solid agreements were reached on restricting harmful pollutants, and in 1997 a treaty on global warming was signed in Kyoto. Pollution remains at the center of the battle to reverse the ecological disasters spawned by modern industry.

2 air pollution

CO_2 emissions from industrial processes and road transportation (tons per annum)

- 0–0.99
- 1–4.99
- 5–9.99
- 10 and above

(1988–89 average in micrograms/m^3 for selected urban areas)

- under 40
- 40–60
- 61–100
- above 100

2 Air pollution is generally concentrated in areas of industrial development (map right). In many metropolitan areas the combination of large cities and surrounding mountains can cause severe smogs, which may be especially damaging to plants, as well as give rise to eye damage.

3 In 1986 a nuclear reactor in Chernobyl in Ukraine exploded, spreading a cloud of radioactive waste around the world (map right). The disaster was the most spectacular of many accidents in the production of nuclear power, which have given rise to growing protests against the use of nuclear fuel. As a proportion of energy generated worldwide, nuclear power has been falling since the middle of the 1980s.

ocean and river pollution: oil slicks and tar balls

- high occurrence
- low occurrence

oceanic pollution

- frequent and severe
- partial and intermittent
- major oil tanker disaster
- oilrig blowout
- natural seepage

river pollution

- severe
- background

3 radioactive fallout from the chernobyl accident, 1986

- pattern of fallout

1 Many areas of the world are severely affected by droughts (map below). Drought can be explained in terms of physical geography—it is caused by lack of rainfall where the climate is dry and variable. However, the impact on human life varies greatly. A drought in California is not likely to have the same impact as a drought in Ethiopia.

1 drought

dry climate regions

- steppe regions
- desert regions

✳ *1971* major droughts since 1965

A curious shift in power has taken place over the past century. In 1900 most people in the world were still utterly dependent on the climate. Drought, frost, hail storms, or floods could destroy homes or ensure crop failure and starvation. National cuisines were tailored to suit climate: most inhabitants of north European countries never saw bananas, oranges, or even coffee. Armies could not move until the beginning of the "campaigning season" (spring). Peasants lived by the weather. It determined their prosperity and rhythm of work: frantic labor to get in a good harvest could be followed by months of inactivity during winter.

Even in a developed country, such as France, Alpine villages might be cut off by snow for part of the year. Even the most privileged sectors of society had to go to some lengths to escape from the impact of climatic change. Kings moved to summer palaces; the British administrators of India retreated from Delhi to the hill station at Simla during the hot season. George Orwell's novel *Burmese Days* describes the obsessive interest taken by the British community in a Burmese town at the arrival of fresh consignments of ice at the local club.

Dependence on climate can still be seen. Countries like Bangladesh are highly vulnerable to floods and typhoons. Droughts can still produce starvation in Africa and hail storms can depress connoisseurs of Bordeaux wine. However, in general, industrialized countries have become less and less dependent on climate. Few people in Western countries would even bother to notice the link between the weather and the

prices that they pay for vegetables in supermarkets. Air conditioning allows investment bankers in Singapore to ensure that their offices are slightly cooler than those of their colleagues in London and has contributed much to the new prosperity of certain cities in the American South.

However, the very technology that has allowed Western countries to gain control over climate has begun to have wider and more dangerous implications. Industrial activity emits a variety of gases (nitrous oxide, methane, and carbon dioxide) that create a so-called "greenhouse effect" by surrounding the earth and trapping heat. The buildup of gases might normally be alleviated by the fact that trees consume carbon dioxide and emit oxygen, but the destruction of the tropical rain forests means that there are now fewer trees, although during the 1990s the pace of deforestation has slackened. The net result is that the overall temperature of the world is slowly rising. It is estimated that the global temperature will rise by about one degree centigrade by 2010 and that it may rise by another two degrees by the end of the next century. This increase is likely, in the long term, to have a variety of effects. It will change agricultural productivity in certain areas and it will melt the polar icecaps, so causing floods and reducing the habitable surface of the globe. Not all the effects of global warming will be negative: most Ethiopians would be happy to receive more rain and many English people would like a climate in which it was easy to cultivate grapes. But widely it is assumed that the effects of global warming

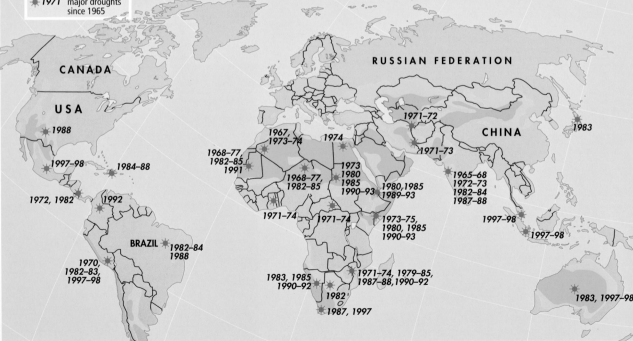

www.globalwarming.org/
Global warming website
www.elnino.noaa.gov/
Web links to el-Niño cyclical climatic change

Map 2: flood damage from 1973

GERMANY
1995, 1997

POLAND
1997

JAPAN
1975–76,
1982–83

NEPAL
1978

KOREA
1984, 1995

PAKISTAN
1973, 1976,
1992

CHINA
1981–84, 1988–89, 1991

EGYPT
1975

INDIA
1973–83, 1985–89,
1991–92, 1996

USA
1976–77, 1979, 1980–84,
1986, 1993, 1995, 1997–98

SUDAN
1988,
1991

SRI LANKA
1989

THAILAND
1988

HONDURAS
1974

BENIN
1985

KENYA
1997–98

SOMALIA
1981, 1997–98

INDONESIA
1973, 1986

BRAZIL
1974–75, 1978,
1985, 1988

TANZANIA
1997–98

BANGLADESH
1973–74, 1976–77,
1986–88, 1991,
1996

PERU
1974, 1982–83,
1986

MALAWI
1991

MOZAMBIQUE
1977

SOUTH AFRICA
1995

Rivers labelled on map: Yukon, MacKenzie, Peace, Nelson, Missouri, St. Lawrence, Colorado, Mississippi, Orinoco, Amazon, Niger, Nile, Congo, Ubangi, Kasai, Zambezi, Orange, Ob, Yenisei, Lena, Amur, Volga, Danube, Yellow River, Brahma-putra, Ganges, Indus, Yangtze, Mekong, Darling, Murray

2 | flood damage from 1973

major river basin

country suffering severe flooding (1973–93). Floods recorded are those resulting in more than 300 deaths and/or more than 40,000 homeless and/or extensive property damage

2 Flooding is the oldest environmental problem. Floods are a hazard for inhabitants of under-developed countries who live near large rivers in order to obtain access to fertile land, but who lack the resources to protect themselves against sudden increases in the water level. The map (above) shows the countries in the world that are prone to flooding. Bangladesh is particularly vulnerable to highly destructive floods.

3 Global warming produced by the emission of gases into the atmosphere may be having a worldwide effect (map right). The result of these emissions is the "greenhouse effect", as heat is trapped by a layer of gases. One consequence is that parts of the two polar ice caps are breaking up. The melting of the ice caps is contributing to a worldwide rise in sea level. The rise in sea level by 2010 will cause grave problems for some low-lying coastal regions.

are to be feared. Countries have discussed measures that may alleviate the problem and the European Union has agreed to prevent further increases in the emission of carbon dioxide after the year 2000, but there are good reasons to doubt that such good resolutions will be implemented. The developing world remains resentful of efforts to curtail their own industrial growth by states which grew rich on industry a century before.

But not all climatic effects are manmade. In 1997–9 the return of the cyclical climate change in the Pacific known as "el Niño" produced exceptionally severe climatic effects, inducing spectacular flooding in America and Africa, and severe droughts in Latin America, Australia, and South East Asia. The droughts played a part in the fires in Indonesia in 1997–8 that destroyed 11,600 square miles (30,000 sq. km.) of forest and created a smog so dense it blotted out the sun. The evidence of nature's own power has persuaded some scientists that global warming is part of a wider natural climatic shift only marginally affected by human agency.

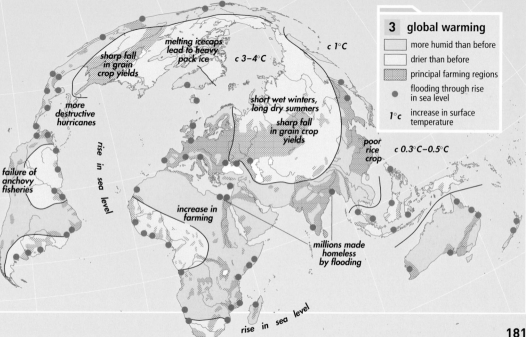

melting icecaps lead to heavy pack ice

c 3–4°C

c 1°C

sharp fall in grain crop yields

short wet winters, long dry summers

sharp fall in grain crop yields

more destructive hurricanes

poor rice crop

c 0.3°C–0.5°C

failure of anchovy fisheries

rise in sea level

increase in farming

millions made homeless by flooding

rise in sea level

3 | global warming

more humid than before

drier than before

principal farming regions

flooding through rise in sea level

1°c   increase in surface temperature

terrorism

1914 Archduke Franz Ferdinand assasinated by Bosnian Serbian nationalist

1934 murder of Yugoslav king and of French Foreign Minister

1978 Red Brigade kidnaps and murders Italian minister of the interior

1979 IRA (Irish Republican Army) assassinates Earl Mountbatten of Burma

1994 World Trade Center in New York bombed

2001 (September 11): members of radical Islamist group Al-Qaeda hijack 4 passenger planes in U.S.; 2 fly into World Trade Center, 1 into Pentagon; 4th crashes

2003 Madrid train bombings

2004 Beslan school massacre, Russia

2 The map (below) shows the locations of terrorist attacks between 1968 and 2001. The figures are deceptive. Attacks are more likely to be reported and recorded in Western Europe or North America than in underdeveloped countries where forces of order may be reluctant to acknowledge the scale of a problem or where victims of terrorism may be unable to report their status. It could be argued that the most effective terrorists are those who are able to hold sway over an area without open displays of violence.

Terrorism is a dangerous word. All governments like to label their violent opponents as "terrorists": the word implies a small, isolated, and irrational group willing to cause immense suffering to innocent civilians in pursuit of its aims. It also implies that such groups can be lumped together regardless of their aims or the context in which they operate.

Changes in political circumstances may make yesterday's terrorist seem like today's freedom fighter. "Terrorists" have often been young men who subsequently went on to enjoy respectable careers. One of the seven men who carried out the single most important act of terrorism in history (the assassination of Archduke Franz Ferdinand, which sparked the First World War) ended his days as director of the Institute of Historical Research in Belgrade. Independence movements in countries such as Cyprus and Kenya were once labeled terrorist by their opponents. Israel, some of whose founders bombed the King David Hotel in Jerusalem, is now seen as the state that confronts the most persistent terrorist problem. In Algeria the Front de Libération Nationale (FLN) once employed terrorist tactics against the French rulers of the country, but has now become a government party that campaigns against the "terrorism" of Islamic militants in its own domain.

In general terms terrorism in the 20th century has been characterized by an awareness that its perpetrators cannot hope to gain outright military victory. Their actions are designed to provide "propaganda by the deed" to draw attention to their grievances and possibly to provoke their opponents into counterproductive repression. Terrorism has been rendered effective by two things. The first is technology, especially in the form of portable high explosives, which has allowed small numbers of determined people to do great damage. The second is the publicity provided first by the media.

Assassinations by anarchist and nationalist groups in France, Russia, and the Balkans during the years leading up the First World War spread the idea of terrorism. During the interwar period there were also some spectacular terrorist attacks, such as the murder of the Yugoslav king and French foreign minister in 1934 in Marseilles. However, repressive regimes, such as those of Hitler, Stalin, and in the early years of his rule, General Franco, were not very susceptible to terrorist threats. Such regimes were impervious to the loss of civilian life and willing to repress terrorism with extreme ferocity.

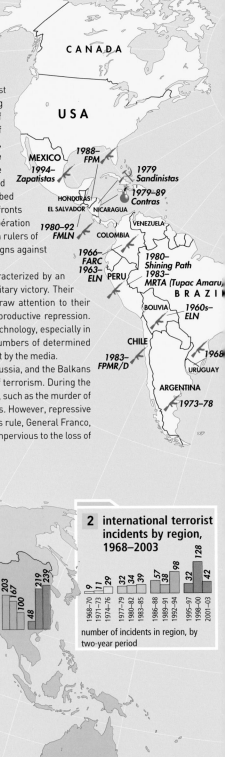

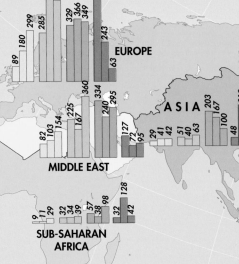

2 international terrorist incidents by region, 1968–2003

number of incidents in region, by two-year period

www.terrorism.com/
Site of the Terrorist Research Center
www.state.gov/s/ct/rls/pgtrpt/
U.S. State Department annual report on terrorist trends

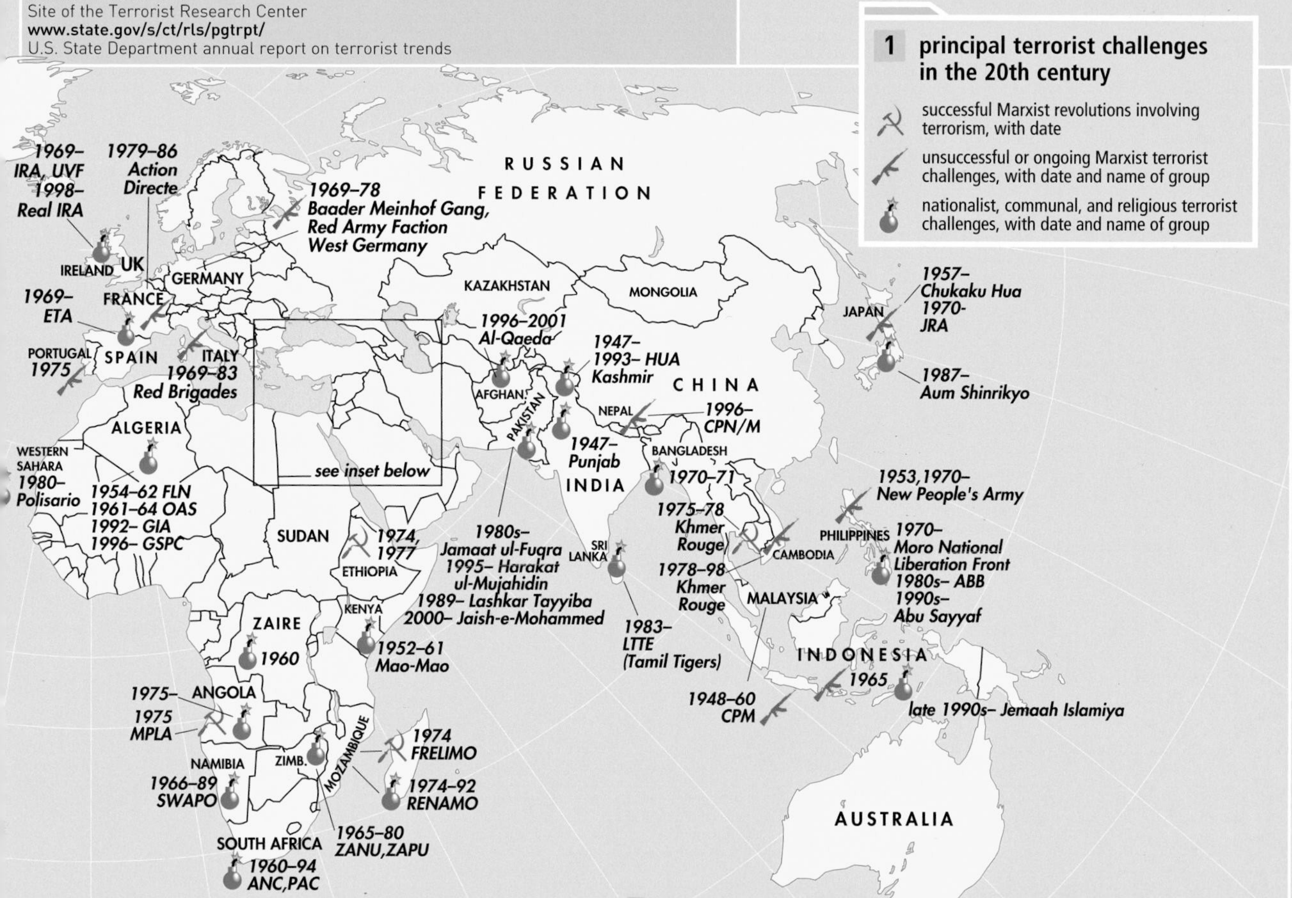

1 principal terrorist challenges in the 20th century

successful Marxist revolutions involving terrorism, with date

unsuccessful or ongoing Marxist terrorist challenges, with date and name of group

nationalist, communal, and religious terrorist challenges, with date and name of group

Map labels (clockwise/regional):

1969– IRA, UVF 1998– Real IRA — IRELAND, UK

1979–86 Action Directe — FRANCE

1969–78 Baader Meinhof Gang, Red Army Faction West Germany — GERMANY

1969– ETA — FRANCE/SPAIN

PORTUGAL 1975

ITALY 1969–83 Red Brigades

WESTERN SAHARA 1980– Polisario

ALGERIA 1954–62 FLN 1961–64 OAS 1992– GIA 1996– GSPC

SUDAN ETHIOPIA 1974, 1977

ZAIRE 1960

KENYA 1952–61 Mao-Mao

1975– ANGOLA 1975 MPLA

NAMIBIA 1966–89 SWAPO ZIMB.

MOZAMBIQUE 1974 FRELIMO 1974–92 RENAMO

SOUTH AFRICA 1965–80 ZANU, ZAPU 1960–94 ANC, PAC

RUSSIAN FEDERATION

KAZAKHSTAN MONGOLIA

1996–2001 Al-Qaeda — AFGHAN.

1947–1993– HUA Kashmir — PAKISTAN

NEPAL 1996– CPN/M

1947– Punjab INDIA

1974, 1977 1980s– Jamaat ul-Fuqra 1995– Harakat ul-Mujahidin 1989– Lashkar Tayyiba 2000– Jaish-e-Mohammed

SRI LANKA 1983– LTTE (Tamil Tigers)

BANGLADESH 1970–71

1975–78 Khmer Rouge 1978–98 Khmer Rouge — CAMBODIA

MALAYSIA 1948–60 CPM

INDONESIA 1965 late 1990s– Jemaah Islamiya

CHINA

JAPAN 1957– Chukaku Hua 1970– JRA 1987– Aum Shinrikyo

PHILIPPINES 1953, 1970– New People's Army 1970– Moro National Liberation Front 1980s– ABB 1990s– Abu Sayyaf

AUSTRALIA

see inset below

1 Terrorist campaigns have taken place across the world since 1945 (maps above and below). In the developing world many of the early terror campaigns were inspired by Marxist revolutionary struggle, but terrorism also existed in Europe either as struggles for national liberation (Northern Ireland, the Basque province in Spain) or against capitalism (Germany, France, Italy). More recently terrorism has been represented by religious conflict: Hindu against Muslim in India; militant Islam against the West; and westernized native elites throughout the Middle East and North Africa.

After the Second World War terrorism began to be practiced by many in the Middle East and, particularly, by Palestinians who wished to attack the state of Israel. Supporters of the Palestinian Liberation Organization launched a spectacular series of attacks during the 1970s and 1980s and gained publicity with a new tactic of hijacking international aircraft. Such attacks excited interest from middle-class students in developed countries who made up the core of movements such as the French Action Directe, the West German Red Army Faction, and the Italian Red Brigades. In 1978 the Red Brigades kidnapped and murdered the Italian minister of the interior, Aldo Moro. These terrorist groups were characterized by a desire to challenge the social order and a sympathy for liberation struggles in the Third World. However, in the long term, such groups were defeated. Left-wing terrorism was undermined by the gradual spread of disillusion with ideologies that had seemed so fashionable in the 1960s, as many young people retreated from political activism altogether.

The terrorism that survived during the 1980s was increasingly linked to various forms of nationalism. Obvious examples were the activities of the Provisional IRA in Northern Ireland and ETA in the Spanish Basque country. Palestinian nationalism also continued to be linked to terrorism, and this nationalism became increasingly associated with Islamic fundamentalism, much of it sponsored by Iran. Groups such as Hamas and Hezbollah have taken the ground vacated by the PLO in its avowed shift to more peaceful operations. The U.S., which had long escaped terrorist action on its own soil, also began to suffer attacks from both new and old forms of terrorism. In 1994 the World Trade Center in New York suffered a bomb attack from Islamic Fundamentalists. Seven years later, on September 11, 2001, a new group calling itself Al-Qaeda, led by Osama bin Laden, destroyed the Center entirely, killing more than 3,000 people. America declared a global war against terrorism.

Inset map (Middle East) labels:

1994– CHECHNYA
GEORGIA ARMENIA AZERBAIJAN
UZBEKISTAN 2002– Islamic Movement of Uzbekistan (UIM)

GREECE 1948–49 ELAS 1971– ELA 1975–2002 November 17

TURKEY 1978– Dev Sol 1984– PKK

2001– Ansar al Islam

CYPRUS 1951–60, 1971–74 EOKA EOKA B

SYRIA 2002– Asbat al-Ansar
LEBANON IRAQ IRAN

ISRAEL JORDAN 1982– Hezbollah

KUWAIT

LIBYA

EGYPT 1970s– Gamaat Islamiya, Islamic Jihad

SAUDI ARABIA

1937–48 Irgun Zvai Leumi, Stern Gang
1956–94 PLO
1967– PFLP
1969– DFLP
1974– Abu Nidal
1987– Hamas, Islamic Jihad
1994– Kach, Kahane Chai
2002– al-Aqsa Martyrs Brigade

183

drugs

In 1988 106 states signed a United Nations Drugs Convention, the most comprehensive program yet devised for combating the traffic in illicit drugs. By the late 1980s the value of the drugs trade was put at $300 billion, half of it from Latin America. By the mid-1990s the trade was estimated to be worth $500 billion, making it the single most lucrative business sector in the world.

There was nothing new about the drugs trade, but its scale and the geography of drug use and abuse has changed over the century. In 1900 narcotic drugs were widely produced and consumed in much of Asia. Their medicinal properties were already known. The trade in morphine (derived from the opium poppy) and in cocaine was legal where it was used for medical and scientific purposes—and large quantities were used in the First World War to dull the pain of horrific wounds. Drugs were also traded illegally to supply addicts, most of whom were to be found in the Far East and southern Asia. It was this traffic that first led to international attempts to control the production and movement of drugs, and to see the whole issue as a "drugs problem."

The first international effort to curb the flow of drugs came in 1912 with a convention signed at The Hague by states keen to eradicate a trade they equated with vice and crime. In 1914 the Harrison Act in the United States made hard drugs illegal—and thereby pushed the whole trade into the hands of criminal syndicates. Further conventions came in 1925 and 1936 as the League of Nations struggled to find ways to enforce control. Production of opium was regulated in British India, but flourished in Iran and China, where in the 1930s an estimated 80 percent of all opium was produced and ten percent of the population—40 million people—were regular smokers of the drug.

The pattern of drug abuse and drug-related crime was affected by political events and social changes, particularly large-scale urbanization, which produced an endless stream of vulnerable new customers. The key political event was the Chinese revolution in 1949. The communist regime began a tough program of eradication of drugs,

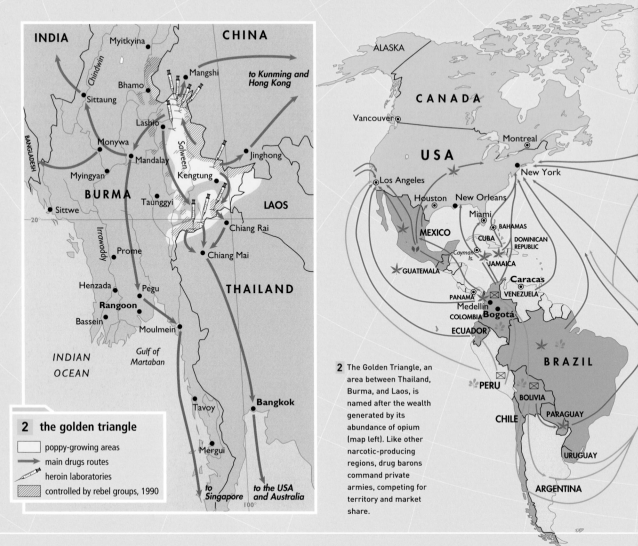

2   **the golden triangle**

☐ poppy-growing areas

➤ main drugs routes

⚲ heroin laboratories

▨ controlled by rebel groups, 1990

2 The Golden Triangle, an area between Thailand, Burma, and Laos, is named after the wealth generated by its abundance of opium (map left). Like other narcotic-producing regions, drug barons command private armies, competing for territory and market share.

www.unodc.org/unodc/en/world_drug_report_2000.html
UN world drug report, 2000
www.cia.gov/cia/publications/factbook/fields/2086.html
Country by country listing of illicit drug productions

which was virtually complete by the 1960s. The center of production of opium shifted to the inaccessible mountainous regions of Burma, Thailand, and Laos (the Golden Triangle) and the bleak and isolated areas of northern Pakistan and Afghanistan (the Golden Crescent). The Burmese trade was protected by remnants of Chiang Kai-shek's Kuomintang army, and run by Chinese syndicates in Bangkok and Hong Kong. With the Chinese market gone, traders looked farther afield. The West became a key market for the opium derivative, heroin (first produced in 1898), which could be flown to Europe or shipped across Asia and the Middle East. Collusion by local officials and police forces made the eradication of the trade almost impossible.

The rise of Western drug markets, which from the 1960s began to consume large amounts of cannabis and cocaine, as well as heroin, transformed the trade. In Mexico, Colombia, and Bolivia, new drugs cartels emerged to supply cocaine to North America. The drug barons wielded enormous power, dominating large parts of central South America. The vast profits from the trade were laundered through offshore banking houses, and ended up in the international financial system as "legal" funds for investment. The $80 million available to the three UN agencies fighting the drugs trade was eclipsed in the 1990s by the vast wealth of the drug traders, able to live beyond the law, in a global underworld with its own power brokers and its own rules.

1 The map (below) shows the pattern of the international drugs traffic. Drugs are produced where the climate is appropriate for the cultivation of plants such as the opium poppy. Cultivation is concentrated in inaccessible hilly areas, where state authority barely exists and where peasant farmers need a cash crop to survive. Large areas of South America, particularly Colombia, have been dominated by drugs cartels, such as the Medellin cartel. The Golden Triangle, an area of South Asia controlled by bandits and guerrilla armies (map far left), is the classic example of such a region.

1 the world drug trade

- major drug-producing countries
- major markets
- ⊠ refineries
- ⇒ principal trafficking routes
- ⊙ money-laundering centers

principal crops
- coca (cocaine)
- opiates (heroin)
- hashish
- marijuana

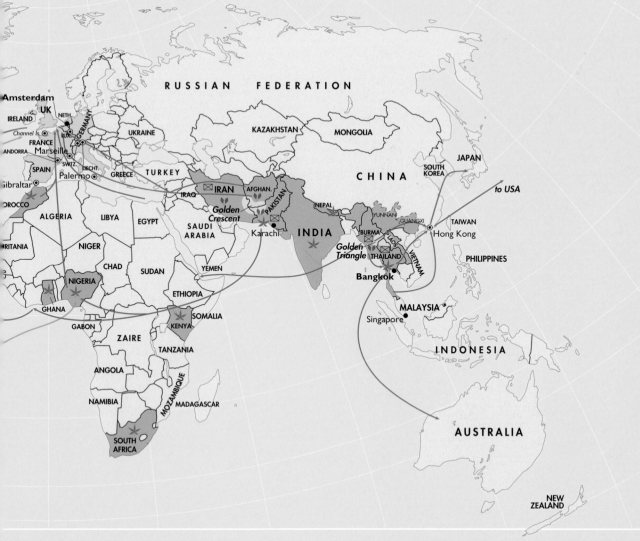

185

space exploration

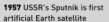

In 1901, British science-fiction pioneer H.G. Wells published *The First Men on the Moon.* **Just 68 years later, U.S. astronaut Neil Armstrong walked on the Moon; by the end of the century, space technology affected daily life and work worldwide.**

The Russian Konstantin Tsiolkovsky published the first scientific study of a spacecraft in 1903, concluding that launching a vehicle into space would be possible with the help of high-energy fuels and staging. Germany's Hermann Oberth published a similar work in 1922. Four years later, the American Robert Goddard flew the first successful liquid-fueled rocket.

In the 1920s and '30s, rocket development was the province of small teams and amateurs who were inspired by Oberth and Tsiolkovsky. The most important of these were the Germans who formed the *Verein für Raumschiffahrt* (Spaceship Travel Society). Their rocket tests were so promising that their leaders—including the 20-year-old Wernher von Braun—were invited in 1932 to develop a military rocket for the German Army.

In 1942 the German team launched the first A-4, also known as the V-2; in 1944 and 1945, some 3172 V-2s were fired at London and other cities. The basic features of the V-2 (engines fed with liquid oxygen and alcohol fuel by a turbine-driven pump; fuel used to cool the rocket nozzle; and steering by gyroscopes and electronics) foreshadowed all the rockets that would follow it.

After 1945, the secrets, hardware, and creators of the V-2 were taken over by the U.S. and the USSR. By the early 1950s, both nations had embarked on the development of inter-continental ballistic missiles (ICBMs) carrying nuclear weapons: They were also large enough to put craft into orbit. In 1957, in a blow to U.S. pride, a modified Soviet R-7 ICBM launched the first artificial Earth satellite, named Sputnik. Sputnik, and the U.S. reaction, kicked off the "space race" of the 1960s. The USSR's Yuri Gagarin became the first man in space in April 1961. President John F. Kennedy responded by committing the U.S. to place an astronaut on the Moon before 1970.

Directed by von Braun and his colleagues, the Apollo project was hugely expensive, including the construction of the Saturn V rocket and its F-1 first-stage engines, and the development and testing of complex rendezvous and docking procedures. The Apollo program achieved its goal in July 1969; the Soviet effort was never close to its achievements.

At the same time, unmanned spacecraft were built and launched for a growing variety of missions. Tiros I, launched in 1960, was the first weather satellite. In July 1962, Bell Laboratories' Telstar satellite beamed live TV from the U.S. to Europe; by 1964, highlights of the Tokyo Olympics were transmitted by satellite to

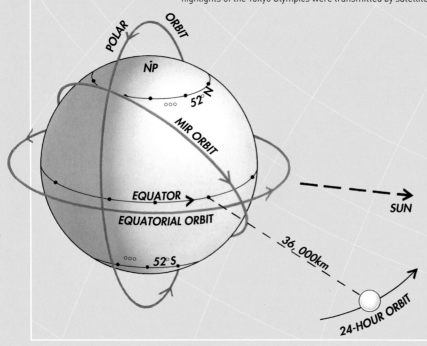

1 The pictures and charts (above and left) illustrate the distances spacecraft have been propelled. A variety of orbits (left) around the Earth have been achieved by artificial satellites since the launch of the Russian Sputnik in 1957. A 24-hour synchronous orbit (first achieved by Syncom 2 in 1963) requires a distance of 22,370 miles (36,000 km) from the Earth. The orbit of the Russian space station Mir passes over all points between 52° N and 52° S. The distances traveled by space probes designed to investigate other planets in the solar system are vastly greater (above right). Travel to the Moon involved a journey of 250,000 miles (400,000 km). The Voyager 1 and 2 probes had to travel thousands of millions of miles in order to reach Jupiter, Saturn, Uranus, and Neptune. It took four hours for pictures of Neptune taken by Voyager 2 to reach the Earth.

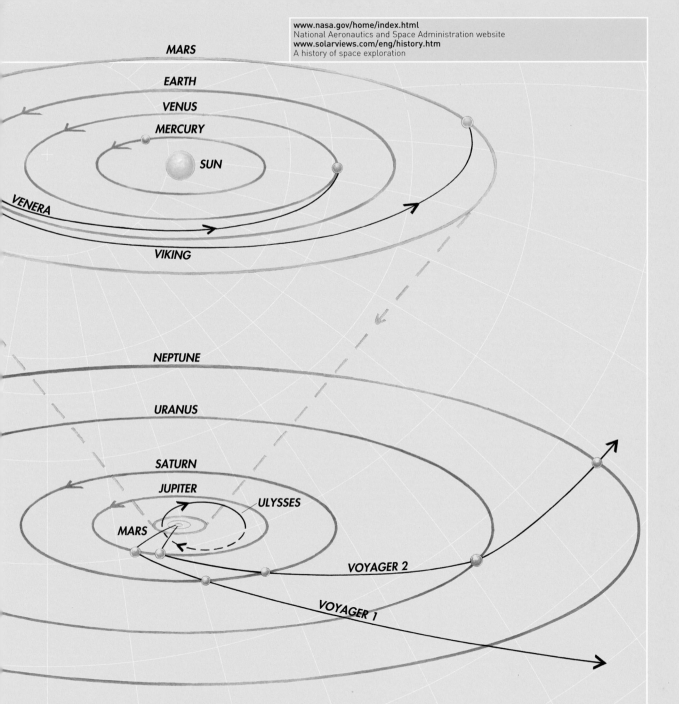

MARS
EARTH
VENUS
MERCURY
SUN
VENERA
VIKING

NEPTUNE
URANUS
SATURN
JUPITER
ULYSSES
MARS
VOYAGER 2
VOYAGER 1

www.nasa.gov/home/index.html
National Aeronautics and Space Administration website
www.solarviews.com/eng/history.htm
A history of space exploration

Europe and the U.S., and the Intelsat consortium completed its round-the-world satellite link in 1967.

On the sidelines of the Moon race, the U.S. and Soviet Union sent robot explorers to Mars, Venus, and beyond. In December 1970, Russia's Venera-7 landed on Venus and became the first craft to return data from another planet. NASA's Pioneer 10 reached Jupiter in 1973 and Voyagers 1 and 2 were launched to Saturn and the outer planets in 1977: both were still transmitting data as the century ended.

After the last Apollo flight to the Moon in 1972, the intensity of the space race subsided. NASA started development of the first reusable spacecraft, the Space Shuttle. It was intended to place satellites in orbit more cheaply than expendable rockets, but turned out to be more costly, complicated, and unsafe.

The vision of a space station was realized in 1970 with Russia's Salyut series (succeeded by Mir in 1986) and the U.S. Skylab. Mir had a fully assembled mass of 125 tons and has been permanently occupied for 13 years.

In the 1970s, Europe and China developed their own space launch vehicles and, with the breakup of the USSR, Russia entered the commerical launch market in the early 1990s.

As lauches became more reliable, and electronics technology advanced, satellite-based communications became ubiquitous. Another universal benefit of space technology was the Pentagon's Global Positioning System satellite constellation, which turned out to be accessible by simple, cheap consumer devices. By the end of the century, though, spacecraft were still being launched by recognizable descendants of von Braun's A-4.

index